MYTH, RITUAL,
AND KINGSHIP

MYTH, RITUAL, AND KINGSHIP

Essays on the
Theory and Practice of Kingship
in the Ancient Near East
and in Israel

EDITED BY

S. H. HOOKE

EMERITUS PROFESSOR OF
OLD TESTAMENT STUDIES IN THE
UNIVERSITY OF LONDON

OXFORD
AT THE CLARENDON PRESS
1958

Oxford University Press, Amen House, London E.C.4

GLASGOW NEW YORK TORONTO MELBOURNE WELLINGTON
BOMBAY CALCUTTA MADRAS KARACHI KUALA LUMPUR
CAPE TOWN IBADAN NAIROBI ACCRA

PRINTED IN GREAT BRITAIN
AT THE UNIVERSITY PRESS, OXFORD
BY CHARLES BATEY, PRINTER TO THE UNIVERSITY

PREFACE

WHEN, four years ago, the volume entitled *Myth and Ritual* had gone out of print, the advisability of bringing out a new and revised edition was discussed. It was felt that during the twenty-one years that had passed since its first appearance so much new knowledge had accrued as to make it preferable to bring out an entirely new book. Hence it was decided to collect a fresh team, and to present those interested in the theme of *Myth and Ritual* with a new symposium on the same theme. Special emphasis has been laid on Kingship, because it has become plain that the place of the king in the myth and ritual of the ancient Near East is now the focal point of the discussion that has arisen over *Myth and Ritual* during the quarter of a century since its publication.

A procedure similar to that followed in the earlier book has been adopted. Through the kindness of Professor Rowley it was arranged that eight lectures dealing with various aspects of the subject should be delivered by the scholars who had been invited to take part in the symposium. These lectures were duly given at the University of Manchester in the autumn of 1955 and the spring of 1956, and are now published, with one addition, under the title of *Myth, Ritual, and Kingship*. The addition concerns Hittite studies. It was felt that the book would not be complete without a contribution on this important but relatively little-known part of the field, and Dr. O. R. Gurney of Oxford has kindly undertaken to fill the gap.

Hence it might be said that this book is an example of one of the elements in the much discussed and much abused 'ritual pattern', namely, the dying and rising god, for it is *Myth and Ritual* Redivivus. One significant change may be observed in this new series of essays: they now have an international character, for two eminent foreign scholars have made valuable contributions to the discussion.

I should like to acknowledge with gratitude the important

part which my friend Professor Rowley has taken in the production of this book, and I would also express my sense of indebtedness to the distinguished scholars who have contributed to it. It is also right to mention that the expenses of the course of lectures at Manchester University were met by the generosity of Mr. Lionel Blundell, who desired that they should be a memorial to his deceased wife, Cissie R. Blundell. I have also to thank my wife for her skill in the preparation of the indexes.

Lastly I have to thank the Delegates of the Clarendon Press for their spirit of enterprise in assisting at the rebirth of one of their own books.

S. H. H.

CONTENTS

viii   *Contents*

ABBREVIATIONS

A.c.O.   *Acta Orientalia.*
A.f.G.M.   *Archiv für die Geschichte der Medizin.*
AfO.   *Archiv für Orientforschung.*
A.J.S.L.   *American Journal of Semitic Languages and Literatures.*
Alliot, *Culte*   M. Alliot, *Le Culte d'Horus à Edfou au temps des Ptolémées* (Cairo, 1949, 1954).
A.N.E.T.   *Ancient Near Eastern Texts relating to the Old Testament.*
Ann. Serv.   *Annales du Service des Antiquités de l'Égypte.*
A.N.V.A.O.   Avhandlinger utgitt av Det Norske Videnskaps-
ii.   Akademi i Oslo, II. Hist.-Filos. Klasse.
A.O.S.   American Oriental Series.
A.R.E.   Ancient Records of Egypt.
A.R.M.   G. Dossin, C-F. Jean, J. R. Kupper, *Archives royales de Mari* (Paris).
A.T.A.N.T.   Abhandlungen zur Theologie des Alten und Neuen Testaments.
A.T.D.   Das Alte Testament Deutsch.
B.E.T.   Beiträge zur evangelischen Theologie.
B.H.T.   Beiträge zur historischen Theologie.
B.I.F.A.O.   *Bulletin de l'Institut français d'Archéologie Orientale, Cairo*
B.J.R.L.   *Bulletin of the John Rylands Library.*
B.Z.A.W.   *Beihefte zur Zeitschrift für die alttestamentliche Wissenschaft.*
C.I.H.   Corpus Inscriptionum Hettiticarum (*Mitt. d. VAG*, 1900. 4, S; 1902. 3, H; 1906. S).
Edfou   Rochemonteix-Chassinat, *Le Temple d'Edfou*, vols. i–xiv (Cairo, 1897–1954).
E.H.P.R   *Études d'histoire et de philosophie religieuses.*
E.O.L.   *Ex Oriente Lux* (Jaarbericht).
E.R.E.   *Encyclopaedia of Religion and Ethics.*
E.T.   *Expository Times.*
Hb.A.T.   Handbuch zum Alten Testament.
H.K.   Handkommentar zum Alten Testament.
H.S.   Horae Soederblomianae.
H.U.C.A.   *Hebrew Union College Annual.*
I.C.C.   The International Critical Commentary.

Abbreviations

J.A.	*Journal Asiatique.*
J.A.O.S.	*Journal of the American Oriental Society.*
J.B.L.	*Journal of Biblical Literature.*
J.C.S.	*Journal of Cuneiform Studies.*
J.E.A.	*Journal of Egyptian Archaeology.*
J.H.S.	*Journal of Hellenic Studies.*
J.M.E.O.S.	*Journal of the Manchester University Egyptian and Oriental Society.*
J.N.E.S.	*Journal of Near Eastern Studies.*
J.P.O.S.	*The Journal of the Palestine Oriental Society.*
J.T.S.	*Journal of Theological Studies.*
K.A.R.	Keilschrifttexte aus Assur religiösen Inhalts.
K.Bo.	*Keilschrifttexte aus Boghazköi.*
K.H.C.	Kurzer Hand-Commentar zum Alten Testament.
K.U.B.	*Keilschrifturkunden aus Boghazköi.*
N.G.G.W.	*Nachrichten von der Gesellschaft der Wissenschaften zu Göttingen.*
N.S.I.	Cooke, *A Text-Book of North-Semitic Inscriptions* (Oxford, 1903).
N.T.T.	*Norsk Teologisk Tidsskrift.*
P.A.O.S.	Publications of the American Oriental Society.
P.E.Q.	*Palestine Exploration Quarterly.*
P.T.	Pyramid Texts.
R.A.	*Revue d'Assyriologie.*
R.B.	*Revue Biblique.*
R.E.	*Revue d'Égyptologie.*
R.E.S.	*Revue des Études sémitiques.*
R.G.G.[2]	Gunkel, *Die Religion in Geschichte und Gegenwart*, 2nd ed.
R.H.Ph.R.	*Revue d'histoire et de philosophie religieuses.*
R.o.B.	*Religion och Bibel.*
R.S.	Ras Shamra Texts.
S.B.T.	Studies in Biblical Theology.
S.E.A.	*Svensk Exegetisk Årsbok.*
S.J.F.T.	*Svenska Jerusalems Föreningens Tidsskrift.*
S.T.	*Studia Theologica.*
Th.R.	*Theologische Rundschau.*
T.Z.	*Theologische Zeitschrift.*
U.H.	Gordon, *Ugaritic Handbook* (Rome, 1947).
U.L.	Gordon, *Ugaritic Literature* (Rome, 1949).
U.U.Å.	Uppsala Universitets Årsskrift.

Abbreviations

V.A.T.   Vorderasiatische Abteilung.

V.T.   *Vetus Testamentum.*

Z.A.   *Zeitschrift für Assyriologie.*

Z.Ä.S.   *Zeitschrift für ägyptische Sprache und Altertumskunde,* Leipzig.

Z.A.W.   *Zeitschrift für die alttestamentliche Wissenschaft.*

Z.D.M.G.   *Zeitschrift der deutsch-morgenländischen Gesellschaft.*

Z.R.G.G.   *Zeitschrift für Religions- und Geistesgeschichte.*

MYTH AND RITUAL: PAST AND PRESENT

by S. H. HOOKE

As the origins of the volume of essays called *Myth and Ritual* are beginning to be lost in antiquity, and myths are even collecting round them, it seems appropriate that, in the introduction to a volume which is a kind of sequel to *Myth and Ritual*, a brief account should be given of how the original book came to be written. Professor Rowley has said in his essay in the present book[1] that *Myth and Ritual* was a *mise au point* of studies which had been going on for some time but mainly outside this country. It is true that such studies had been going on for some time before the appearance of *Myth and Ritual*, especially in Scandinavia, but it was not from them that the impulse came which ultimately resulted in the volume of essays in question. This impulse came from the 'diffusionist' movement connected with the names of Sir Grafton Elliot Smith and W. J. Perry.

Professor Rowley has referred to the late Professor Canney,[2] his own predecessor at Manchester, as one who had developed views about kingship in the ancient Near East, which were akin to those expressed by some of the contributors to *Myth and Ritual*, but quite independently of the so-called 'Myth and Ritual School'. The truth of the matter is that Canney, Hocart (whose book *Kings and Councillors* was published three years after *Myth and Ritual*), and myself were all members of the group who were working with Elliot Smith and Perry; and the kingship 'ideology', as our Scandinavian friends call it, developed by Canney and Hocart, was a product of the views put forward by Perry in his seminars and ultimately published in his book *The Children of the Sun*. Neither Canney nor Hocart contributed to *Myth and Ritual*, although Hocart afterwards contributed to *The Labyrinth*. But my own movement was a 'deviationist' one.

[1] See below, p. 236.　　　　[2] See below, p. 237.

Being somewhat dubious about the pan-Egyptian tendency which the diffusionists seemed to be developing, I had begun to study the cuneiform myth and ritual texts, and, in ignorance at that time of what the Scandinavian scholars were doing, had reached the belief that Babylonian influence on the Semitic-speaking countries of the ancient Near East was more evident than Egyptian. That Babylonian mythology and law underlay Hebrew myths and early Hebrew law had long been recognized, but that Babylonian ritual might have influenced the pattern of early Israelite ritual was an idea which had not yet gained currency in this country. So it was with the purpose of making a further study of the possibility of Babylonian and Egyptian influence on Hebrew religion that a team of contributors was assembled and briefed, and the volume *Myth and Ritual* was published in 1933. Thus it might be said to be a secondary product of the diffusionist movement, and came into existence in ignorance of the Continental studies to which Professor Rowley has referred. I became aware of the important work which Professor Mowinckel was doing after the *Myth and Ritual* project had been started, and I referred to its significance on p. 13 of that book; but of the contributors to *Myth and Ritual* the late Professor Oesterley was the only one who showed any acquaintance with Mowinckel's work, and he definitely rejected that scholar's views *in toto*.[1] The only person who had any connexion with *Myth and Ritual* and was also influenced by Mowinckel's work was Professor A. R. Johnson. He was not, indeed, a contributor to *Myth and Ritual*; but his important essay in *The Labyrinth*, entitled 'The Role of the King in the Jerusalem Cultus', showed the influence of Mowinckel's work, and he has often since acknowledged his debt to that scholar,[2] while he has always strenuously rejected the imputation of belonging to any school. Since the present essay is intended to deal with the past history of the Myth and Ritual movement in this country, I have said this much in order to clear up an obscure point in relation to its real origin.

[1] Cf. W. O. E. Oesterley, *The Psalms*, i. 44 n. 2.
[2] Cf. A. R. Johnson, *Sacral Kingship in Ancient Israel*, p. 54 n. 1.

Criticism of the Myth and Ritual position. The first reactions to the appearance of *Myth and Ritual* were generally favourable. In America Professor Albright expressed a guarded approval. In 1935, under the title of *The Labyrinth*, a second collection of essays appeared whose object was to develop still further the ideas put forward in *Myth and Ritual*. In this volume Professor A. R. Johnson published the essay referred to above, an essay which brought into relief in almost prophetic fashion the theme which was to be the focus of controversy during the next two decades, namely, the place of the king in the ritual pattern of the ancient Near East.

Ten years after the appearance of *Myth and Ritual*, Professor Ivan Engnell published his book *Studies in Divine Kingship in the Ancient Near East*, in which he expressed his agreement with the position outlined in *Myth and Ritual*, and developed it with a great wealth of illustration from the relevant sources. He did not, however, deal with the question of kingship in the Old Testament, promising a further book on that aspect of the subject.

In 1947 Principal Norman Snaith published his book *The Jewish New Year Festival*, which was the first serious critical examination of the problems raised by *Myth and Ritual*. It showed how much work had been done in that field during the fourteen years that had elapsed since the appearance of the original book. In the next year the late Professor Henri Frankfort published his important book *Kingship and the Gods*, in which he dismissed with characteristic dogmatism the work of a number of scholars. But the full force of his attack on the Myth and Ritual position broke out in his Frazer Lecture for 1951, entitled *The Problem of Similarity in Ancient Near Eastern Religions*. This pamphlet has supplied many of the later critics of the Myth and Ritual position with ammunition for their attacks. We shall return to Frankfort's criticisms directly. It is not necessary to mention all the subsequent critical attacks on the position, but those of Professor Birkeland, R. P. de Fraine, and not least of Professor Mowinckel himself, whose *Psalmenstudien* might with justice be regarded as the *fons et origo malorum*, will be considered together with Frankfort's criticisms.

Examination of the criticisms of the Myth and Ritual position.
The main points of Frankfort's attack are as follows:

(*a*) He accuses the contributors to *Myth and Ritual* of a slavish following of Frazer.[1]

(*b*) He denies that the similarities enumerated in *Myth and Ritual* between the myths and rituals of Egypt, Babylon, and the related countries may rightly be described as a 'pattern'.[2]

(*c*) He claims that 'the belief that differences are specific and similarities generic vitiates one's very approach to the evidence'.[3] He goes on to deny that the alleged similarities existed at all.

(*d*) He claims that the contributors to *Myth and Ritual* have 'recklessly' imposed this imaginary 'pattern' upon the religion of Israel.[4]

Taking these points in order, it is obvious, or should be, that anyone dealing with ancient kingship rituals would be bound to show resemblances to Frazer, for the simple reason that he was dealing with the same group of observed phenomena, and to some extent using the same sources. But the whole approach of *Myth and Ritual* was from the first a conscious revolt from what was regarded as the non-historical method of the purely comparative approach. The opening sentences of *Myth and Ritual* contained a criticism of Frazer's definition of mythology as the philosophy of primitive man,[5] and it is relevant here to remark that the Myth and Ritual movement had its origin in a protest against the Tylorian thesis, accepted by Frazer, that similar cultural conditions produce similar cultural phenomena in every part of the world. This is an aspect of the problem of similarity with which we are not now concerned, and which was rebutted years ago by the demonstration that a large number of similarities which had been regarded as independent inventions were in

[1] H. Frankfort, *The Problem of Similarity in Ancient Near Eastern Religions*, p. 7 n. 2.

[2] H. Frankfort, op. cit., pp. 7 ff.   [3] H. Frankfort, op. cit., p. 6.

[4] H. Frankfort, op. cit., p. 8.

[5] S. H. Hooke, *Myth and Ritual*, pp. 1 f.

reality borrowings, the result of culture contacts. Necessity has been called the mother of invention, but she might with better reason be called the step-mother of borrowing. Mr. Harrison pointed out many years ago that man will not invent if he can borrow, and proceeded to prove his point by a number of well-grounded examples. Another point of disagreement with Frazer was our criticism of the undefined concept of 'primitive'. So much for the charge of slavish following of Frazer.

Frankfort's second line of attack relates to what he regards as the illegitimate use of the term 'pattern'. Professor Birkeland has raised similar objections, and these may be considered together with those advanced by Frankfort. In his Frazer Lecture Professor Frankfort quotes with approval Miss Ruth Benedict's use of the terms 'patterns of culture' to denote the determinant values of a particular primitive culture, and goes on to say:

> If 'pattern' is not used in this sense, if the term is not a tool in the search for the systems of value which *distinguish* one Near Eastern civilization from another, a system which, in each case, reveals the coherence of the political, religious, ethical, and artistic norms, then it becomes a rigid scheme. Then 'pattern' means a fixed combination of certain elements which are expected to recur and which are, consequently, postulated even when they have left no trace in our evidence.[1]

Miss Benedict's use of the term 'culture pattern' is a perfectly legitimate one, and is generally recognized as such by anthropologists, but Frankfort's attempt to limit the use of the term 'pattern' in this way is arbitrary and illegitimate, and his assertion that in *Myth and Ritual* the culture pattern there discussed has become a rigid scheme, 'recklessly imposed' on other cultures, is wholly unjustified. The charge that this imaginary rigid scheme has been recklessly imposed upon the religion of Israel will be dealt with later; but for the present let us consider the question of the legitimacy of the term 'pattern' in *Myth and Ritual* to describe the results of the examination of the Assyro-Babylonian ritual and mythological texts. This examination, based on a prolonged and careful study of these texts in the original

[1] H. Frankfort, op. cit., pp. 7 f.

cuneiform, revealed the existence in a definite culture area, namely that called by its occupants Sumer and Akkad, of a group of ritual practices which occurred together at certain important seasonal occasions. The most important of these, and the one for which we have most evidence, was the New Year festival in Babylon, though there is evidence that it was also celebrated in other centres. Now the regular occurrence together of these ritual practices, with their accompanying myth, can legitimately be said to constitute a pattern, as Professor Birkeland concedes when he says, 'There can be no doubt that a common pattern forms the background of the Akkadian and Hebrew conceptions and cultic performances concerning this festival celebrating the enthronization of the god, i.e., the Akkadian *akitu* festival and the Israelite New Year festival.'[1] Professor Birkeland's objections to the view presented in *Myth and Ritual* of the relation between the Akkadian pattern and the religion of Israel are mainly due to his particular definition of 'pattern'. His objections will be dealt with when we come to Frankfort's fourth charge, but his definition may fitly be discussed here. His words are: 'When the word "pattern" is used in this paper, it is in a definite sociological sense, signifying a *complex of traditionally combined manifestations of human behaviour or ideology*, appearing associated with the consciousness of norms.'[2] The context of this statement, and a footnote to it, suggest that the meaning of the term 'pattern' implies a model of some kind. It is this underlying implication of a norm or model in Professor Birkeland's definition of 'pattern' that is the root of his objections to the idea of any real relation between the Assyro-Babylonian cultic pattern, whose existence he admits, and the pattern of Israelite religion as he finds it in the Old Testament. But, while this definition, if somewhat obscure, is perfectly admissible, it is not, as we have already said about Frankfort's definition, the only way in which the term may be defined or used. The 'pattern' envisaged in *Myth and Ritual* was never conceived of or presented as a fixed or rigid scheme which could be imposed on any other

[1] H. Birkeland, *The Evildoers in the Book of Psalms*, p. 19.
[2] H. Birkeland, op. cit., p. 17 and n. 1.

religion or culture area by some kind of social mechanism; nor
was it conceived of as a norm or model with which Israel was
confronted during its settlement in Canaan; but it was a natural
and convenient term to describe an observed group of ritual
practices exhibiting a certain order, and bound together by the
Akkadian kingship ideology. The purpose of *Myth and Ritual*
was certainly not to *postulate* the occurrence of the elements of
the Assyro-Babylonian pattern (to use Birkeland's term) in other
culture areas of the ancient Near East, but to inquire whether
any of the elements of this pattern might be found in the group
of civilizations which made up the larger culture area of the
ancient Near East.

The third of Frankfort's charges need not detain us long. The
question of the relative importance of differences and similarities
will be answered differently according to the point of view of the
answerer, but it still remains true that differences arise from
prior similarities; the genus comes before the species, and the
species is defined by its differences within the larger circle of the
genus. Professor Frankfort stressed, quite rightly, the differences
between Egypt and Babylon because he considered that there
was a danger of essential differences being minimized or disregarded. I think that later on in this book it will be shown that
in one important respect he overstressed the difference. But the
object of *Myth and Ritual* was to establish the existence of
essential similarities between the chief culture areas of the
ancient Near East, without in any way denying or ignoring the
differences; and the increased knowledge of these areas which
we have gained during the last quarter of a century has provided
further evidence of the existence of such similarities. Every
logician would agree, as against Frankfort, that similarities are
generic and differences specific.

The fourth charge is the most serious. Professor Frankfort
has accused the contributors to *Myth and Ritual* of having
'recklessly imposed' upon the religion of Israel an imaginary
and non-existent pattern, and denies the existence in the Old
Testament of any evidence to support the view that traces of the
Akkadian ritual pattern may be found in Israelite religion.

To the first part of this charge the reply can only be a categorical denial. In the first place, nothing was ever imposed by us on Hebrew or Israelite religion, but a careful examination of Israelite ritual was made to see if the presence of certain practices mentioned in the Old Testament could be explained by the theory of culture contacts with other civilizations during the period of settlement or later. In the second place, Professor Frankfort has ignored the significance of the list of prohibited practices contained in the Pentateuchal codes and condemned by the prophets;[1] he has also ignored Mowinckel's demonstration of the evidence in the Psalms for the existence of a Hebrew New Year festival ritual of the enthronement of Yahweh the relation of which to the Akkadian New Year ritual is too obvious to be overlooked. In a characteristically dogmatic way he dismisses in a sentence the work of a number of scholars without proof:

An extreme case of the neglect of the individual nature of distinct civilizations is presented by Ivan Engnell, *Studies in Divine Kingship in the Ancient Near East.* . . . Engnell forces one single pattern upon the extensive material which he has collected, thus destroying the rich variety of pre-Greek thought in the name of 'comparative religion'. The same criticism applies to S. Hooke's *Myth and Ritual* and his *The Labyrinth*; E. O. James's *Christian Myth and Ritual*; and A. M. Hocart's *Kingship*. In different degrees these overshoot the mark of comparative research, which should counteract the narrowness of viewpoint entailed in devotion to a particular field but should not in any way infringe upon the individuality, the uniqueness, of each historical actuality.[2]

Throughout the whole of the chapter in *Kingship and the Gods* from which this note is taken, Professor Frankfort simply rejects, without argument or proof, any interpretation of titles or statements regarding kingship which does not agree with his own theory of the nature of kingship and its associated patterns. He has further ignored the fact that both the Old Testament and the supporting evidence of archaeology show that there were different levels and stages of Israelite religion and ritual practice,

[1] S. H. Hooke, op. cit., pp. 70 f.
[2] H. Frankfort, *Kingship and the Gods*, p. 405 n. 1.

and he has also ignored the fact that the traces of the ritual 'pattern' which he rejects were assigned by the authors of *Myth and Ritual* to the early stages of Israel's religious development when it is generally acknowledged that a certain amount of assimilation with Canaanite religious practices was taking place as Israel gradually passed from a semi-nomadic and pastoral way of life to an urban and agricultural civilization. It is to be regretted that Frankfort included in *Kingship and the Gods* an Epilogue dealing with Hebrew ideas of kingship, since it shows that, admirable field archaeologist as he was, he was not an Old Testament scholar, and his excursion into that domain shows a complete ignorance of the state of modern Old Testament scholarship.

Having dealt with Professor Frankfort's criticisms, we may now turn to those made by Professor Birkeland is his monograph *The Evildoers in the Book of Psalms*. Reference has already been made to his definition of 'pattern', and the principal ground of his objections seems to lie in the fact that he thinks that *Myth and Ritual* maintained that Israel took over the foreign ritual pattern as a whole. But nothing could be farther from the intention of the contributors to that book, though some went farther than I should be prepared to go. Professor Birkeland himself expresses what was the main contention of *Myth and Ritual* when he says:

> Foreign patterns and separate ideas were adopted by Hebrew religion when they could be interpreted so that they fitted into the totality. That is the principle of all cultural borrowings, which are always transformed to fit the new system. Hebrew religion was never confronted with a common pattern. But it was often confronted with concrete religions and their patterns, and from the latter much flowed into its own religious system. These borrowings may appear as disintegrations. But that is only when they are regarded from the standpoint of the producing religion. From that standpoint every borrowing means a disintegration, when the totality is not borrowed. For every borrowed element means a breaking up of an original unity, since the element borrowed has to pass into a new totality to find a new home in new surroundings.[1]

---

[1] H. Birkeland, op. cit., p. 20.

Here Professor Birkeland uses the term 'disintegration', which he had previously criticized me for using, in the exact sense in which I have always used it, and I find myself in almost complete agreement with the passage just quoted. With regard to the effect of the borrowings some qualification would seem to be called for. As will appear later, the prophets regarded these borrowings as a deliberate attempt on the part of Israel to make itself like its surrounding pagan neighbours, and it is doubtful whether such a process should be described as 'passing into a new totality'. I may add that Professor Birkeland will not find in anything I have written the suggestion that the group of phenomena which I have bracketed together under the name of a ritual pattern, was in any sense a model by which the Hebrews were 'confronted' when they began to settle in Canaan. What the two essays which I contributed to *Myth and Ritual* aimed at laying down as a provisional hypothesis was that in early Egypt, in the early city states of Sumer and Akkad, and in Canaanite cities before Hebrew settlement in that area, certain common factors in cult practices and their associated myths were observed to exist, and were characteristic of agricultural communities in the ancient Near East as early as the beginning of the third millennium B.C., and probably earlier. It was not the purpose of *Myth and Ritual* to carry the inquiry into the origin of these practices and ideas back beyond the evidence furnished by the available textual and glyptic material, but it is not unreasonable to suppose that the beginnings of such ideas and practices go back to the earliest beginnings of agriculture in the ancient Near East, and that out of these generic similarities, partly as the result of such culture contacts as I have referred to previously, and partly as the result of the special environmental conditions of each area, culture patterns developed with specific differences characteristic of each of the different areas. In Egypt the peculiar place of the Nile in her economy, and the unique development of ideas about death and the after-life, led to the creation of a religious pattern whose differences have almost submerged those common elements to which I have referred, and whose existence in Egyptian ritual practices has been established quite definitely by Professor Blackman's essay in *Myth and Ritual*, notwithstanding repeated assertions to the contrary. In the same way the special conditions of life in Sumer and Akkad with its numerous city states led to a development of a cult pattern best known from the late texts in which the shape of the Babylonian New Year festival is preserved. The lateness of these texts has been referred to as though it in some way invalidated their evidence; but it is generally agreed by Assyriologists that the late Seleucid texts edited by Thureau-Dangin in his *Rituels accadiens* are copies of earlier documents, though we cannot say how early. But the text known as *Enuma elish,* or the Babylonian Creation Epic, which is the myth that accompanied the ritual of the New Year festival, though it has clearly undergone considerable editing, goes back to Sumerian times, and so bears witness to the very early existence of the New Year, or *akitu* festival, as part of the cult pattern of the city states of Sumer and Akkad. Professor Sidney Smith's essay, which follows this, will describe the ritual patterns which gathered round the institution of kingship in these Mesopotamian city states, and will make clear the existence of those essential similarities denied or belittled by some of the opponents of the *Myth and Ritual* position during the last decade.

The question of what sort of religious pattern had developed in Canaan by the time the Hebrews entered that area is so bound up with the problem of the early religion of Israel that it will be best to discuss them together. Until comparatively recently our chief source of knowledge concerning Canaanite religion was the Old Testament, and when *Myth and Ritual* was published the Ras Shamra texts were just beginning to be studied, so that what was said there about them can now be corrected and amplified from the much fuller light which has been thrown upon them by thirty years of study. Much is still obscure, but it is safe to say that the shape of Canaanite religion tentatively presented in *Myth and Ritual* on the basis of what was then known about the Ras Shamra texts, has been confirmed in the main, though with important modifications, by fuller knowledge of those texts. But Professor de Langhe will be dealing with that subject in his essay, so that it need not be pursued farther here, except to say that Ugarit was, by reason of its position, open to culture contacts from many directions. Its material culture shows the influence of Egypt and Crete; the fact that its alphabetic script was written in a cuneiform of its own devising suggests Assyro-Babylonian contacts which are confirmed by business and state documents in Akkadian; and the pattern of its religion and mythology also suggests, either that it is the product of Assyro-Babylonian influence working upon an indigenous Canaanite pattern, or that both the Ugaritic and the Assyro-Babylonian complex of ritual and myth stem from some such early Semitic agricultural type of ritual as I have previously suggested. I think the former is more probable, but have no wish to be dogmatic on the point. I am also of the opinion that where traces of Assyro-Babylonian influence on the religion and culture of Israel appear, and it is impossible to deny their existence, they have been received mainly through the medium of Canaanite culture, though some borrowings probably took place during the period of Assyrian domination, and later on during the Exile.

Little needs to be said about the criticisms of R. P. de Fraine in his book *L'Aspect religieux de la royauté israélite*, save to remark that his denial of any borrowed elements in Israelite religion would be rejected by almost all Old Testament scholars today; it may be added that the Anglo-Scandinavian school which he has set up as his main target is a myth of his own invention.

With regard to Professor Mowinckel's criticisms, especially those in his recent fine book *He That Cometh*, it may be said that they are mainly directed against the more extreme forms of the 'ritual pattern' as theyhave developed in Scandinavia; and as this essay is concerned with *Myth and Ritual* and its past, all that need be said with regard to the idea which Professor Mowinckel is especially concerned to combat, namely, that Yahweh was ever thought of in Israel as a dying and rising god, is that I have never gone beyond what he himself admits when he says, 'At all events we may not draw conclusions from the wholly baalized cult of the bull-deity at Bethel about the conception of Yahweh in Jerusalem and the cult there',[1] but that, as will be seen later, the baalized cult of Bethel cannot be excluded from the expression 'the religion of Israel' which is so often used by the critics of the Myth and Ritual position. Professor Mowinckel concedes all that I should claim for *Myth and Ritual* when he says: 'At times this may not have held good in some syncretistic circles, and perhaps even in the official cult of the Northern Kingdom. It is also conceivable that in the time of David and Solomon the cult at Jerusalem was considerably more Canaanite than we can prove today.'[2] He also admits that the extant texts have been expurgated of traces of earlier Canaanite tendencies, and adds, 'what is more important is that the rites themselves were expurgated: that must have been a natural consequence of the purification of the cult'.[3] But the existence of rites that needed to be expurgated is implied, and the question of where they came from cannot be avoided.

What is meant by the expression 'the religion of Israel'? In the various criticisms of the Myth and Ritual position such expressions as 'the religion of Israel', 'the genuine Yahwism', 'the official religion of Israel', are of frequent occurrence as a kind of standard by which the suggestions of foreign elements are to be judged and rejected. It may be as well, therefore, to examine the evidence of the Old Testament itself to ascertain what meaning should be attached to these terms. In a passage from the monograph already quoted Professor Birkeland says: 'It must not be forgotten that the religion appearing in the Old Testament is not that of pre-Israelite Canaan surviving in popular notions and practices.'[4] Now 'the religion appearing in the Old Testament' is surely a somewhat vague expression. It is to be presumed that the two earliest streams of Hebrew immigration into Canaan, that represented by Abraham, and that represented by Jacob with his tradition of Aramaean ancestry, brought some kind of religion with them. In his monograph[5] Alt has shown how difficult it is

---

[1] S. Mowinckel, *He That Cometh* (Eng. tr.), p. 457, add. n. viii.
[2] S. Mowinckel, op. cit., p. 88.   [3] S. Mowinckel, op. cit., p. 88.
[4] H. Birkeland, op. cit., p. 19.
[5] A. Alt, *Der Gott der Väter*, in *Kleine Schriften zur Geschichte des Volkes Israel*, i. 1 ff.

to say what kind of religion it was, or what kind of god was the object of the earliest settlers' worship. Then it is generally recognized that only a portion of the original Hebrew settlers migrated to Egypt, experienced the great deliverance under Moses, and received from him, according to the tradition, the religion and cult of Yahweh; while that part of the Hebrew people which had not undergone these experiences remained in Canaan, gradually assimilating the agricultural way of life and its implications which they had met with as they settled there. Thus we have already three strands which must have gone to make up the religion of Israel during the confused period of the Judges, a time when, according to Hebrew tradition, 'every man did that which was right in his own eyes'; these three strands were (*a*) the religion which the original settlers brought with them, the patriarchal religion, (*b*) the religion developed by the settled tribes which did not go down into Egypt: a religion of which we can possibly glean something from the book of Judges, and which was probably largely shaped by Canaanite influences, (*c*) the religion which we can only describe as 'Mosaic', the result, according to tradition, of a special revelation made to Moses in Midian, imparted to the tribes whom he led out of Egypt, and carried by them into Canaan when they entered that country under the leadership of Joshua. How far there was some common and central element in these three historically separate strands which caused them to blend and ultimately develop into what might be called the 'official' religion of Israel is a difficult question. But I am prepared to say now what I should have hesitated to say thirty years ago, namely, that when the eighth- and seventh-century prophets look back over Israel's past and use such language as Jeremiah does when he says, 'I remember for thee the kindness of thy youth, the love of thine espousals; how thou wentest after me in the wilderness, in a land that was not sown. Israel was holiness unto the Lord, the firstfruits of his increase',[1] they are not merely idealizing a past of which they have little real knowledge. The very fact that such a religion as that which shines in the prophets could flower in the soil of Israel shows that

[1] Jer. ii. 2–3.

a vital seed was hidden in that soil. But it was doubtless a prophetic judgement that is expressed in the words of Ps. xcv. 10; 'Forty years long was I grieved with that generation, and said, It is a people that do err in their heart, and they have not known my ways.' In Ezek. xx. 13 we have that prophet saying: 'But the house of Israel rebelled against me in the wilderness: they walked not in my statutes, and they rejected my judgements, which if a man do, he shall live by them.' He goes on to describe what we are entitled to call the religion of Israel after their entry into Canaan, 'For when I brought them into the land, which I had lifted up mine hand to give them, then they looked out for every high hill, and every thick tree, and they offered there their sacrifices, and there they presented the provocation of their offering, there also they made their sweet savour, and they poured out there their drink offerings. Then I said unto them, What meaneth the high place, the name whereof is called Bamah unto this day?' When we add to this the picture of the religion of Israel in the book of Judges, and the implications of the ritual prohibitions in Leviticus and Deuteronomy, prohibitions which must have been directed against prevalent practices, it is difficult to deny that this is, to use Professor Birkeland's expression, 'the religion appearing in the Old Testament'. This is not something recklessly imposed by wicked 'patternists' upon a pure religion of Israel. We may recall Ezekiel's vivid presentation of his people's attitude as expressed in the words, 'In that ye say, We will be as the nations, as the families of the countries, to serve wood and stone' (Ezek. xx. 32). What I have said so far is intended to refer to the early period of Hebrew settlement in Canaan, before the institution of the monarchy; the passage of Ezekiel just quoted shows how far deliberate assimilation of Canaanite cult practices had gone in Israel very shortly after the entry into Canaan, and not even the most violent anti-patternist would venture to accuse Ezekiel of recklessly imposing the Canaanite cult pattern upon the religion of Israel. The Ras Shamra evidence, now so much better understood, shows how definite that pattern was, at any rate in the north-west corner of Canaan, and also how many features in it suggest the influence of Babylon or Assyria, and hence it is a legitimate inference that Israel came under that influence indirectly through its Canaanite contacts.

With the coming of the monarchy certain important changes in the religion of Israel seem to have taken place. The king assumed a place in the cult the significance of which will be discussed by Professor Johnson in his essay; but again the prophetic witness tells us that one of the causes which led to the introduction of this institution was the same desire, stigmatized by Ezekiel, to 'be as the nations'. In the later account in 1 Sam. viii. 5, the people are represented as saying to Samuel, 'Now make us a king to judge us, like all the nations.' In Eissfeldt's analysis[1] chapter viii is assigned to his III source, a later account of the introduction of the kingship than that given in chapters ix and x. It seems to have the stamp of the Deuteronomic point of view, and, leaving out of the question its historic accuracy, it would seem to indicate that from the outset the kingship in Israel had, to say the least, affinities with the pattern of kingship prevalent in Canaan. Have we any grounds then for supposing that under the monarchy we may find that pure Yahwism which rejects all foreign elements? Two points may first be made, concerning which doubt is hardly possible: first, the establishment of a capital and a court created a cult centre of a new kind. Shechem may have been in some sense a cult centre for such an early amphictyonic league as Professor Martin Noth[2] has familiarized us with, and it is not impossible that Baal-berith may have been a title under which Yahweh was designated as the presiding deity of the league.[3] By tradition Shiloh was the chief, though not the only cult centre, at the close of the period of the Judges. According to the account in 1 Sam. ii it would not appear that the cult as carried on there was in a very healthy state. The reference in v. 22 of that chapter to what the editor of the book regards as a particularly heinous sin of the sons of Eli, has been interpreted, and probably correctly, as indicating the presence of *qᵉdeshoth* in attendance at the shrine; further, Jeremiah's

---

[1] O. Eissfeldt, *Die Composition der Samuelisbücher.*
[2] M. Noth, *Das System der zwölf Stämme Israels.*
[3] Cf. E. Nielsen, *Shechem*, p. 118.

reference to the destruction of Shiloh in chapter vii. 12 gives us the prophetic judgement, which must have been based on tradition, to the effect that Shiloh had been destroyed by the Philistines because of Israel's wickedness. Thus we have a confirmation of what has already been said about the state of the religion of Israel in the pre-monarchic period. While David created a cult centre[1] in his new capital by bringing up the ark and housing it in what tradition held to be the original tent which had sheltered it in the wilderness, Jerusalem was not yet the chief cult centre for the united nation. At some point during the reign of Saul or the early years of David, Gibeon had become the chief national shrine, and it remained such until the building of Solomon's Temple. At the beginning of his reign Solomon, we are told by the compiler of the book of Kings, carried out those duties with regard to the cult which had become the function of the king, at the 'great high place' at Gibeon, and the annalist adds, with a touch of disapproval, 'only he sacrificed and burnt incense in the high places' (1 Kings iii. 3). Evidently the writer did not think that what Solomon did at the high places was really pleasing to Yahweh. But when we come to the break-up of the uneasy unity which had been created by David, and, to use Isaiah's phrase, 'Ephraim departed from Judah',[2] it becomes more than ever difficult to attach much meaning to the expression 'the religion of Israel as it appears in the Old Testament'. For we have a form of religion in the Northern Kingdom which the Deuteronomic commentator describes as 'the way of Jeroboam, the son of Nebat, who made Israel to sin'. This brings us to the second of the two points referred to above. The first is the appearance in Israel of a new kind of cult centre in which the king plays an important part, and a large staff of priests and prophets carry on their various official functions; the second point is the creation of a divergence between the urban form of the cult as practised at the Temple in Jerusalem, and what may be called the religion of the high places at various

---

[1] Cf. J. R. Porter, 'The Interpretation of 2 Sam. VI and Ps. CXXXII', in *J.T.S.*, N.S., v, pt. 2, pp. 172 f.

[2] Isa. vii. 17.

centres in the country districts. These local shrines had their own priests and carried on a form of cult which is consistently condemned by the prophets, and which the reforming kings sought with only partial success to eradicate. All this has to be included in the picture of 'the religion of Israel as it appears in the Old Testament'.

A further divergence was created by the schism between North and South. In order to prevent the people of his newly established kingdom from going up to Jerusalem to perform their religious duties, Jeroboam set up two new cult centres; one at the ancient cult centre of Bethel, which had been a Canaanite sanctuary before Israel's entry into the land, and the other at Dan in the extreme north. In these two new centres Jeroboam set up bull-images which he announced were the gods which had brought Israel out of Egypt; hence the cult practised at Dan and Bethel was intended to be a cult of Yahweh. Jeroboam placed priests in these sanctuaries, and arranged for the celebration of an autumn festival like that which was celebrated at Jerusalem, but a month later. When, later, Omri built his new capital at Samaria, that city also seems to have become a cult centre, for Hosea fulminates against the 'calf of Samaria',[1] and we have a vivid picture of Ahab 'inquiring of Yahweh' by what it may be permitted to call a victory ritual, carried out by a staff of 400 prophets,[2] who are evidently regarded by the king as prophets of Yahweh. Meanwhile, in the southern kingdom the cult of Yahweh continued to be carried on at the Temple. But there were high places with their local priests and cult in the country, and the remark frequently occurs in the Deuteronomic comments on the successive reigns, 'nevertheless the high places were not taken away'. It is often thought that the religion of the southern kingdom was purer than that of the northern. But what is recorded of the activities of the reforming kings bears witness that even in the Temple cult itself foreign elements were present, and if we are to believe Jeremiah and Ezekiel there was little to choose between the two. Indeed, Ezekiel goes so far as to assert that Jerusalem, under the symbolic designation of Oholibah,

---

[1] Hos. viii. 5–6.   [2] 1 Kings xxii. 6.

had gone to far greater lengths of depravity than her sister Samaria.[1] Once again it must be repeated that for the period of the monarchy, according to the evidence of Israel's own prophets, this is 'the religion of Israel as it appears in the Old Testament'. What are we to say when we find in the record the gardens of Adonis, Ezekiel's chambers of imagery, women weeping for Tammuz, women declaring that since they ceased baking cakes for the Queen of heaven nothing has gone well with them, the *maṣṣebuth*, the asherahs, the divinations, the 'seeking unto the *elohim*', and numerous other practices? It is surely impossible to deny that all these are foreign elements, some Canaanite, some presumably Assyro-Babylonian, and some possibly Egyptian, and that all these enter into the picture of 'the religion of Israel as it appears in the Old Testament'. It was from the careful analysis of all these elements that there emerged the 'ritual pattern' presented in *Myth and Ritual*. It was not imposed, recklessly or otherwise, upon the religion of Israel as the prophets saw it and contended with it, but although further knowledge has brought about modifications in details, especially in connexion with the kingship, I still find no cause to abandon the main outlines of the position laid down in *Myth and Ritual*. But it may be possible to remove one cause of misunderstanding. I see more clearly than I did thirty years ago that the eighth-century prophets did not create what it is proper to call the true religion of Israel. I firmly believe that God chose Israel to be the vehicle of revelation, and that in the experience of Abraham and Moses there was established a relationship of faith and obedience which was the vital seed that ultimately flowered in Deutero-Isaiah and the Servant Songs, and in such Psalms as the 51st and 139th which express a depth of religious experience without parallel in the religious literature of any other people. But, as we have seen from the evidence of the Hebrew prophets themselves, such a level of religious experience, such a conception of the character of Yahweh, was not to be found in the nation as a whole at any period of Old Testament history, for the prophetic judgement is directed against Israel as a nation, in the wilderness, in the early

[1] Ezek. xxiii. 4–11.

period of settlement, and under the monarchy. Speaking of one element in the 'pattern', Professor Baumgartner has rightly pointed to 'the deeply rooted repugnance to any sexual association with the deity which we find in Israelite religion'; but here again we find this misleading use of the term 'Israelite religion'. The second chapter of Hosea, to take only one example, shows that there were levels of religion in Israel, widely spread throughout the country, in which Yahweh was spoken of as a Baal and was associated in popular thought with those sexual elements in the fertility cults of Canaan whose existence is well attested. If this be denied, Hosea's polemic loses its point, and the poignancy of his transformation of the ritual marriage element in that level of Israelite religion which he is attacking into the magnificent symbolism of the spiritual marriage between Yahweh and a repentant Israel is destroyed. I might be allowed to quote here a passage from *Myth and Ritual* which the critics seem to have overlooked:

> There does not seem to be any reason for rejecting the tradition that Moses, the traditional founder of Hebrew religion, spent the first part of his life in the environment of the Egyptian court. Here he would be familiar with the ritual pattern of which the divine king was the centre in its most elaborate form. When he was obliged to leave Egypt, he spent some years among the pastoral tribes who occupied the steppes of Midian. Here he passed through the experience which is symbolized by the story of the burning bush. This seems to have impressed upon his mind a conception of the nature of God wholly incompatible with the conception of the Egyptian divine king. This might well have produced in him a strong revulsion against the whole ritual system of Egypt and especially against anything in it that implied the making of a man into a god.[1]

This should make it clear that wherever I have spoken of various elements of Canaanite or Babylonian origin as present in Israelite religious thought or practice, I have always had in mind such levels of Israelite religion as are described in the passages which I have quoted from the prophets. Finally I would add that long study of the Old Testament has convinced me that the persistence and

[1] S. H. Hooke, *Myth and Ritual*, pp. 11 f.

preservation of the vital seed in the religion of Israel lay in the principle of the remnant. Long before Isaiah called his son Shear-jashub, and enunciated his doctrine of the remnant, there had always been what St. Paul calls 'a remnant according to the election of grace'. The 'pattern', to use the offending word, of the remnant is found even in the myth of the Deluge; of all the generation that came out of Egypt only Joshua and Caleb survive by their faith to enter the Promised Land; when Elijah in an agony of self-pity cries out, 'I only am left', the Lord replies, 'Yet have I left me seven thousand in Israel, all the knees which have not bowed unto Baal, and every mouth which hath not kissed him.' Isaiah binds up the witness and seals the instruction among the little band of his disciples, and near the end of it all we find one of the latest prophets saying, 'Thus the poor of the flock that gave heed unto me knew that it was the word of the Lord.' It was among such as these that the original revelation to Moses survived, was deepened and enriched by all the experiences that the nation passed through, flowered in the lofty monotheism of Deutero-Isaiah and the figure of the Suffering Servant of Yahweh, and finally provided the humble circle into which Messiah, God incarnate, was born.

THE PRACTICE OF KINGSHIP
IN EARLY SEMITIC KINGDOMS

by SIDNEY SMITH

COMPLAINTS that modern histories of Western Asia in ancient times deal only with drums and trumpets, or fail to explain 'what it is all about', arise from the present condition of the studies involved. The prime need is to ascertain the course of events over an enormous period, before any attempt to give a general account of changing social conditions or to consider underlying causes can be made. The constant increase in the available sources delays even the collection of evidence as to the political constitutions of individual states. They were kingdoms, but the position of the king varied, and the political nature of the states has yet to be classified, for they were of varied origin. One aspect of kingship in all of them is the relation of the king to religious practice.

The kingdoms to be considered were pagan, the region in which they lay extends from the Mediterranean to the Zagros range, from the Taurus to the Indian Ocean. The pagan period in one part of that region, South Arabia, lasted longer than in the north, and our knowledge of the kingdoms there only begins about the seventh century B.C., whereas in the north the independent pagan states ended in the sixth century. Most of these kingdoms started as city states, some were larger units which arose from combinations under a single king, others were confederations recognizing a suzerain, in which individual states retained a measure of independence. Throughout the region the population was mixed. In early Babylonia, about which most is known, and in Assyria and Syria there were elements in it deriving from non-Semitic-speaking stocks. In South Arabia the people were more homogeneous, but the Sabaeans were distinguished from the men of Ma'in and Qataban by their speech, and in all the kingdoms there were northern Arabs with a distinct set of social habits. Kingship is a political institution and need not conform to racial divisions. Pagan religion, though the words used differ according to language, has much more to do with locality than with race, and cannot be rigorously classified even by locality.

The word 'king' needs definition. In modern usage the vague general idea implied, at any rate in the application to the ancient East, derives ultimately from Aristotle, the first to attempt to define kingship.[1] Thus our dictionaries give the meaning 'monarch', and Aristotle treated kingship as the natural form of monarchy, the other being the perversion, tyranny. He also distinguished kingship among barbarians, including all Orientals, from kingship among Greeks. The function of the king, he said, was to protect the minority, the 'better classes', against the populace, the majority. Tyrants were men who began their careers as demagogues or officers of state, seized kingship, and perverted it for their own benefit. The essential difference expressed itself in a simple apposition; the king, ruling by consent, depends on his own people for support and protection; the tyrant represses his subjects with the aid of mercenary troops. Underlying much that is now said of ancient kings there seems to be an impression that an Oriental king was invariably a tyrant.

The distinction Aristotle made between kingship among Greeks and among Orientals arose from his classification of two natural forms of human association, the one typified by the marriage of male and female, or the relation of natural master, and natural slave, the other by the *polis*. The *polis* is a natural form of society because it is a voluntary association to achieve the Good, and it is an essential characteristic of man that he can express, not merely pleasure and pain, like an animal, but judgement as to what is right and wrong, good or bad. Among barbarians there could be no such natural society, for all are slaves, even marriage is only a union of slaves. There can then be no *politikoi*, only a *basileus*. He ends his discussion of this point by quoting with approval verses to the effect that it is right for Greeks to rule barbarians.

[1] *Politics*, I. ii and III. xiv.

During Aristotle's own lifetime Alexander invaded Asia, but did not attempt to apply his master Aristotle's doctrine. Whatever may be thought of Alexander's prayer at Opis that Macedonians and Persians should be united by *homonoia* to live in unity of heart and mind, his policy of fusion of Macedonians and Persians meant the same thing for Orientals; the Achaemenid kings had followed a liberal policy in the provinces which had once been independent states. Seleucus I and Antiochus I followed Alexander's intention; both won support from their subjects. There was something wrong about Aristotle's view even when he wrote the 'Politics'.

Yet it is not easy to distinguish between what is erroneous and what is correct in his statement. All subjects of an Oriental king were his slaves or servants—there is only one word to cover the two states that we distinguish. But then Oriental kings were slaves too—of the gods; and a king's subjects took an oath by the gods to guard and protect him, so that their servitude to him was ultimately a servitude to the gods too. The distinction between the Greek *polis* and any Oriental form of state is extremely doubtful. The city state existed in Western Asia in Babylonia, Syria, and Palestine long before the historical period in Greece, and these states were not village communities, or tribal settlements, but agglomerations of a more composite character than any Greek *polis*. The Babylonians and Assyrians distinguished between the *maḫāzū*, the *ālū*, and the *ālū ṣiḫru*, though they were no more consistent in usage than we are about city and town. The first appellation is applied to only a few even of the great cities, and seems to refer to famous cult centres; it was used later by Christians for the seats of bishoprics. The second, *ālū*, applies to any town, but new documents of the eighteenth century now show that, when the territorial post-fix KI is added, a city state is meant. In such cases a city and the land round it form a natural unit, an enclave. In that enclave, because men were polytheists, the whole pantheon of gods was recognized; but the land was recognized to belong to one god. The conception is found throughout Semitic-speaking lands, in the form of the local *ba'alim*; Robertson Smith even inclined to the opinion that there was no *ba'al* apart from the god of a territory. The Babylonian city states existed in prehistoric periods.

The earliest documents from them are the Early Sumerian temple records. They are, for the greater part, routine business records, not merely dull but of most uncertain interpretation. The only general conclusion from them is that the temple directed every essential activity, not only matters that might be considered religious business, but the 'urban' activities of the craftsmen and traders and the 'rural' employment of farmers, shepherds, poultry-keepers, fishermen, and fruit gardeners. There was not, and in the alluvium could not be, any opposition between an 'urban' and a 'rural' civilization. The administrators were all priests, and the names of some orders show that we should consider their functions secular. There was doubtless some recognized relation in the status of the different orders, but it is practically impossible to deduce such a hierarchy. Each order had its own head, who always seems independent in his own sphere. Duties that we regard as typical of kings, the conduct of military operations or of foreign affairs, were undertaken by one whose title is written PA.TE.SI, read according to the modern fashion INSI, and translated 'governor'. The reason for this translation is that in the documents of the time of the Third Dynasty of Ur, INSI was used of the local rulers subject to the suzerains at Ur. But in the Early Sumerian period INSI alternates with the title LUGAL, literally 'great man', which we translate 'king'. The word LUGAL is not exclusively political in sense; it frequently means simply 'owner', the man with legal right to a possession. EN.TE.ME.NA of Lagash called himself 'INSI of Lagash, great INSI of NIN.GIR.SU, son of E.ANNA.TUM, INSI of Lagash, eldest son of UR.NINA (now often read UR. NANŠE), LUGAL of Lagash',[1] though he and his father ruled more extensive territories than the grandfather, and had no less authority in Lagash. Difference in translations must not be allowed to obscure the factual identity of the two words.

It is certain that the INSI was some kind of priest, just as in the South Arabian kingdoms the earliest-known rulers used

[1] Gadd and Legrain, *Royal Inscriptions* (Ur Excavation Texts), no. 1.

a priestly title, *mukarrib*, 'the bringer of offerings', before *malik* was adopted. The Akkadian translation of INSI, *iššaku*, remained in use throughout the history of the pagan kingdoms, and during one period Assyrian kings preferred it to *šarru*, 'king'. The word is almost invariably followed by the name of a deity or the state. This usage must be connected with its factual sense.

There was a kingship of another kind in the Early Sumerian period, that over Sumer and Akkad. The names of these two lands are written in descriptive ideograms, 'the land of the lord of the reed', not a bad description of the southern part of the alluvium, and 'the two outflows', that is the region where the Euphrates and the Tigris leave the limestone shelf at about the latitude of Baghdad. Whether the two names reflect some distinction in speech in a prehistoric period or not, it is certain that there was not even a tradition that there were two distinct political units; we only know of kings of Sumer and Akkad, the whole alluvium. This kingship was bestowed by Enlil of Nippur, though that city was never the capital of a dynasty ruling the whole of Sumer and Akkad. The kingship itself passed from dynasty to dynasty, from one city to another, the suzerain of Sumer and Akkad was never more than *primus inter pares*; in this his position resembled that of Enlil, acknowledged before Marduk as the lord of the gods, but an equal among the great gods. Kingship over Sumer and Akkad was attained by victory of one city state over others. The gods of the cities were said to strive against one another. Originally, then, there was a distinction; when a king was to be king of Sumer and Akkad, Enlil, the god of a city which remained outside the strife, bestowed the kingship, though the recipient was already the king of a city state, recognized by the local state god. Later, after the time of the First Dynasty of Babylon, and almost certainly after the time of the first Kassite kings,[1] when Marduk was lord of the

---

[1] Hammu-rabi and Samsu-iluna continued to recognize Enlil, so did Gandaš, on the evidence of a text condemned by some as a forgery. Later Kassite dedications at Nippur may imply continued recognition. In the late period mention of Enlil as bestowing kingship in Babylonia is irregular.

gods, kingship of Babylon became indissolubly united with kingship over Sumer and Akkad, and a king recognized by a local
state god became automatically king of the whole land—theoretically, for such a king was not invariably recognized by all those
he claimed as subjects.

The relation between the king and the god can be divined
from the use of the word INSI, *iššaku*, in the time of the First
Dynasty of Babylon, when it was applied to the holders of
allotments on state territory won by conquest; these tenants were
either men entitled for unstated reasons to sustenance from the
king, *epru*, or members of para-military forces and subject to
regular annual terms of service, the allotment being a form of
wage. In effect this system is that found in military colonies
planted in subject territories by Roman Emperors.[1] It was in
existence from a very early period; the first known evidence for
it belongs to the reign of *Man-ištusu* of the Agade Dynasty.
Whatever the etymological meaning of INSI may be, it implied
that the ruler was the tenant farmer of the god. This aspect of
kingship underlies epithets constantly used in royal inscriptions,
in various combinations, *ikkaru kenu*, 'constant field-labourer',
SIPA.ZI, 'faithful shepherd', *irrišu*, 'cultivator', and the like.
Constant repetition robs such epithets of original meaning—the
typical example in the Christian period is *fidei defensor*; but
original meaning there must have been. The king as 'tenant
farmer' was responsible to the god for the use of the god's land.
The terminology, and the conception, belong to a period earlier
than any of which we have historical knowledge.

Anthropologists and travellers continually report cases of rulers
being regarded as responsible for delay in the coming of the
rains, for bad crops, and for other natural, or seasonal, disasters.
The belief that the ruler is responsible in such matters does not
imply that his subjects attribute to him superhuman powers. It
is at this point that the discussion of the relative importance of
similarities and dissimilarities should begin. In Babylonia in some
prehistoric period there existed a belief that the king was responsible for the state of agricultural land, and for the timely occurrence

[1] F. Thureau-Dangin, *Lettres de Hammu-rapi à Šamaš-haṣir*.

of seasonal phenomena, and that belief exists today sporadically over the East. A traveller has told of the Muslim sect in a remote valley of northern Pakistan which blames the ruler for late rains. It is the interior economy of a land that is of importance to the inhabitants; conflict with other states generally arises if factors affecting that economy are interfered with by 'foreigners'. The war between Lagash and Umma illustrates a universal principle. Not all wars arose from dynastic ambition, much less from personal despotism. Little is known about the internal administration of the early kingdoms, but it is certain that it was devoted in no small part to maintaining the productivity of the land and to all connected with it, as well as to collecting revenue. Within the alluvium this was even true of a kingdom which had conquered another state. Hammu-rabi of Babylon annexed the extensive kingdom of Larsa in his thirty-first year; between then and his last, forty-third, year his instructions in letters to the provincial governor, Sin-idinnam, show the extent of the state works carried out. The kingdom of Ešnunna, outside the alluvium, east of the Tigris, was intentionally ruined by flooding during those years. Ma'er's fortifications were dismantled, which meant that the people there had no protection for their crops. The comparison of the measures taken in the three lands shows that Enlil's land was in a special category. Such incidents are a warning against disregard of the practical effect of the conception in the epithets.

There is no mention of this aspect of kingship in the account given by Aristotle of the powers and responsibilities of kings in civilized lands. He held that in the Heroic Age kingship was limited to leadership in war and to certain religious observances. Dictatorship, limited to a period, he regarded as an elective form of tyranny. Kingship of the kind found in Sparta, where it was vested in two different families and was inherited, was simply military leadership with certain privileges at public meals. He admitted that some legal powers belonged to the king of the Heroic Age, and significantly added that the power of the king as judge, when an action involved an oath, was symbolized by the lifting of the sceptre. Such powers as Greek kings had in urban, rural, and foreign affairs were voluntarily relinquished, others were taken away by the masses and finally only the management of traditional sacrifices remained; Aristotle had the *basileus* archon at Athens in mind.

Ancient kingship in Western Asia had all the features thus attributed to different periods in Greece, even that of election; but the selection of kings by vote, as in the case of the dictatorship, was in Western Asia a selection by the gods, in ritual practice by omens. This is expressed in the royal inscriptions by phrases that might seem to be simple metaphors, such as that the gods regarded with favour, or that they formed, such a one for kingship. There are no precise accounts of appointment to, or proclamation of, kingship in Babylonian records, but there is one significant indication that it was connected with the year. The last, broken, regnal year of a king was attributed to him; for his successor the months of the broken year were 'the moment of kingship', *šurru šarruti*, generally translated 'beginning of kingship'.[1] The first year of a reign began with Nisan following the death of the old king. The significance of this can be seen from the rites at the New Year festival in Babylon.

These are known from a copy written in the Seleucid period of a text giving summary instructions. These instructions could only be appropriate while Babylon was still an independent kingdom, and there is no doubt that the original text dated from at latest the Chaldaean dynasty founded by Nabopolassar. The rites themselves must be much earlier, for no member of that dynasty would have introduced changes. On the fifth day of the festival, after the dawn meal of Marduk had been cleared away, a retinue of priests accompanied the king to the chamber of the supreme god, which he entered alone.[2] Then the head of the

---

[1] *s/šurru* is the basic noun in the adverb *šurriš*, 'at this moment, immediately', and in *asuri, issuri*, 'at or in the event, in this case', e.g. in the phrase *issuri šarru iqabbi*, 'at this time (in this event) the king may say'.

[2] Babylonian temples were private households of the gods. The entry to any chapel was from a courtyard, the space at the entry not suitable for public worship. The times when the gods appeared to the public were confined to public processions, and even then they were enshrined. Some chapels had doors in the short side with the statue facing the door; assembled priests in the court could then see it. Some chapels had doors in the long side, not facing the statue at the far, short end. There are occasional cases of

kalu order of priests entered, removed the royal insignia and apparel, placing them before the god, struck the king's cheek, boxed his ears, and made him kneel to recite a sort of negative confession, to the effect that he had not failed to revere the god, had not brought destruction on his city, had not forgotten the rites, had not smitten or humiliated his people or weakened the defences. If the king did not weep when struck, the omen was bad—that is, unfavourable to the naked man who had been king. Psychological explanations of this ceremony must not be allowed to evade an obvious fact. A king without his insignia, naked, is not a king. That is the justification for not accepting the validity of denials that this was an annual submission to re-election by the god.

The extent to which kings were subject to the consent of the gods expressed by omens is perhaps insufficiently realized. It is illustrated in the great archive found at Ma'er, Tall Hariri, which belongs to the eighteenth century, in detailed accounts even of military actions undertaken by subordinates at the order of kings. It was at one time commonly held that the extreme developments of divination were peculiar to the later periods; they represented, it was thought, one kind of degeneration from comparatively simple forms of faith and ethics through the accumulation of superstitions. The degeneration, it was inferred, was progressive, and largely due to the self-interested motives of the priesthood. That view is quite untenable. Not only do the Assyrian kings of the eighteenth century, writing about the dispatch of military forces on campaign, state that the omens are good or bad, but an officer telling of the posting of men at particular points for the defence of a besieged city has to inform the king that he has consulted the omens. Lists of omens from the liver in the Old Babylonian period have now been published. The evidence is conclusive.

Such practices are not necessarily connected with kingship.

the door in the centre of the long side facing the statue. The disposition must in practice have depended on the ceremonial; it was not desirable that the god should be visible from the court in all cases. The distribution of these types in Babylonia and Assyria does not favour the division into distinct 'northern' and 'southern' types. One type secured absolute privacy.

At a time when the children of Israel had no kings, but were led in times of crisis by a *šōpeṭ*, whose office must have resembled that of a censor much more than that of a judge, Judges xx tells of regular consultation at the oracle in Bethel between the attacks of the other tribes on Benjamin. How replies were obtained is not stated; if the story is historical, some form of divination must have been employed. But that wherever there were kings, recourse was had by them to this practice there can be no reasonable doubt. In the South Arabian kingdoms the king in assembly required the assent of the oracle, *mas'al*, like any private person.

The subjection of the individual actions of the king to a procedure—the framing of a question capable of only a positive or negative response, the examination of the liver or the flight of birds or the like, the decision as to how the many omens were to be interpreted to procure a majority of favourable or unfavourable results—shows that no king acted according to his own judgement alone, without the possibility of interference by others. They were themselves well instructed in the devices of divination, to judge by a letter of Išme-Dagan found at Ma'er, in which he denies that some appearance of the liver has been correctly interpreted.[1] But they cannot always have forced measures through, if the diviners were in opposition. The same observation applies to the royal sacrifices, a part of the king's duties everywhere. If the smoke of the burnt sacrifices went the wrong way, if the libations did not meet with the expected response, the disfavour of the gods must have been known publicly. In fact there was a constant succession of tests of the favour of the gods.

These tests were the occasions when the king performed priestly duties. There is a curious illustration of the popular demand that he should act as priest in the story of the first king of the Hebrews. Samuel opposed, but could not prevent, the appointment of a king. After the victory over Agag, the people demanded that Saul should sacrifice the cattle taken in Gilgal, in spite of the instructions of the Lord through Samuel. Samuel never forgave Saul for assenting to the popular demand. In a community like that of the Hebrews, which deliberately cut

[1] *A.R.M.* iv. 54.

itself off from pagan beliefs and practices, the incident is striking. David, when he danced before the ark on its entry into Jerusalem, did what priests did in the processions at pagan festivals. The association of kingship with certain rites was very strong everywhere. With one type of rite, the seasonal festival, the association of the king took peculiar forms. To exemplify this, one seasonal festival will serve, and the one about which most is known is the sacred marriage.

This rite was not confined to Western Asia. When the royal duties at Athens were divided among nine archons—the three principals, namely the First Archon, the *basileus*, the polemarch, and the six juniors, the Thesmothetai—it is to be assumed that there was some special reason for maintaining this rite of the sacred marriage. The *basilissa* or *basilinna*, the wife of the *basileus*, who abode in the *boukolion*, a cattleman's hut, was solemnly wedded to Dionysus at the Lenaion, on the third day of the festival of the Anthesteria, then roughly in February. It was an annual, seasonal rite, and its origin must be considered very early. In later times the day of the celebration given would always fall in the right season of the year. But the point to be considered with regard to a dated festival in early times should always be, what arrangements were made in periods when there was a not inconsiderable oscillation of the official calendar in the seasonal year. A festival of seasonal character held in the wrong season is ridiculous.[1] More than that, days have their own character in early calendars. A festival must not be celebrated on an unsuitable day.

The Jews had to deal with this problem when they finally accepted the determination of the mean solar year for the prognostication of their calendar of lunar months, with intercalations.

---

[1] Egypt might be thought to exemplify the celebration of seasonal festivals out of season, owing to the sliding calendar, but the evidence requires reconsideration. There were three factors in time reckoning. The 'civil' calendar provided a fixed sequence of days, like the Babylonian abstract calendars. Lunar months were observed, and constituted a separate calendar for which the civil calendar nomenclature could be used. Annual observation of the rising of Sirius related both the current civil and the lunar calendar to the seasons. The evidence has been conveniently set out in R. A. Parker, *The Calendars of Egypt*. The late Roman-period calendars must exemplify the way seasonal festivals were kept in their place much earlier.

In order to avoid the coincidence of certain festivals with the Sabbath, rules were adopted for a complicated arithmetical adjustment. Only a long-standing tradition can have required such a provision, still in force for the religious calendar. It is, then, to be expected that such adjustments were known elsewhere.

In the pagan calendars there is no evidence that the days of any sort of week played a part in religious observance, but the numbered days of the observed lunar month did. That is proved not only by the lists of lucky and unlucky days, but also by texts which prescribe sacrifices and tabus for the days of the month. This latter class of texts, now called hemerologies, did not concern the general public; a comparison of them with dated business documents shows that transactions were in fact concluded on days described as 'dangerous' or 'bad'. Letters from the royal archive of the seventh century at Nineveh prove that diviners made calculations each year as to the character of particular days of the lunar months in the current calendar year, and advised the king accordingly. There were of course two factors to be considered, the oscillation of 1st Nisan in the solar year, and the actual lengths of the lunar months, which were regulated by observation. Before the Hellenistic period divination was primarily conducted for state business, whatever type of organized omen-taking it was, by the entrails of sacrificed animals, by the release of birds, or by the heavenly bodies. Only casual omens, or the dreams secured by incubation, were, as a general rule, available for private persons. Decision as to the character of a day, as it affected the state, ruled the conduct of the king, and it is apparent from what is said in some letters that Assyrian kings of the seventh century were impatient of the fastings and other restrictions imposed. Evidence that royal ritual observances were adjusted to the day of the year, rather than to the numbered days of the observed lunar month, indicates that something of the same sort was done in the case of festivals.

The hemerologies, giving general instructions about the daily royal ritual, give calendar dates, by months and numbered days. In each of the twelve months there are thirty days, and there are two months of Nisan. There was never, in Babylonia, a time when, in the Nippur calendar, each of the twelve months had thirty days, for each month began with the evening on which the new crescent was seen. There was never a year of 360 days; that figure is simply a rounding off of the real year to a figure easily manipulated in giving general instructions, and it is found used that way in the posing and solution of the problems which used, in this country, to be set as 'Practice'. There is no evidence that Nisan was ever regularly doubled in embolismic years. The Babylonians arrived at 360 for several purposes. The day was divided into light and night, marked by the disappearance and the reappearance of the sun's limb. The water-clock, a rectangular or cylindrical tank, shallow to avoid so far as possible the error caused by pressure of water, measured time by the weight of water which issued from it, and was adjusted to the equinoctial day, a mina of weight for each of 6 tours of duty by the watch.[1] A mina weight was 60 shekels, so the day had 360 time units. In a text dealing with intercalation, the appended table to instructions shows a year divided like the night into three tours, that is 180 standard time units; the 360 days of the abstract calendar in the hemerologies show that there was an older analogy of the year, not to the night, but to a complete day. Both the days and the year were treated as circles, and the division of the circle into 360 degrees started in Babylonia. The Babylonians never knew how to use mean averages in their calculations; they used approximations, and in texts giving general instructions they were content with the approximate figure that was easy to manipulate; thus they used one-third for the relation of the diameter to the circumference, *pi*, though they knew it was wrong. Tables giving a 360-day year which never agreed with a current year could be written out and compared, as each new moon was observed, with a current year. On the resulting character of each day the king's daily ritual depended. But it was also affected by intercalation.

[1] '3 minas the day-watch, 3 minas the night-watch.' The interpretation of O. Neugebauer, that each tour lasted 3 minas of water from the clock, results in a division of the equinoctial day into 18 time units, for which there is no evidence. The correct interpretation was known to J. K. Fotheringham, whose explanation of the tally from Nineveh was based on it. This Neugebauer rejects.

It is often assumed that intercalation could be administered by observation of the state of the crops or some similar seasonal phenomenon. In pagan Western Asia, however, in the earliest known period city states had their own calendars; essentially they were all the same, but there were different usages. In Babylonia, the name of a month may recur in different calendars, very occasionally in a different order. But there is no evidence that in any of these states the beginning of the calendar year fell in autumn. The Nippur calendar always began with Nisan; there are known cases of the year beginning at Ur with the month that corresponded to Adar, in Elam with Ayaru of Nippur, none later. The Nippur calendar was that of the lord of Sumer and Akkad, who bestowed the kingship over the united land, and for that reason kings who ruled Sumer and Akkad imposed it on all cities; the calendars of the independent cities disappear after the Third Dynasty of Ur. In any land where crops ripen at different times, above all in a land sufficiently extensive to require an interval between the decision whether the next new crescent will be 1st Nisan and the appearance of the new crescent, observation of crops or the like would not be a practical guide.

There were three main guides to reckoning. First, observation of the moon made it possible to guess whether the twelfth month would last thirty or twenty-nine days.[1] There was a totally erroneous rule for calculating the length of the invisibility between the old crescent and the new, but the approximation can rarely have been wrong. Second, continuous observation of the time between sunrise and sunset, compared with the time between sunset and sunrise, was a guide to the approach of both the spring and the autumn equinox. Third, observation of the heliacal risings and settings of the signs of certain constellations, especially those constellations which constituted a lunar zodiac, provided a reckoning in a practically invariable stellar year. In the twelfth month it was then possible to estimate whether certain stars would be visible within a certain number

---

[1] Owing to accidents of visibility observation led to there being months of 31 and even 28 days; such aberrations were corrected by lengthening of months on the late observation of the new crescent.

of days before or after the next new crescent, and about which day the equinox might be expected. If the equinox was likely to fall before the middle of the twelfth month, intercalation was necessary and we know that dispatches to that effect were issued.

Both divination and the administration of the calendar required a system of observation, and the observers required instructions. They had to be taught to measure by standard time, that is by the hours of the equinoctial day, the nychthemeron. A table converting the changing seasonal hours into standard time is inscribed on a fragment of an ivory tally stick from Nineveh.[1] There was also a table of the lengths of fifteenths of the night for days beginning before the 15th Adar and continuing after 15th Nisan, in this schematic calendar the day of the equinox. The progressive lengthening and shortening of the days is represented by an arithmetical progression with the ratio of light to night at the summer solstice 2 : 1, reversed at the winter solstice. This is not only grossly inexact, but was known to the Babylonians to be so, for another text gives the ratio 3 : 2, nearly right; for daylight at the summer solstice in Baghdad lasts about 14 hours 20 minutes. The fifteenths of the night represent, for the days intended, the course of the moon's visibility.[2] This is simply derived from the reduction of the moon's course in any one month to the scheme 'full moon in the sky from sunset to sunrise on the 15th day', which does not correspond to ordinary observation.

---

[1] Published in S. H. Langdon, *Babylonian Menologies*, p. 55; columns C and D were explained by Fotheringham in *The Observatory*, Dec. 1932, pp. 338–40.

[2] On the tally column A has the progression from 13 50 to 13 20. Column B on the left runs from 12 50 to 12 30, on the right from 12 20 to 11 50. These are fifteenths of nights which in A shortened from 3 minas 27 shekels in standard time to 3 minas 20 shekels and in B from 3 minas 6 shekels to 2 minas 57 shekels 30 sixtieths. In the appendix of O. Neugebauer's article in *Isis*, xxxvii. 37–43, there is a transcription of the unpublished second tablet of the 'Plough Star', Obv. ii. 43–44: 'On the 1st Nisan, the (whole) night-watch lasting 3 minas 10 shekels, at 12 quadruple minutes 40 sixtieths, setting of the moon. On 15th Nisan, the (whole) night-watch lasting 3 minas, at 12 quadruple minutes, moon-rise.' Similarly the second tablet of 'Observe the (sky) pattern' series: 'On 1st Adar, (the night being) 3 30, then 3 30 times 4 (a division by 15), 14 quadruple minutes (elapse from sunset) to the setting of the moon. And on the 15th, (the whole night being) 3 20, then 3 20 times 4, 13 20 (elapse from sunset to) moon-rise.' Both texts are based on the scheme: equinox, 15th Nisan. That must apply to the tally.

The series called 'The Plough Star', often treated as if it was a compendium of Babylonian astronomical knowledge, is, like the tables of the length of daylight and night in different months, or of the retardation of the moon, really for instruction, listing the constellations, giving calendar dates for heliacal risings and settings, the intervals between the setting of one star and the rising of another, stating the association of the seasons with the sun's crossing of a belt round the celestial equator. The calendar dates given can never all have been correct in any one year, and the calendar meant is once again the schematic twelve months of thirty days. The text is part of the teaching of observers as to what is to be regularly recorded.

The instructions for deciding whether a year is to end with the twelfth month or to include thirteen months begins with an enumeration of series of celestial and terrestrial omens in which the omens were connected with the calendar dates. The first instruction is to write out the schematic calendar, presumably with the relevant omens, and to reserve the days of the New Year festival. This has nothing to do with an actual epact, or any form of epagomenal days, which were unknown in Babylonian practice. The phrase means, as may be seen from the mathematical texts, that the days of the New Year festival are to be fixed later in the calculation. The observations made during the actual months and days correspond to the three guiding factors, the lengths of daylight and night, the course of the moon, the dates of the risings and settings of certain stars. The final point in the calculation is the instruction to set down the visibility of the new moon in relation to the constellation 'One Acre'. It was that which would determine whether an intercalary month was necessary.

In the tables and texts connected with this matter of intercalation, there are two alternatives for the date of the spring equinox. In one set, it is assumed that the equinox is 15th Adar. In the other, it is 15th Nisan. That is to say, it was considered permissible to adjust the calendar provided that this did not mean that the equinox would occur in the first half of Adar. It was not necessary to intercalate a month unless failure to do so meant that the equinox would occur in the second half of Nisan. The rule was followed fairly faithfully in practice, to judge from those series of years where intercalation can be followed from datings. Occasionally the oscillation exceeded thirty days. Sometimes the administration broke down, and a failure to intercalate in the correct year might require intercalation in two successive years, or even two intercalations in one year. Sometimes the cause of the breakdown is ascertainable, a known political calamity, more often not. The king, whose own daily conduct was ruled by rituals, was responsible to his subjects for the administration of the calendar; his convenience had to be considered.

The instructions for the celebration of the New Year festival at Babylon date the days for the celebration to Nisan 1–12; on the last day the assembled gods returned to their cities. There are two different sets of hemerologies. One was found at Ashur, probably of eleventh-century date so far as the copy is concerned, the other at Nineveh, not earlier than the eighth century, but the original text must be much older. There are differences between the two, not important, but sufficient to show that either the two sets represent the traditions of different temple schools, or that there was correction and revision at some unknown date. Neither set refers to the festivals; they deal only with the daily observances. In the set from Ashur the 'dangerous' or 'bad' character of the first sixteen days—the number is due to the scheme which treats the fifteenth day as that of the full moon—is more precise; this is to be associated with the oscillation of the dates of celestial phenomena in the official calendar. In the set from Nineveh a 'bad' day can be marked 'favourable'; this resembles the contrary apodoses in omens.

On these entries an assumption about the duration of the New Year festival in the earlier periods has been founded, and also about a reform of the observances. The 'bad' or 'dangerous' days are thought to be exactly those of the festival, and thus show that the rites in the eleventh century lasted sixteen days; the further assumption is then made that the different formulae of the Nineveh hemerologies indicate that Ashurbanipal introduced these changes in daily observance. The reduction of the sixteen days to eleven is then attributed to Nebuchadrezzar. There is no positive evidence for all this, and the conclusions are not inherently probable. The Nineveh archive proves that in ritual matters the late Assyrian kings had to do what they were told— a position in which kings have frequently been placed. The early kings of the Chaldaean Dynasty intentionally magnified the importance of the festival, as may be read in their inscriptions; none of them is likely to have curtailed the days of joy and rejoicing, an act that not only would have required the consent of the priesthood, but would have incurred the anger of the populace. Since some importance has been attached to the assumptions about reforms of the calendar by Ashurbanipal and Nebuchadrezzar in criticism of the thesis proposed in *Myth and Ritual*, it is of interest in the present reconsideration of that thesis to distinguish between what is known and what has arisen through modern interpretation.

It has been shown that in general instructions the Babylonian use of calendar dates can be inapplicable to any calendar year, but depends on an abstract scheme for adjustment to an official year. The doubt about the dates in the general instructions for the New Year festival is, then, as to what the calendar dates mean. On 4th Nisan the priest recited 'One Acre, Esagila, heavenly and earthly counterparts.' 'One Acre' was a constellation; the precinct of Esagila, the temple of Marduk, was theoretically its counterpart on earth. The Babylonians had in fact a scheme for relating distances between the stars and distances on earth, which was connected with their inter-relation of time, weight, and distance measurements.[1] On 5th Nisan the chant was 'Divine Bull, glorious light which lightens the darkness', an allusion to the expected heliacal rising of the sign of Taurus. The rites need not mean more than that the constellations were visible on the days of the chants; but when 1st Nisan slides in the solar year to a day over a month earlier than the first day of the rising of the sign of Taurus, the rite is rendered unseasonable. It is possible that 1st Nisan in the instructions simply represents the day on which the festival began in an abstract scheme, unrelated to the days actually selected; and that is the conclusion to which

[1] See the text published by F. Thureau-Dangin in *R.A.* x. 215–25.

the instruction in the seventh-century text about intercalation points. The matter is of slight interest, apart from the fact that the New Year festival at Babylon was really a commemoration of the construction of the temple of Marduk in heaven after he had defeated Chaos and ordered the universe.

The Creation Epic was recited twice at the New Year Festival at Babylon, and the last event in it is the construction of that temple in heaven by the lesser gods. The substance of the Epic is the story of Marduk prior to that event. It is coherent as a story, and its recital at the festival shows that the triumph over Chaos was thought of as an annual event preceding the period of the festival. On the other hand there is no mention of the marriage of Marduk in it. A festival calendar[1] has an entry that 'Marduk hastened to bridal, *ḫadaššutu*', after 11th Nisan, that is presumably after the festival.

The class of texts called 'commentaries' have not, as yet, been studied as a whole. They resemble in some ways the Talmud, and were obviously for the instruction of priests in the temple schools. A commentary on a literary text, for example, gives notes on words and phrases, dissecting the written form, often in the odd way that is found in the Jewish commentaries. There are commentaries on, for instance, month names, generally right in giving the sense, but often indulging in the same queer tricks to explain the written form as will sometimes be found in the reasoning of the rabbis about the use of one word in preference to another. The commentaries on ritual actions connected with the myth of Marduk are ill preserved, and it has frequently been observed that the meaning is obscure; some hold that it is too obscure to permit interpretation. That is just; the story of Marduk belongs to pagan, polytheistic thought,

---

[1] Reisner, *Sumerisch-babylonische Hymnen*, pl. 145, VAT 663, obv. 7–10, transliteration and comments in Pallis, *The Babylonian Akitu Festival*, p. 198: *um* 11 KAN *ina qirib E. ŠIGIŠŠE itenippušu isinnu ... apkallu mati* (?) *danu. iḫiš ana ḫadaš-šutu*. 'On the 11th, they regularly perform the festival in the house of sacrifices ... (to ?) the mighty ancient wise spirit of the land (?). He hastened to bridal.' The context, being broken, is therefore obscure. As the text gives rites of a Marduk festival followed by comments, the inference that Marduk is the subject of *iḫiš* is justified.

of a kind not unfamiliar to anthropologists. Modern Europeans cannot, on rational lines, hope to understand the explanations. But there is no warrant for neglecting what can be gathered from the commentaries as to the events in the myth. It seems quite certain from these that part of Marduk's story included an imprisonment in the 'mountain' of the underworld, that his consort Ṣarpanitum was smeared with blood from his wounds, that the gods rescued him by boring a hole in the door of the mountain. Because Nisan is twice mentioned in this text it has been inferred that all the events were represented in the Nisan rites. The text does not necessitate that view, and all else known conflicts with it, not least the 'joy and rejoicing' at the festival.

Marduk was in fact one kind of year-god, with a cycle that is recognizable, birth, vigorous youth, success over other powers, recognition as supreme, marriage, eclipse, re-arising. This cycle is reflected in his identification with heavenly bodies through the months of the year. In Ṭebitum, the tenth month, he was the star LUGAL, our Regulus in Leo. That cannot be unconnected with the election of Marduk to kingship. In Simanu, the third month, he was the constellation 'One Acre', the 'great square' of Pegasus with α Andromedae, the counterpart of Esagila. In many months he was Jupiter, sometimes *niberu*, 'the star of the crossing-place', certainly not Jupiter. It seems hopeless to attempt to elucidate the riddles; to ascribe all this to 'astrology' and late interpretation is surely wrong, for man related stories about, and elaborated deities out of, the heavenly bodies from the earliest times. Babylonian myths had a similar cycle for all kinds of year-gods; that is why it can be argued that the Marduk myth as we know it was an adaptation of an earlier Enurta myth. Other gods had their New Year festivals, in which the ritual apparently resembled that of Babylon. It is to be presumed that the ritual of the bridal of Marduk and Ṣarpanitum was celebrated at the same time as a seasonal festival, the sacred marriage, elsewhere. Definite evidence that it was celebrated at the New Year festival is lacking, the best witness is the statement that implies a bridal after the festival.

The almost exclusive preoccupation with the New Year

festival in modern studies tends to obscure the round of seasonal festivals celebrated in all the cities. That tendency is partly due to the fact that in themselves the words 'new year', like the Hebrew *Rosh ha-Shanah*, can be understood to mean any festival that inaugurates a new cycle of events. But there was really only one New Year festival, at the beginning of the calendar for a new year, and it was called *zagmukku*, 'the edge of the year'. It was also called *akitum*, also a word of Sumerian origin, but there were festivals called *akitum* in months which were never the first month of the calendar. There were, for instance, *akitum* festivals in *Teśritum* in cities which had the New Year *akitum* in Nisan. It seems a *reductio ad absurdum* to call both New Year festivals; *akitu* were seasonal.

The best account of the sacred marriage is to be found in those inscriptions of GU.DE.A which deal with the marriage of the state god and goddess at Lagash. It is often said that this was celebrated in the first month of the year, because the *tirḫatu*, one of the presents the groom gave to the bride, was received by the goddess in that month. But the gifts preceded marriage; the correct annual season for the rite is indicated by the text which says that when the goddess Baba lay beside NIN.GIRSU, the lord of the territory east of the Tigris in which Lagash lay, the river was in spate. The flood reaches Baghdad late in May; the date on the Shaṭṭ al Hai is of course a little later. The celebration of the connubium at Lagash is then a rather crass form of symbolism; and it has nothing to do, at least immediately, with refructification of the soil for growing crops. Its importance is connected with date plantations, and orchards generally; between the river floods and fruit harvests came the arid summer.

In the royal correspondence from Nineveh, in two letters, one addressed to the king, one to the 'king's son', that is the heir, details are given of the ritual for the marriage of Nabu and his consort Tašmetum at Calah, Nimrud; the date of the festival appears in one letter, 4th to 14th Ayaru. The numbered days have apparently no significance other than would attach to them in a particular year, and it is probable that this is a case of adjustment to the current calendar. The god of Calah was Enurta, identified in the sky with Sirius. Nabu was the son of Marduk, his city was Borsippa; the point is significant, for Ayaru is called 'the month of Ea', the god of magic, of sweet water, of the southern sky, the grandfather of Nabu. The rigmarole is senseless for us; when the festivals were celebrated all this was thought to have a significance. There can be no doubt that at Calah the festival always fell in Ayaru, roughly May. That would accord with the indication of the date at Lagash.

In the documents of the fifteenth century from Nuzu, not far from Kirkuk, there appears a form of the month-name Ayaru, *ḫiaru*, which is early, for it appears as the name of a festival of the state goddess of Alalakh, 'Atšanah, on the northern Orontes, in an account docket of the eighteenth century.[1] The text deals with the issue of sheep for sacrifice, one to a 'king's son' who did not become a king. The last entry reads: 'One sheep when Ḥepat sanctifies (or, has sanctified, *uqaddiš*).' This last entry is a direct reference to a form of the sacred connubium yet to be illustrated. The form *ḫiaru* is a correct phonetic development, in certain dialects, from *ḫayaru*; the *faʿal* form is retained in Ayaru, with dropping of the aspirate for the stopped initial (as in 'Iyyar). The nominal form derives from a verbal root which commonly means 'to sue for a girl in marriage', but is used, in the Creation Epic, of the selection of a husband by a goddess, in that case Chaos herself, Tiamat.

In cuneiform the month-names of the Nippur calendar are generally written in the 'Sumerian' form, and the Sumerian forms are descriptive. Ayaru was GUD.SI.SA, rightly interpreted in an Akkadian commentary as 'bull-driving'. The ritual of the marriage of Nabu at Calah was celebrated on a threshing floor, and ended with the god hunting bulls and lions in a park, *ambassu*; the kind of park meant is illustrated by the reliefs from Ashurbanipal's palace; it is not unlikely that the scenes depicted belong to a ritual hunt.[2] The approach of the hot weather in these

[1] D. J. Wiseman, *The Alalakh Tablets*, no. 346.

[2] The ritual hunt as part of the rites performed by Amenḥetep III as well as of Thutmose IV, in the test for approval of their succession, is mentioned on the stelae from between the paws of the great sphinx. Similar hunts in south Arabian kingdoms have been elucidated by A. F. L. Beeston in *Museon*, lxi. 183–96. In RES 4177 and

lands must always have been, as it still is, a time for laying in stores of meat after the animals had had their spring grazing. Hunting was as much a pursuit of settled man as of the nomads. The reason why the sacred marriage of the *basilinna* at Athens took place from the *boukolion*, otherwise unknown, is illustrated by the connexion of the goddess's festival and bull-driving, though this is found in lands remote from Greece.

A ritual in which a marriage was enacted, followed by a hunt, implies that both male and female parts were played by human beings. There is a record of festivals of NIN.LIL, the consort of Enlil, in a structure given a ritual name, IB.MA.AL, of doubtful interpretation.[1] The form of the text is for the most part simple. The structure repeatedly fell down; it was, then, fragile. A king, invariably a king of Sumer and Akkad, performed some work of restoration described by a verbal form which cannot be interpreted exactly. NIN.LIL led his son and successor into it.[2] The text is imperfectly preserved and begins with the second occasion of restoration, by Gilgamos, the legendary fifth king of the First Dynasty of Erech, himself the son of NIN.SUN, the goddess of Erech. The first structure must have belonged to the time when gods ruled on earth. Gilgamos built steps down to a water channel, GUG.BURRA, *kibis eqi*, so the structure, which was within the precinct of Enlil's temple, must have stood below the main terrace level of the sacred area. NIN.LIL brought his

3946 it was celebrated for 'Athtar, in RES 4176 for Ta'alab. In RES 4177 it was executed by the son of a *mukarrib*, in Philby 64 by a king of Ḥaḍramawt; in CIH 547 the 'community of 'Athtar' and its leader confessed to omission of the hunt for the deity ḤLFN on the occasion of a war, with the result that the god 'made their watercourses to flow in spring and autumn with very little water'. That there is some connexion between the rite in south Arabia and that at Calah seems obvious, but of course the exact relation (derivative ɔr conceptual?) remains obscure.

[1] The interpretation suggested by the position of the site is that IB.MA.AL is a descriptive phrase, IB-*šapliš*, AL-*ritkub*. Nouns derived from the root *rakabu* are used of the stories of buildings. The name suggests to me the dug-out floor below normal ground-level.

[2] The translation by A. Poebel, *Historical Texts*, no. 6, according to which the heir brought the goddess into the structure, has generally been followed because of the order of words, subject–object. Presumably this was thought of as analogous to the king taking the hand of the god to lead him out in procession. The order of words is not inviolable, object–subject can occur; the occasion indicates volition on the part of the goddess.

son and successor into it. This motive, the establishment of a
dynasty by the recognition of the son of the first king, illustrates
the reply of Yahweh to David's inquiry about building a temple
in Jerusalem, 2 Samuel vii. When the bower fell for the third
time it was ANNA.NI, almost certainly A.ANNI.PADDA,
second king of the First Dynasty of Ur, who restored the 'great
garden' of Enlil's precinct; the structure was, then, in a plantation, like the park at Calah. NIN.LIL brought his son and
successor into her bower; within the formal structure of the
text this implies that ANNA.NI was the first king of Ur to be
king of Sumer and Akkad. The structure fell a fourth time, the
first king of the Third Dynasty of Ur restored it, and NIN.LIL
brought in his son and successor ŠUL.GI, one of the most
powerful kings in all Babylonian history. In the time of ŠUL.
GI's successor the goddess did not go to the bower; no reason
is given for this; it may possibly be connected with a disputed
succession, since Bur-Sin seems to have come to the throne by
violence. Then an *enu*-priest was selected by omens at Erech,
and the ritual took place. It would seem, then, that the *enu*-
priests and kings shared this function; the appointment of such
priests in the service of several different gods is mentioned in the
date formula lists. The structure restored by the *enu* for the fifth
time fell, and Išbi-Irra, once a provincial governor of the last
king of Ur, proclaimed himself king at Isin before the Elamites
took Ibi-Sin prisoner. He 'rebuilt with wisdom the house where
the GINA are brought'. GINA, 'things established', is a word
of wide import which can be applied to standard measures of
length and weight, to laws, to rituals, to sacrifices, and to taxes.
What exactly is meant in this text may be guessed, but there can
be no certainty; the use of the word shows that at the time the
text was written the customs of the festival were still well
known and needed no precise description.

Another expression is used of the relation of the goddess to the
king. Owing to a calamity elsewhere, the southern provinces
that Hammu-rabi had gained from Rim-Sin I of Larsa rebelled
against his son Samsu-iluna twenty-one years later, under the
leadership of Rim-Sin II, probably a grandson of Rim-Sin I.

The rebellion was successful for a time and territory that had previously always been within the border of the kingdom of Babylon was invaded. In this period years were dated not by number in the reign of the king but by 'names' which recorded acts of the king in the previous year; when military affairs are referred to, only successes are mentioned. The last formula of Rim-Sin II reads: 'the year that the goddess NIN.MAḤ raised the king Rim-Sin in the temple Kesh, the fundament of Heaven and earth, to kingship over the people everywhere. He did not avert the breast of the enemy to (other) lands.' The first part is normal, and must refer to the year before that of the formula. It is known that Rim-Sin II was finally defeated by Samsu-iluna at a battle near Kish, not far from Babylon; the presence of the rebel army there indicates how successful the revolt had previously been. As a result of the victory Samsu-iluna regained lost provinces, temporarily. The last part of the date formula must have been added after the battle at Kish, before the Babylonian troops re-entered the rebellious area and imposed Samsu-iluna's date formulae.

The expression 'raised to kingship' might seem a simple metaphor. If it were so, then a goddess bestowed some form of kingship. That is contrary to all that is known. The city god in Babylonia bestowed kingship, his consort may be mentioned with him, but not without him; or 'the great gods', including certain goddesses, may assent to the appointment of a king, but the goddesses are never mentioned alone. The phrase clearly indicates some recognition of kingship, just as the phrase in the record of NIN.LIL's festivals does. There is evidence that 'raising' was a technical term.

There was a class of priestesses called *enātu*, the feminine plural of *enu*; there must then be some connexion between the male and female orders. An alternative appellation was *nadātu*, round which there has been etymological speculation; it probably means 'women thrown down', that is surrendered to the god. This class existed in all Babylonian cities, and formed a distinct social group, with independent legal standing. If married, they generally gave a slave girl to their husbands, though exceptional cases of their having children of their own are known. In certain cities, if not in all, there was a supreme *enitu*.[1] It is an accident, due partly to the hazards of excavations, partly to the history of Babylonia, that our information about the supreme *enitu* concerns Ur.

In the reign of the last independent king of Babylon, Nabonidus, there was an obscuration of the moon on 13th Elul, that is the day before, or two days before, the full moon. There was an entry in the state omen books to the effect that this portended the desire of the moon-god for an *enitu*. Recourse was had to the oracles of the sun-god, that is to the celestial body whose course determines the year, and of the weather-god, who determines the seasons, both therefore 'lords of divination', in this case the relevant powers, though there were other gods of oracles; the meaning of the omen was confirmed. Nabonidus then framed another inquiry, and 'entrusted' it, that is submitted it through the diviners. The first alternative was that some daughter of a member of the royal clan, *kimtu*, should be appointed; that was negatived. The corollary, that the priestess should be his own daughter, received an affirmative answer. The text goes on: 'I paid attention to the decree of the great lord, Sin, my god who engendered me, and to the utterance of Shamash and Adad, and I raised my daughter, my own offspring, to the *enu*-priesthood.' There is no doubt what kind of desire Sin expressed by the obscuration, it was 'the desire for *nadātu*-priestesses, the desire of the gods for the human kind'. The person who 'raised' his daughter was Nabonidus himself. The procedure he had followed was twofold; selection of the *enitu*, then her subsequent 'raising'.

The sacred area in which the ritual took place was called the *bit gipari*. It was in ruins, overgrown with palm-trunks and fruit trees.[2] It must then have been in a plantation of the same

---

[1] Regularly spelt *EN-tu*, generally read *entu*. For the phonetic spelling compare, e.g., the description of the mother of Sargon of Agade in the legend as *enītu*, while the father was a 'gardener',—as was Enlil-bani. In the legend *enītu* used to be rendered 'lowly', on the hypothesis that *ēnū*, really 'to change, alter', meant 'to bow down' or the like. There is no justification for supposing that *enītu* means 'lowly' in the sense 'poor'.   [2] See the additional note on the site of E.GI.PAR at the end.

kind as that of NIN.LIL at Nippur. While the site was being cleared, two stelae were discovered. One bore the name of Nebuchadrezzar I, and a relief of an *enitu*, attired in her ritual ornaments and dress; original texts and copies were found too, so that it is to be inferred that the site was stripped of the early foundation deposits. The other stele was that of EN.AN.E.UL, 'the *enu* Heaven has made perfect', the ritual name of the daughter of Kudur-Mabug and the sister of Rim-Sin I, in whose time a wall had been built round the old lying-place of the *enātu*. Nabonidus restored the structure on the old lines, and endowed both the temple and the various orders of priests he re-instituted.

This account is fortunately not subject to the kind of scepticism that sees in almost any report of discoveries of early texts reason for condemnation of them as pious frauds, however unmotivated. A clay copy of EN.AN.E.UL's inscription has turned up, and it confirms the account of Nabonidus. She was the last of a series of princesses who were *enātu* at Ur from the time of Sargon of Agade onwards. The election by omens of some of them is mentioned in date formulae, and is sometimes followed by a formula concerning the 'raising'. The interval seems normally to have been two years. There is then no reason to assign the 'raising' of the daughter of Nabonidus to the month of Elul, or some immediately subsequent month in the same year; he probably followed ancient precedent in this rite. The successive appointments recorded in the formulae also show that the rite was not one celebrated only in years when there was an obscuration of the moon on 13th Elul. That portended the desire for a new priestess. Once installed, the supreme *enitu* conducted the rite annually. There was one case in which the interval between the selection by omens and the 'raising' greatly exceeded the normal, and it can be shown that this was due to political causes.

At the beginning of the reign of Lipit-Ištar at Isin his sister, who bore the ritual name EN.ANNA.TUM, was *enitu* at Ur. In the last year but one of his reign, or thereabouts, his daughter, given the ritual name EN.NINSUN.ZI, was elected by omens.

As NINSUN is the epithet of the state goddess at Erech, the mother of Gilgamos, it would seem that Lipit-Ištar relied for support on Erech and Ur; he was not a member of the dynasty of Išbi-Irra, but descended from a usurper who probably imposed himself on the kingdom. Before his daughter could be 'raised' Lipit-Ištar was driven out of Isin by 'the Amorite', in some war between the states about which there is no other information. EN.ANNA.TUM then transferred her allegiance to the king of Larsa, Gungunu, who came to the throne shortly before or after the expulsion of Lipit-Ištar; this is known from inscriptions of EN.ANNA.TUM found at Ur. EN.NINSUN.ZI was not 'raised' till the 13th year of Gungunu, over a decade after her election. It is clear that the exceptional interval is connected with the exceptional political position of the priestess.[1] The whole incident illustrates the political significance of these appointments.

The connexion of political history and the religious administration is rarely mentioned or considered, largely owing to the division of studies of Babylonia into sections, which arises partly from the sources, partly from the specialization inherent in modern scholarship. Yet there are obvious indications of it, particularly in the facts known about the sacred marriage. The record of the NIN.LIL festivals shows that the occasions when a king of Sumer and Akkad was brought into the bower marked the establishment of different dynasties in the suzerainty. The sporadic appointments of princesses at Ur when that city was compelled to acknowledge the rule of men not of southern origin were obviously due to political motives. Kudur-Mabug, the son of Simti-Šilḫak, was, if not by allegiance an Elamite, at least of Elamite descent;[2] he was the suzerain of both his sons,

---

[1] The length of the interval caused F. R. Kraus in *J.C.S.* iii. 21–24, 26–27, to throw doubt on the figures given in the two distinct king-lists of Isin and Larsa. He did not consider the inscriptions of EN.ANNA.TUM, or the expulsion of Lipit-Ištar. The building made for EN.NINSUN.ZI is recorded in an inscription dated *ud nig.si.sa₈.ki.en.gi ki.uri₈.a i.ni.in.gar.ra.a*, so the year of the election of EN.NINSUN.ZI was that after the issue of the Sumerian laws still extant, now known to belong to the reign of Lipit-Ištar. The building must not be attributed to any year later than the election.

[2] Doubt has been expressed by A. Poebel as to the Elamite descent and connexions

Warad-Sin and Rim-Sin I, kings of Larsa owing to his victories, till he died. The election of his daughter as *enitu* was the sign of the acceptance of foreign rule. Nebuchadrezzar I, though he called himself 'offspring of Babylon', belonged to the Second Dynasty of Isin, by no means well established when he came to the throne; his revival of the ritual betokens an effort to revive, and gain support from, the south, which played no part in events after the fall of the Sea Land Dynasty. Nabonidus was not by birth a member of the Chaldaean Dynasty, but was the son of a prince of Harran; he came to the throne through the deposition of a minor who was himself only a grandson of Nebuchadrezzar II on his mother's side. The revival of the ritual at Ur is connected with the campaign of Nabonidus to restore a more ancient cult than that of Marduk, and that campaign was at once the result and the cause of friction between the priesthood and the king at Babylon. These three kings reverted to ancient religious practices no doubt for their own advantage. At least two of them must have seemed innovators, from the contemporary point of view, but the ritual practices they revived were unquestionably ancient. The conceptions involved had nothing to do with the thought or practice of their own age, either about kingship or rituals, and it is an error to attempt to reconstruct a coherent logical system by combining what is known of the developments in the later periods with the ritual.

Throughout the period during which princesses were *enātu* at Ur the names of kings are not infrequently written with the divine determinative. Routine temple records mention offerings to deified kings. Hymns celebrated them, and these generally contained some reference to the union with a goddess, expressed in terms of mythology.[1] This question of the deification of kings

of Kudur-Mabug and his sons, but his study has not been published. The Ma'er letters prove that a *sukkallu* of Elam was at the head of the alliance against Hammurabi of which Rim-Sin I was a member and Zimri-Lim, finally abandoning his treaty with Babylon, a late adherent. The facts warrant the statement that the father and both sons were connected with Elam.

[1] The nature of these hymns was first adequately summarized by Père H. de Genouillac in *J.A.* Janvier-Mars, 1928. Quotations and discussion in H. Frankfort, *Divine Kingship.*

should not be treated apart from the tradition that is the basis of
the introduction in the king-lists to the dynasties known to be
historical. Gods ruled on earth; then divine, immortal creatures,
brought to an end by the Flood; the survivor of that was the
last of the immortals. The legendary kings, 'heroes', were half
divine and lived beyond the spell of ordinary men. The dynasties
of human men began while some kings were still allowed supernatural lifetimes; then there was deification of kings of Sumer
and Akkad till the end of the Isin Dynasty. It was not a matter of
power, at any rate at the end, for deified kings of Isin were less
powerful than their contemporaries at Larsa and Babylon; it may
have been something to do with recognition at Nippur, which the
kings of Isin controlled. From the beginning of the First Dynasty
at Babylon there was no deification of kings there; after the time
of Hammu-rabi deification is sporadic and very rare. Gradually
texts dealing with the Sumerian tradition are accumulating, but
our knowledge of the continuous story once told is incomplete.
It is merely possible to see in the broad outline the gradual change,
both in civilization and in the practice of kingship.

It is not uncommon to find that, though early beliefs are
gradually abandoned by rulers and nobility, they remain the faith
of others. Belief in the divinity of kings must have remained a
tendency in Western Asia long after the last deification of a native
king. The squabble among the Greeks about the deification of
Alexander, like modern views on the subject, arose from Greek
ideas. The essential fact is that the deification was first mooted
when Alexander had conquered Asia. It is often said that the
Achaemenid kings, by demanding proskynesis, claimed divinity;
the assumption is doubtful, for the Assyrian kings set the example
for proskynesis to the Medes; in any case if there was deification
it was unimportant. But the proof of the endemic belief in some
parts is to be found in the practice of the Sassanian kings, who,
when dealing with subject races, called themselves *baga*, 'god',
a title never used in their dealings with the Romans, and certainly
opposed to their Zoroastrian faith. That there was a sporadic
use of the word 'god' even in those pagan periods when kings
were not deified is exemplified by the client prince who addressed

Zimri-Lim of Ma'er, the contemporary of Hammu-rabi, as 'my lord and my god'.

There were degrees in godhead. Things in contact with gods were deified. The relation of the king to the state god was always close. At Ur the largest building within the temenos was found to have two inscriptions in the walls, one describing it as the temple of the moon-god, the other as the palace. At Khorsabad the palace of Sargon II of Assyria had a court in which were the chapels of two deities. The king of Ur was deified, Sargon was not. There was some change; but it was not radical.

The festival of the marriage of gods and goddesses in Ayaru, the festivals in which a goddess brought a king into her bower, or 'raised' a king, the rite of the marriage of the *enitu* and the god, all seem to be aspects of a single phenomenon during the period in which deification of kings was common. The goddess 'raised' the king, but if the connubium was enacted, who played the part of goddess? In the date formulae it is usually understood that the expression used is in the passive form, the *enitu* 'was raised'. Nabonidus stated that he himself 'raised' his daughter, and it is possible that his words stress the unnatural union.

The reason for associating all three forms of marriage together depends primarily on the crass character of the rite. Then there is the type of building in each form. The IB.MA.AL at Nippur was a fragile structure in a garden in the temple precinct, somewhere near water-level. The lying-place of Baba at Lagash is described as a 'stall', TUR, generally an open court for cattle. The lying-place at Ur was an old fruit plantation. At Calah the structure used was on a threshing-floor adjoining a park. By Ayaru the threshing-floors were clear; cereal crops were delivered in Nisan, to be stored underground during the summer months, apart from immediate needs. The connexion with the rise of the rivers is somehow to be related to the position of the bower near water; the hunters of animals watched for their game by rivers and water channels, a point brought out in the episode of the hunter and Enkidu in the Gilgamos Epic. The Euphrates and Tigris floods are immediately followed by the beginning of sub-tropical summer heat, then by dearth of water. In the myths these are the months of the descent of gods into the 'mountain' or the underworld. With October, roughly Tešritum, 're-ripening', there is a new natural supply of food, the delivery of the date harvest. It was as important to keep 1st Tešritum in certain limits with regard to the autumn equinox as to keep 1st Nisan oscillating before and after the spring equinox. If 1st Nisan fell, say, fifteen days before the spring equinox, 1st Tešritum would be twenty days or more before the autumn equinox; hence the use of an intercalary Elul. That the sacred marriage rite in Ayaru was ultimately connected with the autumn festival in Tešritum is an inference justified by the position of the structures where it was celebrated. It ought never to have been connected with the fertility of meadow and field; the hypothesis that it had to do with childbirth in the cottage of the peasant or the palace of the prince is romantic, but unlikely, in view of what is known about the *enātu*. It had to do with fruit-growing, not agriculture proper. It was a festival celebrated in towns or cities, but one event, the final hunt, is as bucolic as any rite at a rural festival. Above all, on certain occasions the king played the part of the god, his daughter that of the goddess, but not necessarily always. The rite went on annually, and there were priestesses of the same order as the supreme *enītu*, just as there were *enu* priests who acted in the same way as the king. The insistence on the fact that the bower 'fell down' before the time of the new *enītu* is connected with the new appointment.

The god at Lagash was NIN.GIRSU, a territorial epithet which the Babylonians assigned to Enurta. At Ur it was Sin, the moon-god. At Calah it was Nabu. If, as is probable, the marriage of Marduk was celebrated in Ayaru in much the same way, yet a different god shared in the same annual, seasonal rite. Of the myths of Sin[1] and Nabu practically nothing is known; it would be rash to assign that to the absence of any myth. Of Enurta and Marduk the stories are partly preserved; they are sufficiently similar to have given rise to the view that the myth of Marduk was adapted from the earlier myth of Enurta. More superhuman

---

[1] On the birth of Sin in the Enlil–Ninlil myth see S. N. Kramer, *From the Tablets of Sumer*, 79–82.

powers than vegetation gods pass through the same sort of cycle; man's mythopoeic powers, like his inventions of narratives, are limited. The inference that seems indisputable is, that the rite of the sacred marriage goes back to a remote antiquity, and that is the reason why it was included in the cults of distinctly different gods.

Its annual nature seems to be connected with the annual re-appointment of the king, as was the case with the Nisan festival. There was in Assyria a different period of kingship, which could be interpreted as an argument against this association. The history of the calendar in Assyria is imperfectly known. In the documents from Kültepe and Ali̦sar and other sites, of the first half of the nineteenth century and a little earlier, twelve months are named, and the year dates are by the *limu*-eponym. Further precision was obtained by naming the two officials responsible for conducting the affairs of the business centre of any one traders' settlement for a period of five days; these duties, prob-ably onerous, were discharged by the principal merchants in a kind of rota. If the months were lunar, as might seem probable, the lack of any intercalary month in the enormous number of documents implies an improbably short year. In the eighteenth century the kings of the Ekallatum Dynasty at Ashur did not use this calendar, but dated their correspondence by the names of months characteristic of the Ma'er kingdom and the Middle Euphrates. During the fourteenth and thirteenth centuries the old month-names of the documents from Anatolia are found again, but there is no mention of the *ḥamuštum*, the five-day period. The eponym system continued throughout uninter-rupted, and remained the official dating of years after the Nippur calendar was adopted, probably by Tiglathpileser I.

The function of the *limu*-eponym is unknown; the com-memorative stelae found collected and set in rows at Ashur indicate that the office was held at the old capital. During any reign the king normally held office once, either in his first or second year, and his officers of state and provincial governors followed; the rota varied. Election to the office depended on the throw of a die; a specimen was found at Ashur. That the king himself had to throw the die is known from an inscription of Shalmaneser III; he was, then, in this office, *inter pares*. Late Assyrian kings showed their dislike of this; Sennacherib delayed taking the office till his eighteenth year, Esarhaddon and Ashurbanipal did not take it at all. An earlier king, Ashur-nirari IV, at the end of the eleventh century, tried to avoid the difficulty by acting as *limu* for each of his six years of reign; that amounted to converting the Assyrian system into a reckoning by regnal years, the contemporary Babylonian practice. But the precedent was not followed. It is the *limu*-office which is the counterpart of the annual period of kingship in Babylonia.

There was, however, a recognized period of kingship in Assyria, though it was reckoned in two different ways. Tiglath-pileser II in the tenth century was eponym in his second and thirty-first years, an inclusive thirty-year period. Shalmaneser III in the ninth century was eponym in his second and thirty-second years, a thirty-year interval. In the eponym system this constitutes a cyclical renewal of kingship. This thirty-year period is found in Egypt, where the king was, in the words of the Rosetta Stone, κύριος τριακονταετηρίδων, lord of the thirty-year periods; though in the New Kingdom, from Dynasty XVIII onwards, the intervals between *sed* festivals were irregular, there is little doubt that it was the correct interval, and the *sed*-festival was essentially a renewal of kingship, which gave rise to the expression in the Rosetta Stone. In Syria in the fifteenth century a king of Alalakh, after a reign of thirty years, entrusted the administration of his kingdom, and its religious observances, including the ancestral rites, to his son. Only a king, or appointed heir, could have been allowed to conduct the rites for royal ancestors; even if the expression used referred only to these rites, and not to the administration of the kingdom, an arbitrary assumption, it would still be clear that the old king abdicated after a reign of thirty years, and that this is to be connected with the thirty-year renewals of kingship in Egypt and Assyria.[1]

The reason for the adoption of this thirty-year period does

[1] Inscription on the statue of Idri-mi. The categorical statement that this king did not abdicate but merely installed his son to perform certain rites depends ultimately

not seem to be connected with any observable phenomena, or any coincidence of days in a luni-solar calendar. It is just possible that it is one of those analogies between the day, the month, and the year found in texts. In specifying a future month the expression used in some business documents is 'a month of days', that is the perfect month of thirty days, not the shorter or longer month that arose from observation. In certain lands the conception of 'a month of years' for the period of kingship may be a sort of parallel to the Hebrew 'week of years' which played a part in, for instance, servitude.

Assyria thus presents a curious phenomenon. The king, from the earliest period apparently, had to fill an annual office which was also held by his subordinates. That is probably to be connected with the origin and development of the Assyrian kingdom, too often thought to be a constant entity from the beginning. The Ma'er archive has now proved that before and after the reign of Shamshi-Adad I at Ashur there were kingdoms within the kingdom as it was later known, and that owing to the failure of Shamshi-Adad I's son, Išme-Dagan I, to resist successfully the rise of minor kings in the region between the Tigris valley and the Khabur and Euphrates valleys owing to the support given them by Zimri-Lim of Ma'er, the suzerainty imposed by earlier kings was no longer recognized. Shamshi-Adad himself was the son of a king of Ekallatum, not far south of Ashur, and was driven out of his inheritance by the suzerain. The political evidence may warrant the assumption that the parity of king and nobles in the *limu*-system was a recognition of the original rights

on a comparison with the appointment of certain members of the Hittite royal family as 'priests'. When Suppiluliu(mas) appointed Telepinus his son priest in Qizzuwadana to the state goddess, the last independent king of that state had died; the priest Telepinus was the new ruler of a kingdom reduced to the status of the provinces of the Hittite confederation. Ḫattusilis III was appointed priest in the same province that had formerly been ruled by the uncle of Mursilis I; in both cases they were rulers of a state within a state, as appears from the early part of the *apologia* of Ḫattusilis III. The facts should not be quoted in isolation, but only in their context. Little has yet been written to elucidate the interior government under the Hittites, and the inscriptions give sparse information, but it is fairly clear that some provinces resembled the priest-kingdoms of the Hellenistic and Roman periods. Ḫattusilis III sheltered a king expelled from Syria by Muwattallis.

of local kings within a confederation, preserved in some form of religious duty. Side by side with this annual aspect, there was another practice, found in Egypt, and almost certainly in Syria. In many ways Assyria preserved, unchanged essentially though developed, characteristics of an earlier strain of Semitic people than is found in Babylonia, where the Amorite intrusion which began under the Third Dynasty of Ur removed some practices altogether, and changed the language considerably. The Assyrian evidence really confirms the point, which is evident in any case; kingship throughout retained some characteristics that existed at a very early period, prehistoric in the sense that we have no historical knowledge about it. The assumption that annual festivals and the annual re-election of kings by the gods existed in Babylonia is not much affected.

Lest it be thought that the present argument, that kingship was limited in time by the necessity to secure reappointment by the god, does not prove that this was more than a pious theory, without political effect, attention should be drawn to a general observation and to a particular instance. It is well known that in Babylonia the average length of reigns under most dynasties was exceptionally brief. There are two exceptions, the First Dynasty of Babylon and the Kassite Dynasty, so far as that term refers to the actual Kassite succession and is not allowed to include the Aramaean kings who appear in the Babylonian king-list. Both the First Dynasty of Babylon and the Kassites were intrusive, and they depended on a soldiery descended from invaders, settled by right of conquest and therefore bound, in order to maintain themselves, to loyal service in defence of military leaders. The extreme weakness of most kings is noted in the general histories, though it can be obscured by the twofold sense of the word 'dynasty'. That word, like the Sumerian equivalent BAL, can mean a succession of kings of the same family. It can also mean a succession of kings of the same state but not of the same family. The Third Dynasty of Ur is an example of the former, the Isin and Larsa Dynasties of the latter, type. Some of the short reigns, which often form a comparatively long series, were due to conquest by other states. But a considerable number were usurpations by men not of royal birth, rebels, former subjects. When there is, in any state like Babylonia, a proneness to civil dissension, its nature and cause must be of interest. In Assyria there were periods of civil dissension, the cause dissension within the royal family; but Assyria remained faithful to a single dynasty from its foundation by *Adda-si*, the 47th king, to Ashurbanipal, the 113th. In Babylonia the extreme mutability during the same period is so marked, and usurpations so constant, that there must be some feature in the kingship there that will account for the frequent opportunities to displace kings.

The particular instance of such an opportunity belongs to the time of the Isin Dynasty. A passage in an inscription of GU.DE.A of Lagash has often been cited as the proof of a period of 'misrule' during a festival.

> That day when the king (NIN.GIRSU) entered the temple, for seven days, the maid competed with her mistress, the servant was equal to his master. In the town the great and the little slept side by side. An evil tongue twisted its words (to appear) good. (But) all evil was driven out; he (GU.DE.A) paid heed to the laws of the goddess and of the god.[1]

During such days there was a 'substitute' king.[2] Irra-imitti of Isin, 'in order that the substitute should not be established, ordered the "gardener" Enlil-bani to sit on his throne', and placed the orb of kingship on his head. While Irra-imitti supped a brew in his palace, he died. Enlil-bani did not rise from the throne, and was established in the kingship. In the king-lists there are two variants as to this succession. According to one, after the seven-year reign of Irra-imitti there was an interloper, whose name is lost, for six months, followed by Enlil-bani. According to the other, Irra-imitti ruled for eight years, and was followed immediately by Enlil-bani. The two accounts reflect a difference of opinion as to the legitimacy of the reign of the interloper; the king-list confirms the entry in the New

---

[1] The translation follows the interpretation of Th. Jacobsen in H. Frankfort, *Divine Kingship*, p. 174, save that 'all evil was driven out' is taken as adversative apposition to the statement about the 'tongue'.

[2] On this subject see the articles of Labat in *RA* xl. 123–42, von Soden in *Festschrift Viktor Christian*, 100–7, W. G. Lambert in *AfO* xviii. 109–12.

Babylonian chronicle.[1] The story remained famous, for it was
known to Agathias in a mutilated form, but it is a record of
actual political events. A king, certain that he would not be
allowed to remain king, set a man of his own choice on the throne,
not a member of his own family. The substitute or mock-king
was recognized as king outside the palace; the appearance of his
name in one form of the canon shows that his appointment could
pass as regular. In the end the man appointed in the palace won,
after the civil strife that is implied; his party presumably did not
recognize the interloper as king at all, and assigned the beginning
of the year, to which the six-month reign of the interloper must
be assigned, to the last legitimate king. The opportunity of the
interloper was a festival, almost certainly the New Year festival;
this is proved by the description of him as 'substitute'. This
instance should be a reminder that political events and religious
institutions and beliefs are, in some forms of community, more
closely interrelated than modern western Europeans compre-
hend. Recent events in one part of Africa have illustrated that
point in a different way, unwillingness to accept the deposition
of a ruler except in accordance with established custom. In
Babylonia established custom must account for Irra-imitti's certainty that he would not be reappointed; when he installed
Enlil-bani, he took the part played by the chief *kalu* at the annual
ceremony at Babylon on 5th Nisan.

What, if anything, followed the reappointment of the king
in Babylonia is unknown; that there was some ceremony in
which subjects took oaths of allegiance to the king seems probable,
but there does not seem to be even indirect allusion to this in
the texts. But in Assyria there are two accounts of the appointment of a 'king's son', the heir, and both of them are reported
because of the political position that resulted.

When, in the centuries from Tukulti-Enurta I, the thirteenth,
onwards, Assyria came into conflict with Babylonia there was
always a hesitation about policy which did not occur in dealing

---

[1] Kraus believed that any reign beginning in Nisan, or which included Nisan, must
be accorded an integer for that year; he inferred that the six-month reign of the interloper must be assigned to the end of the year, and that the discrepancy as to the reign
of Irra-imitti is due to error, not to views about the legitimacy of the interloper.

with other territories. Tiglathpileser III and his son were recognized as kings in the Canon of Claudius Ptolemaeus, Sargon II during the last five years of his rule in Assyria. Sennacherib, though he reconquered Babylonia after its revolt on his accession, did not take the title of king of Sumer and Akkad, but followed Tukulti-Enurta I's policy of appointing nominees, which twice proved a failure. After he had suppressed the last revolt in his reign he ruled Babylonia directly, but still did not take the steps required for recognition as king of Sumer and Akkad. The years of his direct rule are therefore entered in the Canon as ἀβασίλευτα. But Sennacherib had two legitimate queens, an unusual situation, one of them an Aramaean princess, Naqi'a, 'the pure', and it was her son, Esarhaddon, who was selected as heir. The intention can be inferred from the result; in the Canon Esarhaddon is the acknowledged king from 680 to 668, the whole of his reign in Assyria, and from the start he gave a place in his protocol to 'king of Sumer and Akkad'. The intention of his appointment was to unite the kingship of the two lands. That meant that the claims of the sons of the first legitimate queen to the inheritance in Assyria were passed over, and gave rise to a civil war. Esarhaddon's account of his appointment is circumstantial for that reason.

By command of Ashur, Sin, Shamash, Bel and Nabu, of Ishtar of Nineveh, of Ishtar of Arbela, my father who engendered me raised my head rightfully, *kiniš*, in the assembly of my brothers, saying: 'This is the son (and heir) of my governing power, *ridutu.*' He questioned Shamash and Adad at the oracle, and they answered a constant 'Yes', saying, 'He is your successor, *tēnū.*' He paid attention to their august utterance and assembled the people of Assyria, small, great, my brethren, the (men entitled to the) name of my father's house, in one place. Before Ashur, Sin, Shamash, Nabu, Marduk, the Assyrian gods, the gods who dwell both in heaven and earth, he ordered them to name their (the gods') names (in an oath formula). In a month of favourable omen, on an auspicious day, in accordance with their exalted command, I entered joyfully into the house of governing power, *bit riduti*, the place that compels awe, *ašri šugluddi*, wherein kingship is set, *šikin šarruti*, and a rightful governance, *riddu kinu*, was assigned, *ittasiq*, over my brethren. But those whom the gods abandoned trusted to their own inglorious devices, *ipšeti šurruḫāti* (*quttulu* form indicating defect) plotting evil.

This is followed by a reference to the attempt of the brothers to renew 'angers that had been appeased' in the heart of Sennacherib, whose intention to make Esarhaddon king remained firm, according to Esarhaddon. But Esarhaddon had to fly and remain in hiding till the gods

regarded balefully the doings of the rebels, which were done without the gods' wish, and did not stand at their side, but caused their strength to be dissipated in devilry, and made them bow beneath me. The people of Assyria, who had sworn the oaths, the ban of the great gods, by water and oil, to protect my kingship, did not go to their aid.

The procedure is thus clearly defined. First, there was the family conclave in which the king's decision was announced; that was not binding. Second, the name of the heir was submitted to the same oracular gods as Nabonidus consulted when he appointed his daughter *enītu*. Their assent alone permitted the next step. Third, a general assembly of all Assyrians, of every rank, including not only the king's son, but the whole royal kin, including dependants, was summoned, and it was at that assembly that the summons to take the oath of allegiance in the name of the gods was accepted or not. Whether the assembly was one of representatives of different towns and communities, or consisted of men capable of bearing arms, cannot be said; what is clear is that though Esarhaddon states that the people of Assyria took the oath, he does not say that his rebellious brothers did. In Babylonian and Assyrian law it was never compulsory to take the oath. If, when summoned to do so, an accused or suspect person refused, he was adjudged guilty without ordeal. The brothers did not take the oath of allegiance to Esarhaddon, and if they had been able to prevent the oracles giving a favourable answer, there would have been no chance for Esarhaddon. One interesting detail is that the oath is described as a ban 'by water and oil'. This is the sole reference to the taking of an oath by water and oil, and the addition is implicitly connected with the appointment of a future king. Thutmose III, when he appointed a king in Nuḫašše, La'aš, or Ruj, set oil on his head. That was

the procedure of Samuel on two different occasions, I Samuel x.
I and xvi. 13. In magical rituals the significance of an anointing
with water and oil is frequently apotropaic. This is one of the
minor similarities not so much in ritual as in symbols that concern
the bestowal of kingship. There is another. The assembly in
Assyria where the appointment of the 'king's son' with the
approval of the gods was an occasion which tested the willingness
of the members of the assembly to take the oath of allegiance is
to be compared with the story of Rehoboam, who, after he
became king in succession to Solomon, went up to Shechem;
all Israel came 'for making him king'. That was the time when
Jeroboam, who was still in Egypt, hearing of the assembly, went
to a village in Ephraim.[1] If the excision favoured by some is
accepted, the narrative implies, but does not state, that Jeroboam instigated the condition imposed on the taking of the oath
of service. The Masoretic text on the other hand states that the
returned fugitive led the assembly of Israel. There are two
inferences. The institution of kingship among the Hebrews was
copied from other states; the necessity of an assembly to make the
successor of Solomon king must have existed elsewhere. The
second inference depends on the soundness of the text; if Jeroboam really led the assembly, there must have been something
like a truce of god observed at the time, and we know that such
truces were observed at pagan festivals in Arabia, for example
at Mecca. There is not necessarily any opposition between the
statement that Solomon died and was buried, *waiyimlok* Rehoboam, and the statement that the assembly was gathered to make
him king, provided that it is understood that acting as king did
not mean that the king's subjects would necessarily confirm the
succession. In Assyria, a small party, the older sons of Sennacherib
and their adherents, refused allegiance to Esarhaddon. In the
Hebrew kingdom ten of the twelve 'tribes' refused allegiance to
Rehoboam, and the kingdom ceased to be an entity. The reality
of the procedure in the assemblies of the two nations is not one
always presented in discussions of ancient kingship. It is not

[1] I Kings xi. 43–xii. 4. Generally xii. 2 is inserted between the two halves of xi.
43, and some, deleting the name of Jeroboam in xii. 3, alter the text there.

unlikely that the royal ritual at seasonal festivals, of very ancient origin in any case, is connected with the confirmation of the appointment of a king.

Esarhaddon did not give the name of the month in which he entered 'the house of governance', *bit riduti*.[1] Ashurbanipal in his similar account did. The reason for his formal report of appointment is connected with the same matter of policy as that which led to Esarhaddon's appointment. Either because the union of the kingship of Assyria with that of Sumer and Akkad had proved too difficult for the king himself—the labour entailed must have been immense—or because he dared not risk the appointment in Assyria of a son who would have been acceptable in Sumer and Akkad, Esarhaddon split the kingdoms again. Ashurbanipal was to be king in Assyria and to consent to the kingship of Shamash-shum-ukin in Babylon. That Ashurbanipal did, but he retained direct rule in southern Babylonia, that is over the Chaldaeans. Inevitably friction arose, and the 'brothers' war' resulted. The report of his appointment as heir is a justification. In substance it corresponds to that of Esarhaddon as to the procedure. He was 'engendered of Ashur and Beltis', *binut Aššur u Belit*; Ashur and Sin, that is the god of the Nisan festival in Assyria and the lunar deity, the two main factors in deciding the calendar, had long since proclaimed his name. The two statements seem to us verbiage; the first unquestionably refers to the meaning of *Aššur-bani-apli*, 'Ashur is the engenderer of an heir', and, further, is probably an allusion that would have been understood literally by an Assyrian. Three oracles, those of the sun-god, the weather-god, and of Ishtar, the planet Venus, 'ordered that I should exercise kingship'. The assembly of 'the people of Assyria, small, great, of the Upper (Mediterranean) and Lower (Persian Gulf) Sea' was held on 12th Ayaru. The oaths were administered, and the heir entered the *bit riduti*, 'the place of NAG.DIB, or NAG.TI', an expression of

---

[1] The damaged text of the fragmentary copy, Prism S, was restored by Père V. Scheil to give the month Nisan, and this is still given by Frankfort as the date of Esarhaddon's entry into the *bit riduti*. Campbell Thompson in his edition of the preserved text rightly said that the restoration is almost certainly erroneous; the traces in S are reconcilable with the reading in the preserved copy.

uncertain interpretation, in which both DIB and TI mean 'to take', and NAG may be 'a libation', but in any case has to do with water. There is little reason to doubt that the 'favourable month' and the 'auspicious day' of Esarhaddon were Ayaru and a day corresponding to the 12th in the year of his appointment. The seasonal festival of Ayaru was the sacred marriage, celebrated about the time of high water in the Tigris. The relation of the festival to the appointment of heirs seems clearly defined in the Nippur record.

The existence of rites similar to that of the *enātu* at Ur in states scattered over a wide area is to be assumed from the mention of that or similar orders of priestesses. At Ma'er the Akkadian word used was *ugbabtu* or *ugpaptu*, an *'uf'al* form that may be semantically connected with an Arabic root meaning 'to be dry, withered'. The *nadātu* are mentioned in the routine administrative documents of the eighteenth century at Alalakh. There is no direct evidence that the king or a 'king's son' played a role at either state in the goddess's festival, unless the entry of a sacrificial sheep issued to a 'king's son' in the docket from Alalakh is such; there is also no direct evidence that the king or a king's son played the part in Assyria, unless the letters from the Nineveh archive about the festival at Calah are such. On the information actually available it is possible to make all sorts of distinctions, even to assume that there were differences; when that view is taken, the partial and haphazard nature of the documents available, and the lack of any proof that the differences—which are in themselves probable—indicate basic dissimilarity should be clearly stated.

It might be assumed that, as the mention of the peculiar order of priestesses is confined to cuneiform documents, the wide distribution of the sacred marriage ritual in this particular aspect is due to the Babylonian influence that the spread of cuneiform attests. The assumption is doubtful. The rite of the marriage of the *basilinna* to Dionysus at Athens is not likely to have been due to Babylonian influence, but it was some very ancient rite connected with kingship. In Egypt the institution of the 'god's wife', *ḥm.t nṯr*, is known from the time of the queen Aḥmes

Nefertari, early in Dynasty XVIII. After Dynasty XX the 'god's wife' at Thebes was not the queen, was childless, and adopted her successor; according to a suggestion of Professor Junker the place of this priestess's ritual was called the *wcb.t*, something like 'the pure place', cleansed like the site at Ur by EN.AN.E.UL. The documents from Egypt as elsewhere provide scant information; those who reconstruct a history of the office of 'god's wife' by excluding any consideration of similar institutions outside Egypt may be neglecting a major probability, that it was a very ancient institution not due to a comparatively late stage in Egyptian history. But quite apart from these cases of the sacred marriage outside Western Asia, accident has preserved a fragmentary document inscribed on stone in the language of Ma'in.[1]

The extant part of the text shows that it is a decree, described both as a *fitaḥ*, and as a *matābat*, 'response', a term used where the subject is some special question referred to the king in the national assembly. A still more specific word is used of it in the text, *ṣalwāt*, variant *ṣalāt*, connected with the word for 'prayer', presumably because the subject is a religious practice. The area in which the rite dealt with was carried out was within the territory of two princes, entitled *Dhu* of their tribes, who were responsible for administration, but the reference of the matter to the king in the assembly shows that the subject was of more than local importance. The southern Arabian kingdoms had lunar calendars, which were almost certainly intercalated as the years can be shown to correspond, at a later period, to years in the Antioch calendar. The deity to whose cult the rite was proper was 'Athtar, the male counterpart of the female Ishtar of Babylonia, the morning and evening star, Venus. The order of priests responsible for the execution of the rite is called the *'ahl 'ummanahatan*, 'the people of the *ummanu*', and the *ummanu*

---

[1] Glaser no. 282: Rhodokanakis, *Studien zur Lexicographie und Grammatik des Altsüdarabischen*, i. 60–66: Conti Rossini, *Chrestomathia arabica meridionalis epigraphica*, no. 80: G. Ryckmans, RES vi, no. 3306. The stone was at Saudā. It is not in the British Museum, as stated in the heading to the translation of Rhodokanakis in H. Gressmann, *Altorientalische Texte*.

are known from other south Arabian texts to be men with technical knowledge, whether priests or builders or the like. The beginning of the text is lost, the translation of the extant part subject to many difficulties; but the general sense is sufficiently clear to justify a paraphrase.

And in accordance with the application of this religious instruction the women and the two foremen of the *'ahl 'ummanahatan* and the one who has been appointed with them shall be brought among the *'ahl 'ummanahatan*. And instructions shall be given, if there has been a revelation to them from the sacrifices which (the men of) Ma'in and their daughters dedicated, that the time has come round for such a one among the women that she shall go down when 'Athtar[1] desires. And the sacrifices to him shall be increased to the one that brings a response. If they bring plentiful offerings and (then) 'Athtar makes a revelation from the sacrifices of (the men of) Ma'in and their daughters who have made the dedication to 'Athtar, that the time has come round for that one among the women 'Athtar desires, (instructions shall be given that) they shall deliver a wife at the time that 'Athtar desires that he shall be given a wife. And what is prescribed in the religious instruction shall be accomplished, from the revelation to the decision of the decree.

Date of this decree and the response: 6th. 'Athirat in the eponymy of Hawf-'Il Dhu Wakil, his prior eponymy;[2] hearer,[3] Ya'aws-'Il, son of Sharakh, Dhu Rafzan, with Ya'aws-'Il, son of Hani', Dhu Ganad. Dhu Ganad and Dhu Rafzan have been placed in charge of, and have undertaken an oath concerning, and have received commands for, the writing of the words they heard as hearers.

That the rite was of national importance seems clear from the fact that the dedication of the sacrifices was imposed on the whole

---

[1] Text, *'tr*: if correct, must, as Rhodokanakis took it, be in apposition to *nmy*, with a similar sense. The word is a *hapax legomenon* in that case. I assume a scribal error of omission, for *'ttr*, which simplifies the syntax. It will be noted that the woman is to 'go down', *wrdt*; the distinctive sense of the verbs of motion is always preserved, never insignificant, and this use justifies the inference that the rite was conducted below the level of normal habitation.

[2] This might be the first of two successive years during which the eponym served as *kabir*, or the first six months of his year of office. The distinction only appears sporadically in the eponym datings, which might favour the second alternative.

[3] The procedure in the assembly seems to have been that one man or more had the duty of memorizing the exact words of the decree as agreed in the assembly and announced by the king, the organ of decision, as chiefs are in African assemblies. Rhodokanakis had a different view.

population. The revelation of the god may be some annual phenomenon, but it might be connected with the eight-year period of the planet. The month of the decree was that sacred in the Ma'in calendar to the goddess who seems to correspond to Asherah. The connexion of the order of priestesses, on any one of whom the choice might fall, with the *ummanu*, is to be compared with the reference of EN.AN.E.UL to her brother Rim-Sin I as 'my *ummanu*'. The Ma'in decree will bear detailed comparison with the *enītu* rite at Ur. There are important differences; the god was a planet, presumably, not the moon, and there is no indication that any of the women was a princess. Distance, and a great difference in date, render any assumption that the rite was adopted from Babylonian, ultimately Sumerian, practice, almost impossible.

This section of the reconsideration of *Myth and Ritual*, intentionally restricted to the connexion between the practice of kingship and a single seasonal ritual as an example of others, indicates that the seasonal rituals as we know them in historical periods go back to an earlier date than any period historically documented. The connexion of seasonal rituals with actual calendar arrangements much earlier than the earliest calendars we know in Babylonia, already luni-solar, indicates that there is, in those lands where the kings played a part in the seasonal rituals, an intimate relation between the conception of the king as responsible to the god or to gods for the proper farming of his land and the recurrent need for the approval of the gods to be manifested at seasonal festivals. These manifestations of the favour of the gods are connected with a limitation of kingship in period, with questions about succession, with the undertaking of the people in assembly to take an oath by the gods to guard the king. The institution of kingship was subject to different developments in different periods, but some features were survivals from a prehistoric period. It is possible that kingship varied from one land to another even in the earliest prehistoric period in which it originated. But there are some characteristics of kingship in the earliest form known, that connected with priestly office of a particular type, which seem a matter of the institution rather than the period. There is something in common as to the calendar, between the Chinese book *Yueh Ling*, the monthly observances, and the practice of kingship in Babylonia, and Chinese scholars have frequently stated that in essence the observances go back to the beginning of kingship. It is this point to which the present section on the *Myth and Ritual* thesis would draw attention.

In the original volume of essays the thesis was that certain characteristic ceremonies recur in different lands in Western Asia, sometimes not all in each land, sometimes in different contexts, in a way that forms a 'pattern', that is a coherent sequence. Of one of those ceremonies, the sacred marriage, it is certainly true that it formed a part in a sequence, and that though there is no information to prove that it was mentioned in the complete myth of Marduk, there is strong presumption that it was. The similarities of the sacred marriage in its aspect as the marriage of a god to a girl or woman with rituals or institutions in other lands that have been noted confirm the original thesis. As the sacred marriage was certainly enacted—not all myths were, and it was not originally stated that *all* dramas were acted out myths—it is difficult to see any justification for the dogmatic assertion, 'the "patterns" are postulates';[1] the coherent sequence existed. On the other hand, the evidence does not show that the sacred marriage was invariably part of a calendar New Year festival.

One line of attack on the thesis has been based partly on a theory about the calendar—not one that commands universal assent—partly on a distinction between fertility cults in Palestine and an 'urban' development in Mesopotamia. Babylonian texts show that the marriage rite had to do with a peculiar period, high water in the river (whether Tigris or Euphrates), preceding the apparent death of vegetation in summer, followed by the fruit harvest. 'Urban' or not, this was connected with life in the soil, the fructification of Earth followed by a period of gestation, then reproduction.

The line of criticism which seems most suspect, however, is to be found in the view that 'the comparative method is most

[1] *J.C.S.* vi. 99.

valuable when it leads, not to the spurious equation, but to a more subtle distinction of similar features in different civilizations', and that 'the differences between two countries enable us to define the particular character of each civilization'.[1] If a similarity is spurious, that is does not exist, then it does not belong within the scope of the thesis in *Myth and Ritual*. But an implicit assumption that factual similarities must be subordinated to differences of 'civilizations', and are necessarily to be regarded as developments within particular civilizations and therefore accidental, would only be justified if it could be shown that the similarities could be proved to be of later date than the supposed 'civilizations'. In fact coherent abstracts are invented by this assumption; 'civilization', in any case a difficult term to define, is not in any one land at any one period a coherent, logical unit, in which religious ideas, conceptions of kingship, and the rest are inter-related as in a philosophical system. There is always a body of survivals, a body of later developments, a body of recent innovations incorporated in an incoherent mass of beliefs and practices. Whether the psycho-analysts are right in comparing myth-making to dream processes or not, it is, historically, a fantasy to reconstruct a 'mood of hope rather than trust' as 'characteristic of the feeling of complete dependence which pervades Mesopotamian religion' out of an assumed sequence of ceremonies at the New Year festival at Babylon in the autumn. The real truth is that there are two historical bugbears. One is the anachronism. To start from the assumption that, because Ma'in is not Babylonia, the sacred rite of 'Athtar there must be a peculiar development within Ma'in out of South Arabian 'civilization' of the last five centuries B.C. may be, probably is, an anachronism. The other is incorrect association or dissociation

[1] H. Frankfort, *The Problem of Similarity in Ancient Near Eastern Religions* (Frazer Lecture, 1950), pp. 10, 21. Note also p. 17: 'It is now, I hope, evident that the similarities between Egypt and Mesopotamia are by no means more important than the differences. Nor can it be maintained that they are primordial. If they were, they would become more numerous and pronounced when we go back in time.' The criterion will not do; feudal monarchy could not be treated on these lines. 'Primordial' begs the question, which is the chronological relation of the similarities and the differences in kingdoms of a similar type. My late friend knew that I thought his statements open to severe criticism, both in detail and interpretation.

as to what is coherent. The origin of kingship, the origin of rites of a gross symbolism, the origin of myths—much earlier than the written texts—are all too mysterious for the 'definition of the particular character of each civilization' to be based on them; they characterize man's thought at a particular stage.

The crux of the matter seems to lie in the origin of kingship. It was not a universal institution. We know of peoples who had no kings; some of the peoples who invaded Babylonia either had none or cannot be shown to have had any. The Sumerian tradition was that kingship came down from heaven; inverted, that should mean that what is said about kingship among the gods embodied conceptions about kingship on earth—and they were not quite Aristotle's conception of Oriental kingship. There was, much distorted, an indisputable truth in one tenet of the 'Pan-Babylonian' school, that Babylonians conceived the macrocosmos and the microcosmos as replicas. That is Shamanism, and also a way of life rather than of thought. Gods, kings, rituals, myths—to me a hopeless, incomprehensible jumble, but at some very ancient period a combination that justified, explained, necessitated existing institutions. When the Hebrews had been settled for some generations in Palestine a popular demand arose for the appointment of a king, partly owing to the pressure from the Philistines, partly owing to the internal, 'tribal', disorders described in Judges xix–xxi. The kingship instituted was based on government among other peoples, and there were queer results. The existence of a document like the Song of Solomon, since it was attributed to the son of David, shows that; just as it shows that a literary type known elsewhere, the dialogue without the naming of the *dramatis personae*, belongs to the pagan, not the orthodox Jewish, elements in the composite 'civilization' of Israel and Judah.[1] The Heroic Age kingship in Greece had some odd characteristics; when Odysseus failed to return to Ithaca,

---

[1] The latest discussion of the connexion between the Song of Solomon and the sacred marriage, frequently debated, and mentioned by Professor T. H. Robinson in *Myth and Ritual*, p. 185, is Hartmut Schmökel, 'Heilige Hochzeit und Hoheslied' (*Abhandlungen für die Kunde des Morgenlandes*, xxxi. 4). In this matter Tammuz is generally mentioned. He refused the approach of the goddess, as did 'Aqhat in the Ras aš Šamra text. The difference indicates a different season.

the suitors assumed that whoever married his supposed widow could claim his 'house', his legitimate son was disregarded. Aristotle admitted that kingship in the *polis* arose from consent. Rousseau argued that kingship in general arose from a contract between subjects and king, and that kings perverted their function into despotism. It seems unlikely that the original conception will ever be demonstrable, for kingship preceded civilization of the type found in written documents.

The rectification of criticism is a constant process. For one completely without convictions on the thesis of *Myth and Ritual* the 'sacred marriage' seems a good test of reasoning on the subject. The basic similarities of the rite in different lands in different ages, in spite of differences apparently casual, seem clear. If they are spurious, that should be factually demonstrable. If the same institution can legitimately be assigned quite different origins, that should be demonstrable too; but the argument should not depend on modern reconstructions. What can legitimately be regarded as established is that the marriage rite was a state institution, that kings in practice could not, during some periods, neglect it, and that it belonged to a 'pattern', the sequence of festivals throughout a year.

ADDITIONAL NOTE

THE POSITION OF THE *BIT GIPARI* AT UR

During the seasons 1924–5 and 1925–6 a much-reconstructed and altered complex of buildings south-east of the tower at Ur produced inscriptions which seemed to the excavators to justify the attribution of specific ancient names to individual parts. The complex is on a sun-dried brick terrace of very early construction, which existed before the time of the Third Dynasty of Ur. One coherent element in the complex was named E.GI.PAR by the excavators on the basis of inscriptions of periods later than the Third Dynasty, and the identification seems to have been generally accepted.

The find-spots of the inscriptions are not conclusive evidence. The inscription on Ur-Nammu's gate socket should not be cited, as the stone was admittedly re-used. The gate sockets of Bur-Sin may have been re-used. The clay cones of Lipit-Ištar were found in E.NUN.MAH as well as in the building called E.GI.PAR. The cones of Sin-balaṭsu-iqbi, the governor for the Assyrians, were found in position in the NIN.GAL temple, by the screened space where the statue of the goddess stood. Bricks of Nabonidus with the inscription about the *bit gipari* were found in the pavements of courtyards in two different buildings, that called E.DUBLAL.MAḤ, and the large residence in the north-west corner of the city wall, adjoining the structure called by Sir Leonard Woolley the 'Harbour Temple' because it was at a low level, by the canal system.

From the account of Nabonidus it is clear that he opened gates or doors in the wall of the old lying-places, and found the two stelae inside. It was the whole area within the gates which was in ruins, *ašaršu nadima emi karmiš*; he cut down (*iṣ*)*alamittum inbi ṣippatim*. *alamittum* in the form *elamittum* is equated with *gišimmaru*, *Z.A.* xliii. 239, and is therefore one of the many sorts of palm, not 'Gesträuch'. *inbi ṣippatim* means 'fruit of orchards', the adjective in 'altes Obst' is not justified, and carries an implication not in the text. Nabonidus removed both the trees and the soil, *iṣṣi epiri assuḫ*. The plantation of fruit in the *giparu* was regular; Père Deimel, *Sumerisches Lexikon*, 427/37, quoted *SI.SA eburi napaš* (*il*)*Nisaba ušaḫnabu giparu*, and the verb *ḫanabu* applies primarily to fruit.

EN.AN.E.UL in her inscription twice mentions the 'pure' nature of the area in which the GI.PAR stood, *lu gi.par nam.en.bi.še ki.sikil.la du.a*, 'I who made a giparu for the *enutu*-office in a pure place', *ki.bi ba.ra.sikil . . . ki.bi ḫu.mu.sikil*, 'its site was not clean . . . I cleansed it'. The procedure must be the same as that of Nabonidus. These places were completely cleared and the soil washed when each new *enitu* was appointed. The reports to Zimri-Lim about the house of the *ugpaptu* at Ma'er, *A.R.M.* iii, nos. 8, 42, 84, are to be understood in this connexion, and 42/23–24 emphasizes the point that if the work proposed on the site cannot be carried out, there will be a lack of water, *mat belia mē ibirri*. EN.AN.E.UL found there was no wall, and uses a peculiar expression, *bad nu.um.gu*. The word GU generally means 'a bank', and is rarely used as a verb, but it occurs in the phrase *ŠUB.ŠUB*. *GU* translated *šaqu ša elippi*, which can only refer to the beaching of a boat that had been launched. 'No wall had been banked' is a direct reference to a water-course. In *R.A.* xxxiii. 106, 33, *ina nari gugallum karpatum uttēr* should be translated 'at the river, the bank-officer turned back (-*t*-form) the water-pot', preventing an unclean person performing lustration. Inside the area, EN.AN.E.UL says, *gišimmaru* (for the form of the sign see Labat, *Manuel*, p. 164, a combination of the first and fourth in column 4) (*šim*)*buru ḫe.šub*, 'palms and aromatic plants had fallen down'. The aromatic plant is generally described simply as *šammu* by the determinative, a not unusual alternation; its presence in the area shows that the place was a garden.

Nabonidus says that he built the house of his daughter *ana itē E.GI.PAR*, 'beside the *giparu*'. In the temple identified as E.GI.PAR there was a kitchen, but there was no house beside it that can correspond to the account. There is an obvious discrepancy between the inscription of Nabonidus and the identification of E.GI.PAR by the excavators. That is rather an argument for revising the identification than disbelieving the inscriptions. EN.AN.E.UL certainly did not 'cleanse' the site now called E.GI.PAR.

THE KINGSHIP RITUALS OF EGYPT[1]

by H. W. FAIRMAN

I N Egypt our first certain contact with the institution of king-ship is at that significant period, the First Dynasty, and in the time immediately preceding it. We meet it as a going concern: it is not yet in any way fully developed, but it already possesses many of the characteristic symbols and insignia, some of the elements of the titulary, and is infused with many of the ideas that were fundamental to the Egyptian conception of kingship until the kingship itself perished. It has no prehistory; for the existence of the Red Crown of Lower Egypt in Late Predynastic times[2] is not automatic proof of the existence of the developed Pharaonic type of kingship, and the ingenious and elaborate edifice of prehistoric kingdoms erected by Sethe[3] is now, if not universally discredited, at least sorely battered and assailed, and is without any archaeological support. This ignorance of the beginnings of Egyptian kingship is a severe handicap when we attempt to examine and explain that institution, for we cannot tell how or when it developed. Was it the creation of the men and the foreign influences responsible for the remarkable upsurge of civilization and material culture following the creation of the united kingdom of Egypt, or was it already existing? We do not know. It is clear that some aspects of Egyptian kingship and

---

[1] The following works may be consulted for general reading: A. Moret, *Du caractère religieux de la royauté pharaonique* (Paris, 1902) (quoted as Moret, *Royauté*); H. Frankfort, *Kingship and the Gods* (Chicago, 1948) (quoted as Frankfort, *Kingship*); H. Jacobsohn, *Die dogmatische Stellung des Königs in der Theologie der alten Ägypter* (*Ägyptol. Forsch.*, Heft 8, Glückstadt, 1939); H. Müller, *Die formale Entwicklung der Titulatur der ägyptischen Könige* (*Ägyptol. Forsch.*, Heft 7, Glückstadt, 1938); L. Greven, *Der Ka in Theologie und Königskult der Ägypter des Alten Reiches* (*Ägyptol. Forsch.*, Heft 17, Glückstadt, 1952).

[2] *J.E.A.* ix. 26–33.

[3] K. Sethe, *Urgeschichte und älteste Religion der Ägypter* (Leipzig, 1930). For this reason this paper makes no attempt to deal with these hypothetical prehistoric kingdoms, still less with that of Osiris, cf. A. Scharff, *Die Ausbreitung des Osiriskultes in der Frühzeit und während des Alten Reiches* (*Sitzb. Bay. Akad. d. Wiss.*, Phil.-hist. Kl., 1947, Heft 4).

ritual are African and must surely go back to predynastic times, but it would be more than bold for this reason alone to assume that all the ideas and practices of Egyptian kingship originated and developed in prehistoric Egypt.

The Egyptian of historic times did not have our doubts and difficulties. To him the kingship was not merely part, but the kernel of the static order of the world, an order that was divine just as much as the kingship was divine. The Egyptians believed that the first dynasties were of gods, followed by a dynasty of spirits or demi-gods, the Followers of Horus. It was in these times that justice and the social order were created, so that in later times texts would speak of 'The Ghosts who made the sun-disk, who created all good things in their time. Ma'et (Truth), she descended from heaven to earth in their time, she consorted with the gods, there was abundance of food in the bellies of men, there was no Falsehood throughout the land, no crocodile seized, no snake bit in the days of the Primeval Gods.'[1] The kings of the First Dynasty who united the two parts that make Egypt were Upper Egyptian rulers, worshippers of the god Horus. Each king, therefore, was the Horus, the man in whom Horus was incarnate, and henceforth every king of Egypt was Horus.

From the earliest historic times, therefore, the dominant element in the Egyptian conception of kingship was that the king was a god—not merely godlike, but very god. With the growth of the worship of Rēʿ the king came to be thought of as the Son of Rēʿ; and as Osiris-worship gained favour almost inevitably another conception developed, for Horus was the son, the avenger, and the successor of Osiris, and so every living king was Horus, and every dead king was Osiris, for Osiris was the good king, who had been murdered by his evil brother Seth, but whose throne had eventually been assigned to his son Horus as the result of a lawsuit before the gods themselves. The foundation of the kingship was not merely that the king was divine and descended from the gods who had founded the earth, it was also the legal fact

---

[1] K. Sethe, *Amun und die Acht Urgötter von Hermopolis* (Berlin, 1929), Taf. iv (*Theb. T.* 95*k*); cf. *Edfou*, v. 85, 13–15; Sethe, loc. cit., 90*k*).

that the king was Horus, the legitimate heir of Osiris, whose claim to his father's throne had been vindicated in a divine court of law. The king was a sublime being, immensely remote from his people. Thus in a tomb of the Eighteenth Dynasty we are told: 'Every king of Upper and Lower Egypt is a god by whose dealings one lives, the father and mother (of all men), alone by himself, without equal.'[1] The sun-god we are told elsewhere had appointed him 'to be shepherd of this land, to keep the people alive, not sleeping by night as well as day in seeking out every beneficent act, in looking for possibilities of usefulness'.[2] In theory he was the officiant in every temple in the land; the land itself was in theory his so that every funerary offering or endowment was 'a boon which the king gives'; he was the mainspring of every activity, leader in war and peace; he was the dispenser of justice and also the source of the law, and yet at the same time subservient to the law; his well-being and prosperity were the well-being and prosperity of his people.

The consequence of this concept of kingship was that theoretically everything in religious and secular life was linked with the king, and every religious ceremony and ritual was in a sense a royal ritual. It would obviously be impossible in the space available to deal with all festivals and ceremonies, and I propose that we should concentrate on three main points: first, the making of the king; secondly, the king in action, studying certain ceremonies or festivals celebrated by or for the king; and finally, the passing of the kingship, which will afford us a convenient opportunity to study the cult of the ancestors.[3]

---

[1] N. de Garis Davies, *The Tomb of Rekh-mi-Re at Thebes* (New York, 1943), pl. xi. 18.

[2] P. Berlin 3029, 1, 6 = *Studia Aegyptiaca*, i (*Analecta Orientalia* 17, Rome, 1938), p. 49. For the conception of Pharaoh as shepherd of his people see J. M. A. Janssen, 'De Farao als goede Herde', in *Mens en Dier* (Amsterdam, 1954), pp. 71–79.

[3] In the following pages I devote what some may consider disproportionate attention to the evidence from the Graeco-Roman temples. This is done deliberately because the material from the earlier periods is relatively well known, whereas the bulk of the abundant Ptolemaic material is still to a great extent untranslated and has rarely been utilized in discussions of kingship. Ptolemaic texts on the whole are so firmly based on older traditions that, if used with caution, they throw valuable light on earlier practice and belief.

One of the most striking characteristics of kingship in Egypt was its extraordinary stability: revolutions and conspiracies are relatively unheard of; legitimate heir, usurper or foreign conqueror, each, once something had happened to him, became veritable and recognized king, and, what is perhaps more remarkable, each quite clearly considered his predecessors, apart from such obvious exceptions as the Hyksos and the Amarna kings, as his ancestors. It is quite evident that at some point in the making of the king, in his selection or in his crowning, something happened that ensured his legitimacy, that automatically disarmed opposition and claimed and obtained loyalty, and that simultaneously made him a god and linked him directly with all of Egypt's past.

It is obvious that very many kings came to the throne by the normal operation of the order of succession from father to son. At times this succession could be secured by the invention of special devices, as in the Eighteenth Dynasty, for instance, the creation of the office of God's Wife of Amun, who was the eldest daughter of the king and married the heir apparent, whose claim to the throne was assured by that marriage.[1] If the heir was not of pure royal blood, or if for some reason or other there were doubts about his position, his accession could be assured by oracle, as in the case of Tuthmosis III; or by a dream, as with Tuthmosis IV or the Ethiopian Harsiotef; or by the fiction of the divine marriage, as with Hatshepsut and Amenophis III, it being asserted that the god had impersonated the reigning king and, visiting the queen, had begotten on her the future ruler. This idea of the theogamy goes back to the Old Kingdom when one of the stories in the Westcar papyrus records the birth of the first three kings of the Fifth Dynasty as triplets whom the sun-god Rē' had begotten on the wife of a high-priest: from the Fifth Dynasty onwards, every king had a name as Son of Rē'. For the pure usurper, of course, it was naturally difficult to resort to any of these devices, but it will be found that in practice a usurper took great pains to demonstrate that in fact the god

---

[1] C. E. Sander-Hansen, *Das Gottesweib des Amun* (Kong. Danske Videnskab. Selskab., Hist.-fil. Skr., Bind i, Nr. 1, Copenhagen, 1940), esp. p. 13.

had selected him for the kingship from the time of his birth and that he was tantamount to his son.[1]

In discussing the making of the king we must distinguish between accession and coronation. The accession appears normally to have been at dawn on the day after the old king's death, but the coronation was celebrated after a period of varying length, partly to allow of the necessary preparations, but still more so as to select the auspicious day. In Egypt the proper time for the coronation, and also for the related jubilee or *sed*-festival, was at the beginning of one of the decisive moments in the calendar, the beginning of one of the three seasons, the most favoured date being the first day of the first month of winter (the fifth month of the Egyptian year).[2] The formal accession was speedily followed by the drawing up of the full titulary of the new king, which was proclaimed, and there is little doubt that at once the king assumed effective power; it is not known to what extent he was entitled, at this stage, to carry or wear the usual crowns and insignia. If we are to believe Hatshepsut, between accession and coronation the king made a state progress through the land, and at various places was acclaimed and recognized by gods, men, and the ancestral spirits, but the consensus of modern opinion is that much of Hatshepsut's account is fictitious.

No connected account of an Egyptian coronation[3] has survived and at the best the reliefs give us only a selection of the more significant items, and even the exact order of the ceremonies is uncertain. It is evident, however, that to the Egyptian the death of a king meant the temporary disruption of the union of the Two Lands, and that one of the main purposes of the coronation was to restore that unity and to ensure that the new king became a god. The first ceremony was a purification, the Baptism of Pharaoh as it has been called:[4] the king was purified by the gods

---

[1] A good example is afforded by the coronation inscription of Haremhab: most recent edition by A. H. Gardiner in *J.E.A.* xxxix. 13–31.

[2] *J.E.A.* ii. 122 ff.; xxxix. 23.

[3] Moret, *Royauté*, pp. 75–113; Frankfort, *Kingship*, pp. 105–9. An abbreviated Egyptian version will be found in the coronation inscription of Haremhab, *J.E.A.* xxxix. 13–31.

[4] A. H. Gardiner, 'The Baptism of Pharaoh', in *J.E.A.* xxxvi. 3–12.

of the cardinal points. The purification was not by water alone; the reliefs frequently depict the symbols of life and power or dominion as issuing from the vases, and it would appear that the ceremony was intended to transfer to the new king the powers of the gods of the cardinal points. The king was then led into the Dual Shrines, or the Per-wer and Per-neser, and crowned by the gods, in theory being invested with each individual crown. This was followed by investiture with crook and flail and the presentation of the little casket containing the title-deeds or testament. It was probably at this juncture that the symbolic ceremony of Uniting the Two Lands was performed and it was apparently at this point that Thoth or the Inmutef-priest proclaimed the god's decree declaring that the newly crowned king was his legitimate successor, and the Ennead gave their endorsement. The king was then led towards the god, Thoth proclaimed his full titulary, and Thoth and Seshat, goddess of writings and annals, inscribed his years and life-span on the leaves of the sacred persea tree. Finally, apparently after presentation of a scimitar and perhaps investiture with other regalia, the king was led into the presence of the god[1] who formally adjusted the crown as the king knelt before him, and then there was a banquet. It is obvious that these were only the main rites and that they must have been accompanied by many hymns and by other ceremonies of which we have no suspicion. At some point there was certainly a moment when the new king was publicly acclaimed and praised, and Ptolemaic evidence indicates that this was after the affixing of the crowns,[2] possibly after the proclamation of the decree. Another important ceremony was the circumambulation of the walls,[3] which hitherto has been generally accepted as symbolizing the taking possession of the kingdom. Helck, however, has recently suggested that it is to be equated with the threshing of grain.[4] Its exact position in the coronation ceremonial is uncertain, but if Helck's interpretation of this ceremony

[1] A scene at Edfu indicates that the king was led not only to the presiding god but also to his royal ancestors (*Edfou*, i. 108, 6–109, 6 = xi, pl. 255).

[2] Cf. *Edfou*, vi. 188, 7–189, 2.

[3] Moret, *Royauté*, pp. 96 ff.; Sethe, *Untersuchungen*, iii. 133 ff.

[4] *Orientalia*, xxiii. 408.

and of the Ramesseum Dramatic Papyrus (see below, p. 82 f.) be correct, it should perhaps be regarded as a rite partly protective and partly Osirian, and one would expect to find it early in the proceedings, or on the eve of the coronation.

An interesting sidelight on the coronation is afforded by the annual festival of the selection and coronation of the Sacred Falcon[1] which was celebrated at Edfu in the Ptolemaic Period on the first day of the first month of winter and the four following days. Although ostensibly this festival was that of the coronation of a new Sacred Falcon, who would reign for a year, there can be no doubt that it was intimately connected with the kingship. The very date is significant (see above, p. 78), and the texts leave no room for doubting that throughout the festival the Sacred Falcon, the king, and Horus were as one, and that the festival also celebrated the annual renewal of the coronation of the reigning king.

The festival began with the selection of the new Sacred Falcon, which was effected by Horus by means of an oracle. Then followed the Recognition: the Falcon was displayed publicly from a balcony over the main door of the temple, between the two wings of the pylon, and special hymns were sung, one greeting the New Year that was being inaugurated, and the second being concerned with ensuring the protection of the Sacred Falcon, and the king, from all harm and danger. The actual coronation took place inside the temple and was in two stages: the first stage included anointing, investiture with a ceremonial collar, and the presentation of the symbol of eternity and of four posies; in the second stage the royal insignia were presented, and then an elaborate and comprehensive ritual was celebrated for the protection of the god and everything connected with him. Finally, the Sacred Falcon was taken to his own temple, a special grace before meat was sung, pieces of flesh, symbolizing the destruction of the enemies of the god and the

---

[1] The only detailed study of the festival is that of Alliot, *Culte*, ii. 561–676; an outline in English will be found in *B.J.R.L.* xxxvii. 189–92. A similar festival was celebrated at Philae; cf. H. Junker, 'Der Bericht Strabos über den heiligen Falken von Philae im Licht der ägyptischen Quellen', in *Wiener Zeitschrift für Kunde des Morgenlandes*, xxvi. 42–62.

king, were presented, and lastly there was a banquet, the actual meal being symbolized by the burning of myrrh.

If we attempt to summarize these varied ceremonies, it would seem that the making of the king involved first of all selection by the god. Thereafter the ceremonies were designed to purify the new king; to reunite in his person the Two Lands; to transfer to him divine honours and even divine nature, by purification and by investiture with and presentation of crowns and regalia; to emphasize this by direct decree of the god, ratified by the Ennead and finally sanctified by the direct blessing of the god. At what stage in these proceedings the king became a god is never stated. Probably there was not a particular moment or rite of deification and the effect was cumulative, but if one has to select a particular point, it would seem that of all the ceremonies it was the actual affixing of the crowns and uraei that was really decisive. The subsequent ceremonies are probably confirmatory and protective and henceforward the newly crowned king, whatever his origin, was not only legitimate king, but a god, directly linked to all his royal predecessors, the company of the ancestors that stretched in unbroken line to the first god-king, and his position and authority were unassailable.

It will be noted that no mention has yet been made of the Ramesseum Dramatic Papyrus,[1] although ever since it was first published it has been interpreted as a coronation drama. The existing text is dated to the reign of Sesostris I, the second king of the Twelfth Dynasty (*c.* 1961 B.C.) but is clearly based on a much older original that may go back as early as the First Dynasty. It is composed of forty-six scenes, illustrated by thirty-one drawings. Each scene consists of four elements: a description of some act in the play; the mythological explanation of that act; a conversation between gods embodying words, and puns on them, uttered by the gods on occasions related to the situation described; and lastly a variable number of stage directions. There is no need to give a detailed description of the drama. Let it

---

[1] K. Sethe, *Dramatische Texte zu altägyptische Mysterienspielen* (Leipzig, 1928). An excellent summary, though accompanied by explanations of more doubtful value, will be found in Frankfort, *Kingship*, pp. 123–39.

suffice that the view put forward by Sethe and generally accepted is that this is a drama performed when the king, shortly after his accession, visited the more important cities of Egypt. The essential parts of the drama were the coronation of the king (scenes 26–32) and the burial of his predecessor, ending in a feast (scenes 33–46), the opening scenes (1–25), though containing important elements, being essentially preparatory. It has been claimed that these various acts 'realistically identified the living king with Horus, and the dead king with Osiris, and so perpetuated all that Osiris and Horus meant for Egypt'.[1]

Frankfort, for his part, while accepting Sethe's views in general, considered that the whole drama was a 'Mystery Play of the Succession' and denied that the concluding scenes had any connexion with burial, maintaining that in reality they were concerned with the transfiguration of the king's predecessor.

It has always been recognized that the traditional interpretation of the drama involved very great difficulties: it is not easy to discern any logical development of the drama, and as a coronation play it diverges very greatly from much that we know about the coronation, for it omits many of the most important ceremonies, and even the affixing of the crown is merely given a passing reference and no more. Moreover, the figure of the king, consistently shown in his boat, is never depicted as a living being and the king himself is never clearly stated at any point of the drama to take an active part in it. These and other points have been considered by Helck in a recently published paper.[2] He considers that these difficulties are mainly due to the fact that the extant manuscript does not reflect the original condition and order of the text but is the result of a Middle Kingdom editor turning the badly damaged and broken manuscript (as far as scene 35) and unwittingly grouping the fragments in an order different from the original, only scenes 36–46 being preserved in their original order.

Helck's attempt to reconstruct the original order is based on

---

[1] A. M. Blackman in *Myth and Ritual* (ed. S. H. Hooke), p. 31.

[2] W. Helck, 'Bemerkungen zum Ritual des Dramatischen Ramesseumspapyrus', in *Orientalia*, xxiii. 383–411.

the claim that the scenes in the Ramesseum Papyrus are to be found again, but in a different order, in the famous scenes of the jubilee of Amenophis III in the tomb of Kheruef at Thebes.[1] Briefly, Helck's view is that the reconstructed papyrus is concerned with ceremonies celebrated on the eve of the *sed*-festival and consisting basically of the Opening of the Mouth and the burial of a royal statue representing the deceased king, the king's father. He considers that this must go back to very early times, when, he claims, the *sed*-festival actually marked the accession and coronation of a new king, on the eve of which the old king, killed on attaining the conventional limit of his age, naturally had to be buried. On this view the statue was substituted for the killing of the old king.

Before one can finally accept Helck's views, a rigorous checking of the papyrus with his reconstruction will be necessary. At least, however, his theory removes many of the difficulties in the interpretation of the Ramesseum Papyrus and it does also afford some explanation of the link between the *sed*-festival, traditionally set on the first day of the first month of winter, and the erection of the _Ded_-pillar[2] and the burial of Osiris on the last day of the previous month. It also brings us face to face with the complicated problem of the jubilee or *sed*-festival.

This festival[3] can be traced back to the First Dynasty. It was obviously of very great importance, but we have no manuscript that gives us a connected sequence of scenes, the order of the main rites is quite uncertain, and even the significance of the festival is disputed. The festival is very often associated with a period of thirty years, and having once been celebrated by a king could be repeated every three or four years, but it was not

[1] For many years known only from Erman's sketch reproduced in Brugsch, *Thesaurus*, 1190. The tomb was rediscovered in 1943 and a preliminary publication of the texts and reliefs was given by A. Fakhry, 'A Note on the Tomb of Kheruef at Thebes', in *Ann. Serv.* xlii. 449–508, pls. xxxix–lii.

[2] B. van de Walle, 'L'Érection du pilier *djed*', in *La Nouvelle Clio*, vi (1954), 283–97.

[3] Principal sources: von Bissing, *Das Re-Heiligtum des Königs Ne-Woser-Re*, ii and iii, and the text of Kees in the last volume; von Bissing–Kees, *Untersuchungen zu den Reliefs aus dem Re-Heiligtum des Rathures*; Moret, *Royauté*, pp. 235 ff.; Frankfort, *Kingship*, pp. 79–88.

necessarily celebrated thirty years after the king's accession, and the factor that determined when the jubilee should be celebrated is quite unknown. It is probably true that in essence it was a renewal of the king's power and rule, though, as we have just seen, some authorities hold that in origin it marked the coronation of a new king. The preliminaries of the jubilee were many and complicated and always involved, if not the construction of an entirely new temple, at least the erection of a 'Festival Hall' within an existing sanctuary, the preparation of a Court of Festival, and a 'Palace' which acted somewhat after the manner of a robing-chamber, and shrines of primitive Upper and Lower Egyptian type, of which we possess a remarkable stone model in the Festival Court of the Step Pyramid at Sakkara. These buildings were purified and dedicated, and finally there was a five-day illumination which ended on the eve of the festival. In the meantime, statues of the gods from all parts of the country were brought to the capital, and all the leading officials and nobility assembled, for, bearing archaic titles, many of them had to take part in the ceremonies, in which the reliefs seem to indicate that the whole people was concerned.

The proceedings seem to have started with a great procession of king, divine statues, and other people, accompanied apparently by gifts to the gods. Thereafter there appears to have been for a time an almost incessant series of processions, visits, of expressions of homage and loyalty to the king, of changes of costume, and complex but obscure rites. The general purpose is, perhaps, by demonstrations of loyalty and visits to the gods to emphasize the links between the gods, the king, and his people. A rite of obviously very great importance was the dedication of a field, at which the king in a peculiar sort of dance, first as king of Lower Egypt, then as king of Upper Egypt, crossed the field to the four compass points, and was thereby believed to have dedicated the field, which presumably represented Egypt, and simultaneously reasserted his control over the land. The final ceremonies also include actions by the king in his dual capacity of king of Upper and Lower Egypt: these actions certainly appear to involve rites connected with the coronation; the king sits four times on thrones facing the cardinal points, he is proclaimed to each point of the compass, an arrow is shot to each point, and in general it seems that the king's accession and coronation are proclaimed to the whole world. The last act of the festival seems to be some sort of act of homage to the royal ancestors.

It is obvious that a king such as the Egyptian was regarded as having the deepest influence on his people and his country. The kingship was clearly very closely connected with agriculture and fertility, and the safety and health of the king entailed the safety of Egypt and the health and well-being of its inhabitants. Inevitably, therefore, there must have been numerous ceremonies at which either the king conferred benefits on the land, or in which protective rites on behalf of the king, or the symbolic destruction of his enemies, automatically ensured the same desirable results for Egypt. Some typical rituals of this kind must now occupy our attention.

The great festival of Min[1] in the first month of summer (the ninth month of the year) was in part at least a harvest festival, though separate from the more popular harvest festival celebrated in the same month. It was a festival that clearly concerned not merely Min and the harvest, but also the kingship. The king went in procession to pour libations and burn incense to Min in his temple. The statue of the god was then carried out of the temple, preceded by the king and queen, the sacred white bull, in which the god was supposed to be incarnate, and priests carrying standards and statues of the royal ancestors. The procession wended its way to a temporary shrine erected in the harvest field. Here the rites included the offering of a great oblation, ceremonies for the king, his Ka and his ancestors, the previous kings, the reaping of a sheaf of corn which was presented either to the god or to the bull, the dispatch of geese to the four points of the compass to announce that both Horus, the son of Isis and Osiris, and the king himself had assumed the crown, and there is a possibility that the king and queen may have had intercourse.

---

[1] H. Gauthier, *Les Fêtes du dieu Min* (Cairo, 1931); Frankfort, *Kingship*, pp. 188–90. For the most recent publication of the scenes at Medinet Habu, plus comparative material from other Theban temples, see *Medinet Habu* (ed. Chicago), iv, pls. 196–217.

Here we obviously have a fertility rite, and one that is clearly linked with the king. It is somewhat puzzling to find the incident of the four geese included, for that is a coronation ceremony, but it occurs again in similar circumstances, as will be seen shortly (p. 87), in the Sacred Marriage at Edfu. It cannot be the coronation or accession of the reigning king that is being proclaimed, and it is possible that the incident refers to the beginning of a new year of the fertility god Min, who was also Horus, and was automatically the king. The whole festival would, therefore, have been the annual renewal of the fertility and virility of the king—for the ultimate benefit, of course, of the entire land.

It is appropriate to consider at this point the so-called Sacred Marriage which was celebrated at Edfu in Ptolemaic times over a period of fifteen days, from the new moon to the full moon of the third month of summer (the eleventh month of the year).[1] The ceremonies really began fourteen days earlier when the river procession of Hathor left Denderah. The goddess, after stops at various places on the way, did not reach Edfu until the eighth hour, the afternoon, of the day of the new moon. At the river bank Hathor was greeted by Horus the Behdetite and a deputation from Elephantine: obviously the festival concerned the whole of southern Upper Egypt. There and during the journey by canal from the river to the temple of Edfu, numerous ceremonies were celebrated, including the Opening of the Mouth, the offering of the first-fruits, the driving of the calves, and the offering of Truth: these ceremonies were a combination of essentially funerary or harvest rites with others, such as the driving of the calves, that, in origin harvest and threshing rites, had long since been Osirianized and adapted for the funerary cult. After further ceremonies in the main temple of Horus, the two gods were taken for the night to the Birth Temple, or Mammisi, which was apparently their resting place every night of the festival.

With the second day a new phase of the festival commenced. During the ensuing fourteen days, although Horus and Hathor were inseparable, the emphasis is no longer on the Sacred

[1] Alliot, *Culte*, ii. 441–560; see also *B.J.R.L.* xxxvii. 196–200.

Marriage but on what is called the Festival of Behdet. On each of the first four days of this festival the gods were taken in procession to the sacred necropolis where there was, it seems, a temple or chapel, and a sacred grove concealing four mounds; each day a different mound was visited. Here special ceremonies were performed for the 'Divine Souls'. The procession then returned and further complicated ceremonies were performed. These included the sacrifice of a red ox and a red goat, the dispatch of four geese to the cardinal points, each bearing the message that Horus the Behdetite had assumed the White and the Red Crown, and arrows were shot to south, north, west, and east. There followed other acts symbolizing the destruction of the king's enemies by means of trampling on or otherwise destroying a model hippopotamus, crocodiles, a piece of papyrus inscribed with the names of enemies, and by trampling on fishes. Thereafter there came a public interpretation of these acts and objects which makes it quite clear that the destruction of enemies was portrayed, and then the populace gave themselves up to a night of merriment. On the fifth to thirteenth days of the Festival of Behdet it is probable that the ceremonies were much the same, though possibly on a more modest scale, and finally on the fourteenth day, the fifteenth after her arrival at Edfu, Hathor returned to Denderah after another long series of ceremonies.

The ritual acts thus briefly summarized are of exceptional interest and complexity, and as a whole are a combination unique in our knowledge of Egyptian ritual and festival. In certain festivals it is well known that the people shared in the festivities, but the deliberate attempt publicly to explain the significance of the various episodes is a notable feature of this particular festival. Even more interesting is the clear evidence that the festival was not a unity. That in part it was a Sacred Marriage is certain, but that was neither the sole nor the principal part of the festival; for linked with it are on the one hand harvest ceremonies (but a harvest festival celebrated two or three months after the reaping and threshing had been completed), and on the other hand ceremonies connected with the funerary cult. Throughout there are clear parallels and points of contact with the festival of Min already discussed (p. 85), and throughout it is indisputable that the king and the kingship are involved.

The connexion of some of these ceremonies, e.g. the driving of the calves and the treading of the grain, with the harvest festival is well known.[1] Other texts in the Ptolemaic temples afford additional support for this contention. Thus, at the Festival of Harsomtus at Denderah in the first month of summer, evidently the Denderah harvest festival, the ceremonies included the treading of the burial mounds of the Divine Souls, and the treading under-foot of scattered grain which is explicitly stated to symbolize the destruction of the king's enemies.[2] Similar, and in some cases identical, ceremonies are to be found in the harvest rites of the First Month of Summer at Edfu[3] and Kom Ombo.[4] The linking of the Sacred Marriage and harvest festival thus finds an obvious explanation: both were directly concerned with the fertility and prosperity of the king and people.

The funerary aspect of the ceremonies is also a natural development from the harvest festival, because, of all Egyptian rites, it was the harvest festival that was most speedily and completely Osirianized owing to the intimate connexion of Osiris with grain and agriculture. A long series of supplementary texts at Edfu leaves us in no doubt as to the purpose of the visit to the sacred necropolis. The visit was made in order annually to revivify and make oblation to the 'Divine Souls', or the 'Children of Rē'' as they are sometimes called, who were buried there and whose mortuary priests were Horus and Hathor. These Divine Souls were dead gods, nine in number, of gigantic stature, and are sometimes called 'The Ancestors'. Though none of these gods came from Edfu originally, they were all Upper Egyptian in origin, not one of them comes from the Delta. They came into being before heaven or earth existed, and having travelled

---

[1] A. M. Blackman and H. W. Fairman, 'The Significance of the Ceremony *Ḥwt Bḥsw* in the Temple of Horus at Edfu', in *J.E.A.* xxxv. 98–112; xxxvi. 63–81, esp. pp. 76 ff.

[2] *Edfou*, v. 352, 9–354, 2.

[3] Ibid. i. 384, 11–385, 3 = xii, pl. 330, in part a duplicate of E. Chassinat, *Le Temple de Dendara*, iv. 69, 4–10; cf. also *Edfou*, vi. 280, 18–281, 10.

[4] De Morgan, *Ombos*, ii, p. 52, nr. 596.

through Egypt and 'come to rest in the necropolis in the south of Egypt, they gave birth to inhabitants for Upper and Lower Egypt'.[1] It is said that they were embalmed and buried at Edfu at the express command of Rēʿ 'in order to prosper Egypt by concealing them in their crypt',[2] or, as another text puts it, 'the land was blessed from the very time of their concealment'.[3]

We are thus at last able to discern the true significance of this remarkable feast. The festival we are accustomed to call the Sacred Marriage is in reality a combination of three—the Sacred Marriage, the Harvest Festival, and the Festival of the Ancestors. They were not incompatible, nor was their association at Edfu due to mere chance; for they were all closely connected with each other, with fertility rites, the mortuary cult, and the protection of the king, on whose safe keeping and well-being that of Egypt and her people, in turn, depended. It is important to note that at the centre of all, so to speak, lay the Ancestors.

The ritual of the Sacred Marriage which we have just discussed stipulates, shortly before the dispatch of the four geese to the cardinal points, that four 'books' are to be recited. Three of these are no more than names to us, but the fourth, entitled 'The Subduing of the Nobility', is fortunately better known. The scenes in the temples of the Graeco-Roman period now enable us to identify this 'book' with other similar scenes in the New Kingdom. The earliest example occurs under Tuthmosis III of the Eighteenth Dynasty near the Festival Hall of that king at Karnak,[4] a second is found under Sethos I at Abydos,[5] and a third under Ramesses II at Karnak.[6] In all these three earlier

---

[1] *Edfou*, iv. 240, 5–9.   [2] Ibid. v. 62, 17–63, 1.

[3] Ibid. iv, 84. 3.

[4] Unpublished : location F. 464 (H. H. Nelson, *Key Plans Showing Locations of Theban Temple Decorations* (Chicago, 1941), pl. vii. I am indebted to Dr. G. R. Hughes and Dr. C. F. Nims of Chicago House, Luxor, for copies of Chicago Oriental Institute photographs 3246, 8443. No texts have survived.

[5] South wall, descending passage from the Osireion: some of the texts, but not the reliefs, in A. Mariette, *Abydos*, i, pl. 49, *e–f*. I have used my own notes, and excellent photographs lent me by Miss A. M. Calverley.

[6] South wall of the Hypostyle Hall: Champollion, *Notices descriptives*, ii. 41–42; Alliot in *Revue d'Égyptologie*, v. 110–12; Chicago Oriental Institute photograph 5982.

scenes the texts are very brief and are solely concerned with the offering to the god of birds that have been trapped in a great clap-net; there is no reference to any wider or deeper significance. Three further scenes occur in the Graeco-Roman period at Karnak, Edfu, and Esna and were translated and commented upon a few years ago by Alliot.[1] These late versions are far more developed than the earlier ones and of them all those of Edfu are by far the best and most extensive: it is on Edfu[2] that the following summary is primarily based.

The essential feature of all these scenes is an enormous clap-net which is shown set up in the marshes and being pulled shut by the king and either two or three gods. In the earlier versions only birds are caught in the net, but at Edfu the net somewhat incongruously traps birds, fish, animals such as oryx, ibex, and oxen, and four kneeling human figures with tightly bound arms. At Edfu there are two scenes set exactly opposite each other on the first register of the inner face of the wall to east and west of the main temple. On the east is the 'Book of Subduing the Nobility. Placing the Two Lands and the Banks, and the hill countries of all foreign lands under the feet of the King.' This, it is said, is to be recited 'over figures of four enemies whose names are written on their breasts in green ink and placed on a brazier', four times at dawn and twice at the tenth hour. On the west wall the equivalent scene is apparently entitled 'Affixing the Two-feather Crown', but careful study of the text shows that what is recorded is really three acts: (*a*) the affixing of the Two-feather Crown; (*b*) the presentation of a fillet; and (*c*) a text, whose title is lost, which is basically the same as that on the east wall.

The texts make it perfectly clear that the ceremonies and spells are directed against rebels and enemies of the king, especially when they attack him, and that their effect is to capture these enemies, to render them powerless and ineffective, and to destroy

---

[1] Alliot, 'Les Rites de la chasse au filet aux temples de Karnak, d'Edfou et d'Esneh', in *Revue d'Égyptologie*, v. 57–118.

[2] *Edfou*, vi. 55, 5–58, 2, with xiii, pls. 492, 493; *Edfou*, vi. 235, 4–238, 6, with xiv, pls. 585, 586.

them. The birds, fish, and animals caught in the net are said to represent various enemies in general, and are also identified one by one with various foreign enemies such as Asiatics, Beduin, Nubians, &c. A damaged passage appears to indicate that they were also to be eaten for breakfast, lunch, and supper.

The nature and purpose of these ceremonies is thus quite obvious. In the first place, they are in accord with the Egyptian theory of sacrifice and offering:[1] in Egypt sacrifice bore no implication of atonement, but enshrined a double concept, on the one hand the destruction of the enemy, e.g. by the burning of the slaughtered offering, and on the other hand the absorption of certain desirable qualities and powers by eating the sacrifice. Secondly, these ceremonies were magical and employed the familiar principles of sympathetic magic.[2]

Our texts do not inform us of the particular part of the year at which these ceremonies were performed. It seems a reasonable assumption that they may have been performed at any time when danger or attack threatened: Could they have been performed at the beginning of a foreign campaign? It is also certain, as we have seen, that at Edfu they formed part, in the Sacred Marriage, of the Festival of the Ancestors, where they were linked with other similar ceremonies designed to protect the king and to destroy his enemies. Lastly, the association of the Edfu texts of the Book of Subduing the Nobility with ceremonies of investiture suggests that it may perhaps have formed part of the coronation ritual: although this is not included in any of the surviving

[1] Cf. H. Junker, 'Die Schlacht- und Brandopfer und ihre Symbolik im Tempelkult der Spätzeit', in *Z.A.S.* xlviii. 67–77; H. Kees, 'Bemerkungen zum Tieropfer der Ägypter und seiner Symbolik', in *Nachr. d. Akad. d. Wiss. zu Göttingen*, Phil.-hist. Kl., 1942, Nr. 2, pp. 71–88; cf. also H. Junker, 'Das Brandopfer im Totenkult', in *Miscellanea Gregoriana* (Rome, 1941), pp. 109–17.

[2] e.g. the ceremony of breaking the red vases, *Pyr.* 249; S. Schott, 'Die Zeremonie des Zerbrechens der roten Töpfe', in *Z.A.S.* lxiii. 101; the proscription texts of the Middle Kingdom, K. Sethe, *Die Ächtung feindlicher Fürsten, Völker und Dinge auf altägyptischen Tongefäßscherben des Mittleren Reiches* (Berlin, 1926), G. Posener, *Princes et pays de l'Asie et de la Nubie* (Brussels, 1940), W. C. Hayes, *The Scepter of Egypt*, i. 329, and fig. 217; for Old Kingdom examples of the same practice, H. Junker, *Giza*, viii. 30–38. See also S. Schott, 'Drei Sprüche gegen Feinde', in *Z.A.S.* lxv. 35–42. For a similar practice see Spell 37 of the Coffin Texts (A. de Buck, *The Egyptian Coffin Texts*, i. 146–57, esp. pp. 156–7).

coronation texts, such a ceremony obviously would not have been out of place.

Another example of a protective ritual is afforded by the Festival of Victory, celebrated at Edfu from the 21st to the 25th of the second month of winter (the sixth month of the year).[1] The main texts are found on the first and second registers of the inner face of the western enclosure wall of the Temple of Edfu. On the first register is the abbreviated text of a sacred drama,[2] and on the second register a text of rather different nature usually known as the Legend of the Winged Disk.[3]

The drama, which was acted partly on and partly beside the sacred lake of the temple, is divided into a prologue, three acts, and an epilogue. The purpose of the play was to commemorate the victory of Horus over his enemies, his coronation as king of Upper and Lower Egypt, and his final triumph before a divine tribunal. But since the king himself was Horus, and also one of the actors, the ultimate aim of the drama was to ensure that the king should be victorious over his foes, that he should enjoy a prosperous reign and secure the same triumph that had been won by Horus. Thus the prologue opens with praise of the king and the statement that 'here begins the bringing to pass of the triumph of Horus over his enemies', and the epilogue ends on the same note with the declaration that Horus has triumphed and that the enemies of various gods and cities and of the king have

---

[1] For a brief outline see *B.J.R.L.* xxxvii. 192–6. A detailed study will be found in Alliot, *Culte*, ii. 677–822.

[2] A. M. Blackman and H. W. Fairman, 'The Myth of Horus at Edfu, II: The Triumph of Horus over his Enemies: A Sacred Drama', in *J.E.A.* xxviii. 32–38; xxix. 2–36; xxx. 5–22. That this is a drama has been denied by E. Drioton, *Le Texte dramatique d'Edfou* (*Cahiers des Annales du Service des Antiquités de l'Égypte*, no. 11, Cairo, 1948), and by Alliot in the work quoted in the previous note. Both Drioton and Alliot deny that the text is really dramatic, but are not agreed in their interpretation of the true nature of the text. After careful reconsideration of all the evidence, I find it quite impossible to accept the views of either of the French scholars. All three translations are substantially the same; the dispute is not over translation, but over the nature and interpretation of the texts.

[3] H. W. Fairman, 'The Myth of Horus at Edfu, I: The Legend of the Winged Disk', in *J.E.A.* xxi. 26–36. Also translated and edited by Alliot, loc. cit., who does not consider it to be separate from the dramatic text and attempts to combine the two into a single ritual; this is more than improbable.

been overthrown. Act One is the Harpoon Ritual in which, in five scenes, ten harpoons were thrust into a male hippopotamus, a survival of an ancient ritual that celebrated the victory of the king over his enemies.[1] In Act Two two scenes give the popular rejoicings over the victory and rejoicings over Horus crowned and invested with his insignia, and in Act Three there is a twice-repeated dismemberment of Seth. The king is the beginning and end of the drama. Every Pharaoh ruled over the two lands of Upper and Lower Egypt, and hence many rituals are in a sense double, being enacted separately for each portion of the kingdom. This dualism is clear in Acts Two and Three of the Edfu drama. It is also even more evident, though not previously noted by editors of the text, in Act One in which the ten harpoons, according to the texts accompanying the reliefs, are wielded alternately by Horus, lord of Mesen, and Horus the Behdetite, representing Lower and Upper Egypt respectively. This fact establishes the essential unity of the reliefs and the dramatic text and affords further proof that the drama, as recorded at Edfu, is directly connected with kingship.

The second stage of the festival, the Legend of the Winged Disk, is no drama, and at first sight might appear to have no connexion with the kingship, nor even with the sacred drama apart from the fact that it is concerned with the wars of Horus against Seth. This impression, however, is superficial and misleading. The Legend of the Winged Disk is a propagandist recital, accompanied by innumerable and tedious puns, of the progress of the struggle between Horus and Seth, and invested with a spurious historicity by being couched in the form of an historical document and given a mythological date, the year 363 of the king of Upper and Lower Egypt Rēᶜ-Ḥarākhte. The purpose of this recital is to support the claim of Horus the Behdetite to supremacy. All this, however, is a mere prelude, a convenient peg on which to hang a potent spell for the protection of the king when danger threatens: the recitation of the spell, it is stated, will ensure that the king shall not be afraid and that

[1] Cf. T. Säve-Söderbergh, *On Egyptian Representations of Hippopotamus Hunting as a Religious Motive* (*H.S.* iii, Uppsala, 1953), esp. pp. 25–41.

his enemies shall be destroyed immediately. The two sections of the ritual of the Festival of Victory therefore ensure the triumph of the king over his enemies, secure for him a prosperous reign, and provide him with protection and with a powerful spell to overcome all danger and assault.

It now remains for us to consider the rituals connected with the passing of the kingship. The rituals that accompanied the death of a king must, we are entitled to assume, have been concerned with a double problem. On the one hand the king was a human being: the funerary ritual must therefore have included ceremonies similar to, or identical with, the ordinary funerary ritual, such as the Opening of the Mouth, to ensure the restoration of the vital functions to the dead and to prevent him from dying the second death, or suffering from hunger, cold, and thirst. But, on the other hand, the king was a god and his funerary ritual must have dealt with the problem of his future in the next world and the position which he assumed with regard to the gods and the dead and to the living on earth.

It is a simple matter thus to suggest with some confidence what should have been the theoretical content of a royal funerary ritual, but it is far more difficult to describe what actually occurred, for this is a side of Egyptian practice on which we are singularly badly informed. It is true that we now know of a funerary liturgy that was surely royal and that in origin must have been not later than the beginning of the Third Dynasty, in all probability even earlier, but the surviving text is so fragmentary and incomplete and the wording so concise that it is now impossible to draw a complete picture of the ritual and its development.[1] The enormous mass of inscriptions in the royal tombs of the New Kingdom is of no help at all, for in general the texts are not concerned with the royal hereafter nor with the royal funerary liturgy. The Pyramid Texts should in theory provide us with much of the information we require, information that would be particularly valuable since it would refer to the earlier, formative periods, but unfortunately the tendency in pyramid studies hitherto has been to concentrate more on

[1] A. H. Gardiner, 'A Unique Funerary Liturgy', in *J.E.A.* xli. 9–17.

individual spells and chapters than on complete groups of texts or complete pyramids. This tendency has been encouraged by the fact that the published texts have been printed and numbered in what appears to be the exact reverse of the true and logical sequence, and this has hindered the appreciation of the nature and composition of the rituals contained in the Pyramid Texts and their development. It is only within the last few years that the published studies of Ricke and Schott have suggested an entirely new method of approach to the interpretation and study of the Pyramid Texts.[1]

One of the first fruits of this new approach to the study of the Pyramid Texts can be seen in the recently published attempt by Spiegel to reconstruct the ritual in the pyramid of Unas, the first pyramid to be inscribed.[2] Although this attempt at reconstruction requires further proof and amplification, it is fitting that Spiegel's theory and conclusions should be summarized. First, however, it should be explained that the interior of the pyramid consists of a passage descending from the north and ending in an antechamber from which open out to right and left the burial chamber and the serdab which contains the niches for the statues. Only the burial chamber, antechamber, and the southern end of the passage are inscribed. Spiegel considers that these rooms have a definite significance: the burial chamber represents the underworld, the antechamber the horizon or upper world, and its ceiling the night sky. At the same time, the burial chamber also represents the cities of Ḳus and Buto, the antechamber Middle Egypt, and the serdab Heliopolis. In Spiegel's opinion the burial ritual was celebrated on the last night of the waning moon, beginning at sunset and continuing all night until sunrise; the ideal, but naturally not the invariable, occasion was the last day of the last month of the season of Inundation.

---

[1] S. Schott, *Mythe und Mythenbildung im Alten Ägypten* (*Untersuchungen*, xv, Leipzig, 1945); H. Ricke, *Bemerkungen zur ägyptischen Baukunst des Alten Reiches*, ii, and S. Schott, *Bemerkungen zum ägyptischen Pyramidenkult* (published jointly in *Beiträge zur ägyptischen Bauforschung und Altertumskunde*, Heft 5, Cairo, 1950).

[2] J. Spiegel, 'Das Auferstehungsritual der Unaspyramide', in *Ann. Serv.* liii. 339–439.

The coffin containing the body of the dead king was brought into the burial chamber and there the offering ritual was performed, while the Ka and Ba statues were left lying temporarily in a corner of the antechamber. Afterwards the body was put in the sarcophagus, whose lid was then sealed, and with appropriate prayers the officiants passed through the doorway into the antechamber, performing the breaking of the two red vases as they did so. The Ka and Ba statues were then dragged on bundles of reeds, and each was brought into the serdab, pulled erect and installed in its shrine. Then the doors of the serdab were closed and sealed, a model boat was deposited before them, and the pyramid was left and finally closed up.

This ritual is interpreted as a resurrection ritual. During the burial ceremonies the Ba left the body and, at first an insubstantial wraith in the flickering light of the torches, crosses the underworld (the burial chamber), first acquires tangible form in the statue, crosses the night sky, reaches the horizon and in the serdab joins the Lord of All. The next section of the ritual is concerned with the soul's leaving the grave: the previous section of the ritual is repeated in abbreviated form, threats are uttered against all gods who might prevent the resurrection of the soul, and the boat that is left before the serdab is intended to facilitate the emergence of the soul. Thus the soul leaves the tomb and, as it emerges, greets the newly risen moon that will act as its ferry across the heavens, and with the dawn that follows at once, the ceremonies end.

In commenting upon this reconstruction Spiegel observes that the resurrection ritual is firmly based on the fertility myth and the myth of the dying god who in death begets himself anew and is reborn. At the same time in three ways it is incorporated into the ordinary cycle of Nature. First, it follows the motion of the sun, for sunset signifies death and sunrise rebirth. Secondly, it is also connected with the phases of the moon: the death and resurrection of the king are linked with the waning and waxing of the moon, and since the king was buried on the last night of the waning moon, the new moon in a sense symbolized the new king. Finally, the ritual is linked with the seasonal year: the burial of the king on the last evening of the season of inundation meant that the following day, the first day of winter or seed-time, symbolized both the rebirth of the dead king and the coronation of his successor. It will be appreciated at once how closely Spiegel's theory corresponds to what has already been said above with regard to the coronation, the jubilee festival, and the Ramesseum Dramatic Papyrus.

The pyramid of Unas, according to Spiegel, also contained another ritual, a silent ritual. This is characterized by its pro-pronounced anti-Lower Egyptian and anti-solar tone. It is to a certain degree parallel with the spoken ritual in so far as it also has some concern with resurrection, the journey across the sky, and the ultimate triumph of the dead king, but it is sharply distinguished from the spoken ritual by the fact that whereas the latter is primarily concerned with the union of the soul with the sun-god, in the silent ritual, which also includes the famous Cannibal Hymn, the dead king, by dint of threats and insults directed towards the sun-god, claims the overlordship of the world. The silent ritual was celebrated simultaneously with part of the spoken ritual beginning, as the officiants passed from the burial chamber into the antechamber, with the breaking of the red vases. It would appear that the silent and spoken rituals represent Upper Egyptian and Lower Egyptian rituals respectively, the due celebration of both of which was necessary in the complete royal funerary ritual.

The ritual that has just been outlined is that of the pyramid of Unas. Similar studies of the later pyramids have not yet been made, but Spiegel claims that essentially similar rituals occur in the other pyramids, though not necessarily in such a complete form owing to the state of their preservation, but with differences from pyramid to pyramid in matters of detail and with a tendency increasingly to identify the dead king with Osiris and to stress the Lower Egyptian aspects of the ritual.

The Unas ritual is obviously primarily a resurrection ritual; it has relatively little concern with the royal hereafter as such, except for the general proposition that the king triumphs and acquires supremacy in the next world. The Pyramid Texts incorporate so many conceptions of the hereafter that a complete and satisfactory picture is not yet possible. A clear picture of the destiny of the king in the Osirian hereafter occurs in the pyramids of the Sixth Dynasty:

> Thou standest, O N., protected, equipped as a god, equipped with the aspect of Osiris on the throne of the First of the Westerners. Thou doest what he was wont to do among the spirits, the Imperishable Stars. Thy son stands on thy throne, equipped with thy aspect; he does what thou wast wont to do aforetime at the head of the living by the command of Rēʿ, the Great God; he cultivates barley, he cultivates spelt, that he may present thee therewith. Ho N., all life and dominion are given to thee, eternity is thine, says Rēʿ. Thou thyself speakest when thou hast received the aspect of a god, and thou art great thereby among the gods who are in the estate. Ho N., thy Ba stands among the gods, among the spirits; fear of thee is in their hearts. Ho N., this N. stands on thy throne at the head of the living; terror of thee is in their hearts. Thy name that is on earth lives, thy name that is on earth endures; thou wilt not perish, thou wilt not be destroyed for ever and ever.[1]

This passage clearly demonstrates that the dead king, after the ceremonies of resurrection and transfiguration, took possession of the throne of Osiris and carried out, in the realms of the gods and the dead, all the duties that Osiris had previously performed, while his son, the reigning king, ruled on earth in his stead and maintained the appropriate ritual and offerings for his father. To perpetuate the mortuary cult of his predecessor appears to have been one of the obligations of the reigning sovereign. The implication of this passage appears to be that when the king died he became the reigning Osiris, pushing off the throne his immediate predecessor, hitherto the reigning Osiris, who henceforward became one of that shadowy company of the king's predecessors and ancestors that stretched in unbroken line through the dynasties of men, demi-gods, and gods to the first god-king. This must surely be the idea that lies behind the statements in the Pyramid Texts that the dead king is the Ka of his successor. When, for instance, we read in an address to the Osiris (king) Teti 'Horus is not far from thee, (for) thou art

[1] *Pyr.* 759*a*–764*b*.

his Ka',[1] Horus is not merely the son of Osiris, he is undoubtedly the reigning king. It is not possible here to discuss the exceedingly complex problem of the Ka,[2] but there can be little doubt that among the many meanings that can be attached to the word, not the least important, at least in so far as the king is concerned, is that of 'kingship', and that the king's Ka could on occasion be identified with his kingly office.[3] Thus it may well be that the passage just quoted could be better rendered: 'Horus is not far from thee, (for) thou art his kingship.'

The evidence that has been discussed suggests that the kingship of the reigning king resided in his predecessor. In other words, his kingly office is derived from and inherent in his ancestors, and it was in the establishment and preservation of the direct link with the ancestors that his claim to rule resided. One method of emphasizing that link was undoubtedly the performance of the funerary ritual for his predecessor, and indeed for all the company of the ancestors. In Egypt the funerary ritual was celebrated by the dead man's son: it would be a profitable line of inquiry to seek to discover to what extent inheritance depended on carrying out the burial and mortuary cult of one's father. The king, too, beyond all doubt honoured the cult of his ancestors, the former kings. Is it too much to suggest that the due celebration of the funerary ritual of his predecessor was one of the prerequisites of his claim to be the legitimate king, the living Horus who performed the ritual for his father Osiris?

It is not inapposite in this connexion to recall that in the tomb of Tutankhamun his successor, Ay, is depicted as king performing

---

[1] *Pyr.* 610*d*; for similar expressions see *Pyr.* 102*b*; 149*d*; 582*d*; 587*b*; 647*d*.

[2] The most recent studies are: Frankfort, *Kingship*, pp. 61–78; L. Greven, *Der Ka in Theologie und Königskult der Ägypter des Alten Reiches (Ägyptol. Forsch.*, Heft 17, Glückstadt, 1952); U. Schweitzer, *Das Wesen des Ka (Ägyptol. Forsch.*, Heft 19, Glückstadt, 1956).

[3] See *J.E.A.* xxxvi. 7 n. 2; xli. 141. Cf. also H. Jacobsohn, *Die dogmatische Stellung des Königs in der Theologie der alten Ägypter (Ägyptol. Forsch.*, Heft 8, Glückstadt, 1939). One of the more acceptable conclusions of this work is that the king is the holder and possessor of a divine force, the Ka, transmitted to him by his earthly ancestors, the successors of the god-kings, in order to continue the work of the creator and demiurge.

the ceremony of Opening the Mouth over the mummy.[1] Ay was not of the blood royal. Moreover, Newberry has pointed out that the floral wreaths found in the tomb suggest that Tutankhamun was probably buried between the middle of March and the end of April,[2] which at that period would have roughly corresponded to the fourth month of winter and the first month of summer. If Ay were crowned at the traditional date, he still would have had to wait some eight months for his coronation. We do not in fact know the date of Ay's coronation, but in causing himself to be depicted performing the funeral ceremonies of Tutankhamun he was demonstrating that he was acting as Horus had done for Osiris, and in so doing may well have been producing proof that he was the rightful king and successor.[3]

Our survey has now brought us face to face with the question of the royal ancestors. It is a fortunate circumstance that one example of a ritual of the ancestors has survived in what is now generally called the Ritual of Amenophis I. The two most extensive sources for this ritual are two papyri of the reign of Ramesses II: Papyrus Chester Beatty IX,[4] and another papyrus of which part is in Cairo,[5] and part in Turin.[6] In addition, much shorter and less complete versions of the ritual, which do not mention the name of Amenophis I, occur in the Hypostyle Hall at Karnak (Sethos I) and in the temple of Medinet Habu (Ramesses III): these have been published, together with a survey of the whole ritual, by Nelson.[7]

A survey of all these sources demonstrates that the Ritual of Amenophis I does not contain the episodes of a single ritual

---

[1] *Ann. Serv.* xxxviii, pl. cxvi.

[2] H. Carter, *The Tomb of Tut-Ankh-Amen*, ii. 196.

[3] The suggestion of K. Seele (*J.N.E.S.* xiv. 168–80) that Tutankhamun and Ay were co-regents is not, in my opinion, well founded.

[4] A. H. Gardiner, *Hieratic Papyri in the British Museum, Third Series* (London, 1935), i. 78–106; ii, pls. 50–61.

[5] Cairo 58030, published by W. Golénischeff, *Papyrus hiératiques* (*Cairo Catalogue Général*, 1927), pp. 134–56, pls. xxiv–xxvii.

[6] An edition of the Turin and Cairo portions of the papyrus has been published in Ernesta Bacchi, *Il Rituale di Amenhotpe I* (Turin, 1942).

[7] H. H. Nelson, 'Certain Reliefs at Karnak and Medinet Habu and the Ritual of Amenophis I', in *J.N.E.S.* viii. 201–32, 310–45.

performed on one main occasion in the year or at a particular festival of the dead king. It is at the best only a selection of some of the episodes forming part of a number of rituals and festivals, and there must have been many other ceremonies of which we have no knowledge. About half the episodes (Episodes A–E, 1–31 according to Nelson's numbering) are rites connected with the ordinary daily temple ritual, the episodes being those of the presentation of food, libations, &c., all the toilet episodes being omitted. These are followed by two Heliopolitan (?) rites, spells for libation, and incense to Rē'. Episodes 34–40 are the Reversion of Offerings and commence with the 'Rites performed upon the altar of the kings'. The remaining episodes (41–57) are a miscellaneous collection of spells and hymns: an evening hymn; spells for the festival of Amun; two morning hymns; spells for the festivals of the first and sixth days of the month, for the New Year festival, and for the festival of the goddess Mut.

A new, and hitherto unpublished, fact is of some importance in this connexion. It is now certain that sections of the Ritual of Amenophis I formed the main element in the decoration of at least the eastern section of the Hall of Offerings in the Ptolemaic temple at Edfu.[1] At Edfu, although of course the name of Amenophis I is never mentioned, approximately one-third of the episodes of the Ritual have been identified, either exact duplicates or very close parallels, the series ending, however, with the last ceremony of the Reversion of Offerings (Episode 40). There are in addition many episodes that do not occur in any of the earlier versions of the Ritual, but which must be regarded as having formed part of it. A significant fact is that some of the episodes of the Edfu and earlier versions can now be identified with certain sections of the Osiris Mysteries, some of the ceremonies during the hour-watches of the night.

The Ritual of Amenophis I first became known through the papyrus versions. This has been in a certain sense unfortunate, for it has not unnaturally given rise to the impression that it was

---

[1] Details will be given in my paper 'Survivals of the Ritual of Amenophis I in the Temple of Edfu' which will be published, it is hoped, in *B.I.F.A.O.* lvi. The texts of the Hall of Offerings have been published in *Edfou*, i. 456–505.

merely a ritual in honour of Amenophis I, a ritual that possibly was celebrated above all in his mortuary temple. That it was celebrated for Amenophis I cannot be denied, but that it was exclusively his ritual, or that it was primarily connected with the mortuary temples can no longer be maintained. The papyri, of course, may well have contained abbreviated versions of the ritual or rituals celebrated at various times of the year in honour of Amenophis I; the version at Medinet Habu, the mortuary temple of Ramesses III, may equally well have been intended for that king; but neither Karnak nor Edfu were in any sense mortuary temples, nor were they linked with the name of any one king. It would seem, therefore, that it is only by accident that we have come to link the ritual with the name of Amenophis I, and it would be more accurate to regard it as a ritual of the royal ancestors. This ritual may very probably have been celebrated in the individual mortuary temples, but it was certainly celebrated in others also. If we accept the suggestion that it was a ritual for the royal ancestors, it follows that a ritual of the ancestors was part of the ordinary daily ritual, and of some, at least, of the great annual festivals.

Of particular interest is the association of the Reversion of Offerings with the ritual, and here Edfu helps us. The daily ritual at Edfu was celebrated in the Sanctuary, the façade of which formed the north wall of the 'Central Hall' or 'Place where the Gods Repose', from which only a step or two leads to the Hall of Offerings.[1] At Edfu the scene introducing the Reversion of Offerings (equivalent to Episode 35) is entitled: 'Entering backwards. Reversion of Offerings. Pacifying the gods with the scent of their perfume.'[2] Evidently, after the conclusion of the daily ritual in the Sanctuary, the officiant withdrew backwards from the presence of the god, shut and sealed the doors, and celebrated the Reversion in the Hall of Offerings. It should be noted here that the term Reversion of Offerings has a double sense, expressed in Egyptian by two related but distinct expressions : *wdb (i)ḫt* 'Reversion of Offerings',

[1] See *B.J.R.L.* xxxvii. 169–70 and the plan of the temple that accompanies it.
[2] *Edfou*, i. 501, 16.

and *wdb ḥtpw-nṯr* 'Reversion of Divine Offerings'. As far as I am aware, the former has a predominantly mortuary association and is that used in all versions of the Ritual of Amenophis I in which the Reversion is mentioned. Edfu very clearly and distinctly distinguishes the two terms: the Reversion of Offerings was celebrated only inside the temple, in the Hall of Offerings after the conclusion of the daily ritual; the Reversion of the Divine Offerings was celebrated outside the temple proper when the divine offerings were distributed among the priests after having been carried out through the east door of the Inner Hypostyle Hall.

To summarize this discussion, it seems reasonable to deduce that ceremonies for the royal ancestors formed part of the daily ritual in all temples, and that they were celebrated immediately after the conclusion of the daily ritual before the chief god. Furthermore, it appears that ceremonies for the ancestors were part of many, if not all, of the great annual festivals. In the course of this study we have already seen that the ancestors, or ceremonies for them, figured in the Coronation, the Jubilee, the Festival of Behdet (within the framework of the Sacred Marriage), and in the harvest rites. At Edfu the ancestors also figured in the Osiris Mysteries, the New Year festival, and on other occasions that have not been precisely identified.

We cannot leave the subject of the Ritual of Amenophis I, or the Ritual of the Royal Ancestors as we should perhaps now call it, without some reference to the extraordinary confusions that exist in the papyrus versions of the ritual. The Papyrus Cairo/Turin is obviously a ritual performed for the deified Amenophis I, the officiant being Ramesses II. In Papyrus Chester Beatty IX, on the other hand, the ritual is devoted primarily to Amun in the form of Amun of Opet, a form of Amun that through Kamutef has special connexions with the ancestor cult, the officiant being usually Amenophis I, but sometimes Ramesses II: Amenophis I and Ramesses II are treated exactly as if they were contemporaries performing together the same ritual, though in fact they were separated by some two and a half centuries. This extraordinary situation must imply not merely that the king celebrated the cult of his ancestors, but that he was literally identified with them, and that even in life he was one of them.

It remains briefly to touch on one further point, though space will not permit of an extended discussion. Recent researches[1] have demonstrated that in Ramesside times the Theban mortuary temples appear to have each possessed a resident form of Amun distinct from the state god Amun at Karnak. At Medinet Habu this local form of Amun was Ramesses III; at the Ramesseum he was Ramesses II. The dead king was not merely Osiris, he was identified with Amun and became a part of him. Many of the mortuary temples must have been completed before the death of the king for whose mortuary cult they were destined, but we find that the temple was brought into use as soon as it had been completed and the living king is depicted as offering to himself, the local form of Amun of that temple. It is not known to what extent this is peculiar to Ramesside times and to the Theban temples, but at present no evidence of a similar practice in earlier times is known.

It is not inappropriate that this essay should close with discussion of the royal ancestors and their cult. In the preparation of it I have been increasingly impressed by the immense part played by the ancestors and the ancestor cult in the institution of kingship in Pharaonic Egypt. At the outset we commented upon the remarkable stability of the kingship in Egypt. May not this stability have been due above all to the ancestors? The ancestors may be regarded as a kind of divine corporation of which the king, on dying, became a member. Whatever his origin, the king proved his direct link with the ancestors by performing the funeral ceremonies of his predecessor, thus showing himself acting as a dutiful son. The rites of the coronation not only made him the divine king, the presence of the royal ancestors showed that he was accepted by them, he was of their essence, he was filled with the spirit of the ancestors, and in that spirit he ruled unchallenged and unchallengeable.

---

[1] H. H. Nelson, 'The Identity of Amen-Re of United-with-Eternity', in *J.N.E.S.*, i. 127–55, esp. pp. 151–5; L. A. Christophe, 'La Salle V du temple de Sethi Ier à Gournah', in *B.I.F.A.O.* xlix. 117–80, esp. pp. 172–6, and the conclusions, pp. 177–80.

HITTITE KINGSHIP

by O. R. GURNEY

Our knowledge of the character of Hittite kingship is derived primarily from the royal archives of clay tablets unearthed at the ancient Hittite capital, Hattusas, near the Turkish village of Boghazköy. These, however, are supplemented to some extent by the stone monuments discovered at various places in Anatolia and by the 'hieroglyphic' inscriptions of the late Hittite successor-states.

That the Hittite king was not only leader in war and supreme judge but also chief priest of the national cults, is well established. He 'became priest of the gods' at his accession to the throne, as is clearly shown by the fact that Mursilis II, when addressing the gods of the country in prayer, refers to his accession in just this way.[1] Similarly, Hattusilis III became priest of the weather-god of Nerik at the moment of his appointment as 'king of Hakpis'.[2] Thus the offices of kingship and priesthood were inseparable, whether at a local or a national level.

In the royal archives of Hattusas the number of tablets devoted to the priestly functions of the king is enormous, as compared with any other class of text. Unfortunately most of these tablets are more or less fragmentary, and their very number increases the difficulty of reuniting the broken pieces into continuous texts. The ceremonies which they describe are usually called festivals, and the names of these festivals are many and various. Some are called after the name of a season or portion of the year, others after agricultural processes, such as sowing and harvest. Many have names which are not understood. In most of them the king plays the leading role. Yet despite the apparent variety of these festivals, the actual rituals described are all remarkably

---

[1] Second Plague Prayer, section 1, line 4, in Pritchard, *Ancient Near Eastern Texts*, p. 394; see note by A. Goetze in *Kleinasiatische Forschungen*, i. 221–2.

[2] See Goetze, loc. cit. The statements 'he made me king in Hakpis' and 'he made me priest of the weather-god of Nerik in Hakpis' occur in parallel texts, describing the same event.

similar. They consist invariably of sacrifices and libations to a long series of deities, accompanied by music and formal utterances and actions by subordinate classes of priests. The act of libation is usually expressed by the phrase 'the king drinks the deity', and many of the rock and stone monuments of the empire depict the king in precisely this action of pouring a libation.[1] The offering of an animal is expressed by the verb *šipanti* 'he sacrifices', and when King Hattusilis tells us that he was, in his youth, appointed priest of the goddess Ishtar of Samuha, he summarizes his priestly functions in the one word *šipantaḫḫun* 'I sacrificed'.[2] The elaborate ceremonial which precedes and accompanies the king's offerings is usually described in great detail, but throws no light on the nature of Hittite kingship.[3] The most that we can learn from these rituals is that in nearly all the important festivals the king functioned as priest and performed the normal ritual actions expected of a priest.

A few of the festivals are, however, of special interest. The *purulli* or *vurulli* festival, an ancient Hattic festival of 'the Earth' (*vur*), was celebrated in the spring. The importance of the king's presence at this festival is emphasized when we read in the Annals of Mursilis II how that king, towards the end of his reign, returned to Hattusas in the spring to celebrate the 'great *purulli* festival of Lelwanis' (an underworld deity) before joining his army in the field; and he mentions on this occasion that he had already celebrated such festivals in honour of the weather-god of Hatti and the weather-god of Zippalanda, presumably at or near the town of Marassantiya where he had been spending the winter months.[4] This is one of many examples

---

[1] The phrase 'drinks the god' probably means 'gives the god to drink', though it has also been suggested that it might mean 'drinks in honour of the god' or even 'drinks the god' in a mystical sense: see Güterbock, 'Hittite Religion', in V. Ferm, *Forgotten Religions*, p. 96. Libations are shown, e.g., on the rock-carving at Fraktin and on several reliefs from Malatya (illustrations in Garstang, *The Hittite Empire*, and elsewhere).

[2] 'Apology of Hattusilis', i. 19, in Goetze, *Hattušiliš*, p. 8, and E. H. Sturtevant and G. Bechtel, *A Hittite Chrestomathy*, p. 64.

[3] For an account of the ritual see Gurney, *The Hittites*, pp. 153–5.

[4] *K.Bo.* ii. 5, iii. 38 ff. See Goetze, *Die Annalen des Muršiliš*, p. 189, supplemented by the fragment published by H. Otten in *Mitteilungen der deutschen Orientgesellschaft*, no. 75, 65–66.

showing the lack of centralization in Hittite religion.[1] The
purulli festival at Nerik (the cult-centre of another weather-god)
was also a 'great festival' and must have lasted many days, for
according to a catalogue its ritual covered no less than thirty-
two tablets.[2] If any of these are preserved, they have not yet been
identified; but we possess the text of a myth which is stated to be
the cult-legend of the *purulli* festival of the weather-god of
heaven, as told by a priest of the city of Nerik.[3] This is the myth
of the *illuyankas* dragon.[4] It is related in two different versions;
but the essential nucleus, common to both versions, is that the
dragon first vanquished the weather-god, but that the latter
eventually took his revenge and slew his opponent. Others have
already observed that this myth belongs to the well-known type
exemplified by the Babylonian Epic of Creation, the Egyptian
myth of Osiris, Horus, and Seth, and the English mummers'
play.[5] It is believed that both the Babylonian and Egyptian
myths were represented dramatically at the New Year festival,
the king taking a prominent and significant part in the performance, and it has been claimed that the *illuyankas* myth must have
been similarly performed at the Hittite *purulli* festival, which
occurred at the same time of year. There are indeed other facts
suggesting the existence of a New Year festival at Hattusas
similar to the *akitu* festival at Babylon. That the Hittite calendar
year, like the Babylonian, began in the spring, probably at the
vernal equinox, seems to be proved by a ritual text giving the
duties to be performed by the priest 'when autumn comes
and the year [enters] the eighth month'.[6] A recently published

[1] See Gurney, *The Hittites*, pp. 132 ff.

[2] *K.U.B.* xxx. 42, i. 5–7; cf. E. Laroche, 'La Bibliothèque de Hattusa', in *Archiv
Orientální*, xvii (1949), 3–4, p. 16.

[3] Translated by Goetze in Pritchard, *Ancient Near Eastern Texts*, p. 125. The
translation given by T. H. Gaster, *Thespis*, pp. 324 ff., is unreliable.

[4] The word *illuyankas* is not a proper name but an appellative denoting a kind of
serpent. See E. Laroche in *Orientalistische Literaturzeitung*, li (1956), col. 422.

[5] Gaster, *Thespis*, pp. 317 ff. The statement by I. Engnell, *Studies in Divine
Kingship in the Ancient Near East*, p. 66, that the Babylonian Epic of Creation was
included as ritual text in the Hittite *purulli* festival, is simply a misunderstanding of
the words of Furlani, whom he cites as his authority.

[6] VAT 7700, obv. 8, cited by H. Ehelolf in *Kleinasiatische Forschungen*, i, 149;
cf. Goetze in *Language*, xxvii (1951), p. 467.

fragment contains the following words to be spoken, probably by some priest in a ritual:[1]

> For the weather-god the mighty festival of the beginning of the year, (the festival) of heaven and earth, has arrived. All the gods have gathered and come to the house of the weather-god. If any god has sorrow (?) in his soul, let him dispel the evil sorrow (?) from his soul. At this festival eat ye and drink and be satisfied! Pronounce ye the life of the king and the queen! Pronounce ye [the life] of heaven and earth!

This is an obvious allusion to an assembly of the gods for the purpose of 'fixing the fates'; the scene is laid in heaven, as at the end of the third tablet of the Epic of Creation, but the inference that such a gathering of gods was actually enacted in ritual form, as in the Babylonian festival,[2] can hardly be evaded. The place of assembly may well have been the temple and open-air shrine of Yazili-kaya, about two miles from the capital, as already suggested by others.[3] Whether or not this is so, the assertion that the king 'took the hands' of the god in this festival is based on a mistranslation and cannot be used as evidence for a great religious procession such as took place during the *akitu* festival at Babylon.[4]

The 'Festival of the Year', the ritual of which is not preserved, was celebrated by the king in the winter months. A divination text contains an inquiry about the prospects for the king's health when he 'comes up from a campaign and celebrates the gods, and the king and queen spend the winter in Hattusas, and they perform there the thunder festival of the weather-god of Halap and the Festival of the Year'.[5] However, it was not necessary for the king to return to the capital for this festival,

---

[1] *K.U.B.* xxxvi. 97, discussed and translated by H. Otten in *Orientalistische Literaturzeitung*, li (1956), cols. 102–5. On the analogy of similar utterances Otten thinks that the ritual from which the passage is taken was probably of a magical nature.

[2] See, for example, C. J. Gadd in *Myth and Ritual*, pp. 55–56.

[3] This view was expressed by B. Landsberger, *Sam'al* (Ankara, 1948), pp. 112 ff., and independently by G. R. Levy, *The Sword from the Rock*. H. Otten, loc. cit., considers it to be possible.

[4] Gaster, op. cit., pp. 318 and 330, refuted by Goetze in *Journal of Cuneiform Studies*, vi. 100. On the significance of the act of 'taking the hand' see R. Labat, *Le Caractère religieux de la royauté assyro-babylonienne*, pp. 175–6.

[5] *K.U.B.* xviii. 12, obv. 1 ff.

for at the end of his second year Mursilis II celebrated it while in winter quarters on the Astarpa River.[1] Since it was celebrated in the winter and at the end of the year, this cannot have been the Hittite New Year festival.

The great national deity of the Hittites was the sun-goddess of Arinna, 'who directs kingship and queenship',[2] and it is therefore no surprise to find that her 'regular festivals' were among those for which the presence of the king was essential. Mursilis II tells us that during the prolonged absence of his father, Suppiluliumas, on his Syrian campaigns, he had been unable to return home for this purpose, and so the festivals had lapsed.[3] Mursilis made their celebration his first care on his accession to the throne. The ritual of these festivals is not preserved, unless it is to be recognized in a fragment entitled 'the great festival of Arinna'.[4] The lapsing of such festivals in the absence of the king may be compared to the similar situation which sometimes occurred at the New Year at Babylon.[5]

Another festival which emphasizes the independence of local cults is that named *nuntariyašhaš*. This was celebrated in the autumn, when the king returned from a campaign.[6] For sixteen days, accompanied by the queen and the heir to the throne, he carried out a royal 'progress' (this may be the meaning of the word *nuntariyašhaš*), passing from city to city and offering sacrifices in the presence of a 'great congregation'. The towns of Katapa, Tahurpa, Arinna, Zippalanda, and Kastama are the scenes of such celebrations, and since the whole ceremony is referred to as the 'journey to Nerik',[7] this holy city must have figured in a part of the text which is lost. On the fifth day the king performs sacrifices and libations at Arinna, while the queen

---

[1] *K.U.B.* iii. 4, ii. 48, followed by the statement: 'And this I carried out in one year.' The performance of the festival was therefore regarded as the last act of the year, not as the first of the following year.

[2] *K.Bo.* i. 1, rev. 35, 40, in Weidner, *Politische Dokumente aus Kleinasien*, pp. 26–28.

[3] *K.Bo.* iii. 4, i. 16–18, in Goetze, *Die Annalen des Muršiliš*, p. 20.

[4] *K.U.B.* xx. 76.

[5] See R. Labat, op. cit., pp. 173–4.

[6] *K.U.B.* xxv. 12–14 and ix. 16, colophons; see Goetze, *Kleinasien*, p. 85 with note 6 and pp. 154–5.

[7] *K.U.B.* x. 48, ii. 22–23.

celebrates the sun-goddess of Arinna and the goddess Mezulla at Tahurpa. For this celebration by the queen we have a special tablet which will be discussed below (see pp. 120 f.).

The pious Mursilis tells us that in his ninth year he actually handed over the command of his army to a general in the field and himself proceeded to Kummanni in Kizzuwatna (the classical Comana Cappadociae) to celebrate the festival of the goddess Hebat.[1] This, however, was a special case. Kummanni was not originally a Hittite city, but had been annexed by Suppiluliumas, and it would have been his duty as a conqueror to pay his respects to the famous deity of this holy city.[2] However, he died before he was able to carry this out, and the duty devolved on his successor. Thus by the ninth year of Mursilis the performance of this festival would indeed have 'become urgent' for him (Hittite *nakkešta*). Suppiluliumas, however, did not always neglect his priestly functions, for on one occasion his son, travelling up to meet him at Hattusas, found him celebrating festivals at the city of Uda, possibly the classical Hyde.[3]

Mursilis II is indeed conspicuous for the zeal and piety with which he carried out his religious duties. He is the author of a number of royal prayers, which are happily well preserved and exhibit a remarkably high religious quality.[4] Any offence by the ruler might, according to the beliefs of the time, bring down the wrath of the gods upon his people. If, therefore, the nation suffered some grave misfortune, it was assumed that the cause lay in a sin committed by its representative, the king. Such a disaster was the pestilence which broke out towards the end of the reign of Suppiluliumas and continued to rage for twenty years, carrying off among its first victims both Suppiluliumas himself and his son and successor Arnuwandas II. Faced with

---

[1] Goetze, *Die Annalen des Muršiliš*, pp. 106–9.

[2] Goetze, *Kizzuwatna and the Problem of Hittite Geography*, p. 10.

[3] *K.Bo.* v. 6, ii. 13–14 (cf. Cavaignac, *Les Annales de Subbiluliuma*, 16). Uda is mentioned with Tuwanuwa (Tyana) in *K.Bo.* vi. 28, obv. 9 (in Goetze, *Kizzuwatna*, pp. 21–22). See the discussion by E. Forrer in *Klio*, xxx. 141.

[4] They are translated by Goetze in *Kleinasiatische Forschungen*, i. 161–251, and by Gurney in *Annals of Archaeology and Anthropology* (Liverpool), xxvii (1940); selections in Pritchard, *Ancient Near Eastern Texts*, pp. 394–7. See also Güterbock in V. Ferm, *Forgotten Religions*, p. 98.

this calamity, Mursilis besought the gods to reveal the sin which had been committed, that he might make due atonement. The records were searched and at least three possible causes of the divine anger were found: a certain 'Tudhaliyas the Younger' had been done to death when Suppiluliumas mounted the throne; a treaty with the Egyptians had been violated when Suppiluliumas invaded southern Syria; an ancient sacrifice for the Mala River had been neglected. Only for the last was Mursilis himself in any way responsible, and he promised to carry out this sacrifice without delay.[1] The other two offences had been committed by his father, but he still assumed responsibility for their expiation:

> Ye gods, my lords: whereas ye demanded vengeance for the blood of Tudhaliyas—those who killed Tudhaliyas have already paid the price of their blood-guilt; yea, the blood-guilt has already ruined the land of Hatti. Now, since it has descended on me, I with my family will make amends for it by expiation and restitution.[2]

And in another prayer:

> See, I make a petition to the weather-god of Hatti about the plague. Hear me, weather-god of Hatti and save my life. [I will put it] to you in this way: the bird takes refuge in its nest and the nest saves its life. Or again: if a servant has anything on his mind, he appeals to his master and his master hears him and takes pity on him and puts right what is troubling him. And if a servant has committed an offence and confesses his guilt before his master, his master may do with him whatever he pleases; but because he has confessed his guilt before his master, his master's spirit is appeased and his master will not call that servant to account. And now I have confessed my father's guilt. It is true; I have done it. In the matter of reparation . . . with all the reparation that Hattusas has made through the plague, it has already made reparation twentyfold; yet the spirit of the weather-god of Hatti and the gods my lords is not appeased. If ye demand from me any additional reparation, tell it me in a dream and I will give it.[3]

As representative of his people, the king here comes before

---

[1] *Kleinasiatische Forschungen*, i. 214–15.   [2] Ibid., pp. 172–3.
[3] Ibid., pp. 216–17, and Pritchard, op. cit., pp. 395–6.

the gods in all humility, likening himself to a servant. He claims indeed to be sinless himself, but none the less is willing to assume the guilt of his father in order to appease the anger of the gods.

The attitude of Hattusilis III in the only extant prayer which stands in his name is somewhat similar. Here the cause of divine anger is traced to the impious action of Mursilis in banishing the queen mother, a priestess and the widow of Suppiluliumas, on charges of embezzlement and sorcery. Hattusilis urged that his father was long since dead; that he was a child at the time and had therefore no part in the affair; that on the contrary he had earned great merit by his restoration of the cult of Nerik after its destruction by the Kaska-folk.[1] We miss here, however, the humility and willingness to accept responsibility for further amends, if required by the gods.

The extent to which the welfare of the king was identified with that of the nation may be seen in a prayer which the scribe was instructed to read daily for Mursilis before his god, Telipinu:[2]

To the king and the queen, the princes and the land of Hatti, grant life, health, strength, long years and enduring joy. Grant everlasting fertility to their crops, vines, fruit-trees, cattle, sheep, goats, pigs, mules, and asses, together with the beasts of the field, and to their people. Let them flourish! Let the winds of prosperity pass over! Let the land of Hatti thrive and prosper.

When these royal prayers are compared with those of even such exalted persons as Queen Puduhepa or Prince Kantuzzilis,[3] it may be seen that though many of the same phrases occur, the national character of the occasion is absent. Kantuzzilis prays for his own restoration to health, while Puduhepa pleads for the health of her husband the king. There are also many votive prayers of Puduhepa and other queens for the same purpose.[4]

---

[1] *K.U.B.* xxi. 19 (+xiv. 7). On the affair of the queen mother see Goetze, *Kleinasien*, pp. 87–88; Sommer, *Die Ahhijava-Urkunden*, pp. 300 ff.; and Güterbock, *Siegel aus Boğazköy*, i. 12 ff.

[2] *K.U.B.* xxiv. 2, ii. 12–18 (Pritchard, op. cit., p. 397).

[3] Prayer of Puduhepa, *K.U.B.* xxi. 27, translated by Goetze in Pritchard, op. cit., pp. 393–4. Prayer of Kantuzzilis, *K.U.B.* xxx. 10, translated ibid., pp. 400–1.

[4] *K.U.B.* xv. 1–30, &c., especially the text edited by E. Laroche in *Revue d'Assyriologie*, xliii. 55–78.

An attitude of profound reverence for the gods is exhibited by all the later Hittite kings. The Annals of Mursilis open with an offering of thanks to the sun-goddess of Arinna for granting him victory over his numerous enemies.[1] Hattusilis appears in his narrative of accession as the devoted servant of his goddess Ishtar of Samuha, to whom he ascribes the glory for his success in attaining the kingship.[2] As king of Hakpis he was priest of the weather-god of Nerik and was energetic in restoring the cults of that city after the place had been overrun by the Kaskans. His son, Tudhaliyas IV, is known to have introduced a number of minor reforms in various cults,[3] and it may have been he who inaugurated the carving of the religious sculptures on the walls of the open-air shrine at Yazili-kaya.[4]

In the theocratic world of that time, the authority of the Hittite king was naturally derived from the will of the gods. Indeed it could hardly have been otherwise. The allusions to the divine appointment are sporadic but unmistakable. A small tablet contains the following words to be spoken by a priest when the king worships a deity:[5]

May *Tabarnas*, the king, be pleasing to the gods. The land belongs to the weather-god. Heaven and earth with the people belong to the weather-god, and he has made the *labarnas* [*sic*], the king, his

---

[1] Goetze, *Die Annalen des Muršiliš*, pp. 14–23.

[2] Translation in E. H. Sturtevant and G. Bechtel, *A Hittite Chrestomathy*, pp. 64–83; cf. Gurney, *The Hittites*, pp. 175–6.

[3] *K.U.B.* xxv. 18–24. These texts only concern food-offerings. More extensive restorations of shrines and their furniture, such as *K.Bo.* ii. 1 (Hrozný, *Boghazköi-Studien*, ii. 1–27), do not give the name of the king.

[4] This was the view of Laroche, *Journal of Cuneiform Studies*, vi, 122–3. Güterbock, however, in *Mitteilungen der deutschen Orientgesellschaft*, no. 86 (Dec. 1953), argued that the carvings must be assumed to have been in existence during the second of four building periods at Yazili-kaya, and that to ascribe them to Tudhaliyas IV would leave insufficient time for the architectural changes that took place in periods C and D. The small gallery is probably a mortuary temple dedicated to an earlier King Tudhaliyas; it contains, however, a relief of Tudhaliyas IV (see below, p. 116 n. 4), and although it is possible that this was a later addition, its presence in this position certainly suggests that Tudhaliyas IV was the king who laid out the shrine in honour of his earlier namesake.

[5] *Istanbul . . . Boğazköy Tabletleri*, i, no. 30, translated by Goetze in *Journal of Cuneiform Studies*, i. 90–91. See also Güterbock, 'Authority and Law in the Hittite Kingdom', in *J.A.O.S.*, Supplement No. 17 (1954), p. 16.

administrator and has given him the whole land of Hattusas. Labarnas shall administer the whole land with his hands. Whoever comes too near to the person and domain of Labarnas, the weather-god shall destroy him.

A similar passage is found in a ritual for the building of a new palace:[1]

To me, the king, have the gods, the sun-god and the weather-god, entrusted the land and my house. I, the king, will protect my land and my house. . . . To me, the king, have the gods granted many years. To these years there is no limit.

These two passages are the nearest thing we have in Hittite literature to a philosophy of kingship. The king is the steward of the gods, in particular of the weather-god and the sun-god. In this way he stands in such a close relationship to the gods that his person is taboo and protected from casual contacts with lesser mortals. Protection from defilement is also the purpose of a tablet of instructions to the palace servants, in which they are enjoined to exercise the greatest care in cleansing the water which is offered to the king, and to use only leather from animals slaughtered in the palace for the manufacture of his shoes and his chariot.[2] These instructions appear to the modern reader as simple rules of hygiene; but to the ancient mind impurity had magical associations, and when we read in this text that the discovery of a hair in the king's washing-bowl was punishable with death, the seriousness of this crime on the part of the servant can only be understood in the light of the well-known magical properties of hairs.

The word Tabarnas, or Labarnas, which occurs in the above quotation, is nothing but the personal name of the founder of the royal line. The name is of Hattic origin and seems to have begun with a peculiar consonant, which was rendered in Hittite with

---

[1] *K.U.B.* xxix. 1, i. 17–22, translated by Goetze in Pritchard, op. cit., p. 357.

[2] *K.U.B.* xiii. 3, translated by J. Friedrich in *Mitteilungen der altorientalischen Gesellschaft*, iv. 46 ff. I. Engnell, op. cit., p. 62 n. 12, gives an exaggerated impression of the 'severity' of these taboos. This is the only text of its kind; the elaborate regulations for the king's behaviour contained in the Babylonian hemerologies do not exist in Hittite.

an *l* but in Luwian and Akkadian with a *t*. It was assumed by each king for the period of his reign almost as a surname, but was never applied to deceased monarchs, except in a single religious passage which refers to the statues of 'the former Labarnas's', i.e. all former kings who had once been Labarnas but are so no longer.[1] The conclusion is inescapable that the Hittite king was regarded during his lifetime as the incarnation of his deified ancestor. The spirit of Labarnas lived on in the reigning king, just as the spirit of the ancestor of the Shilluk kings 'is believed to be in every king and to have passed from king to king down the line of his successors'.[2]

We here approach the vexed question of the divinity of the Hittite kings. Shilluk society is usually regarded as almost a classical example of 'divine kingship', and the very similar conception of kingship which obtained among the Hittites might be held to justify the view that their kings also were divine, even though in other respects, of course, there can be no comparison between the two societies. What then can we learn of the beliefs of the Hittites themselves with regard to this problem? They have not left any dogmatic work on the subject, and their views have to be gleaned from scattered allusions and remarks in a variety of texts.

The Hittite king was, as we have seen, set apart from ordinary mortals by virtue of his sacral office. This sacrosanct character was traced by the kings themselves to the special favour of the gods, and every king had his divine patron, by whom he claimed to be 'beloved'. Telipinu was the 'personal god' of Mursilis II.[3] Hattusilis III claims to have been throughout his life the favourite of the goddess Ishtar of Samuha, and as a result of this favour he was a *parā ḫandanza* man, one who lived according to the divine ordinances,[4] and so did not commit the wickedness

[1] *K.U.B.* xxiv. 5, obv. 6. On this and the whole question of the meaning of the Labarnas-name see F. Sommer and A. Falkenstein, *Die hethitisch-akkadische Bilingue des Hattusili I* (1938), pp. 20–29. In exactly the same way Hittite queens took the name of Tawannannas, who had been the wife of King Labarnas.

[2] E. E. Evans-Pritchard, *The Divine Kingship of the Shilluk of the Nilotic Sudan* (Cambridge, 1948), p. 9.

[3] Gurney, *Annals of Archaeology and Anthropology*, xxvii. 45 (on B I. 6).

[4] On the meaning of this expression see Güterbock in V. Ferm, *Forgotten Religions*, pp. 99–100.

characteristic of mankind.[1] Muwatallis was the beloved of the 'weather-god *piḫassassis*',[2] and his seals show him in the embracing arms of that deity.[3] In the well-known rock-relief in the side-gallery at Yazili-kaya King Tudhaliyas is shown in the same relationship to his god Sharruma.[4] Similar scenes in Egypt are held to imply a sharing in the vital force of the embracing deity,[5] but there is no reason to suppose that the Hittite representation was intended to express more than the special love of the god for his human protégé. The effect of such divine favour was exceptional virtue and success, but it does not imply superhuman powers.

More problematical is the relation of the Hittite kings to the sun-god. As an alternative to the name Labarnas, the later Hittite kings, including those of the successor-kingdoms,[6] commonly applied to themselves another title 'My Sun'. There can be little doubt that this title originated as a form of address by the king's subjects, possibly under Egyptian or Mitannian influence.[7] Here, however, a chronological factor enters in. Up to this point the texts of the Old Hittite Kingdom have not been adduced as evidence, because they are almost exclusively of an historical nature and the sacral character of the kingship has no place in them. It is, however, important to note that, whereas the royal name Labarnas is regularly used in them as in those of the Empire, the title 'My Sun' appears in them only once, not as part of the official titulature, but precisely as a form of address put into the mouth of the subjects. The newly adopted heir to

---

[1] 'Apology of Hattusilis', i. 47–50 (cf. p. 113 n. 2, above).

[2] Treaty with Alaksandus of Wilusa, line 1 (Friedrich, *Staatsverträge des Hattireiches*, ii. 50).

[3] H. G. Güterbock, *Siegel aus Boğazköy*, i, nos. 38–40, where the god is named 'weather-god of heaven'.

[4] Illustrated in Gurney, *The Hittites*, pl. 15; M. Vieyra, *Hittite Art*, pl. 25; H. Frankfort, *The Art and Architecture of the Ancient Orient*, pl. 130 B; and elsewhere. On the names of the deity and the king see most recently Güterbock in *Mitteilungen der deutschen Orientgesellschaft*, no. 86, 73–74.

[5] See Frankfort, *Kingship and the Gods*, p. 67.

[6] H. T. Bossert has identified the title 'My Sun' in the Karatepe bilingual and in other Hittite Hieroglyphic texts: see *Oriens*, i. 176 and 189–90.

[7] Sommer–Falkenstein, op. cit., p. 72, and Güterbock, 'Authority and Law in the Hittite Kingdom', p. 16 (cf. p. 113 n. 5, above).

the throne is introduced to the assembly by King Hattusilis I
with the words: 'He is now "the offspring of My Sun" to you.'[1]
This suggests that the identification of the king with the sun-god
was at any rate not an original part of the concept of Hittite
kingship. The usage may have been introduced from Syria or
Egypt and have been adopted by the Hittites as little more than
a form of words. Be that as it may, there can be no doubt that in
the imperial age and in the first millennium the sun-god was in
some sense identified with the Hittite king. Not only was the
winged sun disk placed symbolically above the head of almost
every king (or above his name) on the monuments, from the time
of Suppiluliumas to the last days of the successor-kingdoms; but
when the imperial sculptors wished to carve a representation of
the sun-god in his place among the assembled pantheon at
Yazili-kaya, they produced a figure indistinguishable in every
way from that of a Hittite king in his priestly robes, to such an
extent that until recently this figure was generally regarded as a
deified king.[2] The dress, and the 'lituus' carried by this god, are
in no way characteristic of a solar deity, and can only be understood as derived from the costume of the king, whose office was
not ultimately of solar origin.[3] Moreover, the intimate relationship between the sun-god and the king is expressed in a remarkable passage which has been quoted in transliteration from a still
unpublished Hittite text:[4]

As *marnuwan* and beer have been completely blended for the sun-
god of the gods, so that their soul and heart (i.e. their essences) have
become one, so let the soul and heart (i.e. the selves) of the sun-god and
of Labarnas become one.

Whatever the explanation of the phrase 'sun-god of the gods'
may be, these words evidently express the wish that the spirit of

[1] *K.U.B.* I. 16, ii. 44 (Sommer–Falkenstein, op. cit., pp. 8–9).

[2] It was still so regarded by H. Frankfort, *The Art and Architecture of the Ancient
Orient* (1954), p. 125. But the figure is explicitly designated 'sun-god of heaven'
(Laroche in *Journal of Cuneiform Studies*, vi. 117).

[3] In late Hittite hieroglyphic texts the *lituus* is used as an ideogram for the
sun-god. Bossert (*Archiv Orientální*, xviii. 3–4, 32) argues that it is therefore essentially a sun-symbol. But the usage may be secondary.

[4] Bo. 2544, ii. 18–21, cited by Ehelolf in *Zeitschrift für Assyriologie*, xliii. 176.

the Hittite monarch should become mystically fused with that of the sun-god. It would be interesting to know whether this prayer, which resembles those used in magical texts, refers in any way to the king's investiture or coronation. If that were so, it would imply that, in the later period, the king was believed to be by virtue of his sacred office at least partially divine. If, however, the words are part of some semi-magical ritual not connected with the coronation, this fusion with the divine nature of the sun-god would appear, not as an essential aspect of the kingship, but as something superimposed on it for a special occasion, such as, for instance, the administration of justice.

The ceremony of the coronation is one on which we are not well informed. We know that it was called the 'Festival of Enthronement',[1] or more cumbrously 'the festival when the king sits down on the throne of kingship and the queen on the throne of queenship'.[2] However, the ritual itself is not preserved. Its bare outlines have to be deduced from a text in which a prisoner of war is dressed up as a substitute king and handed over to the gods to avert an evil omen:[3]

> They anoint the prisoner with the fine oil of kingship, and [he (the king) speaks] as follows: 'This man is the king. To him [have I given] a royal name. I have arrayed him [in the vestments] of kingship. I have crowned him with the crown. Remember ye this: that evil omen [means] short years and short days. Pursue ye this substitute.'

In a letter to the King of Assyria, Hattusilis III complained that on his accession the king had not sent him the usual presents, such as 'the royal vestments and fragrant oil for the coronation'.[4] Thus it is evident that the accession of a new king was solemnized by a ceremony which included anointing with oil, clothing in special garments, coronation, and the bestowal of a royal name. All this is in accordance with the sacral character of the

---

[1] EZEN *a-ša-an-na-aš*, *K.U.B.* xviii. 36, 19; also LUGAL-*iz-na-ni a-ša-a-tar*, ibid. 12 ('enthronement for kingship').

[2] *K.U.B.* ix. 10 and x. 45.

[3] *K.U.B.* xxiv. 5, translated by Goetze in Pritchard, op. cit., p. 355.

[4] *K.Bo.* i. 14, rev. 7–10, in Goetze, *Kizzuwatna*, p. 29, cited by Delaporte, *Les Hittites*, p. 137.

royal office, but it throws no light on the problem of the king's divinity.

The succession to the kingship seems to have depended on an act of nomination by the reigning monarch of which the best example is preserved to us in the speech of Hattusilis I from the Old Kingdom.[1] There is in this document no trace of a religious sanction: the will of Hattusilis is declared and his subjects must accept the decision. On the analogy of the Assyrian succession we should expect to find some manifestation of the divine choice, or at least of divine assent. Was this perhaps introduced at a later stage in Hittite history? Such a development might be inferred if a recently published fragment may be restored as follows:[2]

[No]w behold, from among the king's sons [the gods] have nominated [. . .] for the [king]ship; and his brothers, his sisters, [. . .] and the assembly of the men of Hatti shall recognize him.

The subject of the first verb is lost, but the plural form excludes 'the king' as subject, and it is difficult to think of any satisfactory alternative.

The legitimation of the king by the fiction of a divine birth, such as we find in the inscriptions of numerous ancient Mesopotamian kings,[3] does not appear in the Hittite texts. The fact that in the ritual for the building of a new palace quoted on p. 114 the king twice refers to the weather-god as his father is hardly sufficient to prove the existence of such a claim, since the expression stands completely isolated and seems to be merely a figure of speech. In all other texts, including the prayers, the gods are addressed as 'lord'. The phrase 'the son of the weather-god' is used to denote not the Hittite king but the king of Mitanni.[4]

These sporadic hints of divinity are surely outweighed by the fact that the Hittite king 'became a god' at death and cannot

---

[1] Edited by F. Sommer and A. Falkenstein, op. cit.

[2] *K.U.B.* xxxvi. 109. H. Otten, the editor of this text, prefers to take the first verb impersonally ('one has nominated'), but it seems unlikely that the authority responsible for such an important act would not be mentioned.

[3] See Labat, op. cit., chap. iii.

[4] Güterbock in *Zeitschrift für Assyriologie*, xliv. 135. I. Engnell (op. cit., p. 58) again misrepresents his authority (Forrer) here.

therefore have been one during his lifetime. The phrase is standardized for the death of a king throughout Hittite literature, and thus, unlike the isolated passages quoted above, indicates an essential element in Hittite religion. The statues of dead kings were placed in the temples and offerings were regularly made to them by the reigning monarchs. Assertions that living kings enjoyed such divine honours are based on a misunderstanding of the texts.[1]

It is of interest to note that the cult of deceased royalty included queens and other members of the royal family beside the kings,[2] although they are not said to 'become gods'.[3] The doctrine concerning the queen is illustrated by the following passage from the ritual celebrated by the queen at Tahurpa during the course of the *nuntariyašhaš* festival (cf. pp. 109 f.):[4]

> The seer brings eight sun-goddesses of Arinna into the *halentuwa* building. These statues have five sun-disks fixed behind them. They arrange tables, and on them they place [. . .]. They wash the sun-goddesses of Arinna and anoint them and [put] them back on their tables. And the queen comes from the inner room. . . . She washes her hands. She worships the sun-goddesses. And thus she sacrifices to the sun-goddess of Arinna: 7 lambs, among them 2 lambs to the sun-goddess of Arinna of (Queen?) Walanni, 1 lamb to the sun-goddess of Arinna of (Queen) Nikalmati, 1 lamb to the sun-goddess of Arinna of (Queen) Asmunikal, 1 lamb to the sun-goddess of Arinna of (Queen)

---

[1] Engnell, op. cit., pp. 61–62. The reference to 'offerings before the royal statue', when traced to its source in *K.Bo.* ii. 29–30, turns out to concern exclusively the statues of dead kings. There are no 'libations for the king' in the *antahšum* festival, nor does he 'receive' the divine proskynesis: both these actions are 'performed' by him. The statement that a bull was substituted for the king (ibid., p. 64) seems to be intended to suggest that it was so substituted as a cult-symbol; the reference, however, is to a magical text of the scapegoat type. The hieroglyphic texts cited by Engnell on p. 61 from works by Hrozný are completely mistranslated; the alleged deities Apamas and Melasatamas are really words for 'west' and 'east', and the sign in which Hrozný thought he recognized a sacred tree is proved by the Karatepe bilingual to be an ideogram for 'sunrise' (Bossert in *Archiv Orientální*, xviii (3–4), pp. 36–37).

[2] E. Forrer, *Die Boghazköi-Texte in Umschrift*, nos. 24–29.

[3] It is noteworthy that the brother of Mursilis, Shar-Kushukh, the king of Carchemish, whose name appears in the list in Forrer, op. cit., no. 24, v. 16, is explicitly said to 'die' in *K.Bo.* iv. 4, i. 6.

[4] *K.U.B.* xxv. 14, i. 10–31. The broken colophon of this tablet can be restored from the *nuntariyašhaš* text *K.U.B.* x. 48, i. 5–6.

Duduhepa, 1 lamb to the sun-goddess of Arinna of (Queen) Henti, 1 lamb to the sun-goddess of Arinna of (Queen) Tawannannas.

The exact meaning of this curious passage is uncertain, though it suggests that dead queens were in some way identified with the sun-goddess of Arinna. There is, however, no hint of such a belief in any other text. In the case of the deceased kings, the statues of the kings themselves are the objects of the cult.[1]

Such then is the evidence for the nature of Hittite kingship. The belief that the reigning Hittite king impersonated the spirit of the royal ancestor Labarnas appears to date from the earliest times. Since the name of this ancestor is Hattic, it is unlikely that this belief originated with the Indo-European element in the Hittite nation. In theory the king was the steward appointed by the weather-god of Hatti to administer his estate, and must render homage to him by constant prayer and sacrifice. As priest he was the channel through which his people approached the gods. His close connexion with the divine rendered his person taboo and he was protected from too close intercourse with his subjects. The significance of his mystical union with the sun-god, which is mentioned in one passage, is uncertain. All this implies, to be sure, that he was regarded as in some sense superhuman. The fact remains, however, that only at death did he 'become a god', and there is no trace of a cult of living kings.

[1] *K.U.B.* x. 11, iii. 26–30, iv. 1–6, 21–24. *K.Bo.* II. 29, iii. 9 ff., 30, i. 12 ff., 770/b ii. 11 ff. (Otten, *Mitteilungen der deutschen Orientgesellschaft*, no. 83, 58).

MYTH, RITUAL, AND KINGSHIP IN THE RAS SHAMRA TABLETS

by R. DE LANGHE

THOUGH more than twenty-five years have elapsed since the late Hans Bauer published his 'Alphabet of the 5th October', the combined study of the religions and cultic milieu, of the beliefs and rites, which the cuneiform documents of Ras-Shamra-Ugarit presuppose, and which the archaeological finds on the Tell illustrate in a fragmentary and incomplete manner, is still inconclusive. Admittedly we now possess not only editions of the texts, translations, and first commentaries, but other excellent publications which embody and discuss the most significant data. No doubt the most popular of these will be those lucid surveys which claim to present 'some results concerning the gods, myths and ritual of early Canaanite religion' as they are attested in the Ras Shamra tablets; but I hope I shall not be proved rash if I predict that few of these 'results' will become definitely established. For the most part we have to deal only with works of approach, with general and preliminary orientation, with suggestions which though often felicitous are usually limited to a small part of the field.

It must be admitted also that in spite of the successful resumption of excavations at Ras Shamra since the Second World War, archaeological interest in the site has declined. This is, of course, very largely due to the competition of the more sensational discoveries of Qumran and the other Dead Sea sites; the Syrian Tell has suffered by contrast. The flood of publications, besides being often superficial and premature, has shrunk to a trickle; more profound study is left to a handful of valiant survivors.

Before the war eleven fruitful excavations had been carried out on the Tell, the results of which had received widespread comment. In the course of 1948 and 1949 two sounding expeditions were carried out under the admirable leadership of the indefatigable M. Claude F. A. Schaeffer, but it was only in November 1950 that the systematic excavations could resume their normal course and that the new researches concentrated on the royal palace of Ugarit were fully developed. It is already clear that this was one of the grandest and most sumptuous royal residences of its epoch, and we can all welcome unreservedly the recent appearance of volume VI of the *Mission de Ras Shamra*—a splendid precursor of the series which will furnish us with a detailed description of the architecture, furniture, and texts of the palace.

I

In view of the long lapse of time since the first decipherment of the script, and even since the resumption of the excavation of the Tell of Ras Shamra, it may be useful to compare the views put forward in the first enthusiasm engendered by the discoveries with those based on the ampler material provided by the latest campaigns, and with the most recent publications.

Since 1938, when Professor S. H. Hooke published his book *The Origins of Early Semitic Ritual,* the literature relating to Ugarit has very greatly increased. Profiting by the leisure imposed by the interruption of archaeological activity during the war, Professor Schaeffer published his *Stratigraphie comparée et chronologie de l'Asie occidentale (IIIe et IIe millénaires),* followed by his *Ugaritica II. Nouvelles études relatives aux découvertes de Ras Shamra* (Paris, 1949), two works of the utmost importance. As is clear from the dates of publication, these books do not deal with the post-war discoveries, which have been briefly and provisionally described in communications read before the Académie des Inscriptions et Belles-Lettres, in the valuable surveys of *Syria* and the *Illustrated London News,* and finally, in the 'Exposé préliminaire' of the recent volume VI of the *Mission de Ras Shamra* (Paris, 1955), *Le Palais royal d'Ugarit.* As the result of a reclassification and careful revision of the archaeological material, it is now possible to reach a greater precision in the stratigraphy of the site, especially of the first two layers, and to define accurately the Canaanite period of the city.

Publication of the texts which are the special object of our study was far from complete on the eve of the war, and throughout those difficult years M. Virolleaud continued, often under unrewarding and arduous conditions, his brilliant work of decipherment, publication, and interpretation. At the end of the war he was able to announce, not without pride: 'With the exception of III AB,B which will soon be published in this journal, the small fragments which we have collected here are now the only ones still unedited out of all the texts which were discovered at Ras Shamra by M. Schaeffer between the years 1929 and 1939' (*Syria*, 1947). A little later, in April 1948, Dr. Cyrus H. Gordon published in Rome his *Ugaritic Handbook*, comprising a revised grammar with paradigms, all the texts in transliteration, and an exhaustive glossary. At the time of publication all the discovered texts were accessible to scholars, for through the kindness of M. Virolleaud and of Père de Vaux, Dr. Gordon had obtained a copy of the two texts still unedited. For the benefit of the general reader he published in 1949 a comprehensive translation of the poetic and prose texts under the title *Ugaritic Literature*. It is useful to compare this translation with that of Dr. H. L. Ginsberg in Professor J. B. Pritchard's *Ancient Near Eastern Texts relating to the Old Testament*, published in 1950, or with Professor Th. H. Gaster's translation in his *Thespis: Myth, Ritual and Drama in the Ancient Near East* (1950). Another translation which might be mentioned is that by H. E. del Medico (also 1950), which has little to recommend it but its title *La Bible cananéenne*. In this game of comparisons there is a certain appropriateness in the Psalmist's word quoted on the first page of Dr. Gaster's book, 'Surely every man walketh in a vain show', a saying which might be adapted to the occasion by reading, 'The life of every book is no more than a breath.'

Some special points concerning the religion of Ugarit, its mythology and its rituals, have attracted the attention of specialists. In 1948 Dr. Julian Obermann devoted his book *Ugaritic Mythology. A Study of its leading Motifs*, not, as the title might suggest, to a summary of Canaanite mythology but mainly to a 'study of the texts relating to the goddess Anat and to the passages which refer to the construction of the palace of Baal'. Previously, by way of preamble to his exhaustive translation of all the texts, Dr. Cyrus Gordon in 1943 had translated and annotated *The Loves and Wars of Baal and Anat and other Poems from Ugarit*. The far-famed goddess Anat was discussed in 1953 by U. Cassuto under the title *The Goddess Anath. Canaanite Epics of the Patriarchal Age. Hebrew Translation, Commentary and Introduction.*

Other gods of the Ugaritic pantheon have also engaged the attention of scholars. To the industry of Professor Otto Eissfeldt we owe *Ras Shamra und Sanchunjaton* (1939), *Taautos und Sanchunjaton* (1952), and *Sanchunjaton von Berut und Ilumilku von Ugarit* (1952). The same scholar has also examined in greater detail the role of the god El in the mythology of Ugarit, and his important place in the different mythological texts, in *El im ugaritischen Pantheon* (1951), this interesting theme has also attracted the attention of Professor Marvin H. Pope, *El in the Ugaritic Texts* (1955). Another important divinity of Ugarit is Baal; Arvid S. Kapelrud has devoted to him a monograph published in 1952, *Baal in the Ras Shamra Texts*. Lastly, out of many monographs, mention may be made of M. H. Largement's careful study of the poem *La Naissance des dieux gracieux et beaux* (although I cannot agree that he has solved its problems); and of that edited by Dr. John Gray, following H. L. Ginsberg and others under the title *The Krt Text in the literature of Ras Shamra. A social Myth of Ancient Canaan* (1955). More general studies are *Introduction to Old Testament Times*, by Cyrus H. Gordon, and *The Oldest Stories in the World*, by Th. H. Gaster (both 1953).

In Ugaritic literature much still remains obscure. But here we have for our help the *Untersuchungen zur Grammatik des Ugaritischen* of Professor Joseph Aistleitner (1954), and the dissertation written by Izz-al-Din, *The Lexical Relation between Ugaritic and Arabic* (1952); also, dealing with less difficult problems, *Marriage and Family Life in Ugaritic Literature*

(1954) by A. van Selms, of the University of Pretoria in South Africa. From a special point of view, the valuable material in *Studies in Divine Kingship in the Ancient Near East* (1943) by Professor I. Engnell calls for notice.

If one wants to be up to date on Ras Shamra studies this whole list, from which the review articles have deliberately been omitted, is not sufficient. Hundreds of tablets have been discovered since the resumption of the excavations. In a single season—the most fruitful in the whole history of the Ras Shamra excavations—tablets were exhumed bearing five different types of script and texts in eight languages. The sensational character of these finds was enhanced by the discovery that the Cypro-Minoan and Hurrian tablets are most probably bilingual. It is therefore possible that these Ugaritic texts may furnish a new key to the decipherment of Hurrian and perhaps yield a brilliant confirmation of the results obtained by the late M. Ventris for the Minoan Linear Script B. It is even possible that the pseudo-hieroglyphic texts of Byblos, found by M. Dunand and published in his *Byblia Grammata*, of which M. Dhorme claims to have given a completely satisfactory reading, will receive from the tablets of Ras Shamra the additional light necessary for their decipherment. MM. Virolleaud and Nougayrol have spoken of these texts before the Académie des Inscriptions et Belles-Lettres of Paris, and in volume VI of *Mission de Ras Shamra*, already mentioned, M. Nougayrol has identified 176 tablets of judicial fragments, 40 economic documents, 23 letters, 6 school texts, one small fragment of incantation, 3 illegible or insignificant fragments, and 2 anepigraphic tablets, all in Akkadian and coming from the ruins of the royal palace. Moreover, publication is promised in the near future of the alphabetic texts recovered from the eastern, western, and central archives, to be followed by two other volumes containing the international texts of the southern archives and diverse documents relating to the interior affairs of Ugarit. These new contributions will help us to wait patiently for the appearance of the complete and revised corpus of alphabetical texts found before 1940.

II

Many, therefore, are the scholars to whose Ugaritic studies we are indebted. Even if their assertions, suggestions, and conjectures have not always been readily accepted, they deserve our gratitude for their conscientious and often inspiring work. Even if in recent years a certain lassitude has begun to appear, neither their talent nor their productive zeal should be blamed. The documents themselves by their fragmentary state, and the various enigmas which they continue to present to researchers, constitute in this particular field of oriental studies a discipline which evokes humility and resignation. In 1938 Professor Hooke declared: 'There are still so many unsolved problems both in the matter of text and interpretation';[1] and Engnell, five years later, acknowledged in his turn: 'The more work one expends on them the less one understands them.'[2]

One comes up against this difficulty as soon as one tries to make a systematic classification of the Ugaritic texts by grouping them according to the contents of the tablets. Such an arrangement presupposes, indeed, a satisfactory interpretation of all the texts. But often we are far from the goal. Dr. Gordon was doubtless wise to content himself in his *Ugaritic Handbook* with classifying the documents according to the order of their first publication. In order to understand the vocabulary of Ras Shamra, we are bound to look for comparisons and equivalents in all Semitic languages. But sometimes these adduced parallels can be fallacious and misleading; often the meaning of the roots varies and changes from one group of these languages to another; frequently a derivative meaning, the only one known, has replaced the primitive and original sense, the tradition of which has been lost. Moreover, it sometimes happens that the texts contain words which cannot be related to any known Semitic root. Finally, the morphology and the syntax still provide many enigmas. If anyone still needs convincing how little is known

[1] S. H. Hooke, *The Origins of Early Semitic Ritual* (the Schweich Lectures of the British Academy, 1935, London, 1938), p. x.

[2] I. Engnell, *Studies in Divine Kingship in the Ancient Near East* (Uppsala, 1943), p. 109.

about this Canaanite literature, he should glance at the translations of the passages regarded as least doubtful even in the most recent attempts: they are interspersed with blanks, punctuated with question marks, and completed conjecturally with terms and expressions in italics. Although distinguished specialists have laboured over these texts, too many passages have remained unintelligible. One could say with Père de Vaux[1] that we often agree upon the import of a term or expression, sometimes on that of a short passage, but rarely on the general sense of a poem or of a song. Generally we hold different views about the sequence of ideas, the course of the action, the number of actors, their secular or divine status, their degree of relationship, and even their names.

I think it will not be superfluous to remind readers of the mutilated state of most of the tablets and our incomplete, defective, and consequently disputed and disputable, exegesis. This double fact, which we can deplore but not ignore, confronts every scholar and makes his deductions and reconstructions inevitably provisional and hypothetical.

Let us turn to the religious texts (using the word in the widest sense), where there is a possibility of recovering the memory of the Canaanite myths and rites of Ugarit. A long tradition of the French school has accustomed us to the expression 'Mythological and legendary texts' in the sense which an informed reader cannot fail to understand. When employing this formula, the authors who use it do not mean to pass judgement on the ultimate meaning or on the current use which was made of these documents in the liturgical ceremonies of the Ugaritic temples. Nevertheless, the application of it to these texts has been disputed. Several authors, and certainly not the least important, prefer new descriptions: rituals, ritual chants, liturgies, cult-dramas, cult-myths, cult-rituals.[2] These designations raise an extremely important problem, before which each study relating to the cult and religious

---

[1] R. de Vaux, 'Les Textes de Ras Shamra et l'Ancien Testament', in *R.B.* xlvi (1917), pp. 530–7.

[2] I. Engnell, op. cit., pp. 97–109. He discusses briefly the designations suggested by S. H. Hooke, Ch. Virolleaud, R. Dussaud, W. C. Graham, H. G. May, T. H. Gaster, O. Eissfeldt, D. Nilsen, J. Pedersen, F. Hvidberg, and A. Kapelrud.

milieu of Ugarit must needs pause. Here we are dealing, not simply with a dispute about terminology but with the fundamental problem of the nature of the texts, their *Sitz im Leben*, involving necessarily their *Sitz im Kult*: What ends did these chants serve? At what occasions were they recited, prayed, chanted, declaimed, perhaps even acted? Many such questions present themselves even to one who prefers to speak of 'myths' or 'legends'.

In view of our imperfect knowledge of the contents of the texts, there is a temptation to consider the problems raised as insoluble. But against such an attitude is the fact that other scholars who possessed only the same data claim to have reached solutions. Nevertheless, in order to reach their solutions, such scholars have appealed to parallels attested elsewhere. This is perhaps justified, yet it is necessary to test the soundness of this appeal to foreign cult-traditions by a strict analysis of the texts cited in support of their interpretations.

In 1938 Eissfeldt attacked the problem. In *Theologische Blätter* he published an article 'Religionsdokument und Religionspoesie, Religionstheorie und Religionshistorie', a study which was followed up in his book *Ras Shamra und Sanchunjaton*. If his conclusions be accepted, a provisional classification of the religious texts is possible. The author distinguishes 'Religionsdokumente', that is to say, in his own words, 'immediate deposits of living faith', from 'Religionspoesie' or 'Kultpoesie' which is defined as 'poems on religious or cultic themes, in which aesthetic interest outweighs the directly religious, or at least accompanies it'. The proposed distinction seems to me justifiable, save that the fundamental problem is hardly touched upon and the assigning of a particular text to the first or the second category is disputable. It is clear, for example, that the tablets which in the edition of Hans Bauer are classified under the following titles: 'Designations of Offerings, Lists of Materials for Temple Needs, List of Sanctuaries, Divine Names, List of Officials of one of the Temples of Ugarit, A Kind of Sacrificial Tariff, Enumeration of Four Classes of Priests' (if we accept the interpretation which he gives to them), can certainly be included among the *Religionsdokumente*;

their interest, moreover, rests mainly in the enumeration of the divine names, temples, animals suitable for sacrifice, names of classes and of persons. On the other hand, there will not be general agreement on the assignment to the same category of the texts which were entitled 'Hymns and Prayers'. Consider, for example, the text which M. Virolleaud has called 'Hymn to the god Nikkal and to the goddesses Kosharot',[1] which is some-times known as 'The marriage of Ḥiriḫibi, king of the summer'.[2] In such pieces one may stress either the character of 'immediate deposits of living piety', or the literary and artistic aspect of the composition, or the part played by the mythological elements or, finally, the mention of acts and gestures which may suggest the cultic activity of the reciter or the officiating priest. According to whether we emphasize one or the other aspect, and make more or less successful comparisons, more or less felicitously, with similar rites attested more fully in other cults, our interpretation of the texts will vary considerably. It is here that we join issue with the adherents of the *kulthistorische Schule* and the defenders of the 'mythical-ritual pattern in civilization'.

A discussion on purely theoretical lines is not of much value, and, moreover, it easily tends to go beyond our objective, which should be the analysis of the texts, as they are handed down to us, and the synthesis of data established with certainty, or at least with probability. The undoubted merits of this school must, however, be acknowledged. There was a time—not so long ago—when it was thought necessary to explain everything by aetiological myths. Today we frankly recognize that the method of explanation by the cult-ritual constitutes a definite progress. It may be admitted that the relationship postulated between the cult and the temples on the one hand, and the poems which the excavations have revealed to us on the other, is now, at least in principle, firmly established. At Ugarit, in the exhumed temples of Baal and of Dagon and the small sanctuary of the royal

---

[1] Ch. Virolleaud, 'Hymne phénicien au dieu Nikal et aux déesses Kôšarôt provenant de Ras Shamra', in *Syria*, xvii (1936), pp. 209–28.

[2] A. Herdner, 'Ḥiriḫibi et les noces de Yariḫ et de Nikkal', in *Semitica*, ii (1949), pp. 17–20; cf. C. H. Gordon, *Ugaritic Manual* (Rome, 1955), ii. 194 and 153.

quarter, texts have been recovered which were there recited or sung or, some would add, performed and mimed.

It is when we pass from theory to the evidence of actual practice in the local cult of Ugarit that the difficulty begins. Specific roles are assigned to presumed actors who would be the god and the goddess, or the high-priest and his wife; the acts performed by each are defined, the rites to be carried out by the personages present are described, the roles assigned to the divinities as expressed by the actions of their human representatives are interpreted. If all this is not to degenerate into mere imaginative reconstruction it must be required of the authors that they adhere strictly to the known data of the texts. It is very doubtful whether much is to be gained by a rash imaginative use of parallels from other sources. Results obtained by a careful analysis and sound philological interpretation of the texts are more likely to be of permanent value.

There are various reasons for an attitude of sympathetic reserve towards the results of the ritual and cultic interpretation of the texts. In the first place the dogmatic and speculative character of some of these reconstructions raises doubts concerning their soundness. Secondly, while the study of the myths and ritual practices of so-called primitive peoples has in some cases revealed a close relationship between the myths and the rituals, it is equally true that it has also shown the existence of myths which are unaccompanied by any ritual performance. Between these two extremes many intermediate types can be attested. In view of the existence of this demonstrated diversity it is difficult to accept the theory of the existence of a uniformity of ritual pattern in the west-Semitic world. Moreover, according to Baumgärtner, in the interpretation of these great poetic texts from Ugarit the aesthetic element must be taken into account: 'Poetic forms of religious ideas and experiences in artistic phantasy and colour, that is, aesthetic interests, stand side by side with religious interests in these works.'[1]

In the library of the temple of Ugarit we have, then, according to Baumgärtner, 'cult-legends which, composed in literary style,

---

[1] W. Baumgärtner, 'Ugaritische Probleme und ihre Tragweite für das Alte Testament', in *T.Z.* iii (1947), pp. 89–91.

offer a continuous description and narrative, and which can be understood and enjoyed for their own sake'. Babylonian literature offers many texts of a similar character. Finally, no one claims to have recovered in such texts a complete reproduction of the rituals of the Tammuz, Osiris, or Adonis cults, nor of the Babylonian New Year festival; we are even told that the beliefs and religious practices of the Canaanites revealed in the Ras Shamra texts were only an offshoot, an imperfect imitation of the Babylonian models. Some scholars, basing themselves now on an epithet, now on the mention of an action, claim to have found among foreign models the information which is lacking in the tablet which they are interpreting; and with these sporadic and detached elements they claim to have re-created the mosaic, of which the design and colour had been lost. The method sometimes has its good points; occasionally it has led to ingenious and unhoped for results; but a striking parallel is not necessarily proof of an identical concept. It may be relevant here to quote S. Mowinckel: 'It is urgently necessary to see each separate religion as a unique structural whole; all the separate elements which it contains derive their contents and meaning from the whole, whose parts they form, and not from that which they signify in another whole.'[1] With or without reference to presumed parallels, it is from the texts themselves that we have to discover the key to their mysteries.

III

It would be difficult to find a more attractive and more alarming book than *Thespis: Ritual, Myth and Drama in the Ancient Near East*, by Theodor H. Gaster.[2] We find there a thesis presented with clarity and acuteness, a choice of texts admirably selected and translated, commentaries which show great skill, and scholarly notes, where all the legends, all the rites, all the folk-lores of the world are summoned to present their evidence.

[1] S. Mowinckel, *Religion und Kultus* (Göttingen, 1953), p. 137; cf. J. de Fraine, *L'Aspect religieux de la royauté israélite* (Rome, 1954).
[2] New York, 1950.

The learned author first outlines his thesis. Everywhere in antiquity we find the drama side by side with the ritual and the myth. What, then, is the relationship between the three, and what is the underlying idea which explains them? The drama through the medium of the myth takes its origin from the seasonal rituals.

In all nature religions there exist festivals of participation in the unfolding and alternating of the rhythms of the world. The alternation of the seasons with the equinoxes and solstices, with the development of plants and animals, with the evolution of human life itself, are not simple external happenings in which man is only a passive participant. On the contrary, he enters into them actively by means of the functional rite; he seeks to capture the spirit of life, to renew his own vitality and that of the cosmos. This, says Gaster, is the essential meaning of the seasonal rituals. They bring man, both as an individual and as a community, into relationship with the renewal of nature. The purely ritual act is projected directly on to the plane of the ideal; and this is how myths are born. The myth translates the real in terms of the ideal, the temporal and the concrete in terms of duration and transcendence. Finally, the ritual, by the transposition brought about through the myth, is itself transformed into drama. We can go even farther: the ritual 'form' survives not only in the complete drama but also in the structure of hymns and certain literary compositions.

At the base of everything, then, we find a seasonal ritual. This requires essentially two phases: first, a release from the past realized through rites of mortification and purgation; then the acquisition of a new vitality, realized through the rites of invigoration and jubilation. All these rites were first celebrated by the community as a whole, then by its best qualified representatives, especially by the king, who frequently allowed himself to be replaced by a provisional or substitute king for the ceremonies of mortification and purgation. In order to explain, justify, and render efficacious this seasonal ritual, an appeal is made to the myth. This implies that the community or its head reproduce by their acts the primordial act performed by the gods and re-enacted in the seasonal rhythm of nature.

This synthesis has its merits.[1] Nevertheless, it also has its dangers, for nowhere do the ancient writers describe this mechanism of transposition. It was therefore necessary to reconstruct a pattern which had been lost, to remake a mosaic, the design of which had been broken up. Gaster's concept is certainly impressive, but its exaggeration is obvious. We listen with scepticism when he declares:

All the tales wherever they come from draw their interest quite as much from that which is implicit as from that which is said explicitly, and for this reason we have attempted here, by comparing them with other documents, to recover the ideas and associations of thought which these tales had to bring about originally among those who heard them and which had to give to simple words all their value, as a rich gown confers its quality on the mannequin who wears it. Further, since one of these stories has reached us in an incomplete state we have endeavoured to supply what was missing, sometimes by establishing parallels with the stories of other countries, and sometimes by our own intuition. We do not claim, of course, that such additions are necessarily exact.[2]

The justice of this last remark may best be illustrated by an examination of three important texts.

1. *The birth of the gracious and beautiful gods.* For this text, which is among the most difficult of a literature which, as we

---

[1] For reactions to Gaster's book, cf. S. Thompson in *American Journal of Archaeology*, lv (1951), p. 472; R. Follot in *Biblica*, xxxiii (1952), pp. 139–42; W. Baumgärtner in *Gnomon*, xxiv (1952), pp. 63–65; H. J. Rose in *J.H.S.* lxxii (1952), p. 145; C. J. Bleeker in *Nederlands Theologisch Tijdschrift*, vi (1951), pp. 165–6; H. Frankfort in *Review of Religions*, xvi (1951), pp. 163–6; R. T. O'Callaghan in *Orientalia*, xxii (1953), pp. 418–25; A. Goetze in *J.C.S.* vi (1952), 99–103; S. Stein in *P.E.Q.*, lxxxv (1953), pp. 138–43; R. Pettazzoni in *Studi e Materiali di Storia di Religione*, xxiii (1951), pp. 169–70; see also J. de Fraine, 'Les Implications du "patternism" ', in *Biblica*, xxxvii (1956), pp. 59–73.

[2] T. H. Gaster, *Les Plus Anciens Contes de l'humanité. Mythes et légendes d'il y a 3500 ans (babyloniens, hittites, cananéens), récemment déchiffrés et avec des commentaires* (Paris, 1953), pp. 9–10. Cf. by the same author, *The Oldest Stories in the World* (1952), pp. ix–x: 'What is here offered, however, is neither a bald and mechanical translation, nor a loose paraphrase. All stories anywhere depend just as much on what is implied as on what is said, and an attempt has therefore been made to recapture, with the aid of comparative material, that host of ideas and associations which the tales evoked in their original hearers and which served to clothe the bare skeleton of words. Moreover, where a story has come down to us incomplete, an effort has been made to restore what is lost, sometimes on the basis of hints and clues, sometimes from parallels in other lands, and sometimes by sheer intuition.'

have already said, could not be considered simple, we have purposely chosen the title which M. Virolleaud gave to it when publishing it for the first time.[1] In spite of its literary resemblance to the hymns to Anat and to Nikkal, the poem does not belong to the same cycle; it is, on the contrary, a single example of an aspect, or perhaps of a stage of evolution, in the Ugaritic religion. This is the only text hitherto known, which is devoted to El and to Asherat. Moreover, all the gods who are depicted in it are different from the gods of other cycles. Baal, notably, does not appear; nor does his sister Anat, at least not under her usual name, though she may be concealed under the name of Raḥmiya. A problem is thus presented regarding the pantheon, to which two hypothetical solutions have been offered. Either we have in this poem a group of divinities, that of the god El and his court, representing a different type, an older stage than those who appear in the other texts; or it may be suggested that 'El' might represent Baal, a solution which no doubt would not find many supporters.

Three interpretations of the myth have been offered. The first is less an interpretation than an attitude of reserve towards a text whose translation is uncertain and which may not even be a unity. The poem, indeed, comprises two distinct parts, of which the first, divided by various rubrics, appears to be a ritual, while the second, more continuous, suggests the myth or the epic. However, many authors do not adopt this negative attitude. According to whether they emphasize the first or the second part of the poem, they arrive at two different solutions. One group sees in it a ritual illustrated and extended by a mythological fragment— that is the ritualistic interpretation; the other group explains it as a sort of mythological epic, translated through a ritual—that is the mythical interpretation. According to the former group we have a fertility ritual supported by the recitation of the original myth, and according to the latter we have a theogony recited and acted in a liturgy.

[1] Ch. Virolleaud, 'La Naissance des dieux gracieux et beaux', in *Syria*, xiv (1933), pp. 128–57. For recent bibliography, cf. R. Largement, *La Naissance de l'aurore. Poème mythologique de Ras Shamra-Ugarit traduit et commenté* (Louvain, 1949); G. R. Driver, *Canaanite Myths and Legends* (Edinburgh, 1956), pp. xi–xiv; C. H. Gordon, *Ugaritic Manual* (*Analecta Orientalia* 35), Rome, 1955.

Here, then, are many possibilities for a single text. Some have gone even farther. M. R. Largement believes[1] that he can show that the ritual and mythology contained in this poem are intended to attract towards the city all the material resources of the surrounding country, the riches yielded by the sea coast, the cultivated fields, and the steppes where game abounds. According to another expositor, M. R. Follot,[2] El, the great primordial god, lives alone presiding over the resources of nature, lord of the secrets of hunting, fire, and cooking; round his hearth he creates the family by mating with womankind; he creates a divine succession by giving birth to the gods of sky and sea. These gods live at first by gathering the natural products of the sky and the ocean, namely, birds and fishes. They enter into the desert for seven years, whence they penetrate the region of agricultural civilization to the farthest limits of field and steppe. Thus they become identified with all the activities and needs of an agricultural and pastoral culture. According to this interpretation the poem is a ritual using all its liturgical resources to secure fertility and fecundity; it is based on a theogony which explains the birth, growth, and functions of the divinities of nature, but its character is fundamentally urban. So we have a picture of the Canaanite city living under protection of the primordial father-god, illuminated by the divine twins, Dawn and Twilight, together with the sun and the stars; fructified by the divinities of nature, and receiving from their bountiful hand bread and wine, the symbols of civilization and objects both of the ritual and of its mythology.

After assuring us that he has here offered only suggestions, and not certainties,[3] instead of contenting himself with the data provided by the poem mentioned above, the author turns aside

---

[1] R. Largement, *La Naissance de l'aurore* (Louvain, 1949), pp. 49–55.

[2] R. Follot, review of R. Largement's book in *Biblica*, xxxii (1951), pp. 317–19.

[3] R. Follot, op. cit., p. 319: 'Tout ceci ne représente que des suggestions, non point des preuves ni des certitudes. Toutefois, si l'on consente à monter le long escalier des suppositions, aux marches souvent fragiles, on débouche sur une plate-forme, provisoire sans doute, mais qui s'ouvre sur des perspectives magnifiques, d'autant plus magnifiques peut-être qu'elles restent entrevues dans le clair-obscur de la vérité seulement pressentie.'

to discuss the poem of Gilgamesh, the wild man, enticed from the steppe to the city, and civilized by bread and wine. Hence we have here an example of the unsound method of adducing a parallel from an extraneous source. While it may be admitted as a possibility that fertility and fecundity rituals and myths exist in the text, there can be no doubt that they exist in the minds of the commentators.

2. *The cycle of Baal and Anat.*[1] Many tablets of Ugaritic religious literature are concerned with the figure of Baal, who had a temple dedicated to him in the city. The god bears many names: B'L, 'AL'EYN B'L, BN DGN, B'L ṢPN, and others, which testify to his ever-growing popularity and the devotion which the people of Ugarit paid to him. If we may rely on the evidence of the text, Baal is the son of the god Dagon, the corn-god and storm-god. At the period when the songs were composed, the young god had to a great extent supplanted his father, who himself also possessed a temple in the town. His consort, some-times known as 'AHT the 'sister', is the celebrated goddess Anat, the goddess of war and of love,[2] distinguished by the epithets BTLT, the 'virgin' and RḤMY, the 'compassionate one'. Some texts present her as the daughter, others as the lover and the wife, of the god El, whom we have met in the preceding poem. It is not impossible that the couple Baal–Anat may represent in the local cult of Ugarit the syncretism of two originally distinct pantheons, the one having as its head the old Semitic divinity El, being in a fair way to become a *deus*

---

[1] R. Dussaud, 'Le Mythe de Ba'al et d'Aliyan d'après des documents nouveaux', in *Revue de l'Histoire des Religions*, cxi (1935), pp. 1–65; Ch. Virolleaud, *La Déesse 'Anat. Poème de Ras Shamra* (Paris, 1938); A. S. Kapelrud, *Baal in the Ras Shamra Texts* (Copenhagen, 1952); U. Cassuto, *The Goddess Anath. Canaanite Epics of the Patriarchal Age. Hebrew Translation, Commentary and Introduction* (Jerusalem, 1953). For texts, translations, and studies, see R. de Langhe, *Les Textes de Ras Shamra-Ugarit et leurs rapports avec le milieu biblique de l'Ancien Testament* (Paris-Gembloux, 1945); C. H. Gordon, *Ugaritic Manual (Analecta Orientalia* 35) (Rome, 1955); G. R. Driver, *Canaanite Myths and Legends* (Edinburgh, 1956).

[2] C. H. Gordon, *The Loves and Wars of Baal and Anat and other Poems from Ugarit* (Princeton, 1943). Cf. the same author's *Ugaritic Literature. A Comprehensive Translation of the Poetic and Prose Texts* (Rome, 1949); H. L. Ginsberg, 'Poems about Baal and Anath', in J. A. Pritchard, *Ancient Near Eastern Texts Relating to the Old Testament* (Princeton, 1950), pp. 129–42; Th. H. Gaster, op. cit.

otiosus,[1] the other making use of the name Dagon, who had already appropriated the prerogatives of Hadad. It is not difficult to discern traces of enmity between the two divine groups;[2] among the antagonists of Baal figure the god YM, commonly designated by the formula MDD'EL, and MÔT, who is frequently presented to us as MT YDD'EL, which would suggest that the god El found favourites in the group of Baal's enemies. Even the legitimate consort of El, the goddess '*Aṯtrt*, sometimes dissociates herself from her divine husband in order to procure the favours of the young conqueror god. By contrast we learn few details about the origin of Baal; among his daughters only PDRY plays any conspicuous part, while HYN and KTR WHSS are his associates, always ready to help him, especially in the building of his palace or the temple,[3] the outward signs of his supremacy.

In order to establish his domination the god Baal is continually compelled to fight battles which constitute so many episodes of the cycle which is dedicated to him:

(i) YM, the king and lord of the waters, represented by seas, rivers, and springs, is his primordial adversary, whom he succeeds in subduing;

(ii) the rhythm of the seasons is the occasion for new combats with another figure, the god MÔT, who should not be represented as the god of sterility, since he is undoubtedly only the *Gegenspieler* of the god Baal, or may perhaps be only another of his aspects, intended to complete the figure of the favourite god;

(iii) the combat against the serpent Lotan, where the supremacy of the gods is in the balance, and where there are perhaps reminiscences of a myth of creation;

(iv) finally, thanks to the help which Anat brings him and with the concurrence of his loyal associates, Baal succeeds in showing to the assembly of the gods and

---

[1] O. Eissfeldt, *El im ugaritischen Pantheon* (Berlin, 1951); Marvin H. Pope, *El in the Ugaritic Texts* (Leiden, 1955).

[2] B. Nielsen, *Ras Shamra Mythologie und Biblische Theologie* (Leipzig, 1936).

[3] Cf. J. Obermann, *Ugaritic Mythology* (New Haven, 1948).

men that his supremacy is complete through the construction of a temple-palace where he will install himself while awaiting new combats.

There are in the cycle of Baal other episodes in which we cannot always see the bond which unites them with the rest of the cycle. In spite of that, the character of Baal emerges clearly: 'Baal is a young warrior god, and at the same time a god invested with sovereign power, and further the ever-changing god of Nature, which is under his control in meteorology, vegetation, and agriculture.' His adversaries can threaten him for a moment and attack his supremacy, but the god always recovers himself in the end, and re-establishes his momentarily endangered supremacy. The attempt to set up a transitory usurper in the person of ʿAṮṮAR quickly proves unsuccessful. Neither ʿAṮṮAR nor MÔT can finally menace the incontestable rule of the god Baal.

The commentators on the Ras Shamra texts are for the most part agreed on this general presentation. But here, as in the other texts, the problem arises of the cyclic recurrence of the rituals: is it a mythological poem with varied episodes, or a cult ritual which was performed or mimed at the New Year festival, at the time when the first rains heralded the longed-for return of fertility to fields, animals, and men? No doubt, if we adopt the ritual interpretation, the great role of Baal is taken by the king, the *rex sacrorum*.

We cannot deny the possibility of cultic rituals at the time of religious festivals in the temple of Baal. Nevertheless, the cycle of Aliyan Baal is essentially a series of poems with varied episodes from which liturgical or rubrical indications are totally absent. If the end of the summer and the announcement of the rainy and fertile season were celebrated in Ugarit by religious ceremonies of thanksgiving, it may be surmised that the tablets of the cycle of Baal, brought out from their archives, were read or recited by the high-priest or the king. In the representation of the fight between Aliyan Baal and his adversary MÔT, the worshippers could recognize the fundamental ideas—the succession

of the seasons, the end of the suffocating dry heat, the announcement of the beneficial rains, the promise of a good harvest,
Corresponding to other episodes of the cycle—the construction
of the palace, Anat and the heifer, the fight against the master of
the sea and lord of the river, Lotan the tortuous serpent,—there
were undoubtedly other hopes and preoccupations of the devout
population, hopes which a patient exegesis may perhaps one day
reveal to us. But in all this it is not necessary to go beyond the
theory of the myth as an expression, not of deeds and actions,
but of ideas, hopes, and aspirations. But when we assume the
existence of mimes or dramas, we go beyond the evidence of
the texts.

Hence I cannot agree with Kapelrud, who by reversing the
roles, expects scholars who are opposed to his views to prove the
non-cultic character of our texts: 'The AB texts were cult
texts. This is actually so likely that the burden of proof ought to
rest on the scholars who maintain that these texts are not cult
texts.'[1] Taken out of its context, to which it forms a sort of
conclusion, this assertion cannot but cause surprise. Yet, in
order not to misrepresent the attitude attributed to Kapelrud,
I think it right to follow his exposition and to discuss the meaning of the terms used.

'It is evident', he writes, 'that seen from a purely literary point
of view the greater part of the so-called AB cycle may be called
epics. They are composed in a poetical form and features characteristic of epics.'[2] And further: 'Seen according to their context
the texts may very well be called myths. That designation implies
that we have a story concerning super-human beings. . . .'[3] We
could even concede that 'Our texts are not "L'art pour l'art",
they were not told just for the enjoyment of the audience'. But
is it necessary to go farther and regard our texts, following
Hvidberg, Pederson, Mowinckel, Engnell, and Gaster, as *cult-
dramas*? Goetze's remark, that there is 'Nothing in the literary
form of the poems that would justify such an assumption' merits

[1] A. S. Kapelrud, *Baal in the Ras Shamra Texts* (Copenhagen, 1952), p. 27.
[2] A. S. Kapelrud, op. cit., p. 14.
[3] A. S. Kapelrud, op. cit., pp. 14–15.

attention and links up with the views expressed above. The ritual explanation is not helped by Engnell's admission: 'We can naturally not expect "Scenarios", with indications of who has to utter a certain cue or to perform a certain action, etc. Such things are in a living tradition of a cultic "place in life" so obvious that they need not be specially noted.' Yet many would like to have further information about the existence and the import of this 'living tradition'.

Apparently Kapelrud has deferred to this legitimate wish. In order to fix the *Sitz im Leben* of the texts AB, he first recapitulates 'Some facts concerning the place where they were found and the surroundings of this place'—we know that the texts come from the library or the school of the scribes of Ugarit, which formed an annex to the great temple of Baal and Dagon, adjoining each other in a quarter which was clearly distinct from the royal quarter. If it is perhaps true that 'it is no accident that one temple is dedicated to the god who plays the main role in the AB texts', it is not enough to remark that 'the temple needed its cult texts, and cult texts need a temple', in order to establish the cultic character of the cycle of Baal. If we accept the premise: 'I shall only mention that the temple of Baal and the building of this temple is a central theme of the AB cycle', it still does not necessarily follow that 'nobody can doubt that these texts were recited or used for dramatic performance in the temple they mention so frequently'. For the existence of these 'dramatic performances' needs to be proved, otherwise than by the presence of the cycle in question. It is no doubt true that no one would think of calling in question the existence of the temple of Baal, the custom of offering him sacrifices, the outstanding place of the god Baal in the pantheon of Ugarit, and his decisive role in maintaining and renewing the fertility and well-being of persons and things. One might even admit *a priori* the possibility of 'dramatic performances' at regular intervals. But the question still remains: what role did the cycle of texts AB play in it? The only answer yielded by the examination and analysis of the texts under discussion is: a myth with epic aspects. All the rest dissolves into hypothesis.

3. *Divine Kingship in the Ras Shamra texts.*[1] Every informed reader, we are told, will find in the Ras Shamra texts all the documentation needed for the description and illustration of the sacral role of the 'divine' king. According to Engnell, the chief exponent of this view, the matter is beyond doubt. He does not hesitate to employ as a title 'The evidence of the Ras Shamra texts'—evidence which he endeavours to impart to his readers in the course of more than seventy pages.

To begin with, it is surprising that the author, wishing to describe the sacral position of the king, considered it necessary to study and comment on the majority of the Ugaritic texts. Not all the tablets have the same importance for this theme. A more systematic, and hence more comprehensive, exposition would, no doubt, permit of a better arrangement of the texts according to their direct bearing on the problem, and an assessment of the scope of the assumptions which underly the construction. But as we have it the work presents a sequence of commentaries on the religious texts of Ugarit, in the midst of which the central theme is unfortunately swamped.

Engnell's conclusions are clear and definite:

. . . we have thus also in Ras Shamra found most of the elements in the kingship ideology displayed in the antecedent: the king divine of origin and enthronement, his identity with the high god, and in particular, with the fructification deity, having power over rains and crops; his being the object of cult, his functioning in the cult, in divination and purification rites, and especially in the annual festival as suffering, 'dying' and reviving, and as performer of the hierogamy. We have seen him in sham fights, and in the ideology as dragon-killer and rescuer-god, as ideal law performer, have met with his collective responsibility, with his insignia of power, and his substitutes the bull and the lamb (p. 173).

All this is to be found in the writings of Engnell and other authors. Nevertheless, I maintain that after twenty years of Ugaritic studies I do not find these ideas and representations in

[1] Cf. I. Engnell, *Studies in Divine Kingship in the Ancient Near East* (Uppsala, 1943); J. de Fraine, *L'Aspect religieux de la royauté israélite. L'institution monarchique dans l'Ancien Testament et dans les textes mésopotamiens* (*Analecta Biblica* 3) (Rome, 1954); and 'Les Implications du "patternism" ', in *Biblica*, xxxvii (1956), pp. 59–73.

the Ugaritic texts. And Engnell himself, in a recent review, admits of reservations in regard to some of the theories which he used to enunciate with equal assurance: 'The present reviewer is also quite willing to admit that his own survey of the material in his *Studies* may contain certain exaggerations and generalisations. But this does not in any way hit the essential, which is the living on of the ideology in the tradition.'[1] It is true that this applies only to the Mesopotamian material; yet it is to be hoped that this may be the beginning of a *revocavi* extending also to the Ras Shamra texts.

As it is impossible to discuss, with textual support, all the statements relating to the sacral character of the kingship, we shall confine our attention to the Keret text. In 1936 M. Virolleaud published a first tablet of this cycle which combines three; he chose the title: *La Légende de Kéret, roi des Sidoniens*, which, as Baumgärtner had no difficulty in showing, was based on a false restoration of a mutilated passage. *Syria* of 1941 and of 1942–3 contained the following: 'Le roi Kéret et son fils (II K)' and 'Le mariage du roi Kéret (III K)'; it was evident that III K should precede II K. Let us note first that nothing in the text suggests that Keret was a king of Ugarit, the founder of a royal dynasty, except perhaps the fact that the tablets were discovered at Ras Shamra. Moreover, the date of the composition of the tablets does not prevent us from relating to a remote past the unfolding of the scenes described, which it may be convenient here to specify.

Whatever might be said about the contents of the tablets III and II K, which were greeted with enthusiasm as constituting a brilliant confirmation of the royal ideology deduced from I K, there remains the incontestable fact that only the first tablet has withstood from all angles the assault of the most informed criticism, and that it is to this that we have to look primarily for information as regards the role and the nature of Keret's kingship. Now, the result of this examination seems to me today, as it did ten years ago, to refute utterly the attempts at a cultic explanation. It remains for me to prove this.

According to Engnell, tablet I K contains a double description of a series of rites and scenes having a unique bearing on the cult.

[1] *Svensk Exegetisk Årsbok*, xviii/xix. 208.

We witness successively a *bit-rimki* rite, an ablution rite, a sacrifice, and, in the guise of immediate preparation for the *sukkot* festival, a rite of the preparation of bread. Then follows the celebration of the festival properly so called. We find the king at the head of his men setting out—for the festivities are celebrated in the open air in the desert. But before celebrating the marriage Keret must engage in a mock combat with the substitute king, a part played by the high-priest, whose wife plays the role of the goddess-queen. At the conclusion of this drama, the king brings out the wedding presents, and in the midst of general rejoicing he celebrates the sacred marriage, the culmination of the cultic festival.

Here, by contrast, is the interpretation which I still defend. The king, Keret, informed in a dream of coming events, prepares himself by an ablution and a sacrifice for the success of the enterprise upon which he is about to embark (II. 62b–79a = 157–71a). Then he takes precautions for the troops of the expedition and for those who remain in the city of his residence (II. 79b–94a = 171b–9). At the moment of departure, the population as a whole comes to acclaim its king and to wish him success (II. 92–103a = 180–91). After seven days of marching, Keret arrives in the neighbourhood of Udm, the residence of King Pebel-Melek (II. 106–9 = 207–11). The journey to Udm is interrupted after the third day's march by the dispatch to the sanctuaries of Tyre and Sidon of a delegation commissioned to convey to the goddesses of these cities Keret's promise of an offering (II. 197–206). Having reached the end of his journey, the double city of Udm—actually the double site of Khirbet ed-Dâmiyeh near the lake of Tiberias in Galilee—Keret surrounds the capital of Pebel-Melek both on the north and on the south with his troops, and by a clever strategy he occupies a city, fields, and a spring (II. 110–114a = 212–217). We should note that all the localities described in the text, with one exception, can be located on a modern map of Galilee and that the proposed identifications do not cause any difficulty from either the archaeological or the philological point of view.[1] After seven days of

[1] R. de Vaux, 'Le Cadre géographique du poème de Keret', in *R.B.* xlvi (1937)

siege, Pebel-Melek begins negotiations (II. 114b–125a = 218–30). Again, the second part of the tablet, which contains an account of the fulfilment of the events dreamed, presents a text which has no parallel in the account of the vision, but there is unfortunately a lacuna between ll. 230–67. When the text is resumed, at line 268, the account corresponds to line 125b. The envoys of Pebel-Melek come to Keret, and present to him in the name of their king gold, silver, horses, and choice gifts (II. 125b–136a = 268–80). Nevertheless, Keret reveals the real purpose of his campaign: he wishes to marry Mṭṭ-hry, the daughter of Pebel-Melek, who will give him the desired inheritance (II. 136b–53 = 281–300a). The text of the vision stops here, but the account of the fulfilment continues the narrative by indicating that the envoys of the king of Udm depart to consult Pebel-Melek (II. 300b–306). This is the end of tablet I K. The continuation of the negotiations might no doubt be found on a tablet which has not yet been discovered. There can be no doubt concerning the happy outcome of the expedition, since tablet III K tells us of the festivities accompanying the celebrations of the marriage of Keret with Mṭṭ-hry.

Reading the two versions of the contents of tablet I K, anyone who is not familiar with the Ras Shamra-Ugarit texts, will have some difficulty in seeing there résumés of one and the same text. Our conviction that we have in the text of Keret a very human account of a king in search of a fiancée and wife rests on the philology and exegesis of the text. Engnell, for his part, probably thinks the same about his interpretation. The results obtained on each side are diametrically opposed. Which of the two is right? No doubt an impatient reader would like to be given a brief and irrefutable proof of the soundness of the proposed solution. Alas! it must be admitted that we cannot offer a conclusive proof which will be generally acceptable. Possibly an infallible proof does exist. Anyone who will take the texts and study them for himself, and consult the dictionaries and the numerous studies which have already appeared on this question,

pp. 362–72; R. de Langhe, *Les Textes de Ras Shamra-Ugarit et leurs rapports avec le milieu biblique de l'Ancien Testament* (Paris-Gembloux), ii. 97–147.

L

will, I am sure, reach the conclusion which I have presented elsewhere and briefly repeated here.[1]

In order to guide him in his studies and to stimulate his interest, let me point out finally that the passages of I K which are easily translated by accepting the historico-legendary interpretation—*claritas sigillum veri*—are declared to be *very obscure* by the exponents of the cultic theory, and that the translations proposed therein are described as *purely tentative*. The following example speaks for itself. Although opposed to any geographical localization of the events described, the exponents of the cultic interpretation admit the existence of occasional geographical allusions which clearly cannot be explained as merely forming part of a list of stopping-places along the route of the exodus to the desert. Consider first a passage according to the cultic interpretation:

> And they rest in the 'city' (-ies)? of *šrn,*
> the 'town(s)'? of *s·t.*
> In the field is hewing of wood,
> on the threshing-floors gathering in of *s't* (grain?),
> in the well drawing of water,
> at the spring filling up.

This passage, in which Engnell sees 'rites pertaining to the sukkot-festival', describes the stationing of the troops of Keret all around the residence of Pebel-Melek, the double site of Udm = Khirbet ed-Dâmiyeh:[2]

---

[1] R. de Langhe, 'Het Ugaritisch Keretgedicht. Legende, Mythus og Mysteriespel?' in *Miscellanea historica Alberti De Meyer* (Louvain, 1946), pp. 92–108; and 'L'Enclitique cananéenne -*m(a)*', in *Le Muséon*, lix (1946), pp. 89–111; and review of Engnell, in *Bibliotheca Orientalis*, x (1953), pp. 18–22.

[2] For the purpose of comparison I give also the texts as read by Driver and Gray:

G. R. Driver	J. Gray
'He did attack the cities	'They abode at the city,
(and) destroy the towns,	They watched at the town.
he did sweep (?) from the fields	To and fro in the fields plied
the women gathering (sticks)	the women cutting wood,
and from the threshing-floors those	Congregating in the open spaces.
seeking (straw),	To and fro at the well plied
did sweep (?) from the fountain the	the women drawing water,
women drawing (water) and from	Filling (the jars) at the spring.'
the spring those filling (buckets).'	

And they station themselves in the city of Sharona,
in the city of *Sa͑t,*
in the fields of *Htb(h),*
in the plains of *Hpšt s͑t*
near the fountain of Shebt,
near the spring of Mimlat (II. 110–14a = 212–217).

Suffice it to note that this distribution of forces shows excellent strategy on the part of Keret: to the north of the besieged capital he ordered a town, fields, and a well to be occupied; to the south a similar manœuvre: a town, plains, and a spring. Moreover, in a radius of less than 15 kilometres there are to be found in Galilee the double site of Khirbet ed-Dâmiyeh (= *udm rbt* and *udm trrt*), that of Sarona (= *šrn* or *šarna*), Khirbet es Sa͑d (= *s͑t*), Kefr Sabt (*šebt*), and Khirbet Mimla (= *mmlat*). The coincidence between the modern geographical names and those of the poem of Keret is surely too striking to be simply the result of chance. But if the Galilean thesis is sound it may enhance the probability of the soundness of the historico-legendary interpretation of the poem of Keret.

Recently Dr. John Gray has devoted an important monograph to the Keret texts.[1] The marriage of Keret, recognized as the theme of the first tablet, might be 'a reminiscence of the symbiosis of Semitic and Hurrian in North Syria, which is attested by the administrative texts of the 15th–14th century from Ras Shamra. From that point onwards the text is concerned with domestic history.' As regards the *Sitz im Leben,* the learned author asserts that the text 'served a practical purpose in the community where it was current, to achieve some desired end or to conserve certain accepted values'. These values would be especially of a social order and there would be the same motive for preserving and repeating them as for the values of the cosmic, seasonal, animal, and vegetable order. We should find these usages sanctioned and these customs accepted in the society of Ugarit. The title 'social myth' is thus all the more justified as the description of a text which, for example, on the

---

[1] J. Gray, *The Krt Text in the Literature of Ras Shamra. A Social Myth of Ancient Canaan* (Leiden, 1955).

occasion of royal marriages at Ugarit, reminded worshippers of the divine benedictions which attended those rites and institutions imposed on the community by tradition.

Just as we do not know on which occasions and at which festivities the priests of Ugarit recited the great myths of Ras Shamra, we also do not know what use was made of the tale of Keret. But such as it is, in spite of its merits, it reveals little of the emotions and beliefs which gave it birth. It is possible that the problems solved by similar texts 'are certainly not to be solved out of the lexicon, or, as some have alleged, out of the whole gamut of Semitic lexica'. But at least we have there an efficient and reliable means of control.[1]

In conclusion: an historic stele of Amenophis II discovered at Memphis reports that 'His Majesty the Pharaoh came once to Ugarit and subdued there all his enemies and following this His Majesty set out again with an easy and gay heart having taken possession of all the country'. We have certainly been less fortunate: we have certainly not taken possession of all that Ugarit has revealed; there remain enigmas and problems, which are so many enemies. But we take leave of them 'with an easy and gay heart'.

[1] We have noticed with great satisfaction the conclusion of Professor G. R. Driver: 'That some nucleus of historical fact lies behind the story of Keret appears indeed probable, but how much may be fact and how much fiction can hardly be determined in the present state of knowledge' (*Canaanite Myths and Legends* (Edinburgh, 1956), p. 5).

EARLY HEBREW MYTHS AND
THEIR INTERPRETATION[1]

by GEO WIDENGREN

ARE there any Hebrew myths, and is it at all possible to speak of any interpretation of these perplexing entities? A review of the history of their actual interpretation will probably teach us something about early Hebrew myths and their explanation.

It is now exactly eighty years since a real start was made in the discovery and interpretation of Hebrew myths when Ignaz Goldziher, later so famous as an Arabist, published his work on Hebrew mythology.[2] The unfavourable reception given to this book caused Hebrew and Old Testament studies to lose that great Semitic scholar, with a corresponding gain to Arabic and Islamic studies. We should not forget in this connexion that it was Goldziher who was the real founder of Islamology—the historical interpretation of Islam.

To be sure, it is not at all difficult to understand the unfavourable impression Goldziher's treatment of Hebrew mythology created among his contemporaries, but at the same time it must be stressed that our modern criticism is of quite a different character from that directed against him eighty years ago.[3] The defects of Goldziher's work are easy enough to detect; it is less easy to observe its merits, although they obviously exist.

Goldziher is completely dominated by the idea that behind

[1] For general surveys the reader is referred to the following articles, occasionally somewhat out of date, because written before the utilization of the Ras Shamra texts: Gunkel, *R.G.G.*[2] iv. 381–90, 'Mythus und Mythologie: III A Im AT.'; Peters, *E.R.E.* iv. 151–5, 'Cosmogony and Cosmology (Hebrew)'; G. Margoliouth, *E.R.E.* vi. 656–8, 'Heroes and Hero-Gods (Hebrew)'. My distinguished predecessor (as a contributor on the present theme) Professor T. H. Robinson wrote the essay 'Hebrew Myths' in Hooke, ed. *Myth and Ritual*, Oxford, 1933. This article will of course often be quoted in what follows.

[2] Goldziher, *Der Mythos bei den Hebräern und seine geschichtliche Entwickelung*, Leipzig, 1876. An English translation has already been published (1877), but this edition not being available to me my references are to the original German edition.

[3] Goldziher himself later on in life disclaimed responsibility for this book!

the tales of the patriarchs there are to be found old myths. His work is further characterized by the thought that myth is the linguistic expression of the impression made on man by the various phenomena of nature. Also the contrast between nomads and agriculturists is, for him, very important. Moon-mythology, concerned with the moon and stars of the night sky, is held to be characteristic of nomad culture, whereas sun-mythology, concerned with the burning sun and the day sky is thought to be equally characteristic of an agricultural people. On points of detail we should note that Goldziher mentions such mythological figures as the winged Šaḥar, the Dawn, Ps. cxxxix. 9 and the Sun as a young hero in Ps. xix. 6.[1]

Goldziher also refers to the role played by the moon calendar among the nomads in contrast with the sun calendar prevailing among tillers of the soil.[2]

He had already put forward the interpretation of Jonah as a sun-hero.[3] He further distinguished as a special category of myths the so-called culture-myths, to which he devoted a whole chapter.[4] Last but not least, he conceived the remarkable notion of myth developing either into religion or into history.[5]

Goldziher drew his comparative material chiefly from Arabian culture, but by no means neglected the wider field including Indo-European mythology.[6] For this reason we should call his method phenomenological rather than historical, although his use of the Arabian way of life of course has a genetic aspect too.[7]

---

[1] Cf. Goldziher, op. cit., pp. 135 f. and 134.

[2] Cf. Goldziher, op. cit., pp. 75 ff.

[3] Cf. Goldziher, op. cit., p. 120.

[4] Cf. Goldziher, op. cit., ch. vi, pp. 242–80.

[5] Cf. Goldziher, op. cit., p. 301. When Goldziher assumes a development from myth to history he is in a way in line with those modern scholars who speak of 'the historicization of myth', undoubtedly a real and often recurring phenomenon, cf. below, p. 201 n. 1.

[6] This was, of course, partly due to lack of concrete data from the Semitic field at the time when Goldziher wrote, but one is rather astonished to see Syrian pagan religion so completely neglected. One is under the impression that Goldziher's ideas of interpretation did not come from carefully collected and sifted material but rather preceded and determined this very collection.

[7] The comparison between Hebrew nomads and nomad tribes of pre-Islamic Arabia has been classical among scholars like Wellhausen and others of his generation.

The next really important step in the interpretation is marked by Gunkel and his school, above all Gressmann, Schmidt, and Mowinckel.[1] Gunkel, perhaps the greatest Old Testament scholar of this century, was dominated by the idea that myth was younger than folk-lore, and for this reason was deeply influenced by it. This assumption was common among folk-lorists of his day and may be found even in our own time.[2] Gressmann, next to Gunkel the dominating figure among Old Testament exegetes in modern times, shared unreservedly the general convictions of Gunkel which led him to a similar and regrettable neglect of the ritual aspects of myth. For in folk-lore the emphasis is on word and not on ritual action; myth is predominantly conceived of as 'a story of the gods', *Göttergeschichte.*[3] Accordingly myth was chiefly interpreted by this school as a kind of cosmological, anthropological, and cultural speculation. Emphasis was laid on myths of origin, such as creation-myths, paradise-myths, or myths of nature such as sun-myths, or finally aetiological myths, which played a very great role in the interpretation of the texts.[4]

In the main it was denied by Gunkel that the patriarchs originally were mythical figures, ancient gods, as had been asserted not only by Goldziher, but also by Winckler representing the Pan-Babylonian school,[5] and by the great historian Eduard Meyer, who made a most interesting attempt to establish an association between the patriarchs and the many cult-places mentioned in connexion with them in the sagas of Genesis.[6]

Gunkel followed Goldziher in his interest in the so-called culture-myths.[7] Gunkel's chief fault was his acceptance of the

---

The nomad Hebrew tribes of the times of Moses are often supposed to have been something very akin to Arab *badawis.*

[1] Gressmann, Schmidt, and Mowinckel may all be called real followers and pupils of Gunkel who was the founder of a veritable school.

[2] Cf. Gunkel, *Genesis*, 3rd ed. (Göttingen, 1910).

[3] Cf. Gunkel, op. cit., p. xiv; *R.G.G.*[2] iv, p. 383.

[4] Cf. Gunkel, op. cit., pp. xv, xx ff.; *R.G.G.*[2] iv, pp. 382 f.

[5] Cf. Gunkel, op. cit., pp. lxvi ff. Winckler, as a typical representative of the Pan-Babylonian school, advocates ideas that cannot possibly be taken seriously in our day.

[6] Cf. Meyer, *Die Israeliten und ihre Nachbarstämme* (Halle, 1906), pp. 249 ff. Behind Meyer we find Nöldeke who was always a champion of the same opinion.

[7] Cf. Gunkel, op. cit., p. xvi, with a reference to Gressmann, *Z.A.W.* xxx (1910).

prevailing opinion that myth is a later development of the tale. But his special merit was his willingness to make comparisons above all with surrounding ancient cultures, e.g. Mesopotamia and (to a lesser extent) Phœnicia and Egypt, whereas the comparative material from Arabia, so popular among the scholars of an older generation like Goldziher, was more or less ignored by him.

While Gressmann made some original contributions to interpretation[1] it must be said that Schmidt in his great work on Jonah did not do more than trace the mythical motifs (which still survive in that book).[2] In his case we cannot speak of any interpretation of actually existing early Hebrew myths.

Mowinckel, although like Schmidt a pupil of Gunkel, has freed himself in so many respects from his master's influence, and at the same time has been so deeply influenced by other Scandinavian scholars, that he must rather be classed as belonging to the so-called Scandinavian school.

We come next to the British 'Myth and Ritual School', which is, of course, not a school in the same sense in which we can speak of Gunkel and his school.

This British line of research was started by Professor Hooke by means of a combination of exegetical, anthropological, and folk-loristic methods. The influence of Frazer (and to some extent Hocart) is conspicuous everywhere. Frazer himself had demonstrated his interest in the Old Testament by publishing his work *Folk-lore in the Old Testament*, but it is quite obvious that his general views of so-called 'primitive' conceptions or of mythology were not at all accepted by Hooke, the inspiring force of the 'school'.[3] Hocart, himself a contributor to the literary products of the 'school', was mainly influenced by the work of

---

[1] Cf. *Z.A.W.* xxx (1910), pp. 9 ff. and *Mose und seine Zeit* (Göttingen, 1913), *passim*.

[2] Schmidt, *Jona* (Göttingen, 1907); we have already indicated that this was an old idea, cf. above, p. 150 n. 3.

[3] Cf. Hooke, *Myth and Ritual*, pp. 1 f. where some clear criticisms were presented. For Hooke as the 'starter' of the whole 'Myth and Ritual School', cf. op. cit., p. xiv of the preface written by Simpson. The term 'school' is used here for convenience because it has been customary in literature to speak of 'the Myth and Ritual School'.

Perry.[1] This influence manifested itself *inter alia* in a complete denial of the evolutionary principles so characteristic of British anthropologists of an older generation (and with typical British conservatism still cherished in some quarters with admirable piety towards tradition). The leader of the 'school', Hooke, by profession an Old Testament scholar, had also received an anthropological training, and another of the leading members, Professor James, can be classified also as a professional anthropologist besides being an historian of religions.

Accordingly it is the emphasis on anthropology and folk-lore which constitutes the special mark of this British 'Myth and Ritual School'. The predilection for folk-loristic methods is thus a trait shared with the school of Gunkel, but while Gunkel above all is interested in folk-stories, Hooke and his followers are more concerned with popular customs. Another common trait is the presupposition that the ancient Near East was the home of the mythical conceptions met with in the Old Testament. Egypt, Mesopotamia, and pre-Israelitic Canaan are invoked to assist in the interpretation of difficult passages, where a Hebrew myth is assumed to be found. The special contribution of the school is, however, the theory of a general pattern of myth and ritual in the Ancient Near East, including Israel.[2] In this we are reminded of the American anthropologist Ruth Benedict's 'patterns of culture',[3] and the trend in modern cultural anthropology represented by her; though it is very doubtful whether her influence can be traced here.

Compared with the definition of myth given by Gunkel we have to note a great advance, for emphasis was laid by Hooke

---

[1] Hocart, who published his book *Kingship* in London in 1927, worked rather independently, as Professor Hooke has told me (letter of 22 Oct. 1955). He is quoted by Hooke, op. cit., p. 6, and was associated with Hooke's collaborators in the collection of essays presented in *The Labyrinth*, ed. Hooke (London, 1935), to which he contributed the paper 'The Life Giving Myth', pp. 261–81.

[2] Cf. Hooke, *Myth and Ritual*, pp. 1 ff. 'The Myth and Ritual Pattern of the Ancient East'.

[3] It should be observed that Benedict did not publish her book *Patterns of Culture* until 1934. Hooke speaks, op. cit., p. 5, of 'culture patterns'. Professor Hooke has told me (letter of 22 Oct. 1955) 'that Ruth Benedict had no influence whatever on the Myth and Ritual movement'.

on the cultic aspect of myth: 'the original myth, inseparable in
the first instance from its ritual, embodies in more or less symbolic fashion, the original situation which is seasonally re-enacted
in the ritual'.[1] This definition of the essence of myth has played
a dominating role in subsequent discussion.

The Scandinavian school is still less a school in the true German sense of the word than the British 'Myth and Ritual School'.
It can be said to be a certain trend, in a way running parallel
with the two schools already mentioned and at the same time
in its later phases being partly, sometimes deeply, influenced by
the British scholars.[2] The Scandinavian school starts from the
strong influence exercised by the Danish philologist and historian
Grönbech and his interpretation of cult as a ritual drama, and
this influence is met with especially in the important works of
Mowinckel and Pedersen.[3] From the very outset the cultic
aspect of myth accordingly prevails to the utmost degree among
Scandinavian scholars in their interpretation of myth and legend,[4]
thanks to this influence of Grönbech. Some scholars in Uppsala
who had been deeply influenced by the works of Mowinckel
and Pedersen, were later to a certain extent influenced also by
the British 'Myth and Ritual School'.[5] If anything can be said

---

[1] Hooke, op. cit., p. 3.

[2] Engnell has declared himself a convinced 'patternist'. The present writer has
often, especially in the various volumes of the series 'King and Saviour', declared
his adherence to the principles advocated by Hooke and his followers. On the whole
all members of the so-called Upsala school (the term is used here for convenience)
have learnt much from British scholarship in this regard.

[3] Cf. the work of Grönbech, *The Culture of the Teutons* (London, 1931), with the
essay on 'Ritual Drama', ii. 260 ff. As to Grönbech, cf. Widengren, 'Die religions-
wissenschaftliche Forschung in Skandinavien in den letzten zwanzig Jahren',
Z.R.G.G. v (1953), ii, 'Die dänische Forschung', Heft 4. In *The Old Testament and
Modern Study*, ed. Rowley (Oxford, 1951), p. 189, Grönbech is called 'anthropologist'.
He was, however, above all a philologist, trained by Vilhelm Thomsen, and published
his thesis on a Turkish subject and afterwards became a university lecturer in English.
On the influence exercised by Grönbech on Mowinckel and Pedersen cf. Anderson,
'Hebrew Religion', *The Old Testament and Modern Study*, pp. 292, 295; Widengren,
op. cit., pp. 320 f. Both Mowinckel and Pedersen expressly acknowledge their
debt to Grönbech.

[4] For this reason the cultic aspect is emphasized also by many New Testament
scholars of Uppsala, not least those of an older generation, e.g. Gillis Wetter.

[5] This holds true especially of the present writer.

to be characteristic of this Scandinavian school it is that it was dominated by studies in Semitic languages and cultures, rather than by folk-lore and anthropology, and that the history of religions, based on an accurate philological interpretation of the texts, was given priority over general comparisons based on folk-lore and anthropology. This fact is due, of course, to the education and training received by the Scandinavian scholars. A marked anti-evolutionary trend is conspicuous everywhere, except in Mowinckel, who also stands more aloof from Pedersen and the younger Swedish scholars.[1] The theory of a general myth and ritual pattern was accepted, in some quarters with enthusiasm, in others with more reserve.[2] Again Mowinckel took his own course by explicitly criticizing the hypothesis of a Near Eastern pattern in myth and ritual.[3]

The discovery of the Ras Shamra texts and their interpretation exercised a great influence on both the British and the Scandinavian schools. In the Ugaritic mythological poems a connecting link was found between Israel and Canaan, with the ancient Near East providing the general cultural background. It was this Canaanite–Syrian literature that provided us with definite proof that Canaan and Israel belonged to the same culture area as Mesopotamia.[4] It was now possible to demonstrate in detail

[1] For a discussion and criticism of the principles of evolutionism cf. Widengren, 'Evolutionism and the Problem of the Origin of Religion', *Ethnos*, x (1945), pp. 57–96.

[2] For some criticisms cf. Widengren, *R.o.B.* ii (1943), p. 50 where it is said that the Old Testament passages have not been sufficiently analysed and that for this reason the work of the school sometimes suffers from a certain schematic and 'constructive' character. (It belongs to 'life's little ironies' that the same charge was eventually brought against me too!) But I ought to have observed the obvious fact that the books published were intended chiefly to introduce a point of view.

[3] Cf. Mowinckel, *Han som kommer* (Copenhagen, 1951, Engl. transl. 1956), pp. 26 f., where the criticisms presented by Frankfort, *Kingship and the Gods* (Chicago, 1948), are accepted. He seems to be more positive in his book *Offersang og sangoffer* (Oslo, 1951), p. 36, but on p. 61 he denies the thesis that there ever existed a common Near Eastern royal ideology (if I have understood him correctly, his terminology being very loose, because he speaks of 'the king in all oriental religions', but no one has included other religions than those of the ancient Near East).

[4] Incidentally it may be observed that this term 'culture area' was used both by Hooke, *Myth and Ritual*, p. 5, and by Widengren, *Ethnos*, p. 95 (with a reference to Goldenweiser, *Anthropology* (London, 1937), pp. 457 ff.). I am not quite sure whether

that Israel had been profoundly influenced by the old inhabitants of Canaan; this had, of course, been assumed long ago, but demonstrations had fallen short of convincing proof. Incidentally it is curious to observe to what extent the convincing demonstrations were made by scholars outside the British and Scandinavian schools. Of course many contributions were furnished by members of these schools also, but so far as the British 'Myth and Ritual School' is concerned it would seem as if the Second World War had a devastating effect, for since 1940 its members have published very little on the same lines as before. The more welcome therefore is the present volume.

The chief value of the Ugaritic texts from a more general point of view of myth-interpretation lies in the fact that they so clearly exhibit the ritual aspects of myth. This has been emphasized among others by Pedersen.[1] For this reason these mythological poems possess typical value for the interpretation of ancient Hebrew myths.

This short and admittedly very incomplete survey of the history of interpretation has shown us myths in their close association with rites and ceremonies, as part of a ritual. Further, the theory of a general myth and ritual pattern of the ancient Near East has proved a very useful clue and must obviously be given the most careful consideration. At all events we have to look upon Israelite Canaan as part of a vast culture area of the Near East, dominated by Babylonian culture patterns, and this not only in the field of religion but in spiritual and material culture in general.[2] Egypt, which certainly exercised a considerable

---

Professor Hooke considers the whole ancient Near East one vast culture area with Mesopotamia as its centre and with *one* general myth and ritual pattern, cf. *Myth and Ritual*, p. 70, or if he thinks of several developments of a common, older pattern, cf. *The Origins of Early Semitic Ritual*, The Schweich Lectures of the British Academy 1935 (London, 1938), p. 57. (The difference of opinion has been observed by Anderson, op. cit., p. 294 n. 1.) Widengren, *The Accadian and Hebrew Psalms of Lamentation as Religious Documents* (Stockholm, 1937), pp. 1 ff., esp. p. 17, emphasized that Palestine and Syria were only offshoots of Babylonian civilization.

[1] Cf. Pedersen, ed. *Illustreret Religionshistorie* (Copenhagen, 1948), pp. 200, 202 f., 204 f., 206 f., 210; 'Canaanite and Israelite Cultus', *A.c.O.* xviii (1939), pp. 1–14.

[2] The spread of cuneiform writing and literature, of Mesopotamian seals, of cosmology, of temple architecture and symbolism, of art patterns, &c., as well as of many Babylonian loanwords would seem to be most typical.

influence on Canaan, constitutes an entirely separate culture area.[1]

Myth as a literary creation has to be seen as older than those popular tales, stories, sagas, and legends where corresponding motifs are found.[2] There has been a certain tendency in modern interpretation of Hebrew myths to neglect their speculative force and importance.[3] But actually cosmological myths have played a considerable role in the religious life of Israel and it would seem to be quite obvious that myth in Israel as elsewhere is very often on the verge of developing into a kind of theory of the world and of life.[4] Even in an agricultural society there was room for thought about more things than 'certain practical and pressing problems of daily life'.[5]

The question we put forward in our introductory sentence can without any doubt be answered in the affirmative. The history of interpretation of what scholars have called Hebrew myths has already achieved much, demonstrating in the most convincing way that there once existed in Israel a very rich treasure of myths—real, i.e. ritual myths—playing a central role

[1] Thus far we may admit that criticisms (e.g. Frankfort, Mowinckel, &c.) were right to a certain degree. But from a more general point of view, when, e.g., the whole culture area of Egypt and the Near East is considered, both these smaller culture areas can be regarded as constituting *one* single culture area as contrasted, for instance, with the Mediterranean culture area. In this case the lack of orientation in cultural anthropology in its modern aspect (perhaps coupled with apologetic inclinations) have caused a certain bias and much unnecessary bitterness in polemics, e.g. on the side of Frankfort and Mowinckel.

[2] For a general survey cf. Widengren, *Religionens värld*, 2nd ed. (Stockholm, 1953), pp. 151–62.

[3] But already Gunkel, *Genesis*, pp. xv f. had stressed the 'philosophical' implications of some of the Old Testament myths.

[4] It is to Radin that the credit should be given of having shown the importance of the speculative element among non-literate peoples, cf. *Primitive Man as Philosopher* (New York, 1927). For Africa we may refer to the various interesting publications of Griaule, cf., e.g. (together with G. Dieterlen), 'The Dogon', *African Worlds* 1953, pp. 83 ff.; 'Mythe de l'organisation du monde chez les Dogons du Soudan', *Psyché*, vi (1947), pp. 443 ff.; 'Descente du troisième verbe chez les Dogons du Soudan', ibid., xiii–xiv (1947), pp. 3 ff., and many articles in *Journal de la Société des Africanistes*, 1948–50, 1952. Among ancient Indo-European peoples the speculative spirit in myth is most conspicuous, cf. the many epoch-making works of Dumézil and for this question in general Widengren, *Religionens värld*, pp. 133, 151 f

[5] Hooke, *Myth and Ritual*, p. 2.

in the religious system and life of the Hebrew people. I should like to stress the word 'system', for in Israel as elsewhere in the Ancient East there existed a real system of ideas, a veritable *Weltanschauung.*

When mentioning cosmological myths we have already touched upon *one* kind of myth, incontestably preserved among older parts of Old Testament literature. Although Israel, according to the judgement of Gunkel, was unfavourably disposed towards myths[1] we nevertheless meet with a great many passages in the Old Testament containing allusions to cosmological myths, as indeed Gunkel himself has demonstrated.[2] Actually there is here a confusion, which recurs rather often, between the Old Testament and Israel itself. We must not lose sight of the fact that the Old Testament, as it is handed down to us in the Jewish Canon, is only one part—we do not even know if the greater part—of Israel's national literature.[3] And, moreover, this preserved part has in many passages quite obviously been exposed to censorship and correspondingly purged.[4] In such circumstances it is in fact quite remarkable that we are still able to detect so many traces of myths in the Old Testament. It surely calls for notice that Old Testament poetry has kept intact some ancient Near-Eastern myths to a considerably greater extent than its prose narratives, and it is astonishing to find so many traces of myths also in those poetical parts of the Old Testament that may almost certainly be dated to exilic and post-exilic times.[5] To these poetical parts must, however, be

---

[1] 'Israel ist den Mythen nicht günstig gewesen', *R.G.G.*[2] iv. 381. This is better expressed in his *Genesis*, p. xiv: 'Der eigentliche Zug der Jahve-Religion ist den Mythen nicht günstig.'

[2] Above all in his classic work *Schöpfung und Chaos* (Göttingen, 1895); 2nd impr. 1921.

[3] Cf. Pedersen, *Z.A.W.* xlix (1931), p. 161: 'Fragen wir, was das AT ist, muß die Antwort zunächst ganz einfach lauten: Es ist die nationale Literatur des jüdischen Volkes, wie sie etwa 1–2 Jahrhunderte vor dem Anfang unserer Zeitrechnung vorlag.'

[4] For this criticism of myth cf. Peters, op. cit., p. 154 b; Gunkel, *Genesis*, p. 119 f., and in general Oesterley-Robinson, *Hebrew Religion, its Origin and Development,* 2nd. ed. (London, 1937), p. 173; cf. also Gressmann, *The Expositor,* ser ix. 3 (1925), p. 417.

[5] Above all in Isa. xl–lxvi and in Job.

added Genesis, although there are certain arguments in favour of the hypothesis that Genesis as far as its mythical material is concerned is largely based upon epic traditions.[1] But on the whole it is in the poetry rather than in the prose that we are confronted by Hebrew myths. How, then, can we explain, in a text admittedly rather late like Job, the astonishingly large number of allusions to ancient Hebrew myths? This question has been the subject of discussion[2] and we shall revert to the problem.

First of all when treating of existing Hebrew myths we should not forget—as is usually done—that the description of the appearance of Yahweh himself is based upon mythical notions and very often possesses a definite mythical-anthropomorphic colouring.[3] We have in Deut. xxxiii. 2–3 a short, unfortunately rather enigmatic, description of Yahweh's triumphal procession in old times from Sinai.[4] Here it is said that He comes from 'Myriads of Holy Ones', which may be taken as the name of a place[5] or as a designation of His divine court. At any rate this expression must be associated with other similar passages, describing God as surrounded by His royal household or His assembly: (e.g.)

> El is a terrible master in the great council of the Holy Ones,
> and awe-inspiring above all those round about him.
>
> (Ps. lxxxix. 8)[6]

These Holy Ones in Ps. xvi. 3 appear in an obscure context,

---

[1] Sievers's old theory of an original metric version of Genesis went too far, but that traces of poetic texts have been discovered by Gunkel in his commentary is well known. Through the work of Cassuto the whole problem has received a fresh stimulus and ought to be examined anew. We hope to be able to revert to this problem. (Professor Burney also attempted to prove the metrical character of Genesis.)

[2] Cf., e.g., Gunkel, *Schöpfung und Chaos*, pp. 158 ff., 162; Robinson, in *Myth and Ritual*, p. 176. It is a matter for regret that the thesis of Feinberg, 'Ugaritic literature and the Book of Job' (Baltimore 1945), remains unpublished, for obviously such a problem must have been treated there. For the solution offered by Albright cf. below, p. 202.

[3] It should be observed that, e.g., Eichrodt, *Theologie des Alten Testaments* (Leipzig, 1935), ii. 3 speaks of 'der Form naturmythologischen Denkens'.

[4] A detailed philological and historical commentary on this passage was given by Nyberg, *Z.D.M.G.* xcii (1938), pp. 320–44.

[5] Cf. Nyberg, op. cit., p. 336.   [6] Ibid.

but obviously in this passage too they are thought of as independent, divine beings.[1] In Zech. xiv. 5 we further read:

> And Yahweh, my God, will come,
> all thy Holy Ones with thee.[2]

In Daniel viii. 13 the seer is listening to the conversation between two of the Holy Ones.[3] Cf. also Ecclus. xlii. 17.[4] Just because the Holy Ones constitute the assembly of Yahweh He is glorified as unsurpassable among them as we see from Exod. xv. 11:

> Who is like thee among the gods, Yahweh,
> who is like thee, glorious among the Holy Ones?[5]

This passage is especially valuable when compared with Ps. lxxxix. 6 f., where in the two stichoi immediately preceding the already quoted passage it is said:

> The heavens praise thy miracle, Yahweh,
> yea, thy faithfulness in the assembly of the Holy Ones.
> For who in the clouds is equal to Yahweh,
> can be like Yahweh among the sons of the gods.

Here we can clearly see that 'the assembly of the Holy Ones' is the same as 'the sons of the gods', i.e. according to usual Hebrew and Semitic idiom 'the gods'.[6]

Very impressive indeed is the scene depicted in Ps. lxxxii, where God (El) is standing in the assembly of the gods, judging

---

[1] An attempt at emendation and reconstruction of the text by Nyberg, *Studien zum Hoseabuche*, U.U.Å. 1935: 6, pp. 118 ff.

[2] Cf. Nyberg, op. cit., p. 336.

[3] Cf. Montgomery, *The Book of Daniel*, I.C.C., 1927, pp. 231 f. (rather unsatisfactory).

[4] The text: 'Nor have the Holy Ones of God been able to tell the wonders of Yahweh.' Smend, *Die Weisheit des Jesus Sirach* (Berlin, 1906), p. 44, adopts the marginal gloss גבורותיו instead of ייי. Usually Job xv. 15 is compared with the passage in question.

[5] It is not necessary to emend מי כמכה נאדר בקדש if we take קֹדֶשׁ as an abstract substantive possessing the value of a broken plural, cf. Nyberg, *Z.D.M.G.* xcii (1938), pp. 335 f. (it is true that Nyberg did not quote this passage, but the omission was perhaps only due to an oversight).

[6] I cannot find any reason for emending אֱמוּנָתְךָ in v. 6. It goes without saying that it would be more correct to translate בני אלהים as 'gods'. The conventional translation is used here. Cf. also Winter, *Z.A.W.* lxvii (1955), pp. 40 ff.

them.[1] Yahweh is accordingly the highest god in a council or assembly of gods, called 'the Holy Ones', or 'the Holy Ones of God' or simply 'the gods' ('the sons of the gods').

This assembly of the Holy Ones is found in Canaanite mythology. In the Phoenician inscriptions there is, for instance, such a passage as Esmunazar inscr. 11. 9, 22, where the phrase 'the(se) holy gods'[2] occurs; or, still more interesting from our point of view, 'the congregation of the holy gods of Byblos', Yehimilk of Byblos 11. 4–5.[3] In the Ugaritic texts, moreover, the expression 'the Holy Ones' is synonymous with 'the gods' (texts no. 137: 20 f., 38; 2 Aqhat i. 4, 9, 14).

In the case quoted from the Yehimilk inscription the word for assembly is *mpḥrt*, which corresponds to the same term in Ugaritic where we meet with the corresponding expression 'the assembly of the sons of El (the gods)', *mpḥrt bn il*, which has a synonymous term in *pḥr bn ilm* or *pḥr ilm*.[4] In the Ras Shamra texts this conception of an assembly of the gods recurs very often and it is clearly thought of as being under the leadership of El, 'the father of the gods'.[5]

---

[1] In the text I have left out the passage Hos. xii. 1, which is difficult. For interpretation and translation cf. Nyberg, *Studien*, pp. 92 f. No emendation being necessary I would rather like to translate: 'But Judah is seeking pasture with El, and with the Holy Ones she is faithful', interpreting this saying somewhat differently from Nyberg (who, however, *Z.D.M.G.* xcii (1938), p. 336 n. 2, admitted that the lower Canaanite deities might be alluded to by the prophet). I would suggest that because El and the Holy Ones together constitute the assembly of the gods there is no opposition between them in this passage and that רד and נאמן for this reason must possess a synonymous meaning. Therefore I take רד in the meaning of Arabic رٰاد (but in another sense than Nyberg). The meaning would be that Judah is seeking refuge with El and is clinging to his assembly, the Holy Ones. For Ps. lxxxii cf. Morgenstern, 'The Mythological Background of Psalm 82', *H.U.C.A.* xiv (1939), pp. 29–126; Nyberg, *Studien*, pp. 122–5.

[2] Quoted from *N.S.I.* No. 5: האלנם הקדשם אל and האלנם וקדשם. For the plural meaning cf. op. cit., p. 24 note to no. 3: 10, and Harris, *A Grammar of the Phoenician Language* (New Haven, 1936), p. 77, s.v. אל 'these'.

[3] Quoted from Harris, op. cit., p. 77, s.v. אל 'god', and Albright, *J.A.O.S.* xvii (1947), pp. 156 f.

[4] Quoted from Gordon, *U.H.*, Glossary, p. 262: 1629. There is a second expression for assembly, viz. *'dt ilm*, *U.H.*, Glossary, p. 255: 1455, and a third one *dr bn il*, *U.H.*, Glossary, p. 224: 560 (add to the references 128, iii. 19).

[5] Cf. the text 2 in Gordon, *U.H.*, l. 33 *lab bn il*. The father of the sons of El (God) cannot possibly be any other god than El himself.

Behind the Canaanite idea of a high god and his assembly of holy gods, where he is as it were the president and redoubtable leader, we discern without any difficulty the Mesopotamian conception of Marduk and the assembly of the gods, the *puḫur ilāni*, as it occurs especially in the Epic of Creation, *Enūma eliš*, tablet IV. In Mesopotamia we also have abundant proof of the idea that the high god is considered the father of the gods.[1]

So the mythical idea of God surrounded by his assembly has evidently been taken over from the Canaanites, who shared this conception with the inhabitants of Mesopotamia.

We may now pass on to the various forms of the epiphanies of Yahweh. It is well known that He is a god associated above all with storm, lightning, and thunder. His epithets or the invocations of him give sufficient indication of his character, for he is 'the rider on the clouds', Ps. lxviii. 5, or 'the rider of heavens', Deut. xxxiii. 26 (Ps. lxviii. 34), or 'the rider on the cloud', Isa. xix. 1. With a still stronger mythical colouring it is said that he is riding on the Cherub, 2 Sam. xxii. 11; Ps. xviii. 11. In Hab. iii. 8 Yahweh is even depicted as borne on His horses. Among these passages, as has been observed long ago, Ps. lxviii. 5 is of special interest, for the Hebrew expression runs: *rōkēḇ bā'arāḇōt*. This epithet was not understood until the Ugaritic exhibited in several passages the corresponding epithet *rkb 'rpt*, given to Ba'al.[2] In this case too the mythical image has been inherited by the Israelites from Canaan, though we can trace the same conception back to Mesopotamia. Here the godhead is sometimes depicted as riding in the sky in his car,[3] or as riding on the storm or hurricane,[4] or on the typhoon.[5] This is true especially of Adad, the East-Semitic counterpart of the West-Semitic Hadad, whom we meet in the RS texts as Ba'al.[6] This would

---

[1] Cf. Tallqvist, *Akkadische Götterepitheta* (Helsingfors, 1938), p. 1, s.v. *abu*.

[2] Observed already by Bauer, *Z.A.W.* li (1933), pp. 88 ff. Cf. further Gordon, *U.H.*, Glossary, p. 259: 1539.   [3] *rākib iṣnarkabti.*

[4] (*rākib ūmi =*)*ud.da u₅.a*; (*rākib ugalla =*)*u₄.gal.la u₅.a.*

[5] *rākib abūbi.* All these epithets are indexed in Tallqvist, op. cit., p. 175, s.v. *rakābu.*

[6] Cf., e.g., Kapelrud, *Baal in the Ras Shamra Texts* (Copenhagen, 1952), pp. 50–52. The identification of Hadad with Ba'al is clearly expressed in the Amarna

seem to be of special importance as we shall see from what follows.

In the magnificent picture of Yahweh's epiphany in Hab. iii, the Canaanite background of which was demonstrated by Cassuto in 1938, we read:

> Before him Pestilence marched,
> and Plague went forth at his feet.
>
> (Hab. iii. 5)[1]

We find here two of the bodyguards of the Israelitic high god, Rašaf and Dabar. Of these Rašaf is a well-known west-Semitic deity,[2] and presumably Dabar is another, minor deity.

In the same poem in Hab. iii the lightnings of Yahweh are also mentioned in verse 11 as His arrows and His spears.[3] The same image of Yahweh as the thundering and lightning god is met with in Pss. xviii. 14–15 and xxix, whose Canaanite background has long been recognized.[4] In the RS texts Ba'al with his mace and his spear, the symbol of lightning,[5] furnishes us with a good illustration of Hab. iii. 11.

---

letters, cf. the discussion by Gressmann, *B.Z.A.W.* xxxiii (1918), pp. 191–216, where, however, the conclusions should be supplemented and corrected in the light of the RS texts.

[1] Transl. Albright, 'The Psalm of Habakkuk', *Studies in Old Testament Prophecy Presented to Professor Theodore H. Robinson* (Edinburgh, 1950), p. 12. Albright assumes vv. 3–7 to be 'taken with little alteration from a very early Israelite poem on the theophany of Yahweh as exhibited in the south-east storm', and vv. 8–15 to be 'adapted from an early poem or poems of Canaanite origin', op. cit., p. 8.

[2] Cf. Albright, *Archaeology and the Religion of Israel* (Baltimore 1946), 3rd ed. 1953, p. 79 with references p. 196 n. 24 (also an article by Vincent, *R.B.* 1928, pp. 512 ff.). The mythological background of Hab. iii. 5 was pointed out by Oesterley, in *Myth and Ritual*, pp. 119 f. Cf. also my thesis *The Accadian and Hebrew Psalms of Lamentation*, p. 256. Rašaf is now found also in the Karatépé inscription.

[3] This verse causes no philological difficulties.

[4] Cf. Albright, *Archaeology and the Religion of Israel*, p. 129. As to Ps. xxix we refer to Ginsberg, *Atti del XIX Congresso Internazionale degli Orientalisti*, 1938, pp. 472 ff. 'As shown by Ginsberg this psalm swarms with Canaanitisms in diction and imagery; there can be no doubt that it is a relatively little changed adaptation of a Baal hymn to the cult of Yahweh, probably in or about the tenth century B.C.', Albright, op. cit., p. 6. In this connexion it should be noted that 'the Sons of God' are found in Ps. xxix. 1.

[5] Cf. *Syria*, xiv (1933), pl. xvi; Dussaud, *Les Découvertes de Ras Shamra (Ugarit) et l'Ancien Testament* (Paris 1937), p. 41.

To the retinue of Yahweh there also belong other divine beings met with in Canaanite mythology, namely the hypostases Ṣaeḏaeq and Mišpāṭ, Šaḥar and Šālōm (Šālēm).[1] Now Ṣaeḏaeq and Mišpāṭ have their counterparts in the Sydyk and Misor of Philo Byblius (Eusebius, *Praeparatio Evang.* i. 10, 14), while Šaḥar and Šlm appear in the same form in the Ugaritic poems. There are also traces of another deity, the Dew, Ṭal, in the Old Testament texts.[2]

Enough has been said to show that the oft-repeated saying that the monotheistic spirit of Yahwistic religion did not tolerate any mythology certainly needs some qualification. In older times Israelite religion was a rather complex entity, embracing also—as we have seen—the idea of God surrounded by His divine assembly and council, and accompanied by His bodyguards. In this polytheistic trend there was a tendency to express more fully all the richness of divine essence and to get it more concretely visualized.

We may now proceed to the habitation of Yahweh. This is originally Sinai, but with the conquest of Jerusalem Yahweh also takes His seat on Sion. Now this mountain of Sion is explicitly identified with Ṣāfōn in Ps. xlviii. 3.[3] Here the mountain of the gods is situated, to which we shall now direct our attention. This mountain is the earthly paradise, surrounded by the paradise rivers which stream forth from below it, and including the garden of paradise where Primordial Man is its ruler. God has His seat here on the top of the cosmic mountain which is, as it were, His throne.[4] But this mountain of Ṣāfōn is

---

[1] Cf. Widengren, *The Accadian and Hebrew Psalms of Lamentation*, p. 71; *Psalm 110*, U.U.Å. 1941 : 7, 1, p. 10; a detailed discussion in Ringgren, *Word and Wisdom*, (Uppsala, 1947), pp. 86, 150 ff., where all the divine hypostases are investigated.

[2] Cf. Widengren, *Psalm 110*, pp. 9 ff. Engnell, *Studies in Divine Kingship in the Ancient Near East* (Uppsala 1943), p. 82 n. 5, has added a reference to proper names composed with *ṭal*.

[3] The qualification *ịarkeṭē ṣāfōn* is given to Sion in spite of the fact that Sion is not at all situated in the north. It is a foreign geographical perspective adapted to Jerusalem as is the case also in Ps. lxxxix. Cf. Gunkel, *Die Psalmen* (Göttingen 1926), p. 206 (comparing Isa. xiv. 13 f.), and Widengren, *Psalm 110*, p. 24.

[4] Selected literature: Wensinck, *The Ideas of the Western Semites concerning the Navel of the Earth*, Amsterdam 1916; *Myth and Ritual*, p. 180; Widengren, *Psalm*

well known from Ugaritic literature where it plays a central role in mythical cosmography. Here we have the place of the divine assembly where Ba'al is enthroned as ruler.[1] It seems indisputable that the intruding Israelitic tribes have taken over all this mythical geography from Canaan,[2] where it had been introduced in its turn from Mesopotamia. For it is only there that we find it fully elaborated and set in its proper context. Here too we find a common pattern underlying the mythical ideas in question.

As is well known, the Hebrew Paradise story in Gen. ii–iii exhibits all the distinctive features of an original myth; this has been demonstrated by Gunkel with a wealth of evidence that still commands respect.[3] By comparing it with other Old Testament passages Gunkel was able to show that it had lost much of its original colouring and become emasculated. In the early form of the story Primordial Man is a divine or semi-divine being, the snake a demon, and paradise the abode of God Himself; but in Genesis, while the special properties of the two trees in paradise are retained, that of its water has disappeared, and even the expression 'the Garden of God' is no longer used.[4]

For Gunkel's demonstration the famous passage Ezek. xxviii was of primary importance.[5] Because this text from various points of view is still one of the key texts and much labour has been expended on both its textual and ideological elucidation, we quote here in our own translation the relevant passages.[6]

110, pp. 5–7, 15, 24 (literature indicated p. 15 n. 3); *The King and the Tree of Life*, U.U.Å. 1951: 4, pp. 11, 44 f., 56 ff., 64 with fig. 22 on p. 66; *Religionens värld*, pp. 278 ff.

[1] Cf. Eissfeldt, *Baal Zaphon, Zeus Kasios und der Durchzug der Israeliten durchs Meer* (Halle, 1932), pp. 20 ff.; Kapelrud, op. cit., pp. 57 f. and *Joel Studies*, U.U.Å. 1948: 4, pp. 93–108.

[2] Cf. Eissfeldt, op. cit., p. 20: 'Zu den Elementen, die Jahwe anderen Göttern, Kulten und Mythen entwindet und sich zu eigen macht, gehört auch die Vorstellung von einem in den Himmel ragenden Berg, dem Zaphon, der Sitz und Thron des Baals dieses Berges ist; der Baal wird entthront, und Jahwe nimmt seinen Platz ein.'

[3] Cf. Gunkel, *Genesis*, pp. 25–40.   [4] Cf. Gunkel, op. cit., p. 39.

[5] Cf. Gunkel, op. cit., p. 34; Robinson, *Myth and Ritual*, pp. 180, 182; Hooke, op. cit., p. 11.

[6] A detailed commentary was given in Widengren, *Psalm 110*, pp. 15 ff.; *The Ascension of the Apostle and the Heavenly Book*, U.U.Å. 1950: 7, pp. 26, 94–97.

Thou wast a sealer of the preserved (thing), full of wisdom and accomplished in beauty.

In Eden, the Garden of God, thou wast, every precious stone being thy cover,

ruby, chrysolith, diamond, topaz, shoham, jasper,

sapphire, malachite, beryl, hyacinth, agate, amethyst and gold.

The works of thy settings and thy trappings on thee, the day thou wast created they were prepared.

Thou wast a cherub, oh, what an anointed of the Shadower, and I placed thee on the holy mountains.

A god thou wast, in the midst of stones of fire thou didst walk.

(Ezek. xxviii. 12–14)

We should note in this text the following important points: in the Garden of God, situated 'on the holy mountain', there was dwelling a divine being, anointed by God, who is called 'the Shadower', either because the godhead is overshadowing him with his wings (cf. Pss. xvii. 8; lvii. 2; lxi. 5; lxxiii. 8)[1] or because the deity is thought of as a mighty tree in the shadow of which he is living (cf. Hos. xiv. 9; Ezek. xxxi. 2–9; Dan. iv. 7–9).[2] This divine being is called a 'cherub' and an 'anointed (one)', the former epithet indicating his association with the garden as its guardian (Gen. iii. 24) and with God as that upon which the Deity rides (Ezek. x. 6 ff.),[3] the latter his royal status, because he has received his anointing from God—just like a corresponding Mesopotamian figure, the Primordial Man called Adapa.[4] And we should not forget that the whole description applies to the king of Tyre (Ezek. xxviii. 1). Accordingly the Phoenician ruler from the point of view of royal ideology is both the guardian of the Garden of God and God's anointed. His garment reflects his wonderful nature, being set with twelve

---

[1] Cf. the discussion in Widengren, *The Accadian and Hebrew Psalms of Lamentation*, p. 253.

[2] Cf. Widengren, *The King and the Tree of Life*, pp. 56 ff. When not the godhead but the king is depicted with the traits of this symbol we meet with the same phenomenon as in Mesopotamia, where the king as 'Tammuz' has taken over the symbols of this god, cf. Widengren, op. cit., pp. 42 ff.

[3] For the mythical being called 'Cherub' cf. Lods, *Israël des origines au milieu du VIIIᵉ siècle* (Paris, 1932), p. 533. The English transl. was not accessible to me.

[4] Cf. Widengren, *The King and the Tree of Life*, pp. 21 n., 59 f.

precious stones, and he is walking about in the midst of 'stones of fire', i.e. the stars. He was not only 'accomplished in beauty' but also 'full of wisdom', and 'a sealer of the preserved (thing)', just as Marduk in the Mesopotamian Epic of Creation sealed the tablets of destiny, *Enūma eliš*, iv. 122.[1] Actually it can be shown without difficulty that the Primordial Man wears the same pectoral as the Israelite high-priest wears in virtue of his office (Exod. xxviii. 17–20), the twelve jewels in both cases being exactly the same. We know further that Phoenician and Mesopotamian rulers really were equipped with a pectoral.[2] Such a pectoral has been found in the excavations of Byblos, in the same square form as that worn by the high-priest of Yahweh, and moreover inlaid with twelve (?) stones.[3] For this reason it is quite conceivable that the Palestinian princelets before the Israelite conquest of Canaan were equipped with such a pectoral, taken over by the Davidic ruler of Jerusalem. But the mythical significance of this garment lies above all in the fact that the Urim and Thummim, contained in the so-called *hošæn mišpāt*, correspond to the Mesopotamian Tablets of Destiny. Accordingly Primordial Man, the mythical exemplar of both the Phoenician and Israelitic ruler, was wearing the Heavenly Tablets, deciding the destinies of the world. They were fastened to his breast in a pouch in exactly the same manner as Marduk wore them in *Enūma eliš*, iv. 121–2 (cf. i. 156–7). But these tablets are in reality—as was seen long ago—nothing but the Tablets of Law, delivered by God to Moses.[4] By means of the possession of these Divine Tablets the Primordial Man in paradise in fact was—what he is called—'a sealer of the preserved (thing), full of wisdom'. Here another detail calls for notice. The Israelite king on the day of his enthronement received a copy of the Law,

---

[1] This idea lives on in the Jewish notion of the 'heavenly tablets', Enoch xciii. 2; Book of Jubilees v. 13; xvi. 9; xxxii. 21 and ultimately in the Qur'ānic *lauḥ maḥfūz*, cf. Widengren, *Muḥammad, the Apostle of God and His Ascension*, U.U.Å. 1955: 1, pp. 117 ff.; *The Ascension of the Apostle*, pp. 27 f., 36 ff.

[2] For the following cf. Widengren, *Psalm 110*, pp. 13 ff.; *Sakrales Königtum im Alten Testament und im Judentum* (Stuttgart, 1955), p. 27.

[3] Cf. Montet, *Byblos et l'Égypte* (Paris, 1929), pl. xciv.

[4] Cf. Widengren, *The Ascension of the Apostle*, pp. 22 ff.; *Psalm 110*, p. 19 n. 3 (with references).

that is these same Heavenly Tablets, given by Yahweh to Moses. This is accordingly the perfect ritual counterpart of the mythical conception we have been tracing here. The Israelite king is also as the possessor of the Tablets of Law 'full of wisdom', a proclaimer of God's revealed will. We cannot, however, pursue farther this line of thought.[1] Here we should only like to point out the fact that the legendary Mesopotamian king Enmeduranki of Sippar on the occasion of his enthronement in the temple Ebarra was given 'the tablets of the gods, the bag with the mystery of heaven and earth'.[2] For this reason we think that in this case too it has been possible to trace the myth and ritual pattern from Israel via Canaan back to Mesopotamia, even if in this case the interpretation of the Ugaritic texts does not yield any really reliable results.[3]

We have already hinted at the fact that Primordial Man is conceived of as the guardian of paradise. He is therefore also the Gardener *par excellence*. The paradise garden contained within it not only the Tree of Life but also the Water of Life, a fact inferred from the references collected by Gunkel.[4] For the ritual background of this mythical conception it is important to note that we find in Palestine a connexion between water and tree, between temple basin and sacred grove, which clearly reflects the Water of Life and Tree of Life in paradise. Once more we are carried back to Mesopotamia where this association has its special *raison d'être* in the Ea-Eridu circle.[5]

Primordial Man as the Gardener is a widespread mythic-ritual conception in the ancient Near East, especially associated

---

[1] Cf. in addition to *Psalm 110*, pp. 13 ff., and *The Ascension of the Apostle*, pp. 22 ff.; also *Sakrales Königtum*, pp. 28 ff. and above all *J.S.St.* ii (1957), pp. 1 ff.

[2] Cf. Widengren, *The Ascension of the Apostle*, pp. 7 f.

[3] Attempts to find parallels have not been lacking, cf. Widengren, *Psalm 110*, p. 13, where Gaster, *Iraq*, vi (1939), p. 136, is quoted, but cf. on the other hand *Sakrales Königtum*, pp. 91 f., where strong scepticism is expressed.

[4] Cf. Gunkel, *Genesis*, p. 36 with the following references: Ezek. xlvii. 1–12; Joel iv. 18; Zech. xiv. 8; Rev. xxii. 1 f. Cf. further Widengren, *Psalm 110*, pp. 23 f., with reference to Ps. xlvii. 5, and *Sakrales Königtum*, p. 104 (a slip there should be corrected: the text of course should be read קדש משכני עליון).

[5] Cf. Widengren, *The King and the Tree of Life*, p. 36.

with royal ideology. The king in Mesopotamia, for example, is the living representative of the mythical Gardener in paradise.[1] The Tyrian ruler, as the incarnation of Primordial Man in paradise, carries on this mythical tradition and in the Israelite combination of Primordial Man and ruler the idea is still living, the Saviour-King of future Messianic times having acquired traits which connect him with the First Man, Adam.[2] In the Ugaritic text depicting the life of the hero Krt, the high god El is called *ab adm*, 'the father of Adam (Mankind)'. Adam, Primordial Man, is accordingly the son of El.

Curiously enough, the sacral king may be looked upon symbolically not only as the Custodian of the Tree of Life, a branch of which he is carrying in his hand as his sceptre,[3] but even as this tree itself.[4] Obviously this holds true of both Syrian-Canaanite and Israelite culture. Above all would seem to be important in this case the idea of the coming Saviour-King as 'the Shoot', *ṣæmaḥ*, a notion found in Phoenician inscriptions as well as in the Old Testament. There is even an exact parallel to 'the righteous shoot' (Jer. xxiii. 5; xxxiii. 15) in Phoenician inscriptions, where the same term is found,[5] as we might have expected, for this mythical idea a wider context is to be seen also in Mesopotamia.[6] It was one of Gunkel's special merits to have devoted a great monograph, now a classic, to the investigation of Yahweh's activity as a creator.[7] He had no difficulty in

---

[1] Cf. Widengren, op. cit., pp. 9 ff.

[2] Cf. Widengren, *R.o.B.* ii (1943), pp. 71, 74. A detailed elaboration of this idea was later on given by Bentzen, *Messias-Moses Redivivus-Menschensohn* (Zürich, 1948). The English transl. *King and Messiah* (London, 1955), was not accessible to me.

[3] Cf. Widengren, *The King and the Tree of Life*, pp. 27 ff.

[4] Cf. Widengren, op. cit., pp. 49 ff.

[5] Cf. Widengren, op. cit., pp. 51 f., צמח צדיק corresponding to Phoenician צמח צדק.

[6] Cf. Widengren, op. cit., pp. 42 ff.

[7] Gunkel, *Schöpfung und Chaos*. Gunkel's methods were criticized by no less a person than Wellhausen in his *Skizzen und Vorarbeiten* (Berlin 1899), vi. 225 ff., so far as the interpretation of apocalyptic literature was concerned. But in this case, too, Gunkel on the whole saw more clearly than Wellhausen, whose criticisms were answered by Gunkel, *Zum religionsgeschichtlichen Verständnis des Neuen Testaments* (Göttingen, 1903), pp. 11 ff. Wellhausen's criticisms were quoted with approval by Bentzen, *Moses Redivivus-Messias-Menschensohn*, p. 24, evidently without knowledge

reconstructing an old Israelite myth, according to which Yahweh had conquered the Primordial Dragon—the rebellious waters of Primeval Chaos—split it asunder, and created cosmos out of chaos. For the necessary background of his reconstructive work, by means of which he had to piece together many mythical fragments and allusions in the Old Testament, Gunkel out of sheer necessity was forced to rely almost exclusively on Mesopotamian mythical poems, above all on the great Epic of Creation, *Enūma eliš.* In our days, thanks to the important new Ugaritic material, we are in a position to compare the Israelite myth with corresponding Canaanite mythical themes. Actually this may be said to be the point of contact where we are able to analyse with most reliability the historical connexions between Israel and Canaan.

The *locus classicus* for Yahweh's fight against the Dragon is found in the Psalms and was quoted by Oesterley in his essay on 'Early Hebrew Festival Rituals'.[1]

God is my King from of old,
   achieving victories in the midst of the earth.
Thou didst split in twain the Sea in thy strength,
   Thou didst break in pieces the heads of the dragons in the waters.
Thou didst smash the heads of Leviathan,
   Thou wilt give him for food, for food to the people of the desert.
Thou didst cleave fountain and flood,
   Thou didst dry up ancient rivers.

(Ps. lxxiv. 12–15)[2]

The best-known name for this redoubtable enemy of Yahweh is Leviathan, which we meet with in this passage. Another name for the Dragon is Rahab, found, for example, in another famous

---

of Gunkel's refutation. Actually what Gunkel has to say in this connexion is in our day still more relevant (against Bentzen and Mowinckel). Of modern studies on this theme we may mention Gray, *Transact. Glasgow Univ. Oriental Society*, xiv (1950–2), pp. 47 ff.
   [1] Cf. *Myth and Ritual*, p. 129 and Robinson, op. cit., p. 176 n. 3 (only a reference).
   [2] Some slight changes have been introduced in the translation given by Oesterley. The conjecture לְאֲמְלָצִי יָם in Köhler-Baumgartner, *Lexicon*, p. 715 b, 'to the sharks of the sea' apart from philological difficulties—the word being only hypothetically constructed—only yields a rather trivial meaning.

passage, Ps. lxxxix. 10–15. Here emphasis is laid on the great
deed of creation which Yahweh achieved by conquering Rahab.
A third term is Behemoth, met with, for instance, in Ps. lxviii.
30, as 'the beast of the reeds', to quote what is probably the
oldest extant passage.

The great Primordial Dragon is accompanied by other ser-
pent- or dragon-like monsters, Tanninim, the leader of which
is sometimes called Tannin, taken in the sense of a proper name.
We may refer to Ps. lxxiv. 13 f. (already quoted) and Job vii.
12. Now these accompanying monsters are often called 'the
helpers of Rahab', *ōzᵉrē Rahaḇ*:

> God doth not turn back his anger,
> the helpers of Rahab did stoop under him.
>
> (Job ix. 13)

But we also meet with more general designations such as
Tehom, 'the Deep', or the Sea, Yam, or River, Nahar.[1] We
may compare for Tehom the most famous of all creation-texts,
Gen. i. 2 (and Ps. civ. 6); for Yam and Nahar the magnificent
description of the divine epiphany in Hab. iii. (already alluded
to), where we read in verse 8:

> Is against the River(s) enflamed, oh Yahweh,
> yea, against the River(s) thy wrath,
> or against the Sea thine anger?
>
> (Hab. iii. 8)[2]

Special details call for notice. Thus we should first of all note

---

[1] A survey of the different terms is found in Gunkel, *Schöpfung und Chaos*, pp. 30
ff., 41 ff., 61 ff., 69 ff., 81 f., 91 ff., 97; *Genesis*, p. 121; Robinson, *Myth and Ritual*,
p. 176. For the terms for 'Sea' cf. above all Gunkel, *Schöpfung und Chaos*, pp. 91 ff.

[2] The Hebrew text runs:

הבנהרים חרה יהוה
אם בנהרים אפך
אם בים עברתך

I think we can translate the MT as it stands. For this reason I cannot follow Albright in his very drastic reconstruction of the text, cf. *Studies in Old Testament
Prophecy*, p. 11, though he may be quite right in reading the sg. נהרם (with enclitic
ם⁻), the plur. used in v. 9 being נהרות. On the other hand Hebrew, like other
Semitic languages, prefers variation. It should be mentioned that Albright's emen-
dations on the whole have no support in the versions. Cf. also the general trend in
Mowinckel's article in *Theologische Zeitschrift*, ix (1953), pp. 1–23.

that Leviathan has several heads, Ps. lxxiv. 14. Secondly, when conquering the Sea-Dragon or the Deep, Yahweh before the fight rebukes, *ga'ar*, his adversary. So in the following passage:

> He rebuketh the Sea and drieth it up,
> and the rivers he causeth to run dry.
>
> (Nah. i. 4)

For this motif we should also compare such passages as Ps. civ. 7; cvi. 9 and Isa. xvii. 13.[1]

Thirdly the epithets of Leviathan, *nāḥāš bārīᵃḥ 'aqallāṭōn*, Isa. xxvii. 1, deserve special mention.

As will soon be seen these three details are of primary importance.

Gunkel when writing his monograph had access only to Mesopotamian material, Phoenician texts at that time being non-existent. Now, thanks to the RS texts, we are able to check the results achieved by Gunkel.

We may, then, state that, as the result of recent comparative researches into the Hebrew myth of the Dragon-fight and the corresponding motifs in Ugaritic mythological texts, a perfect parallelism between the two has been demonstrated. It has been rightly said that we meet here with one of the most striking points of agreement between Ugarit and Israel.[2] The text III AB especially furnishes us with many details of the fight between the high god Ba'al and his opponent Prince Sea, Zabul Yam.[3] There are, however, in the other texts also some allusions to the same myth, so that we can elucidate the three points in the Hebrew myths just singled out as especially significant. Thus we find that the exact equivalent of Leviathan, here called (Lawtan >) Lotan, is described as having seven heads, *šlyṭ dšbᶜt rašm*, Anat. iii. 39. He is further called *ltn bšn brḥ/bšn 'qlṭn*,

---

[1] Cf. Gunkel, *Schöpfung und Chaos*, p. 108; Haldar, *Studies in the Book of Nahum*, U.U.Å. 1946: 7, pp. 99 ff.

[2] Cf. Baumgartner, *Th.R.*, N.F. xiii (1941), p. 162.

[3] Text published *U.H.*, no. 129+137+68; transl. *U.L.*, pp. 11–17; *A.N.E.T.*, pp. 129–31. The 'historical' interpretation tentatively proposed by Obermann, *J.A.O.S.* lxvii (1947), pp. 205 f. would hardly seem to be acceptable in the light of comparative evidence from Israel and Mesopotamia.

A i. 1–3, 27–30, and accordingly receives the same epithets as in the Old Testament.[1] The verb 'rebuke', *gʻr*, also recurs in the same myth, though not exactly in the situation we should expect. Here we still have to rely on the passage *Enūma eliš*, iv. 76 ff., where Marduk before engaging in the battle with Tiamat makes his accusations against her.[2] The 'helpers' of Rahab likewise have their only counterpart in the 'helpers' of Tiamat,[3] who by the way is the Accadian etymological counterpart of Tehom, as was seen long ago.[4]

We should also observe that Ugaritic material confirms the view that various myths, circling around the motif of the fight against the Sea, had been spread in Canaan and taken over by the Israelites. Thus, for example, the battle against the River is obviously an independent myth in both Ugaritic and Israelite mythology, though it was ultimately merged in the other myths of the fight against Primordial Ocean.

This mythical battle in the Old Testament texts is described as ending in Yahweh's victory over his enemies, followed by his creation of the world, Gen. i (and many other passages).[5] There is, moreover, another myth of creation, describing the original state of the scene of the Creator's activities as 'an uninhabited waste, untilled by man, and without rain or the vegetation which rain produces'.[6] This myth, too, has a clear Canaanite background, the fertilization of the soil being thought of as dependent upon the rains sent by Yahweh to bring fertility.[7]

---

[1] On the meaning of *brḥ* = *bārīaḥ* cf. the discussion in Albright, *Studies in Old Testament Prophecy*, p. 2 n. 9, where he argues with good reason for the meaning 'primordial'. It is usually rendered 'fleeing, gliding', so in Köhler-Baumgartner, *Lexicon*, p. 149 b.

[2] Already observed by Gunkel, *Schöpfung und Chaos*, p. 113: 'Scheltrede'.

[3] Observed by Gunkel, op. cit., p. 38; cf. *Enūma eliš*, iv. 105 ff.; as in Job ix. 13, they are not killed but subdued and fettered.

[4] *Tehōm* = **tihām*, cf. Arabic *tihāmat^un*: Accadian *ti'āmat*. One could of course invoke the fact that Prince Sea in the Ugaritic poem has his helpers, i.e. his 'pages' or 'knights' (not 'lads') who act as his messengers, but we do not know whether they assist him in battle.

[5] Cf. Ps. civ. 5–9, and the commentary given by Gunkel, *Schöpfung und Chaos*, pp. 91 ff., where related passages are quoted.

[6] Hooke, *In the Beginning* (Oxford, 1948), p. 24.

[7] Cf. Hooke, op. cit., p. 24 f.; Gunkel, *Genesis*, p. 5.

There also comes forth from the ground a river or a source of water, *ēd*, watering the whole surface of the earth, *adāmāh*. Then Yahweh formed earthly Man, *ādām*, out of earth, *adāmāh*, as dust, *'apar*. This statement with its play upon *ādām* and *adāmāh* indicates that Man was fashioned by God from the red dry particles of earth, *adāmāh* meaning the red arable soil.[1] Now this pun takes us of course back to Canaan, where we find *ādām* not only as the designation of mankind but also as the name of a deity of earth,[2] and where in the RS texts El is called *ab ādām*, as was indicated above.[3] This manner of creating mankind by fashioning a being out of the dust of earth is a well-known theme in Mesopotamian mythology[4] and we are taken back once more to Mesopotamian mythical stories, at the same time clearly discerning the specific Canaanite colour of the narrative in Genesis ii f.

While one tradition (Gen. i. 26) considers this Primordial Man the image of God, another statement (Gen. ii. 7), which we have just mentioned, says that Yahweh breathed into him His breath of life. At any rate the connexion between God and Primordial Man is very intimate and we may find here a faint trace of the original Canaanite idea according to which El was the father of Adam, Mankind. Primordial Man would then be entitled to be called the Son of God, as has been noted already. We saw that for this mythical conception a ritual association was found in so far as the king was looked upon as a living incarnation or representative of this Primordial Man. Now, certain hints in both Ugaritic and Old Testament texts would seem to indicate that the ruler as son of the godhead was given the special designation of 'firstborn', cf. Ps. lxxxix. 28, where God gives the following proclamation concerning David:

> I shall put him as the Firstborn,
> as the Highest one for the kings of earth.

---

[1] Cf. Köhler-Baumgartner, *Lexicon*, s.v. אָדָם, p. 12 a (the Ethiopic word *'adama* is misprinted), and s.v. אֲדָמָה, p. 13 a.

[2] Cf. Lidzbarski, *N.G.G.W.*, Phil.-hist. Kl. (Göttingen, 1916), pp. 90 f.

[3] Cf. above, p. 169. For Phoenician אָדָם, man, cf. Harris, op. cit., p. 74.

[4] Cf. the manner in which Aruru created Man, *A.N.E.T.*, p. 437 (the *Ludlul bēl nīmēqi* text) = Langdon, *Babylonian Wisdom* (London, 1923), p. 63, and above all the Epic of Gilgameš, 1 Col. ii. 34. In this case the material is clay, cf. Dhorme, *La Religion assyro-babylonienne*, pp. 183 f.

This proclamation assumes that it is possible to elevate a person to the position of the firstborn (cf. the story of Esau and Jacob). Actually in the Ugaritic Krt text the same institution appears in a context which shows a remarkable coincidence with Ps. lxxxix. 28.[1] What is of primary importance is the fact that Krt is depicted entirely as a Primordial King. The connexion between Primordial Man and the actual ruler for this reason cannot be doubted and therefore the mythical conception of paradise and Primeval Man has played a considerable role in royal ideology, the king being as it were the Son of God, just because he is the representative of Primordial Man.[2] Such is the case in Mesopotamia too, where the king may be styled, 'man, the son of his god'.[3]

The creation story of Genesis is enacted during seven days and this fact has been compared to the seven tablets of the Babylonian Epic of Creation as well as with the seven days of the Israelitic Festival of Booths. It has been surmised by Humbert that the Hebrew story of creation was used as a cult text or at least served 'a liturgical purpose'.[4] For this hypothesis the close resemblance between part of the creation story in Genesis and Ps. civ with its unmistakable liturgical background is a strong argument.

---

[1] Cf. Krt. iii. 13–19:

> Be most exalted, oh Krt!
> In the midst of the Rephaim of the earth,
> in the assembly of the gathering of Datan,
> I shall make the youngest of them the firstborn.

A detailed commentary cannot be given here; it may suffice to point to the legend 1 Sam. xvi, where David as the youngest of Jesse's eight sons is elevated above them. In the Krt text 'seven, yea eight' sons are announced to Krt (the number 'seven, yea eight' being significant). For the notion of the firstborn cf. Widengren, *Sakrales Königtum*, p. 54. The connexion with the Datan of Num. xvi is still enigmatic. Gordon, *Introduction to Old Testament Times* (Ventnor, N.J., 1953), p. 294, pointed out the general agreement between the Ugaritic and Old Testament passages. The Ugaritic text, however, refers to a female being.

[2] Cf. above, p. 169 n. 2, the references to the opinions of Widengren and Bentzen.

[3] Cf. Widengren, *R.o.B.* ii (1943), p. 55.

[4] Cf. Humbert, *R.H.Ph.R.* xv (1935), pp. 1–27, and Hooke, *In the Beginning*, p. 36, whence I have borrowed the expression 'a liturgical purpose'.

Loosely attached to the stories of creation and origins are other mythical fragments and allusions as, for example, the Fall of the Angels and the story of the Great Flood.

The Fall of the Angels is preserved in the Old Testament in a very fragmentary state but the Ethiopic Book of Enoch gives some supplementary details which cannot possibly be ascribed to the imagination of later generations. The passage in 1 Enoch vi. 1 ff. is also of considerable interest because it is held to belong to an Apocalypse of Noah, of which fragments are found in 1 Enoch. Especially valuable is the fact that the angels are located on Mount Hermon, thus furnishing us with a definite local background to the myth in question. Conceivably a clear indication is found here of a Sidonian or Tyrian origin of this myth which accordingly would seem to have been taken over by the Israelites from the former inhabitants of Canaan as is the case with so many other Hebrew myths. It should not be forgotten that Hermon is definitely outside Israelite territory in Palestine; at the same time it plays a role in some psalms for which a North-Israelite adaptation of Canaanite psalms may be presumed.[1] Similarly the famous myth of Hēlal ben Šaḥar and his casting down belongs to the circle of myths treating of the fall of divine beings.[2]

In his essay on 'Hebrew Myths' in *Myth and Ritual*, Professor Theodore Robinson made the following statement when dealing with some special topics of the myth and ritual pattern. It deserves quoting in full:

We turn now to another, which springs out of the Creation myth, and which seems to have exercised a very deep influence on the cultus, not only of Mesopotamia, but also of Palestine. This is the 'Tammuz' story. It suggests the annual death and renewal of nature, and is thus, in a sense, a development of the Creation myth itself. Two elements are prominent in it, that of the dying god and that of the divine marriage which assures the fertility of the earth for the ensuing year.

This subject has been closely studied in recent years, and it is

---

[1] Cf. Morgenstern, *The Mythological Background*, pp. 113 f., and in general, pp. 86 ff.

[2] Cf. Gunkel, *Schöpfung und Chaos*, pp. 132–4.

generally (though not universally) agreed that a ritual involving a dying God, a divine marriage, and a ceremonial procession, was found in Israel. It would be strange if it were not so, for some such ceremonial is almost universal among agricultural peoples, though in many instances it has lost one or more of its characteristic features.[1]

Professor Robinson then goes on to point out 'that the representation of the sacred marriage involved features which were repulsive in the extreme to the mind of the nomadic element in Israel'. He further thinks that 'some of the practices eliminated by Josiah seem to have been associated with this cult'. As to the traces left in the Old Testament of such a mythology he rightly observes that 'for the most part we have to rely for our information on occasional references whose full import is realized only in the light of comparative mythology'.[2] I should like to emphasize this methodological remark with which I fully agree but which is obviously not everywhere accepted.[3]

Professor Robinson further proceeds to enumerate the general indications of the once existing sacred marriage in the Israelite myth and ritual pattern. He refers to Ps. xviii. 11 and Isa. iv. 6, where he finds possible references to a 'booth', 'which', as he states, 'may have been originally derived from one feature of the festival'. He points out secondly the fact that it has 'been conjectured that the Song of Songs is based on a collection of hymns used in this ritual'. In this case he is, of course, alluding above all to Professor Meek's epoch-making articles. And he further mentions that 'it has, again, been plausibly suggested that much of Hosea's language and metaphor is based on this cult', referring

---

[1] Cf. *Myth and Ritual*, pp. 183 f. Cf. also Hyatt, *The Journal of Bible and Religion*, 1942, pp. 67–75, and especially p. 74, where he says: 'The myth of the dying–rising god was undoubtedly known to the Hebrews and there are many passages in which it is possible to see echoes or influences of the various elements in this myth. The following passages are offered as possibilities: (*a*) the death of the god, Hos. v. 6–7; v. 13–vi. 3; xiii. 1 ff.; (*b*) the mourning rites, Hos. vii. 14–16; 1 Kings xviii. 28; Jer. vi. 26; xvi. 6; Ezek. viii. 14; Amos viii. 10; Joel i. 8; Zech. xii. 10 f.; Judges xi. 38 ff.; (*c*) the search for the god, Hos. ii. 7 f.; x. 12; and (*d*) the resurrection of the god, Hos. vi. 2; xi. 7; xiii. 14.'

[2] Cf. *Myth and Ritual*, p. 184.

[3] Cf. Johnson, *E.T.* (1950), p. 41. I hope to be able to discuss in another connexion the questions of method in the field of Old Testament exegesis.

to the pioneering article of Professor May. Lastly he emphasizes the often overlooked fact that in the Jewish community possessing the temple at Elephantine in Egypt in the fifth century a goddess Anat was worshipped in association with Yahweh, obviously 'carried by the Jewish immigrants from Palestine into Egypt with Yahweh'.[1]

After these observations the following conclusion is offered.

From our Old Testament alone we should never have guessed that Israel associated a goddess with Yahweh, even popularly, but the conclusion is irresistible, and we are justified in assuming that she played her part in the mythology and ritual of Israel. It is difficult to avoid the conclusion that rites, similar to those found elsewhere, were observed in pre-exilic Israel, and that these included a recital or a representation of the annual marriage of Jahweh and Anath. Details are entirely lacking, and no useful purpose would be served here by endeavouring to supply them conjecturally; the bare fact is sufficient to suggest that the normal pattern was broadly followed.[2]

We might compare this statement with that given by Professor Hooke in his Schweich lectures of 1935 (published 1938). There he stresses three main points: the original significance of the booths made of greenery at the Feast of Tabernacles, the existence of a goddess Anat-Jahu in Elephantine, and 'the very frequent occurrence in the prophetic literature of the representations of the relation between Yahweh and Israel as that of husband and wife', which according to his opinion, 'bears indirect evidence of the sacred marriage as part of Hebrew ritual at an earlier period'.[3]

Comparing this conclusion with that arrived at by Robinson we observe at once the general agreement. The reference to the Song of Songs has been dropped but references to the erotic symbols in the book of Hosea are also adduced by Hooke.

In the same year as Professor Hooke published his Schweich lectures there was printed in Copenhagen a most important book which, being accessible only in Danish, has by no means received

---

[1] Cf. *Myth and Ritual*, p. 185.
[2] Ibid., pp. 185 f.
[3] Cf. Hooke, *The Origins of Early Semitic Ritual* (London, 1938), pp. 54 f.

from scholars outside Scandinavia the attention that it deserves. This is Professor Hvidberg's monograph *Weeping and Laughter*.[1]

Hvidberg takes as his *point de départ* the traces of an older ritual in Israel, but he is of course of the opinion that these ritual ceremonies presupposed certain myths with which they were linked. From the point of view of method his starting-point is in every case Ugaritic literature, which he has subjected to a careful analysis, stating that in the mythical and ritual life as expressed in these texts there were two emotional climaxes, that of laughter, associated with the celebration of the resurrection of the deity and his sacred marriage, and that of weeping, attached to the death of the deity.[2] The allusions to a ritual weeping and laughing found in the Old Testament are generally so intertwined that it is difficult to isolate them from each other. We are therefore in most cases referred to passages mentioning both jubilation and sorrow, e.g. Hos. x. 5–8.[3] The celebration of the Feast of Tabernacles according to Neh. viii. 10 included eating of the choicest food, drinking of the sweetest wine, giving of gifts, and above all 'joy of Yahweh', *hædwat̠ Jahwæh*.[4] Psalm cxxvi has also been invoked by Hvidberg as a cultic reminiscence of the mythical situation, depicted in the text I AB i. 16 f. (with its presupposed jubilation over the resurrection, belonging to a context which is unfortunately lost to us):

> Restore, Yahweh, our fate like that of the streams in Negeb.
> They that sow in tears, they reap with jubilation.
> Weeping he goeth forth, bearing the bag of seed,
>   he cometh home with jubilation, bearing his sheaves.
>
> (Ps. cxxvi. 4–6)[5]

To the references given by Hvidberg to Hosea we should add those adduced by May, who has treated such passages in the book of Hosea where possible allusions to the death and resurrection

---

[1] Hvidberg, *Graad og Latter i det Gamle Testamente* (Copenhagen, 1938).
[2] Hvidberg, op. cit., p. 7.
[3] Hvidberg, op. cit., pp. 82 ff.
[4] Cf. Hvidberg, op. cit., p. 85.
[5] Cf. Hvidberg, op. cit., p. 115.

of the godhead are to be found.[1] Other contributions in the same direction were made by Graham as far as the book of Micah is concerned.[2]

The mythical-ideological background of the symbol of marriage between Yahweh and Israel has been analysed by Nyberg in connexion with his studies on the book of Hosea. He stresses the fact that a central role in Semitic tribal culture is played by the worship of the divine ancestor, *'amm*, who is the chief deity of the tribe. In Old Testament proper names compounds with *'amm* are common (such a name as 'Ammïel, 'My Amm is El', being significant, we may add, as referring to the position held by El as the father of Man).[3] The tribe according to this ideology is looked upon as the outcome of the legitimate marriage between the god-ancestor and a wife, herself a divine being and the common mother of the whole tribe, in a way the personified tribe, the tribe as a collective entity.[4] In Hosea this idea is coupled with the notion of a covenant entered into by Yahweh, the lover, who seeks His bride and after finding her concludes a legitimate marriage with her. Israel, when deserting the worship of Yahweh, commits the sin of adultery, so often sharply rebuked by the prophets.[5]

Nyberg did not refer in clear words to the ritual background of this idea, but it goes without saying that the ritual aspect is of primary importance in this respect, because it shows us how the festival of the sacred marriage could be understood in Yahwistic circles in Israel.

Indeed, some of the epithets given to Israel, to Ephraim, to Judah, or to Sion are most significant, for in Hos. iv. 16 Israel is likened to a young cow, *pārāh*, and Ephraim to a heifer, *'æḡlāh*. We should compare here the fact that Yahweh was worshipped in northern Israel as a bull,[6] and that in Ugaritic

---

[1] Cf. May, *A.J.S.L.* xlviii (1931–2), pp. 73–98.

[2] Cf. Graham, *A.J.S.L.* xlvii (1930–1), pp. 237–58.

[3] Cf. above, p. 169.   [4] Cf. Nyberg, *U.U.Å.* 1941 : 7, 2, pp. 26 ff.

[5] Cf. Nyberg, op. cit., p. 28. On p. 30 we find the observation that Yahweh is jealous, the root קנה being used in this very meaning, with references to Gen. xxx. 1; Num. v. 14; Song of Songs, viii. 6.

[6] For Yahweh worshipped as a bull in Dan and Bethel cf. the well-known text

mythology Ba'al is the young bull, the calf (El being the old bull), while 'Anat is symbolized as the heifer or a young cow, exactly corresponding terms being used, *prt and 'glt*.[1] In Israel other female symbols too occur in the texts. Judah is called 'a virgin', and so is Sion and also Israel, Jer. xviii. 13; xxxi. 4, 21; Amos v. 2. But in the RS texts even the goddess 'Anat can be depicted also as a young woman and called 'the virgin 'Anat', *btlt 'nt*.[2]

Another designation given especially to Sion is that of 'bringer of good tidings', *meḃaśśæraet*, Isa. xl. 9, which also corresponds to the epithet given to 'Anat in Ugarit where she is the bringer of good tidings, *bśrt*.[3]

It is hardly possible to believe that these epithets, still found—at least partly—within their mythic-ritual context, were not taken over by Yahwistic circles from the ancient Canaanite cultus.

In this connexion the interpretation of the Song of Songs gains renewed importance. It has been shown that the description of the hut given there (i. 16) quite fits the ritual pattern found in Mesopotamia, where the arbour for the celebration of the sacred marriage between the king and the goddess is described in Sumerian royal liturgies.[4] The hut in the Song of Songs is just an arbour of the same kind:

> Behold, thou art fair, my beloved, yea, pleasant,
>   and our bed is green.
> The beams of our house are cedar,
>   and cypresses our rafters.

---

1 Kings xii. 28–29; further Hos. iv. 15; Exod. xxxii. 4, 8. The interpretation of Albright (and of others before him), *Archaeology and the Religion of Israel*, p. 156, that the image was thought of only as the postament of the godhead is in itself attractive, but it overlooks the words of Aaron, Exod. xxxii. 4: 'This is Thy God Israel.' How could this be said if the deity were invisible and not at all to be seen in the symbol of the bull? Cf. Hempel, *Gott und Mensch im Alten Testament*, 2nd ed. (Stuttgart, 1936), pp. 265 f.; *Z.A.W.* lvii (1939), p. 77.

[1] Cf. the passage I *AB v. 17–19.

[2] About twenty-five passages, registered by Pritchard, 'Palestinian Figurines in Relation to Certain Goddesses known through Literature', *A.O.S.*, xxiv, 1943.

[3] Cf. the passage IV AB iii. 34–35.

[4] Cf. Widengren, *Religionens värld*, p. 192; *Mesopotamian Elements*, p. 113. Gressmann, *The Expositor*, Ser. 9: 3 (1925), p. 431 was unaware of the existence of such an arbour but rightly surmised its existence.

.. That it is said of Yahweh that He possessed His 'hut', *sukk*,
Ps. lxxvi. 3 or His 'booth', *sukkāh*, Ps. xxvii. 5, in Jerusalem, has
been stressed before in this connexion by Oesterley.[1] Obviously
Yahweh at the Feast of Booths, Sukkōt, like His worshippers
had an arbour, *sukkāh*, to dwell in.[2]

In Israelite Canaan we accordingly find both the tabernacle
of greenery and the male deity living in it during the Sukkōt
festival. But can the passage in the Song of Songs i. 16 really
allude to the sacred marriage? When trying to answer this
question we must first of all bear in mind the fact that it
has already been indicated that Yahweh possessed a consort in
the goddess 'Anat. The mythical fragment in Ps. xix. 5–6 hints
at the wedding chamber, for it is said of God, El:

> For the Sun he has there set up a tent,
>   and as a bridegroom he is going forth from the canopy,
>   rejoicing as a hero to run a course.[3]

That in this passage we have to do with a mythical fragment
from 'a morning hymn, praising the glory of El in the heavens'
would seem to be generally recognized.[4] We should also note
here that El himself is not the bridegroom, but the Sun, thus a
god, inferior to El, with the original Canaanite hymn taken over
by the Israelites.[5] It is thus a younger god who in this place is
thought of as the partner in the Hieros Gamos.[6] Important
also is the fact that we meet with the wedding hut in clearly
mythical surroundings.

That the divine bride must have been such a goddess as 'Anat

---

[1] Cf. *Myth and Ritual*, p. 136 with a reference to Thackeray, *The Septuagint and Jewish Worship*, Schweich Lectures 1921, p. 69. For the passage in question cf. *Midrash Rabbah, Genesis*, transl. by H. Freedman (London, 1939), i, p. 500. Detailed discussion in Riesenfeld, *Jésus transfiguré* (Uppsala, 1947), pp. 146 ff.

[2] Beside *Myth and Ritual*, p. 136 cf. also Gressmann, op. cit., pp. 423 ff.

[3] In the text בהם in v. 5 creates some difficulty. It is generally understood as referring to השמים in v. 1. Cf. the commentaries.

[4] This characterization is borrowed from Briggs, *The Book of Psalms*, I.C.C. i. 162.

[5] For the adaptation of Canaanite psalms in general cf. Albright, *Studies in Old Testament Prophecy*, pp. 3 ff. Cf. above p. 163 n. 4.

[6] Cf. in general Engnell, *Studies in Divine Kingship*, pp. 9, 22, 54 f., 171, but also my critical remarks *R.o.B.* ii (1943), pp. 66 f.

or Aštart, a figure of much the same type, stands to reason.[1] The latter goddess was officially worshipped by Solomon in her special form as the deity of the Sidonians, 1 Kings xi. 5, a fact very often overlooked in modern discussion. In much later times there was a goddess called the Queen of Heaven(s), to whom official sacrifices were offered by kings and princes, both in Jerusalem and in other cities of Judah, Jer. xliv. 17—one more fact that discussion seemingly is inclined to pass by in silence. Now, this Queen of Heaven(s) cannot possibly be any other goddess than Aštart, who accordingly as late as *c*. 600 enjoyed official worship in the kingdom of Judah.

That the sacred marriage should bring as its fruit the birth of the Saviour-King is in accordance with the general myth and ritual pattern and for this reason we will now try to analyse some relevant passages in Old Testament literature, where we find this royal-divine birth alluded to. Here the pre-natal history of Isaac comes to the fore.[2] The traditions in question are now scattered over the chapters Gen. xvii–xviii and xxi, the literary analysis of which must be postponed to another occasion.

The birth-oracle given by God, Elohim, to Abraham, is as it were a model oracle of the birth-oracles of the Old Testament in general, for when God promises a son to Abraham He says:

> Nay, but Sarah, thy wife is bearing to thee a son,
> and thou shalt call his name Yiṣḥāq.
> I shall establish my covenant with him,
> for a covenant in eternity for his seed after him.
>
> (Gen. xvii. 19)

---

[1] Cf. Widengren, *R.o.B.* vii (1948), pp. 23 f.

[2] It has been alluded to in two short notices by Engnell, *Studies*, p. 133 n. 7, where it is referred, in connexion with Isa. vii. 14 *inter alia*, to Gen. xvii. 19 and he says: 'In reality it is conceivably the divine-royal εὐαγγέλιον-formula'; cf. also p. 175 n. 4 with a reference to Gen. xxi. 1. Obermann, 'How Daniel was blessed with a Son. An incubation scene in Ugaritic', *P.A.O.S.*, Offprint Series, No. 20 (New Haven, 1946), p. 28 n. 64, in connexion with his investigations in the Ugaritic motif found in the Aqhat text (published by Virolleaud, *La Légende phénicienne de Danel*, Paris, 1936), gave more attention to the birth of Isaac, underlining some resemblances to the RS texts. The stylistic analysis of the birth oracles owes much to Humbert's article, *AfO*. x (1935), pp. 77 ff. He did not, however, think of the same 'setting in life' as that worked out by me in my article *R.o.B.* vii (1948), pp. 28 ff. (thanks to a comparison with corresponding Egyptian oracles, quoted below).

In this oracle from the deity we meet with three stylistic elements, always recurring in this connexion:[1] (1) Communication concerning the conception. (2) Order concerning the child's name. (3) Prediction concerning the coming deeds of the child.

The continuation of the action is easily found in Gen. xviii. 1 ff., especially vv. 9–14. Here we have the description of the visit paid by God together with his two followers. When Abraham had entertained his unknown guests it is related that they asked for his wife Sarah, whereupon Abraham pointed to his tent, where she was standing. God now promised her a son, but Sarah, listening to His words 'laughed within herself', whereupon God repeated his promise, Gen. xviii. 14. The happy fulfilment does not follow until the beginning of chapter xxi, where it is said:

> And Yahweh visited Sarah, as he had said, and Yahweh did to Sarah as he had talked. And Sarah conceived and bore to Abraham a son to his old age, at the time about which God had spoken to him. And Abraham called the name of his son born unto him, whom Sarah had born unto him, Yiṣḥāq.

(Gen. xxi. 1–3)

Now it is a well-established fact that Middle Hebrew uses the verb *pāqaḏ* not only in the sense of 'visit', but also with a special meaning, namely to visit a woman in the sexual sense of the word.[2] If this special shade of meaning is assumed in this place the original meaning of the passage in question would be that the visiting deity had sexual intercourse with Sarah. It is generally recognized that Sarah is to be understood as *śārāh*, the same word as Akkadian *šarratum*, meaning queen, princess.[3] This interpretation would imply an Israelitic adaptation of an ancient Canaanite tradition of the visit of a deity to the queen, the sacred marriage, the oracle about the birth of the royal-divine child, the naming of the child, and the prophesying of its

---

[1] Cf. Widengren, op. cit., p. 31, compared with p. 29.

[2] Cf. Levy, *Neuhebräisches und Chaldäisches Wörterbuch*, s.v. פקד ; for the meaning of 'visit' in general cf. 1 Sam. xvii. 18.

[3] Nöldeke, *Im Neuen Reich*, i. 1 (1871), pp. 509 f., was of this opinion.

future great deeds, and last of all the account of the birth itself. In the light of what has been said before about the sexual meaning of the 'laughter', the root being *ṣāḥaq*, the various puns on this root in our traditions and the very name of Yiṣḥāq call for special notice.

While discussing the same topic we may briefly mention such passages as the birth-oracle given to the wife of Manoah, concerning the birth of Samson (one more example of the mythical elements in the Samson story),[1] Judges xiii. 3–5, and to Hannah, 1 Sam. i, two oracles deserving more space than can be allotted to them in this essay, in order to pass on to the famous, much discussed text Isa. vii. 14–17,[2] which must be quoted here in full because of its importance.

Therefore, the Lord himself will give to you a sign:
Behold, the young woman is pregnant and beareth a son,
   and calleth his name 'God-with-us' (Immanuel).
Curds and honey shall he eat,
   when he knoweth to reject the bad and choose the good.
For before the boy knoweth to reject the bad and choose the good,
   shall be deserted the land, of whose two kings thou art in dread.
Yahweh shall bring upon thee and upon thy people and upon the
      house of thy father
   days such as have not come since the day, when Ephraim with-
      drew from Judah.[3]

That this oracle belongs to the same category as the other birth-oracles has already been stated by Humbert.[4] The latest example of the same pattern is actually found in the birth story of the Gospels, the general Jewish background of which was

---

[1] Cf. the discussion in Burney, *The Book of Judges*, 2nd ed. (London, 1930), pp. 391 ff.

[2] All these oracles (but in Genesis only xvi. 11 ff.) were treated by Humbert, op. cit., pp. 77 ff.

[3] For a detailed exegesis of this text cf. Hammershaimb, *S.T.* iii (1951), pp. 124 ff., with whom I agree in all essentials. His interpretation has been criticized by Stamm, *V.T.* iv (1954), pp. 20 ff. I trust the impossibility of Stamm's position will be further made clear by the present exposition with its comparative material. My preliminary remarks on Isa. vii. 14–17 were presented *R.o.B.* vii (1948), p. 33.

[4] Cf. Humbert, op. cit., p. 78.

emphasized also by Gunkel. Here again we meet the constantly
recurring three points of prediction.[1]

In the Isaac-oracles we assumed a Canaanite mythical motif
and it can easily be demonstrated that the very literary category
of the oracle about the birth of the divine-royal child goes back
to a Canaanite pattern. The definite proof is furnished, as nearly
always, by Ugaritic literature, where we refer to the oracles
given to Danel and to Krt. In the Aqhat text we read the blessing
communicated by El to Danel:

> He blesses Danel, Man of Rapi,
>   strengthens the Hero, Man of Harnem:
> Danel, Man of Rapi, shall get life in (his) soul,
>   the Hero, Man of Harnem, in (his) power.
> [In his chamber] he shall surely become potent,
>   to his couch he shall ascend [and crouch].
> As he kisses his wife, [she shall conceive,]
>   as he embraces (her), she shall conceive [and become preg]nant,
>   conceive and bear [to the Man of Rap]i .
>
> (II D i. 36–43[2])

This wedding motif plays a great role in another of the
Ugaritic epics, the Krt legend. An important point in the plot
is when the king Pabil-Melek offers the hero all kinds of gifts
which are declined. Instead of that the royal princess is demanded
for wife:

> But what is not in my house mayest thou give,
>   give me the girl Hry,
> the sweetest of progeny, thy firstborn,
>   whose charm is like 'Anāt's charm,
> whose beauty like Aštart's beauty,
>   whose pupil is a fruit of lapis-lazuli,

---

[1] Cf. Gunkel, *Festgabe für A. von Harnack* (Tübingen, 1921), pp. 43–60. Humbert
ends his exposition with the oracles given to Mary in the Gospels. The Semitic background enables us to clear up a philological difficulty, cf. Widengren, op. cit., pp. 34 f.,
where the Syriac versions were adduced for this purpose. It was further shown that
a bridge has now been established between the interpretations offered by Humbert
and those of Norden in his famous work, *Die Geburt des Kindes*.

[2] Cf. Obermann, op. cit., p. 6 (text p. 4). Some slight changes have been made here
in his translation. Other translations are offered in *A.N.E.T.*, pp. 149 ff., and in
Gordon, *U.L.*, p. 86, but I do not think them as good as Obermann's.

the eyelid a bowl of precious stone,
   whom El gave in my dream,
   in my vision the Father of Man:
      that a scion be born unto Krt,
   yea, a lad unto the Servant of El.
         (I K 287–300; *Syria*, xxv (1946–8), p. 162b)[1]

Accordingly, in this text too the high god gives an oracle of blessing to the future father, not to the mother. For El proclaims to 'the Lovely One, the Servant of El', the following oracle:

The wife thou takest, o Krt,
   the wife thou takest to thy house,
   the young woman thou causest to enter thy court,
      she will bear thee seven sons,
   yea, octuple (an) eight(h)!
   She will bear thee Yṣb, the boy,
      he will suck the milk of A[ṯt]art,
      he will suckle the breasts of the virgin ['Anāt],
      he will get food [from the goddesses (?)].
            (II K 21–28; *Syria*, xxv (1946–8), p. 164a)[2]

We see, then, how the birth of the royal child may be considered an essential motif in Canaanite epics, and that the three stylistic elements, typical of the birth-oracle, also recur in the RS texts. A characteristic detail may also be pointed out. We noted in the Isaac legend the pun on the root *ṣḥq*, leading up to the explanation given of the name Yiṣḥāq, 'he laughs'. Now it is a most typical trait of El in Ugaritic mythical literature that he 'laughs', *yṣḥq*, and this detail here certainly calls for notice for it furnishes us with a *raison d'être* for the name of Isaac, Yiṣḥāq.[3] It cannot be denied that this laughter, as Hvidberg has emphasized concerning 'laughter' in general, possesses an erotic

---

[1] Transl. in all essentials in agreement with Herdner in *Syria* xxv.
[2] *Idem.*
[3] Cf. Eissfeldt, *El im ugaritischen Pantheon* (Berlin, 1951), p. 34, where the passages are registered. Ginsberg, *J.P.O.S.* xvi (1936), p. 140 n. 3, was the first to note the importance of El's 'laughter' in this connexion, saying 'I am not aware that anybody has yet pointed out that the theophorous personal name which the biblical hypocoristicon Yiṣḥaq (Isaac) presupposes could only have been inspired by this Canaanite theology.'

touch; compare, for example, the episode in the Ba'al-'Anat cycle (text 75 i. 12). So also Danel 'laughs' when a son is born unto him, 2 Aqhat ii. 10. Another detail of terminological parallelism, already several times underlined, is the fact that the young woman in Isa. vii as well as in Ugaritic texts is called *'almāh* (Hebrew) = *ġlmt* (Ugaritic). Further the term 'Servant of El' calls for notice, because it is parallel to the well-known expression 'Servant of Yahweh' in the Old Testament.[1] And lastly the role played in Old Testament literature by 'the good tidings', already alluded to, may be correctly explained from the RS texts,[2] as has often been emphasized by many scholars in this very connexion. The birth of the divine-royal son is the content of the good tidings brought to Ba'al, II AB v. 88; IV AB iii. 34 ff. and 1 Aqhat.

Behind these Canaanite birth-oracles, given to the god or to the royal-divine hero, with their literary framework of fixed phraseology, special stylistic elements, and ever-recurring ideology, we are, however, able to discern an unmistakable pattern in Egyptian royal ideology. It is now some years since attention was called to the famous scene of the temple reliefs of Deir al-Bahri with their accompanying hieroglyphic text,[3] where we read *inter alia* how Amūn-Rēʿ in the shape of the reigning Pharaoh has intercourse with the queen.[4] Afterwards he himself gives an oracle to the queen concerning the child to be borne by her.[5]

Utterance of Amūn, Lord of the Two Lands,[6] before her:
Khnemet-Amūn-Hatshepsut shall be the name of this thy daughter,
   whom I have deposited in thy body . . .
She shall exercise this excellent kingship in this whole land.

[1] Cf. Virolleaud, *La Légende phénicienne de Keret* (Paris, 1936), p. 8 n. 3. Cf. further, e.g., Mowinckel, *N.T.T.* xliii (1942), pp. 24–26.
[2] Cf. Virolleaud, *Syria* xvii (1936), p. 172 n. 1; Mowinckel, *N.T.T.* xl (1939), pp. 205–7; Engnell, op. cit., Topical Index, s.v. 'the glad tidings'.
[3] Cf. Widengren, *R.o.B.* vii (1948), pp. 28 f.
[4] Cf. Blackman, in *Myth and Ritual*, p. 36. This essay on the Egyptian myth and ritual pattern as far as I am able to judge is still the best treatment of that subject.
[5] Humbert, who is infinitely better acquainted with Egyptian literature than I, did not compare this essential moment in his article already quoted.
[6] The Two Lands are upper and lower Egypt.

My soul shall be hers, my [power][1] hers,
my authority[2] shall be hers, my crown[3] hers.
She it is that shall rule the Two Lands, leading all living (beings).
(Sethe, *Urkunden*, iv. 1, pp. 102 f.; Breasted, *A.R.E.* ii. 80, § 198)[4]

As will be seen immediately, this oracular message contains just the three points met with both in Canaanite and in Old and New Testament literature and here at last—at least for chronological if not for other reasons—we have obviously found the real pattern of the legend of the royal birth with its well-defined oracular formula. This does not at all mean that corresponding traits could not be detected in Mesopotamian texts, for there is indeed a close correspondence with the bovine symbols for god and goddess as partners in the sacred marriage.[5] But hitherto, so far as the oracular announcement of the birth of the child is concerned, it has not been possible to find so exact a parallel to Canaanite ideology and literary expression as that found in the Deir al-Bahri reliefs.

In concluding this section of our essay we should like to emphasize that the ritual background in this kind of myth has been shown to be found in the institution of sacral kingship, adding the observation that to the texts already adduced the 'royal' interpretation of the Song of Songs would supply still more important details.[6]

We have already spoken of Hvidberg's work on weeping and laughter as parts of an older Israelitic ritual, and having dealt with the laughter we may now proceed to the ritual weeping. It is not necessary to examine anew all the passages in the Old Testament so thoroughly analysed by Hvidberg, Graham, and May. Suffice it here to remind the reader of a few of the most significant texts, where the mythic-ritual colouring has not yet

---

[1] Egyptian term: *šḫm*.   [2] *Idem*: *wśś*.
[3] *Idem*: *wrrt*.
[4] Transl. according to Sethe but using Breasted's phraseology.
[5] Cf. *R.o.B.* vii (1948), pp. 26 f. with references to I *AB v. 18–22; IV AB iii. 20–22; IV AB iii. 33–38; Nikal-Košarot 7, and also to the Akkadian text published by Ebeling, *AfG.M.* xiv (1923), pp. 69 ff., transl. also by Böhl, *E.O.L.* 1–5, pp. 203 f.
[6] Cf., e.g., Widengren, *Sakrales Königtum*, pp. 78 f.; Schmökel, *Z.A.W.* lxiv (1952), pp. 148–155; Ringgren, ibid. lxv (1953), pp. 300–2.

entirely faded away. Such are the passages in Hos. x. 5; Judges xi. 30–40 (the story of Jephthah's daughter);[1] Micah i. 10;[2] Isa. xv. 1–9, xvi. 7–12, xvii. 10–11; Zech. xii. 9–14; Jer. ix. 9, l. 5; Joel i. 8.

Very significant is such a passage as Joel i. 8:

> Lament like a virgin, sackcloth-girt,
> for the husband of her youth.

In this place we meet with the terms *bᵉṯūlāh* and *baʿal nᵉʿūræhā*, both reminiscent of the RS texts.[3] But the whole book of Joel is full of such reminiscences, as has been shown in recent years.[4] What is especially striking is the fact that in Old Testament lamentation texts the lack of rain is so often alluded to, and that the withering away of plants is so often mentioned. Such is the case not only in Joel i–ii but also, for instance, in Jer. ix. 9 and Isa. xv. 6. The parallels to the RS texts have been carefully noted by Hvidberg.[5] And we should not forget the two essential words 'seeking' and 'finding', so characteristic of the Adonis cult and so often found both in Hosea and in the Song of Songs.[6]

According to the myth and ritual pattern, however, the death of the young god is characterized also by the fact that he has deserted his temple and city, which—as is said in the litanies—are conquered by the enemies and devastated, left in what has been styled a 'state of chaos'. In this case it is possible to place the ritual weeping for the god in a wider perspective. In the Old Testament psalms, especially in the so-called 'lamentations of the people', and in the whole collection called Êkā, as well as in Isa. xxiv–xxvii, we find a great many such motifs. A detailed comparison with corresponding Mesopotamian texts would sufficiently demonstrate that the same mythical motifs recur in the Old Testament texts just mentioned as in the so-called

---

[1] Goldziher, op. cit., pp. 113 f. has hinted at a mythical motif behind this story.
[2] Cf. Graham, op. cit., pp. 244 ff.   [3] Cf. Hvidberg, op. cit., pp. 122 f.
[4] Cf. Hvidberg, op. cit., pp. 120 ff.; Widengren, *S.E.Å.* x (1945), p. 76; Kapelrud, *Joel Studies, passim*.
[5] Cf. Hvidberg, op. cit., pp. 107 ff.
[6] Cf. May, op. cit., pp. 81 ff. and the Song of Songs iii. 1 ff., cf. also Haller, *Hoheslied, Hb.A.T.* i. 18 (Tübingen, 1940), p. 30.

Tammuz-liturgies.[1] We are thus able to assert that there was just such a ritual mourning in Israel as there was in Mesopotamia after the 'death' of Tammuz, and that this lamentation festival was celebrated in connexion with the Feast of Booths, after the jubilation ceremonies of the sacred marriage. The description given in Neh. viii–ix is quite illuminating in this respect, as was seen by Hvidberg.[2]

With all this we have not shown that there really was a mythical conception of Yahweh as a dying and rising deity, for it could always be argued—as indeed it has been—that this motif in the myth and ritual pattern was so foreign to Yahweh that when traces of that idea are met with in Israelite religion it is due to the fact that Ba'al in some quarters and some periods was worshipped instead of Yahweh.[3]

Against this view recent research has attempted to prove that there really existed in some Israelite circles a worship of Yahweh as a dying and rising deity, and further that passages in the Old Testament where such mythic reminiscences are found testify to a closer correspondence between Hebrew and Ugaritic phraseology and technical terms than was hitherto recognized.

Thus we do find not only the expression 'Yahweh liveth' in some pregnant passages, above all in Ps. xviii. 47 (one of the 'Canaanizing' psalms), an expression exactly corresponding to the cultic cry of jubilation in the RS texts, 'Aliyan Ba'al liveth', I AB iii. 8–9, but, moreover, the cultic exhortation, 'awake', addressed to the god in the sleep of death and directed even to Yahweh in Ps. xxxv. 23; xliv. 23; lix. 4.[4] A mythic situation, in which Yahweh is thought of as being dead, is accordingly presupposed in the cult. Actually there are many allusions to such a moment both in psalms and prophetical texts.[5] Here Ps. lxxviii.

---

[1] Such a detailed comparison is still a desideratum; for the time being cf. Widengren, *Sakrales Königtum*, pp. 63 ff., where the chief motifs are registered with references to some corresponding passages in Mesopotamian literature.

[2] Cf. Hvidberg, op. cit., pp. 85 f. Gressmann, op. cit., p. 422, was on the right track when pointing out how mourning and rejoicing succeed each other at the Feast of Booths.

[3] Cf., e.g. Pedersen's article, *A.c.O.* xviii (1939), pp. 1–14.

[4] Cf. Widengren, *S.E.Å.* (1945), pp. 76 f.; *Sakrales Königtum*, pp. 66 ff.

[5] Cf. Widengren, *R.o.B.* vii (1948), pp. 43 ff.; *Sakrales Königtum*, pp. 66 ff.

61, 65–66 occupies a place in the focus of our interest. This psalm describes the mythic situation, hinted at before, when God's wrath causes His whole people to be delivered up into the hands of its enemies, the 'state of chaos', as we styled it before.

> And he delivered up his strength to captivity,
> and his ornament into the hand of the adversary.
>
> (v. 61)

Then follows the description of the 'state of chaos', verses 62–64.

But when the visitation is at its most terrible, then the situation is suddenly completely changed.

> Adonai awaked like a sleeper,
> like a hero, overcome with wine.
> He smote his adversaries backward,
> an everlasting shame he made them.   (vv. 65–66)

We know from Mesopotamian literature these two motifs, sleep and drunkenness, as symbols of the death of Tammuz. While the 'state of chaos' is reigning on earth and above all in the holy courtyard of the temple, the god is slumbering the heavy sleep of death, a mythic-cultic situation corresponding to that found in Ps. lxxviii. 61–64. We should also note the epithet *gibbōr*, hero, given to Adonai—this very name is probably significant—because we are reminded of the same epithet, hero, in Akkadian *qarrādu*, associated with the young god, who like a hero sets out for battle, when descending into the nether world.[1] For this reason we may say with some confidence that we find in Ps. lxxviii. 65–66 a clear description of Yahweh as emerging in might from the mythic-ritual state, depicted as sleep. In this connexion it should also be carefully noted that the two Hebrew expressions used for 'to sleep' and 'to awake' exactly correspond to those used of the Tyrian Ba'al of Carmel[2] in 1 Kings xviii. 19 ff.[3]

---

[1] Cf. Widengren, *R.o.B.* vii (1948), p. 44 and *Sakrales Königtum*, p. 67.

[2] Concerning this Ba'al cf. the discussion in Albright, *Archaeology and the Religion of Israel*, pp. 156 f. with notes referring to literature, and p. 229 n. *47 with a reference to the article of R. de Vaux, *Bulletin du Musée de Beyrouth*, v (1941), pp. 7–20.

[3] In 1 Kings xviii. 27 the verbs used are יָשֵׁן and יָקַץ, in Ps. lxxviii. 65 יָשֵׁן and יָקַץ cf. Widengren, *Sakrales Königtum*, pp. 68 f. and p. 109 with n. 31.

It is only against the background of Ps. lxxviii that we are in a position to understand another mythical passage in the Psalms, where Yahweh is exhorted to arise and take vengeance on his enemies:

> Arise, oh Yahweh, in Thine anger,
>   lift Thyself up in outbursts of rage against mine adversaries,
> and awake, oh my God,
>   judgement Thou hast commanded.
> May the congregation of peoples surround Thee,
>   and Thou, above it, return to the height.
>
> (Ps. vii. 6–7)[1]

The leading themes are quite clear. First we have the awakening and arising of the deity. Secondly we meet with the idea that God is surrounded by the congregation of the peoples. Thirdly the notion that Yahweh, enthroned on this congregation, returns to the height (where as we have seen He has His throne).[2] That the first motif is found in the Ugaritic texts goes without saying. The second motif is also common there.[3] The third motif is found in RS literature when Baʿal ascends to the height in the North, where his throne has its place.[4] Furthermore, we should not forget the linguistic parallels. The Hebrew *mārōm*, height, corresponds to the Ugaritic *mrym*, just as the Hebrew *šūb*, return, appears in the same form in Ugaritic *šb*, and the peoples, *leʾummīm*, are the equivalent of Ugaritic *lʾimm*.[5] In this connexion the significance of the Hebrew verb *ʿālā*, ascend, used of Yahweh in the enthronement psalms, must be stressed, for it has its equivalent in the verb *ʿly*, which is used when it is said in the RS texts that Baʿal 'ascends' to the height in the north.[6]

The situation in the myth and ritual pattern, when the return to life of the dead god is announced by his messenger, is also

---

[1] Cf. Widengren, *R.o.B.* vii (1948), pp. 44 f. and *Sakrales Königtum*, pp. 67 f.

[2] Cf. above, p. 164.

[3] Cf. Patton, *Canaanite Parallels in the Book of Psalms* (Baltimore 1944), p. 24, where passages are registered.

[4] Cf. Patton, op. cit., p. 19.

[5] Cf. Gordon, *U.H.*, Glossary, p. 242: 1061.

[6] Cf. Gordon, op. cit., p. 256: 1485, and Gunkel–Begrich, *Einleitung in die Psalmen* (Göttingen, 1933), p. 105 (cf. Ps. xlvii. 6; lxviii. 19).

reflected in some Old Testament passages. Above all Mal. iii.
1 would seem to be important, for there it is said:[1]

> Behold I send my messenger,
> and he will prepare the way before me,
> and suddenly will come to his temple
> the Lord whom ye are seeking.

This messenger is the same figure as that found in the Mesopotamian ritual of the New Year festival. The key word of the
Malachi text is the verb 'seek', *biqqēš*, this idea being met with
repeatedly in Hosea, but also in the Song of Songs as was intimated above.[2]

With the passage in Malachi is to be compared the passage
Nah. i. 15:[3]

> Behold upon the mountains the feet of the bringer of good tidings,
>   of one proclaiming peace:
> 'Celebrate thy feasts, oh Judah,
>   fulfil thy vows!
> For not again will Belial pass through thee,
>   he will be wholly cut off.'

The return of God, announced by the bringer of good tidings,
the same root *bśr* being used as in Ugaritic mythological literature,
implies in accordance with the pattern the restoration of peace.
The 'state of chaos' is ended, destruction and war finished.
This same motif recurs in Isa. lii. 7:[4]

> How beautiful upon the mountains are the feet of the bringer of good
>   tidings,
> that proclaimeth peace, bringeth good tidings,
>   sayeth unto Sion: 'Thy God is King.'

[1] Cf. Haldar, *Associations of Cult Prophets among the Ancient Semites* (Uppsala,
1945), pp. 128 f.; Widengren, *S.E.Å.* x (1945), p. 78. We cannot enter here upon a
reply to the criticisms directed against this interpretation. The whole gist of our
exposition with its many references to various aspects of the problem must serve as a
provisional answer.   [2] Cf. above, pp. 177 f.

[3] Cf. the reference in Widengren, op. cit., p. 78 n. 32, and the detailed treatment
by Haldar, *Studies in the Book of Nahum*, U.U.Å. 1946: 7, the passages being indexed
p. 160.

[4] Cf. Haldar, *Associations of Cult Prophets*, p. 129; Widengren, *S.E.Å.* x (1945),
p. 78.

Here a new motif enters the action: the proclamation of God as King, the enthronement of Yahweh upon Sion. We should note here the striking similarity in phraseology between this passage in Isaiah and that in Nahum.[1]

That this kingship of Yahweh is a mythic trait, taken over by the Israelite population from the Canaanites and ultimately from the myth and ritual pattern of the ancient Near East has been explained with so many details in the volume *Myth and Ritual* that we may content ourselves with pointing out some special features. First of all it should be stressed that while earlier scholars (Mowinckel, Wensinck) had to find their parallels in Mesopotamia, the discoveries at Ras Shamra in this case as in so many others have furnished us with abundant material for the mythic-ritual idea of the enthronement of God. This has been shown in detail by Kapelrud.[2] The idea of God as King was so intimately bound up with the Canaanite conception of the deity that the word *mælæk*, king, could pass from an appellative to a proper name. So we meet with the Phoenician divine name Milk and the god Milkom among the Ammonites.[3] This being the case it is sometimes difficult to establish with certainty the exact meaning of the word *mælæk* in the Old Testament. Is it Yahweh as King, Ba'al as King, or the earthly king?[4] This obscurity prevails in the difficult text Isa. lvii. 9 f., where it would seem, however, that we find the god Mælæk, to whom oil and ointments are brought. Because it is said that messengers were sent far away and that Judah, here depicted as a woman, went down to Sheol, the situation described would seemingly be that the god Mælæk is to be found in Sheol. Judah, the woman, seeking her lover Mælæk in the nether world and

---

[1] Cf. the expression על ההרים רגלי מבשר Nah. i. 15 with על ההרים רגלי מבשר Isa. lii. 7, and משמיע שלום Nah. i. 15 with משמיע שלום Isa. lii. 7. We are confronted with a very fixed cultic terminology, recurring in poetic texts, cf. below, p. 201.

[2] Cf. Kapelrud, *N.T.T.* xli (1940), pp. 38 ff., esp. pp. 44–55, where the relevant Ugaritic passages are quoted.

[3] Cf. Nyberg, *Studien zum Hoseabuche*, Index, p. 139, s.v. מֶלֶךְ; U.U.Å. 1941 : 7, 2, pp. 39 f.

[4] This problem has been discussed above all by Nyberg, op. cit. It should be noted that the expression מלכנו Hos. vii. 5 has its exact parallel in Ugaritic, cf. below, p. 196.

bringing him the oil of life in order to restore him to life—so the original mythic situation is probably to be reconstructed.[1] For the prophet himself this god Mælæk is obviously a foreign deity, because he says that Judah has deserted Yahweh (v. 8), but for the Israelites worshipping him he was presumably only Yahweh, somehow merged in the Canaanite god Baʿal-Mælæk.

The idea of the kingship of Yahweh dominates the whole Israelitic pattern. '*Yahwaeh mālak*', thus runs the proclamation, as in Assyria *Aššur šar*,[2] or in Canaan *mlkn aliy[n] bʿl šptn*, II AB iv. 43–44, 'Our King is Alʾiyān Baʿal, our Judge!' In this Ugaritic proclamation formula there is a faint trace of the idea of the god as a judge, an idea that in Israel played such an immense role in the picture of Yahweh Himself, sitting on His throne, judging the nations.[3]

The idea of the kingship of Yahweh in Israel as in Canaan possesses cosmic significance. His battle with the Chaos powers, the Sea-Dragon and her helpers, and His victory over them has enabled Him to take His throne as highest ruler of the cosmos, which He has now created out of chaos. This notion is constantly recurring in the Hebrew psalms of enthronement, where we read such hymns of praise as the following:

> Yahweh is King,
> > majesty he hath put on,
> > Yahweh hath put on.
>
> Yea, the world is established
> > and doth not waver.
> Thy throne is established from of old,
> > from eternity art Thou.
>
> The streams have lifted up, oh Yahweh,
> > the streams have lifted up their voice,
> > > the streams lift up their crashing.

[1] Space does not allow a detailed treatment of the important text in question. For the whole situation cf. Ištar's descent (*A.N.E.T.*, pp. 52 ff., 106 ff.) and for the oil of Life as a revivifying anointment Maqlū vii. 37, and above, p. 166 n. 4. In Ugarit we meet with the theme of ʿAnāt's walking on the mountains and in the valleys in order to find the dead Baʿal.

[2] Cf. Müller, *Das assyrische Ritual. Teil I. Texte zum assyrischen Königsritual* (Leipzig, 1937), p. 8(9) = KAR 216 i. 29. *Aššur šar, Aššur šar!*

[3] Cf. Kapelrud, op. cit., pp. 51 f.

More than the voices of many waters,
magnificent more than the breakers of the sea,
magnificent in the height is Yahweh.

(Ps. xciii)[1]

When Yahweh has conquered his adversaries and enthroned himself on high, it implies that all the universe is in perfect harmony; *tēbēl* does not waver, as the common expression runs.[2] Yahweh has created an orderly cosmos, Ps. xcv. 4; xxiv. 2; xxxiii. 6–9. Then He can judge the peoples with justice, Ps. xcv. 10; xcviii. 9. Also another trait dominates this trend of mythical ideas, namely the notion of the fertilization of the earth by the rains which Yahweh sends. Yahweh's enthronement thus also means the fertilization of the country.[3]

Oesterley in his essay in *Myth and Ritual* stated that the mythical ideas we have treated in this section found their ritual expression in the New Year festival. 'The popular Hebrew name of this festival was, and still is, Sukkot.'[4] No doubt is possible as to the New Year character of this feast,[5] since it was celebrated 'at the going out of the year', Exod. xxiii. 16, or, as it is also said, 'at the turn of the year', Exod. xxxiv. 22. 'As the most important of all the feasts we find it spoken of as "the Feast" ', Oesterley emphasized. It is therefore rather astonishing to meet in some quarters with the contention that there was no New Year festival in pre-exilic Israel and that the existence of such a festival is only a gratuitous hypothesis, for which Mowinckel is mainly responsible.[6]

We have already pointed out the importance the Sukkot festival once possessed for the myth and ritual pattern in Israel. Reference was specially made to its intimate connexion with the sacred marriage and the rites of jubilation, its 'laughing',[7] but

[1] For the interpretation of this psalm cf. Mowinckel, *Psalmenstudien* (Kristiania (Oslo), 1922), iii. 215 f.
[2] For the interpretation of v. 3 cf. Widengren, *Sakrales Königtum*, pp. 62 f., where the passage I AB v. 1–6 in the Ugaritic poems is compared.
[3] Cf. Mowinckel, op. cit., pp. 93 f., 168–70.
[4] Cf. *Myth and Ritual*, p. 122.
[5] Cf. *Myth and Ritual*, pp. 122 f.
[6] For recent discussion cf. Johnson, *The Old Testament and Modern Study*, pp. 190 ff.
[7] Cf. above, pp. 179 f.

also with the rites of mourning as expressions of the sorrow felt by the worshippers at the death of the young god.[1] That the enthronement of the god too was connected with this festival would presumably be quite clear from the description of the final moment of the feast as given by Oesterley, how 'the great procession with Yahweh in His chariot, when it had reached its destination, halted, and Yahweh left his chariot and entered into His "tabernacle" in the temple'. A Babylonian parallel was also alluded to by Oesterley.[2] As we saw, the enthronement of Yahweh was also intimately associated with the idea of Him as the Creator of the universe, a creation involving the maintenance of its order *inter alia* by the bringing of rain and fertilization. Oesterley in this connexion referred to the fact that Rabbinic Judaism 'discerned a relationship between the Feast of Tabernacles and the Creation'.[3] And the sending of the rains was one of the mythical traits that found a corresponding expression in ritual, in both older and later times, in the water libations carried out at this festival.[4] This ritual, symbolizing the falling of the rain, possessed, however, another meaning also, associating it with the sacred marriage; for an analogy was drawn between the consummation of marriage and the fertilization of earth by means of the rains.[5]

We have found that in some passages in the books of the prophets there are unmistakable allusions to the triumphal return of the god to his city and his temple,[6] allusions obviously inspired by the mythic-ritual ideology of the New Year festival, as was shown by Mowinckel.[7] In the book of Jeremiah there are actually many allusions also to the ritual practices connected with the Sukkot festival, above all with the dances, music, and jubilation carried out at the dancing place, *māḥōl*, encircling the vineyard, where the booth, *sukkāh*, was erected.[8] We may

---

[1] Cf. above, p. 191.   [2] Cf. *Myth and Ritual*, p. 136.
[3] Cf. *Myth and Ritual*, p. 124.
[4] Cf. Widengren, *Sakrales Königtum*, p. 41 with the notes 46–48 on p. 100.
[5] Cf. Widengren, op. cit., p. 112 n. 76.
[6] Cf. above, p. 194.
[7] Cf. Mowinckel, op. cit., pp. 238 ff.
[8] Cf. Widengren, *R.o.B.* vii (1948), pp. 20 f.

now state briefly the connexion between the king and the mythical
ideas we have treated here. We have seen that the king acts in
the ritual as the representative of the god, who is dead, but rises
again, is conquered by his enemies, but is at last victorious over
them, and returns in triumph to his temple, creating cosmos,
fertilizing earth, celebrating his marriage, sitting enthroned in
his holy Tabernacle upon the mountain of the gods.[1]

It has accordingly been argued that the so-called 'misery-
descriptions' in the royal psalms of lamentation reflect the
mythical situation, when the god finds himself imprisoned in
the nether world, surrounded by wild, demonic creatures.[2] It
was likewise contended that the king in ritual form was con-
summating the sacred marriage because he was the representative
of the god, and that this position of the king is reflected in the
Song of Songs.[3] We should here add a reference to Ps. xlv, the
inclusion of which in the collection of the canonical Hebrew
psalms surely gives food for thought.[4] The triumphant return
of the god at the head of the great procession was held to be
reflected in the king's position as the 'collector of the dispersed'.[5]
The god's fertilizing of the earth would seem to find its ritual
expression in the king's water libations, which have a last echo
in the Samaritan liturgies, part of which describes the ritual
actions undertaken by the north-Israelite ruler.[6] That the
mythical enthronement of the god finds its ritual parallel not
only in the celebration of Yahweh's kingship, but also in the
coronation ceremonies of the Israelite-Jewish king would seem

---

[1] I give below in an appendix a short summary of some headlines under which the
mythical and ritual themes, recurring in prophetical literature could be summed up.
Many of these motifs have been treated by Mowinckel, op. cit., pp. 228 ff., others by
Haldar, *Studies in the Book of Nahum*, pp. 88 ff., others by myself in *Sakrales Königtum*,
pp. 65 f. as far as Lamentations are concerned, and Gray, *J.M.E.O.S.* xxv (1947–53),
treated the motif of sacrifice.

[2] Cf. Widengren, *S.E.Å.* x (1945), pp. 66–81; *R.o.B.* vii (1948), pp. 37–46. Here
attention should be called to such a typical 'Tammuz-motif' as that found in Ps.
cxxix. 1–3.

[3] Cf. Widengren, *R.o.B.* vii (1948), pp. 17–37 with references; *Sakrales Königtum*,
pp. 78 f. and the articles of Ringgren and Schmökel, cf. above, p. 189 n. 6.

[4] Cf. Widengren, *Sakrales Königtum*, p. 78.

[5] Cf. Widengren, *R.o.B.* ii (1943), pp. 70–73; *Sakrales Königtum*, pp. 57 f.

[6] Cf. Widengren, *Sakrales Königtum*, pp. 34–43.

probable.[1] All this must, however, in future be developed in detail in order to show the real importance of sacral kingship for Hebrew myths and vice versa.

Arriving at the end of our exposition we should like to touch briefly upon some problems more or less closely connected with our main theme.

First of all there is, of course, one question that immediately presents itself to our minds, viz. what after all was the *real* importance and significance of early Hebrew myths in the social and cultic life of ancient Israel? The difficulty of answering such a question is due to the fact that only *one* comparatively small portion of that Israel is allowed to speak freely in the Old Testament texts in their present form, whereas the opinion of opposing portions, surely comprising the overwhelming majority of the nation, finds expression only in scanty fragments and in partly disguised allusions or in the distorted polemics of its adversaries. This difficult situation has already been alluded to in our introductory remarks.[2]

This much can, however, be said without hesitation: there was a positive and a negative reaction in Israel towards the supposed myth and ritual pattern. This is generally recognized. On the one hand, wholehearted acceptance among the majority of the people and in all governmental and official circles in north Israel, and probably during many periods of Israelite history in Judah too; on the other hand, a rejection at least as convinced and wholehearted by the conservative elements of the people, those sections of the population who adhered to the old ideals and the old worship of Yahweh. We should, however, be careful not to identify the so-called 'reactionary prophets' with these circles, for even among the prophets of reaction we find assimilation and adaptation of the myth and ritual pattern, though everywhere transformed, spiritualized, and more or less detached from the cult.[3]

---

[1] Cf. Widengren, *Psalm 110*; H.S. i. 3, pp. 1–12; *Sakrales Königtum*, pp. 44–53. Cf. also above, pp. 174 f. on the idea of the king as the Firstborn.

[2] Cf. above, p. 158.

[3] Cf. our Appendix and our remarks above, p. 199 n. 1. Cf. also the following statement: 'The prophets did not merely react against the cult, but they

Another difficult problem is the question of how Hebrew
mythical ideas could be reconciled with the dominating Hebrew
conception of history. This is a most interesting problem
which we regret we have not space to treat in this connexion but
which will be taken up for discussion on another occasion.[1]

In the course of our exposition we also—at least indirectly—
came across a third problem. How did these older mythical ideas
survive in ancient Israel? In what form were they preserved?
Here the answer is ready to hand, as has been indirectly indicated
in our exposition. The fact that technical expressions and whole
phrases belonging to the mythical sphere recur not only in
psalms but also in prophetical literature and wisdom-literature
has been repeatedly established. We have seen that there once
existed a Canaanite epic tradition as well as cult-lyrics with epic
reminiscences and mythical allusions. When traces of such
mythical traditions are found in Hebrew literature it would seem
quite natural to assume the existence of a now lost Hebrew epic
literature of mythical content, glorifying the deeds of Yahweh,
a literature having left its heritage in the present Old Testament.
Let us remember that in the case of cult-lyrics the process of
Hebrew adaptation of Canaanite psalms has been clearly demonstrated.[2] Here the importance of north Israelite psalms should
be duly recognized. The case of epic-mythical traditions, thanks
to the researches of Cassuto, is conceivably on the verge of being
established in a satisfactory manner, for Cassuto has made it
probable that the Israelites took over and adapted parts of once-
existing Canaanite epics.[3] We must not forget in this connexion
that Gunkel discovered some poetical fragments in the more
mythical parts of Genesis. In view of these facts it becomes
increasingly probable *a priori* that, for instance, the Book of
Job, full as it is of mythical allusions, would not constitute an
exception to the general rule. For this reason it does not seem

took bodily from it many of their highest ideals and most of their significant symbolism', May, op. cit., p. 98.
  [1] In a paper read at University College, Bangor, I treated the subject 'Myth and
History in Israelite-Jewish Thought'.
  [2] Above all by such scholars as Albright, Gaster, and Ginsberg.
  [3] Cassuto, *Hā-ēlāh ʿAnat* (The Goddess Anath), Jerusalem, 1951.

very likely that the author, instead of being a link in an old-established chain of Hebrew tradition, was directly 'dependent on lost Phoenician sources of the Iron age', living 'in the cosmopolitan atmosphere of the sixth or fifth century B.C.' and 'conversant with a wide range of lost pagan north-west Semitic literature'.[1] Such a hypothesis would isolate Job from other specimens of Israelite poetry, where a related phraseology recurs. Nor does it seem very likely that these mythical ideas made their way into Israel thanks to 'a general archaeological revival'.[2] The vitality of the myth and ritual pattern is attested throughout the Old Testament itself. Religious ideas, furthermore, seldom owe their effective strength to some 'archaeological revival'.

There are in early Hebrew myths some speculative implications of far-reaching consequences, as was intimated in our introduction. In our Essay we have not entered upon a discussion of these more philosophical-theological aspects, because such a subject in itself would have required nearly all the space allotted to our treatment of Hebrew myths, the subject being extremely delicate and difficult to handle—if we want to avoid modernizing as well as archaizing tendencies of interpretation. What we have tried above all to do is to establish the position of Hebrew myths within the framework of the supposed Myth and Ritual pattern of the ancient Near East and to demonstrate the importance of the Ras Shamra finds for the understanding of these early Hebrew myths.

APPENDIX

SOME NEW YEAR FESTIVAL THEMES IN PROPHETIC LITERATURE

I. *The State of Chaos.*

   1. The victory of the enemies in city and temple.
   2. The drought and famine.

---

[1] So Albright, *Supplements to V.T.* iii (1955), p. 14.
[2] So Gaster, *Thespis. Ritual, Myth and Drama in the Ancient Near East* (New York, 1950), p. 146.

3. The god's deserting his city and temple.
4. The dispersion of the people.
5. The imprisonment.
6. The sleep of the god.
7. The drunkenness.

II. *The Return of God and People.*

1. The glad tidings brought by the messenger.
2. The awakening of god and people.
3. The return of god and people (survival of the rest).
4. The battle.
5. The defeat of Death.
6. The liberation of the people.
7. The gathering of the people.

III. *The Victory Banquet and Enthronement.*

1. The sacrifice.
2. The victory banquet.
3. The enthronement.

HEBREW CONCEPTIONS OF
KINGSHIP

by A. R. JOHNSON

IT is now well known that two different standpoints appear in
those parts of the books of Samuel which describe in so much
detail and often in so picturesque a way the origin of the
Hebrew monarchy. The earlier standpoint shows a favourable
attitude to the institution of kingship and represents it as designed
by Yahweh Himself for the well-being of the tribal confederation
which owned allegiance to Him. The later standpoint shows a
more critical attitude towards the monarchy, and there is reason
to believe that we have here a line of thought issuing in the work
of the Deuteronomic School.[1]

Both points of view have this in common, however, that they
find the immediate cause of the founding of the monarchy in the
need for unified leadership felt by the Israelite tribes in seeking
to meet the attacks of their neighbours; and, indeed, the trend
is already discernible in the stories of the local heroes whose
exploits are recorded for us in the book of Judges. Thus Saul
first came to the fore as a political leader by rallying his country-
men in an effort to free Jabesh-gilead in Transjordan from the
attacks of the Ammonites,[2] although it was obviously the constant threat from the Philistines to the west which brought
matters to a head and forced the Israelites to think in terms of
a political leader of the same type as was in evidence among the
settled peoples about them.[3] This, of course, was the figure

---

[1] Cf., for example, R. H. Pfeiffer, *Introduction to the Old Testament*, 1941, pp.
338 ff.; and, for some wise comments on the attitude of the Deuteronomist to the
kingship. particularly the Davidic dynasty, see G. von Rad, *Deuteronomium-Studien*,
E.T., 1947, pp. 52–64, *Studies in Deuteronomy*, S.B.T. ix (1953), pp. 74–91.

[2] 1 Sam. xi.

[3] Cf. 1 Sam. xiii. 2–xiv. 46 : and see further, for example, A. Alt, *Die Staatenbildung
der Israeliten in Palästina*, 1930, reprinted with slight modifications in *Kleine Schriften
zur Geschichte des Volkes Israel*, 1953, ii. 1–65; W. O. E. Oesterley and T. H. Robinson, *A History of Israel*, 1932, i. 137–238; M. Noth, *Geschichte Israels*, 1950,
pp. 121–77.

denoted by the term *melek*; and, if the term in question appears to have the primary meaning of 'counsellor',[1] the role which he fills in actual practice is clearly that which we understand by the term 'king'.

From what has already been said it is obvious that for the Hebrews an important, if not the most important, aspect of the king's function was that of being a leader in war. That is to say, primarily it was his duty to defend his people from aggressive action on the part of their neighbours; and, while some allowance should perhaps be made for the part played by personal ambition, it seems clear that it was in fulfilment of this aim that David, after finally defeating the Philistines, made his kingdom still more secure by subduing Moab,[2] Edom,[3] and the Ammonites.[4] The story thus begun with Saul and David was continued under Solomon by the building of fortifications at strategic points throughout the realm[5] and by the development of the standing army, notably in the raising and maintaining of a strong force of chariotry;[6] and, of course, it finds ready illustration in so much of what survives of the royal annals of both the northern and the southern kingdoms as preserved in the books of Kings. Indeed, as one would expect, if the king could not hold off the enemy by force of arms, he was prepared, like Jehu and Menahem in the north or like Hezekiah in the south,[7] to resort to the expedient of buying what measure of freedom he could; for, while he may have been actuated in such a case by no more than a desire to save his own skin, theoretically it was his responsibility to do whatever he could to defend his people from the aggressor or, in other words, to safeguard the liberty of the state. It is significant

---

[1] Cf., for example, M. Buber, *Königtum Gottes*, 2nd ed. rev., 1936, p. 197 (= p. 49, n. 3).

[2] Cf. 2 Sam. viii. 2. [3] Cf. 2 Sam. viii. 14.

[4] Cf. 2 Sam. x–xii. [5] Cf. 1 Kings ix. 15 ff.

[6] Cf. 1 Kings ix. 19, x. 26 ff.: and see further, for references to the important, if disputed, archaeological data from Megiddo, J. A. Montgomery and H. S. Gehman, I.C.C., 1951, loc. cit.

[7] Cf. 'Babylonian and Assyrian Historical Texts', trans. A. L. Oppenheim, in *Ancient Near Eastern Texts relating to the Old Testament*, ed. J. B. Pritchard, 1950, pp. 280 f. (Shalmaneser III and Jehu), 283 (Tiglath-pileser III and Menahem), and 287 f. (Sennacherib and Hezekiah).

that, when the local heroes of the Book of Judges are described as the 'saviours' of their people,[1] and when the armies of Israel are said to have gained the victory on the field of battle,[2] the terminology employed is that which carries with it the implication of having preserved one's freedom or liberty (EVV. 'salvation': √*yšʿ*).[3]

Another and equally important aspect of the Hebrew view of kingship is that of being responsible for the administration of justice within the realm.[4] This aspect, too, is prominent from the first and, like that of acting as leader in war, not only fills out the picture of living beneath the 'shadow' of the king[5] but is wholly in line with the theory of kingship elsewhere in the ancient Near East.[6] The story of the woman of Tekoa whom Joab sent to David to plead in parable fashion the cause of Absalom affords a clear indication of the right of appeal to the king which was enjoyed by even the humblest in the land;[7] and it may be illustrated yet again in the case of David by the way in which Absalom sought to stir up disaffection by waylaying those who were coming to Jerusalem to plead their causes before the king and deploring his father's lack of concern for the rights of his subjects.[8] The same right of appeal is also evident in the famous story of the dispute between the two alleged mothers which was told in illustration of the gift of wisdom which Solomon had received from Yahweh;[9] and it may be seen yet

[1] Judges iii. 9, 15, 31, &c.　　　　[2] e.g. Judges vii. 2; 1 Sam. xiv. 45.

[3] Cf. S. R. Driver, *Notes on the Hebrew Text and the Topography of the Books of Samuel*, 2nd ed. rev., 1913, pp. 118 f.; J. Pedersen, *Israel: its Life and Culture I-II*, 1926, pp. 330 ff.

[4] Cf. Prov. xvi. 10 and the prevalence of this thought in association with the Messianic Hope, e.g. Isa. ix. 5 f. (EVV. 6 f.); xi. 1–5, xvi. 5; Jer. xxxiii. 15: also the treatment of the subject by N. W. Porteous in his attractive essay on 'Royal Wisdom', in *Wisdom in Israel and in the Ancient Near East* (H. H. Rowley *Festschrift*), ed. M. Noth and D. W. Thomas, 1955, pp. 247–61.

[5] Cf. Judges ix. 15; Lam. iv. 20.

[6] Cf. the examples given and the authorities cited in my monograph *Sacral Kingship in Ancient Israel*, 1955, p. 4 n. 1.

[7] 2 Sam. xiv. 1–20: cf. 2 Kings viii. 1–6.

[8] 2 Sam. xv. 1–6.

[9] 1 Kings iii. 4–28. For the story itself, see now the discussion by M. Noth, 'Die Bewährung von Salomos "Göttlicher Weisheit"', in *Wisdom in Israel and in the Ancient Near East*, pp. 225–37.

again in what the Chronicler has to say about the attempt made
by Jehoshaphat to establish a judicial system on a national scale
at all the important centres throughout the country.[1] Accordingly
the years immediately preceding the institution of the monarchy
could be described by a later writer as the time when 'there was
no king in Israel: every man did that which was right in his
own eyes'.[2] All in all, therefore, it is abundantly clear that, in
theory at least, it was the king's responsibility, not only to safeguard the liberty of the state, but also to defend the rights of his
individual subjects.[3]

A third aspect of the prevailing Hebrew conception of kingship which stands out clearly in the Old Testament records is
that which centres in the king's relations, not with his subjects,
but with Yahweh as the national God; for in the last resort that
which bound together the confederation of tribes which went to
the making of the Israelite nation was a common loyalty to
Yahweh. We may recall, for example, the condemnation of
Meroz for failing to play its part in the campaign against the
Canaanite forces under Sisera, which is to be found in the Song
of Deborah, itself almost certainly contemporary with the events
it describes and, as such, one of the oldest examples of Hebrew
literature:[4]

> Curse Meroz, saith the Angel of Yahweh,
> Curse, curse the inhabitants thereof;
> Because they came not to the help of Yahweh,
> To the help of Yahweh against the mighty.

The fact that the king held office as Yahweh's agent or vice-
gerent is shown quite clearly in the rite of anointing which marked
him out as a sacral person endowed with such special responsibility
for the well-being of his people as we have already described.
Accordingly the king was not merely the Messiah or the
'Anointed'; he was the Messiah of Yahweh, i.e. the man who
in thus being anointed was shown to be specially commissioned

---

[1] 2 Chron. xix. 5–11.   [2] Judges xvii. 6, xxi. 25.
[3] Cf., too, Jer. xxii. 1 ff., 13 ff.
[4] Judges v. 23.

by Yahweh for this high office:[1] and, in view of the language which is used elsewhere in the Old Testament with regard to the pouring out of Yahweh's 'Spirit'[2] and the symbolic action which figures so prominently in the work of the prophets,[3] it seems likely that the rite in question was also held to be eloquent of the superhuman power with which this sacral individual was henceforth to be activated and by which his behaviour might be governed. The thought of such a special endowment of the 'Spirit' is certainly implied by the statement that, when David was selected for this high office,[4]

> Samuel took the horn of oil and anointed him in the midst of his brethren; and the Spirit of Yahweh burst upon David from that day forward.

It is true that this passage is commonly regarded as unhistorical;[5] but, even so, there is no reason to doubt that it reflects the traditional viewpoint with regard to the rite in question, for the obviously early stories of the exploits of the local heroes in the period immediately prior to the institution of the monarchy,[6] as indeed those which deal with David's predecessor Saul,[7] are likewise coloured by the thought of just such outbursts of Yahweh's 'Spirit'.[8] Accordingly it should be no matter for surprise

[1] i Sam. xxiv. 7, 11 (EVV. 6, 10), xxvi. 9, 11, 16, 23; 2 Sam. i. 14, 16, xix. 22 (EVV. 21); Lam. iv. 20.

[2] Cf. Isa. xliv. 3; Ezek. xxxix. 29; Joel iii. 1 f. (EVV. ii. 28 f.): also Isa. xxxii. 15; Zech. xii. 10.

[3] e.g. 1 Kings xi. 29 ff., xx. 35–43; Isa. xx; Jer. xiii. 1–11, xix. 1 ff., xxvii–xxviii, li. 59–64. Cf. 1 Kings xxii. 11 (= 2 Chron. xviii. 10); 2 Kings xiii. 14–19.

[4] i Sam. xvi. 13: cf. Isa. lxi. 1.

[5] Cf., for example, K. Budde, K.H.C., 1902, pp. 113 ff.: and see further *Sacral Kingship in Ancient Israel*, p. 13 n. 5.

[6] Cf. Judges vi. 34 ff. (Gideon), xi. 29 ff. (Jephthah), xiii. 25, xiv. 6, 19, xv. 14 (Samson).

[7] Cf. 1 Sam. x. 1, 6 ff., xi. 6 ff. (cf. xvi. 14).

[8] Cf. C. R. North, 'The Religious Aspects of Hebrew Kingship', *Z.A.W.* l (1932), p. 17, who, after rejecting the thought that in 1 Sam. xvi. 13 we have 'an accidental "throw-back" to primitive conceptions', adds: 'We are rather to think of a communication to the king, by contact with the sacred oil, of the very spirit and life of Yahweh himself. The rite was not merely symbolical, but something that we can only describe as sacramental.' Cf. what I have to say in 'Living Issues in Biblical Scholarship: Divine Kingship and the Old Testament', *E.T.* lxii (1950–1) pp. 41 f., about the conception of the king as a *potential* 'extension' of the personality of Yahweh: and see

that the king's person was regarded by the pious followers of Yahweh as sacrosanct; so that, as David himself recognized when he had Saul in his power, one should beware of stretching out one's hand against Yahweh's Messiah.[1] Indeed the very cursing of the king was something to be condemned in the same breath as the cursing of Yahweh Himself.[2]

The foregoing association of the gift of the 'Spirit' with the office of king may be seen again in the short poem known as 'The Last Words of David', in which the royal responsibility for the administration of justice again finds clear expression; and we may note in passing that no convincing argument has yet been advanced against the view that at least the body of the poem is rightly attributed to the founder of the Davidic dynasty.[3] The poem in question may be rendered as follows:

> Oracle of David, the son of Jesse,
>   And oracle of the man who was raised on high,
> The Messiah of the God of Jacob
>   And the hero of Israel's psalms.

> The Spirit of Yahweh speaketh through (*or* in) me,
>   And His utterance is upon my tongue;
> The God of Israel hath said,
>   To me the Rock of Israel hath spoken.

> A ruler of men must be righteous,
>   Ruling in the fear of God
> And like the light of morning at sunrise,
>   A cloudless morning which maketh the grass
>   Glisten from the earth after rain.

> Nay, but is not that how my house stands with God,
>   Since He hath granted me an everlasting covenant,

---

further on this whole point O. Procksch, *Theologie des Alten Testaments*, 1950, p. 120; S. Mowinckel, *Han som kommer*, 1951, pp. 50 and 54 f.; J. de Fraine, *L'Aspect religieux de la royauté israélite*, 1954, pp. 193 ff.

[1] 1 Sam. xxiv. 7, 11 (EVV. 6, 10), xxvi. 9, 11, 23; 2 Sam. i. 14, 16: cf. 2 Sam. xix. 22 (EVV. 21).

[2] 1 Kings xxi. 10, 13: cf. Exod. xxii. 27 (EVV. 28) (E); also Prov. xxiv. 21.

[3] 2 Sam. xxiii. 1–7. See further, on the question of the authenticity of the poem and the soundness of the consonantal text, *Sacral Kingship in Ancient Israel*, pp. 14 ff.

Set forth in detail with proper safeguard?
Yea, doth He not bring to growth
My complete salvation[1] and every wish?

Whereas evil must be like thistles, all running wild,
For these are not removed by hand,
But the man who cometh into touch with them
Must be complete with iron and spear-shaft,
And they must be burned with fire on the spot.

These words also serve to draw our attention to the fact that, whatever may have been the fate of kingship in the north after the disruption of the monarchy, it was regarded from the first as hereditary so far as the southern kingdom was concerned.[2] That is to say, it was recognized as a privilege and a responsibility which had been entrusted to the House of David and had been given legal sanction in the form of a covenant, carefully worded, between Yahweh as the national God and David as the founder of the dynasty. This covenant may be regarded as the correlative to that whereby the general confederation of Israel's tribes agreed at Hebron to accept David as their king;[3] and something of the continuing importance attached to this thought of a specific covenant is to be found in the statement that at the coronation of the boy king Jehoash he was invested with 'the crown and the testimony (*or* testimonies)'.[4] The Hebrew term employed in the latter connexion is the technical one in use to denote the solemn promises or pledges to which one was committed under the terms of a covenant; and it seems clear, therefore, that at his coronation the king was made to wear as a part of the insignia of office a document embodying, in principle at least, the terms of Yahweh's covenant with the House of David. If this seems a little odd, it should not do so; for we may compare the way in which the devout Jew binds upon his arm and brow at morning prayer the words of the Shema, i.e. the basic principle

---

[1] See above, p. 206 n. 3.
[2] Cf. A. Alt, 'Das Königtum in den Reichen Israel und Juda', *V.T.* i (1951), pp. 2–22, reprinted in *Kleine Schriften zur Geschichte des Volkes Israel*, ii. 116–34.
[3] 2 Sam. iii. 21, v. 1–3 : cf. 2 Kings xi. 17.
[4] 2 Kings xi. 12 : cf. 2 Chron. xxiii. 11.

of the Sinaitic covenant as defined in the Book of Deuteronomy.[1] Indeed, here again we have what appears to be an eloquent piece of symbolism, the rite itself being indicative of the responsibilities which the king was thus agreeing to bear or the obligations which he thus undertook.[2]

All these positive aspects of the king's responsibility for the well-being of his people have their counterpart in the fact that any catastrophe on a national scale could be attributed to the fact that he had overstepped the mark and offended Yahweh in some way. Thus the three years of famine which occurred in the reign of David were attributed to Saul's murderous attack upon the Gibeonites in violation of the long-standing covenant between the people of this Canaanite city and the invading Hebrews,[3] just as the census of the nation which took place under David is found to have as its consequence an outburst of plague which should serve to teach David and his subjects a lesson in humility.[4] Similarly, some 400 years later when the Hebrew monarchy was almost at an end, Jeremiah saw in the impending doom of the southern kingdom the inevitable outcome of the lawless reign of Manasseh but a few decades earlier.[5]

All this serves to show how important it was to maintain satisfactory relations, not only with neighbouring peoples and amongst one's subjects, but also with Yahweh as the guardian deity of the nation; so that it should be no matter for surprise to find that throughout the 400 years of the Davidic dynasty, from

---

[1] vi. 4 f.

[2] See further my elaboration of this point, with special reference to Ps. lxxxix and cxxxii, in *Sacral Kingship in Ancient Israel*, pp. 17 ff.

[3] 2 Sam. xxi. 1–14: cf. 1 Kings xvii. 1, xviii. 17 f. The principle which the narrator has in mind in 2 Sam. xxi. 1–14 is clear enough, even though the exact implications of his story are regarded as a matter for discussion. Cf., for example, A. Malamat, 'Doctrines of causality in Hittite and Biblical Historiography: a parallel', *V.T.* v (1955), pp. 1–11; A. S. Kapelrud, 'King and Fertility. A Discussion of II Sam. 21: 1–14', in *Interpretationes ad Vetus Testamentum pertinentes Sigmundo Mowinckel septuagenario missae*, 1955, pp. 113–22 (= *N.T.T.* lvi (1955), pp. 113–22); H. Cazelles, 'David's Monarchy and the Gibeonite Claim (II Sam. xxi, 1–14)', *P.E.Q.* (May–Oct. 1955), pp. 165–75.

[4] 2 Sam. xxiv. 10–25: cf. Gen. xx. 4, 9 (E). See further, for example, A. George, 'Fautes contre Yahweh dans les livres de Samuel', *R.B.* liii (1946), pp. 177 f.

[5] Jer. xv. 4.

the time when David brought the Ark to his new capital city of Jerusalem until that of Josiah's attempt at religious reform, the king is to be found superintending the organization of worship in all its forms.[1] Indeed we find that the king is described as himself leading his people in their worship on a number of important occasions in the national life. We may compare, for example, the way in which David escorts the Ark to its new home in his royal city; for he is described as doing so with a procession in which he obviously fills the leading cultic role, wearing a linen ephod, beginning and ending the procession with an act of sacrifice, dancing wildly before the Ark as it is borne along, and finally, when it has reached its destination, following up the concluding sacrifice by pronouncing a blessing upon the people in the name of Yahweh.[2] Moreover, this story has its parallel in that which tells how David sought to allay the aforementioned plague by offering sacrifice on the threshing-floor of Araunah the Jebusite, i.e. the spot which was ultimately to enjoy peculiar sanctity as the site of Solomon's Temple.[3] Indeed such references to the king's offering of sacrifice are by no means rare. Thus, to take one more example, it is also told of Solomon that he offered sacrifices at the great 'high place' of Gibeon;[4] and, what is more, in the account of the dedication of the Temple it is said of him, not only that he turned around and blessed the people, as his father had done before him on the memorable occasion already mentioned,[5] but also that, from his position before the

---

[1] See 2 Sam. vi (1 Chron. xiii, xv, xvi), xxiv. 18–25 (1 Chron. xxi. 18–xxii. 1); 1 Kings v. 15 (EVV. v. 1)–viii. 66 (2 Chron. i. 18 (EVV. ii. 1)–vii. 10), xv. 12–15 (2 Chron. xv. 1–18); 2 Kings xii. 5–17 (EVV. 4–16) (2 Chron. xxiv. 4–14), xviii. 4 (2 Chron. xxix. 3–xxxi. 21), xxii. 3–xxiii. 23 (2 Chron. xxxiv. 3–xxxv. 19): and the Chronicler's emphasis upon David's preparations for the building of the Temple and his organization of the musical side of its worship, 1 Chron. xxii. 2–19, xxv (cf. 1 Chron. xv. 16 ff.; 2 Chron. xxix. 25 ff.). Cf., too, 1 Kings xii. 26–32 (2 Chron. xi. 14 f.); 2 Kings x. 18–28, xvi. 10–18 (2 Chron. xxviii. 22–25).
[2] 2 Sam. vi (as compared with 1 Chron. xiii, xv, xvi).
[3] 2 Sam. xxiv. 18–25 : cf. 1 Chron. xxi. 18–xxii. 1.
[4] 1 Kings iii. 4 : cf. 2 Chron. 1. 6. See further, for example, 1 Kings iii. 15, ix. 25 (2 Chron. viii. 12 f.), x. 5 (2 Chron. ix. 4 : LXX); also the obviously tendentious story in 2 Chron. xxvi. 16–20. Cf., too, 1 Kings xii. 32–xiii. 10; 2 Kings x. 18–28, xvi. 10–18 (2 Chron. xxviii. 22–25).
[5] 1 Kings viii. 14 (2 Chron. vi. 3).

altar, he proceeded to offer prayer in intercession for both the dynasty and the nation,[1] and then, rising to his feet, again pronounced words of blessing over the assembled worshippers.[2] Further, the Chronicler, who lays such emphasis upon David's preparations for the building of the Temple and his organization of the musical side of its worship,[3] also tells how Jehoshaphat opened his campaign against the invading forces of the Ammon- ites and Moabites from Transjordan with a great act of worship leading up to a special act of prayer on the part of the king and culminating in a prophetic oracle, delivered by a member of the Temple choirs, which gave the king and his followers the desired assurance of victory.[4]

I suppose that the argument as to whether the statements in the Old Testament text require one to infer that the king him- self might perform the act of sacrifice with his own hands, or permit one to hold that the rite was always performed on his behalf by the members of an official priesthood, or even perhaps, under certain conditions, a prophetic order, will continue to be argued indefinitely;[5] but, for my own part, it seems to me that the correct conclusion to be drawn from the available evidence is that, originally at least, the king enjoyed the right of officiating at the altar in person and actually exercised this right on certain special occasions.[6] Indeed, while I am on this point, I should add that equal uncertainty exists as to whether or not one is justified in seeing the survival of royal traits in the figure of the high-priest of the post-exilic period; and here I must draw attention to the theory advanced by Dr. Julian Morgenstern with regard to the role of the king at the autumnal New Year festival, for this is probably the most elaborate example which I can give of this line of approach.[7] Dr. Morgenstern seeks to show

---

[1] 1 Kings viii. 22 ff. (2 Chron. vi. 12 ff.).
[2] 1 Kings viii. 54 ff.
[3] See above, p. 212 n. 1.
[4] 2 Chron. xx. 1–30. Cf., for further examples of the king at prayer in his role as the national leader, 2 Kings xix. 14 ff. (Isa. xxxvii. 14 ff.); 2 Chron. xiv. 8–14 (EVV. 9–15).
[5] Cf., for example, de Fraine, op. cit., pp. 320 ff.
[6] Cf., for example, North, op. cit., pp. 17 ff.; George, op. cit., pp. 172 f.
[7] See 'A Chapter in the History of the High-Priesthood', *A.J.S.L.* lv (1938),

that behind the legal and historical records of the Old Testament, notably the post-exilic regulations concerning the role of the high-priest on the Day of Atonement[1] and the Chronicler's account of the sin of Uzziah,[2] it is possible to trace a time when the altar fire in Solomon's Temple was annually extinguished in anticipation of its being rekindled with appropriate ceremony at the festival in question. On this theory the Temple was so orientated that each New Year's Day the rays of the sun, as they first shone into the Temple, served to mark the fact that the 'Glory' of Yahweh was entering the sanctuary; and the king (or, occasionally perhaps, his surrogate), acting as the chief priest of the nation, had to enter the Holy of Holies, censer in hand, and there secure, apparently at some personal risk, the flame which was necessary for the rekindling of the altar fire and the carrying out of an annual rite of expiation. The theory is worked out in a very ingenious way and, indeed, presented in quite graphic fashion; but, while I have no doubt that the symbolism of the sun played an important part at the autumnal festival in Jerusalem,[3] it seems to me that arguments of this kind, based upon the role of the high priest in the post-exilic period, are dependent upon evidence of too circumstantial and too indeterminate a nature to carry conviction save perhaps in a few small particulars.[4] Accordingly, for the purpose of this short survey, I propose to restrict myself to evidence concerning Hebrew ideas of kingship which is of a more direct kind.

Now enough has already been said to show with what justification the king could be regarded, in theory at least, as the light[5] or life[6] of his people; but it will have been observed that so far I have confined myself to the evidence afforded by the historical books of the Old Testament, and in so doing I have been following the practice which was current, say, at the beginning

pp. 1–24, 183–97, 360–77; *Amos Studies*, parts i, ii, and iii, 1941, pp. 127–60 (= *H.U.C.A.* xii–xiii (1937–8), pp. 1–34).

[1] Lev. xvi.   [2] 2 Chron. xxvi. 16–21.
[3] Cf. *Sacral Kingship in Ancient Israel*, pp. 84 f.
[4] Cf. de Fraine, op. cit., pp. 315 ff.
[5] Cf. 2 Sam. xxi. 17.
[6] Cf. Lam. iv. 20.

of this century[1] and indeed persists, remarkably enough, in the strangely superficial epilogue to the late Henri Frankfort's otherwise able study of the ideas of kingship in Egypt and Mesopotamia, which was published less than ten years ago.[2] I describe this as remarkable, because already quite early in the century the great German scholar Hermann Gunkel, who did so much to draw attention to the importance of recognizing the different types of literature to be found in the Old Testament[3] and, above all, the different types of composition to be found in the Psalter, had drawn attention to what he described as 'royal psalms' with obvious analogies in both the Egyptian and the Assyro-Babylonian royal texts. In short, as early as 1904[4] and more emphatically in 1913[5] and 1914[6] (i.e. long before the appearance of his monumental commentary on the Psalms)[7] he had indicated the advantage which the student of Hebrew religion might derive from seeing these royal psalms in what appeared to be their original and, for the most part, their cultic setting, i.e. corresponding to just such characteristic events in the life of a king as those about which we may read in the aforesaid historical books; so that they serve to reinforce the data offered there for our understanding of the Hebrew conceptions of kingship. The settings which Gunkel recognized for the psalms in question are as follows:

(a) The anniversary of the founding of the Davidic dynasty and the establishment of the sanctuary on Mount Zion, corresponding to the story which we have already noted of David's escorting the Ark to its new home in the royal city (Ps. cxxxii).

[1] Cf., for example, A. L. Williams, art. 'King (The Office of, in Israel)', in *A Dictionary of the Bible*, ed. J. Hastings, ii (1899), pp. 840–4.

[2] i.e. *Kingship and the Gods. A Study of Ancient Near Eastern Religion as the Integration of Society & Nature*, 1948, pp. 337–44.

[3] See in general, for example, 'Die israelitische Literatur', in *Die Kultur der Gegenwart*, ed. P. Hinneberg, i. 7 (1906), pp. 51–102 (2nd ed. rev., 1925), and in particular *Genesis*, H.K., 3rd ed. rev., 1910, pp. vii–lxxx.

[4] *Ausgewählte Psalmen*, 4th ed. rev., 1917.

[5] Art. 'Psalmen', in *Die Religion in Geschichte und Gegenwart*, iv (1913), cols. 1927–49, 2nd ed. rev. (1930), cols. 1609–27.

[6] 'Die Königspsalmen', *Pr.J.B.* clviii (1914), pp. 42–68.

[7] *Die Psalmen*, H.K., 1926. See also its companion volume, completed after Gunkel's death by his pupil J. Begrich, *Einleitung in die Psalmen*, 1933, pp. 140–71.

(*b*) A king's enthronement or coronation (Ps. ii, ci, and cx).

(*c*) The anniversary of such an enthronement or of some other important occasion such as the king's birthday (Ps. xxi, lxxii).

(*d*) A royal wedding (Ps. xlv).

(*e*) A public act of worship in which the king implores Yahweh's aid before leading his troops into battle, i.e. a scene like that which we have already noticed in what the Chronicler has to say about the reign of Jehoshaphat (Ps. xx, cxliv. 1–11).

(*f*) A corresponding act of worship in which the king offers thanksgiving for victory and a safe return (Ps. xviii).

This is not to claim any great originality for Gunkel's interpretation of the foregoing psalms. What was important in Gunkel's approach was the fact that psalms of this type were recognized as forming a distinct class; for, once this was done, it had as its consequence the fact that the psalms in question were no longer studied in comparative isolation but, being taken together, made it possible for one to arrive at a fuller appreciation of the more obviously religious aspects of the kingship in ancient Israel. A typical example is that which is furnished by Psalm xx. The scene is obviously laid in Solomon's Temple, and the wider setting is clearly one of impending battle. The central figure in this act of worship, which in Hebrew would be described as calling upon the Name of Yahweh,[1] is equally clearly the king, who is present in his role as leader of the national forces; and the psalm itself falls into two quite distinct parts, the first of which takes the form of a petition and shows that we have to think of its being preceded or accompanied by an act of sacrifice:[2]

> May Yahweh answer thee in a day of distress!
> May the Name of the God of Jacob be thy safeguard!
> May He send thee help from the sanctuary,
> And from Zion support thee!
> May He be mindful of all thy gifts,
> And find thy burnt-offerings acceptable!
> May He grant thee the desire of thy heart,

[1] Cf., for example, Gen. iv. 26 (J); Jer. x. 25; Zeph. iii. 9.
[2] Verses 2–6 (EVV. 1–5).

And fulfil all that thou dost plan!
May we have cause to applaud thy victory,[1]
Proving triumphant through the Name of our God!
May Yahweh fulfil all thy requests!

At this point the petition comes to an end; for the lines which follow offer an assurance that Yahweh has listened favourably to the king's appeal for help, and they are introduced so dramatically as to warrant the inference that something has intervened to justify so confident an assurance of Yahweh's readiness to help:[2]

Now I know that Yahweh hath granted victory to His Messiah!
He will answer him from His holy heaven
    With the mighty saving deeds of His Right Hand!
These invoke horses, and these invoke chariots;
    But we invoke the Name of Yahweh our God.
These are bowed down and fallen;
    But we are risen and continue as we were!
Yahweh ⌐hath¬[3] granted victory to the king,
    Answering us on the day that we call!

Such language points to the fact that Yahweh's favourable response has been expressed at the appropriate point in the service in the form of a sign, and it has been suggested that this was found in some form of divination associated with the attendant sacrifices.[4] I myself hold that a case can be made out for thinking rather of a piece of creative symbolism of the type associated with the cultic prophets;[5] but that is an argument which must be left for another occasion. Enough has been said at present to show how important it is to examine psalms of this type, if we are to arrive at anything like an adequate appreciation of the part played by the king in the worship of ancient Israel.

Of course the interpretation of these royal psalms is sometimes a much more difficult matter. The language of Psalm xx is

---

[1] See above, p. 206 n. 3.   [2] Verses 7–10 (EVV. 6–9).
[3] The reading of the M.T. ('Grant victory, O Yahweh, to the king!') appears to be due to dittography.
[4] Cf., for example, Gunkel, H.K., in loc.
[5] Cf. my monograph *The Cultic Prophet in Ancient Israel*, 1944, pp. 35 ff.

comparatively straightforward; but what is one to make of the highly coloured and sometimes obviously mythological language which is to be found elsewhere in these psalms? Let us take Psalm ii, for example, which many students of the Old Testament, following Gunkel and those who thought like him, now commonly regard, not as some prophetic anticipation of the coming Messiah (save, perhaps, in a secondary or 'typical' sense), but as, in origin at least, a poem composed for the occasion of a king's enthronement. It runs somewhat as follows:

> Why did the nations become insurgent,
>> And the peoples fall to useless plotting?
> The kings of the earth took up their stand,
>> The rulers conferred together,
>>> Against Yahweh and against His Messiah.
> 'Let us snap their bonds asunder,
>> And let us fling their cords off from us.'
> He who is throned in heaven doth laugh;
>> The Lord maketh mock of them.
> Then He doth speak to them in His anger,
>> And in His wrath He doth dismay them.
> 'But I, as you see, have set up My king
>> Upon Zion, My sacred mountain.'
>
> Let me tell of Yahweh's decree!
>> He hath said to me, 'Thou art My Son;
>>> This day have I begotten thee.
> Ask of Me, and I will make
>> The nations thine inheritance,
>>> The ends of the earth thy possession.
> Thou shalt crush them with a rod of iron;
>> Thou shalt smash them like a potter's vessel.'
> Now, therefore, ye kings, show prudence;
>> Take warning, ye rulers of earth.
> Serve Yahweh with fear;
>> With trembling kiss 'His Feet';[1]
> Lest He be angry, and ye vanish away,
>> For His anger is quickly kindled.
>
> Happy all those who seek refuge in Him!

[1] Cf. A. Bertholet, *Z.A.W.* xxviii (1908), pp. 58 f., 193.

Here the obvious question is the degree to which the theory that this is an accession psalm requires one to take seriously (*a*) the initial implication that the change in the succession to the throne has been the signal for revolt amongst the subject nations in an empire of world-wide proportions, and (*b*) the claim made by the king that, on being raised to the throne, he has become the adopted 'Son' of Yahweh.[1] The answer given by Gunkel in the light of his study of the analogous royal texts from the Egyptian and Assyro-Babylonian fields was that we have here simply an example of the court style (*Hofstil*) characteristic of the ancient Near East, and that such language must not be taken at its face value but must be regarded as no more than poetic fiction. Gunkel's views in this respect were taken up enthusiastically and developed still further by such representative German scholars as Hugo Gressmann[2] and Lorenz Dürr;[3] and, as I hope I have sufficiently indicated, it marks an important stage in the attempt which students of the Old Testament have been making to evaluate this further evidence for the part played by the king in the worship of ancient Israel.

Meantime, however, Gunkel's emphasis on the need to recognize royal psalms as a quite distinct type had been taken up enthusiastically by the Norwegian scholar Sigmund Mowinckel who, in a short but very attractive little study published in 1916,[4] sought to extend the number from a mere ten or so to twenty-two or twenty-four. In one important respect, however, Mowinckel's exposition was markedly different from that of Gunkel; and, significantly enough, this was due to the fact that, under the influence of the Danish anthropologist Vilhelm Grønbech, Mowinckel claimed to find valuable comparative data, not merely in the field of archaeological discovery as represented by the royal texts from Egypt and Mesopotamia, but also in the data furnished by our growing knowledge of the

---

[1] Cf. 2 Sam. vii. 14; Ps. lxxxix. 27 f. (EVV. 26 f.).
[2] e.g. 'Ursprung der israelitisch-jüdischen Eschatologie', *F.R.L.A.N.T.* vi (1905), pp. 250 ff.; 'Der Messias', *F.R.L.A.N.T.* xliii (1929), pp. 1–63.
[3] e.g. *Ursprung und Ausbau der israelitisch-jüdischen Heilands-erwartung*, 1925, pp. 74 ff.; *Psalm 110 im Lichte der neueren altorientalischen Forschung*, 1929.
[4] *Kongesalmerne i Det gamle Testamente*.

forms of thought and behaviour characteristic of the so-called
'primitive' societies of our own day.[1] As a result Mowinckel
became convinced that such exaggerated language as we have
been noting (e.g. the claim to world sovereignty and the
thought of the king as the 'Son' of Yahweh) must be taken
quite seriously as marking an important element in the faith and
worship of ancient Israel. That is to say, what we have here is
not poetic fiction (or, if you like, polite fiction) but cultic reality;
and such seemingly exaggerated language, although it might not
be true, say, for the historian, was real enough for the worship-
per. In short, Mowinckel claimed, we have in these royal psalms
evidence for the existence in Israel of a form of divine kingship;
and, he affirmed, this appears quite explicitly in Psalm xlv, which
was obviously composed in celebration of a royal wedding, for
there the king appears to be told in language which from
Mowinckel's point of view is no mere lip-service, 'Thy throne,
O god, is for ever and ever.'[2]

This point of view found expression again in Mowinckel's
now famous series of studies in the Psalter, published in 1922–4;[3]
and here a place was found for the king in the ritual of the
autumnal festival in Jerusalem, as Mowinckel sought to reconstruct it on the basis of the two types of comparative material
to which I have already referred, particularly that which was
afforded by the Babylonian *akitu* festival and the partially similar
ritual of the Osiris–Horus complex.[4] Beginning with Ps. xlvii,

---

[1] In the preface to the work in question Mowinckel makes special reference to a series of lectures given by Grønbech at a vacation course for clergy during the summer of 1916 under the title 'Sakrament og mystik i de primitive religioner'. Cf. Grønbech's article 'Primitiv Religion', in *Illustreret Religionshistorie*, ed. J. Pedersen, 1948, pp. 11–74. Perhaps I should add in this connexion that, while I am quite certain that students of the Old Testament have something to learn from modern anthropological study, I find little that is convincing in the use made of such comparative data by R. Patai, 'Hebrew Installation Rites', *H.U.C.A.* xx (1947), pp. 143–225.

[2] Verse 7 (EVV. 6). Op. cit., pp. 28 f.

[3] *Psalmenstudien I–VI* (Videnskapsselskapets Skrifter II. Hist.-Filos. Klasse, 1921, No. 4; 1921, No. 6; 1922, No. 1; 1922, No. 2; 1923, No. 3; 1924, No. 1).

[4] See especially *Psalmenstudien II. Das Thronbesteigungsfest Jahwäs und der Ursprung der Eschatologie*, 1922; but note also the preliminary study, 'Tronstignings-salmerne og Jahves tronstigningsfest', *N.T.T.* xviii (1917), pp. 13–79. Cf., too, Mowinckel's restatement of this theory in 'Le Décalogue', *E.H.P.R.* xvi (1927), esp. pp. 121 ff.

xciii, and xcv–c, as a group of hymns which celebrate the Kingship of Yahweh, Mowinckel rejected the earlier attempts to interpret these psalms against an historical background or in purely eschatological terms, and, again arguing for cultic reality rather than poetic fiction, sought to show that they, and indeed a grand total of more than forty psalms, had been composed for use at the autumnal festival which we know as the Feast of Tabernacles.[1] This festival (on Mowinckel's theory) bore the character of a New Year celebration;[2] and, as such, it marked the recurrent point in the circling years when Yahweh dramatically repeated His original triumph over the primeval ocean or chaos of waters, reasserted His Kingship over the gods,[3] and created the world anew. This ritually enacted victory, which also meant Yahweh's triumph over the kings and nations of the earth (regarded, like the gods and indeed like the Egyptians at the time of the Exodus, as the allies of the primeval chaos), was followed by a procession in which the Ark, as the symbol of Yahweh's presence, was borne in triumph to the Temple; and there Yahweh was acclaimed as the proven, universal King, who was now in a position to execute judgement on the defeated gods and nations of the earth. In this way, having vindicated the faith of His followers and seen to it that, as being a new creation, everything was 'all right' ($\sqrt{sdk}$) with them once again, Yahweh showed

---

[1] i.e. in addition to those already mentioned, Ps. viii, xv, xxiv, xxix, xxxiii, xlvi, xlviii, l, lxv, lxvi. 1–12, lxvii, lxxv, lxxvi, lxxxi, lxxxii, lxxxiv, lxxxv, lxxxvii, cxiv, cxviii, cxx–cxxxiv, cxlix; also Exod. xv. 1–18.

[2] This point needs to be stressed, because Mowinckel's choice of a title for the monograph under discussion has proved somewhat unfortunate. The fact that he writes about 'The Enthronement Festival of Yahweh' has made it possible for his theory to be dismissed far too summarily on the ground that the Old Testament records offer nothing to support the view that such a festival ever existed. It should be recognized, however, that Mowinckel is dealing throughout with but one aspect of the autumnal festival which is familiar to us all as the Feast of Tabernacles. See, for example, Mowinckel's own comments in *Psalmenstudien III. Kultprophetie und prophetische Psalmen*, 1923, p. 111, and *Religion und Kultus*, 1953, pp. 76 and 148 (n. 222).

[3] Mowinckel insists that, on the analogy of the language used in connexion with the accession to the throne of an earthly king, the recurrent expression *yahweh mālak* must be rendered as 'Yahweh *has become* King'. Cf. Ps. xciii. 1, xcvi. 10, xcvii. 1, xcix. 1; also xlvii. 9 (EVV. 8). See, however, *Sacral Kingship in Ancient Israel* p. 57 n. 2.

that He was prepared to restore their fortunes in the year that
lay ahead and, in particular, to bestow upon His people the gift
of rain and all the blessings of fertility. Accordingly He renewed
His covenant with them and (what is particularly important for
us to note) with the House of David as represented by the
reigning king, who was the governing factor in maintaining
right relations between Yahweh and His people and, as such,
could be described by Mowinckel as 'an incarnation of the
national god' or 'the channel through which the divine blessing
flows into the people'.[1]

Several other important points emerge from Mowinckel's
argument. The first is the quite revolutionary view that the
psalms which celebrate the Kingship of Yahweh, notably Ps.
xlvii, xciii, and xcv–xcix, far from being dependent upon Isa.
xl–lv, are pre-exilic in origin and have themselves contributed
materially to the formulation of what Deutero-Isaiah had to
say. A second point which needs to be mentioned is Mowinckel's
argument that the story of the removal of the Ark to the City
of David, which is given in 2 Sam. vi (cf. 1 Chron. xv–xvi),
and that of the transfer of the Ark to its final home in Solomon's
Temple, which occurs in 1 Kings viii (cf. 2 Chron. v–vii), are
both based on what was for the authors the familiar procedure
at this annual festival. A third point which merits attention
is the way in which, on Mowinckel's theory, the associated
mythology was given an historical application, as when Yahweh's
deliverance of the Hebrews from the Egyptians at the time of the
Exodus and their safe passage of the Red Sea were interpreted in
terms of Yahweh's triumph over Rahab (i.e. the chaos monster),
or when Deutero-Isaiah forecast the Return from Babylon in
terms of a second Exodus and with the thought of Yahweh's universal Kingship as his leading motif.[2] Finally, the last important

---

[1] *Psalmenstudien II*, p. 301.

[2] For the use of the term 'Rahab' with reference to Egypt, see (a) Isa. xxx. 7;
Ps. lxxxvii. 4: (b) Isa. li. 9 f. Cf., too, *Le Décalogue* (as cited above, p. 220 n. 4), in
which Mowinckel seeks to prove that behind the J and E narratives of the events at
Sinai we should see the influence of the autumnal festival at Jerusalem in its aspect
as the enthronement festival of Yahweh and the occasion for the annual renewal of
the covenant between Yahweh and His chosen people. See also A. Bentzen, 'The

point which emerges from Mowinckel's argument is the conclusion that Israel's eschatological hopes came into being as
an outcome of the bitter disillusionment wrought by the passing
years. That is to say, through recurrent disappointment the
forward look characteristic of this festival, which was originally
restricted to the ensuing cycle of twelve months, was extended
in such a way as to provide for the possible realization of these
unfulfilled hopes in a more distant future.

Although there is much in Mowinckel's thesis and its presentation which must be regarded as unsound, there can be no
reasonable doubt that a great part of what he had to say will
prove to be of lasting value.[1] It marks an important and, as
events have proved, a successful attempt to arrive at a more
balanced appraisal of the records than that which has been
characteristic of so much critical study of the Old Testament;
for the emphasis on the value and importance of the canonical
prophets, which was a distinguishing feature of the so-called
Wellhausen School, had obviously been reached without paying
due regard to Israel's forms of worship and with a corresponding
failure to appreciate the significance of its associated ritual and
mythology. Nevertheless, in view of his emphasis upon the role
of the king in connexion with this festival, it is somewhat remarkable that he made so little use of the royal psalms in the
development of his theory, clinging for the most part to the
thought of a setting for these psalms in some distinctive historical
event rather than that which he elsewhere describes as cultic
reality.[2] In fact, he practically confined himself in this respect to
Psalm cxxxii, which, as we have seen, Gunkel had already linked
with the founding of the Davidic dynasty and the establishment

Cultic Use of the Story of the Ark in Samuel', *J.B.L.* lxvii (1948), pp. 37–53, and
J. R. Porter, 'The Interpretation of 2 Samuel vi and Psalm cxxxii', *J.T.S.* n.s., v
(1954), pp. 161–73, where the principle in question is used as a means of clarifying
the connexion between Psalm cxxxii and the story of the Ark in the books of Samuel.

[1] See my remarks in *The Old Testament and Modern Study*, ed. H. H. Rowley,
1951, pp. 191–5.

[2] This is the more strange in view of Mowinckel's comment on the psalms which
celebrate the Kingship of Yahweh: 'Daß die zeitgeschichtliche Deutung verfehlt
ist, geht erstens aus dem völligen Mangel an konkreten geschichtlichen Hindeutungen
und Reminiszenzen hervor.' (*Psalmenstudien II*, p. 12).

of the royal sanctuary on Mount Zion.[1] However, this somewhat strange omission was speedily recognized by Hans Schmidt,
who, accepting Mowinckel's theory in principle, restated it in
1927 along somewhat broader lines and with more attention to
the part which appeared to have been played by the king.[2]
Schmidt's treatment of the subject is too sketchy for one to
obtain anything like a clear picture of the festival as he envisaged
it;[3] but it is noteworthy for the fact that he thought of Ps. ii,
xx, xxi, lxxxix. 2–19 (EVV. 1–18),[4] cx, cxxxii, and the so-
called prayer of Hannah in 1 Sam. ii. 1–10 as being indicative
of the fact that the enthronement of the earthly king was repeated annually at this time in association with the corresponding
enthronement of Yahweh.[5]

In 1932 the general situation with regard to the religious
aspects of Hebrew kingship was reviewed to date by Professor
C. R. North in a valuable article, in which, as I think, he rightly
accused Mowinckel of 'arguing to particular conclusions from
a very debatable major premise'.[6] That is to say, in North's
opinion Mowinckel commits a basic error of method in that 'he
interprets O.T. religion as a whole by working inwards from
the wide circle of a primitive and general Semitic *Umwelt*,

---

[1] See *Psalmenstudien II*, pp. 112 ff., 298 ff. Note, however, that Mowinckel also
drew attention to the prayer for the king in Ps. lxxxiv as well as Ps. cxxxii, and even
entertained the idea that Ps. lxxii and ci may have been connected with this autumnal
festival. Op. cit., pp. 178 and 327 ff. Further, in *Psalmenstudien III*, p. 113, he suggested that the king, as being the representative of the people, may have been the
speaker in the case of Ps. cxviii, if this is to be regarded as pre-exilic (but see *Psalmenstudien II*, pp. 92 f., 120 ff., 192), and Ps. cxx, cxxi, cxxx, and cxxxi.

[2] *Die Thronfahrt Jahves am Fest der Jahreswende im alten Israel*.

[3] A comparison of this monograph with what Schmidt has to say on the same
subject in *Die Psalmen*, H.A.T., 1934, suggests that, while he regarded many other
psalms as being connected in one way or another with the autumnal festival, the
following are those which finally came to be linked in his mind with that part of the
festival which dealt with the actual enthronement of Yahweh (cf. p. 221 n. 2):
Ps. xxiv. 7–10, xxix, xlvi, xlvii, xlviii, lxviii, lxxvi, lxxxii, lxxxvii, xciii, xcvi, xcvii,
xcviii, xcix, cxiv, cxlv, and cxlix.

[4] Strictly vv. 2–3, 6–19 (EVV. 1–2, 5–18).

[5] In *Die Psalmen* Schmidt added Ps. xviii. 32–51 (EVV. 31–50), lxxii, lxxxiv,
lxxxix. 20–52 (EVV. 19–51), ci and cxliv to the psalms of this type.

[6] 'The Religious Aspects of Hebrew Kingship', *Z.A.W.* l (1932) (as cited above,
p. 208 n. 8), p. 35.

instead of outwards from the centre of the prophetic consciousness.[1] While I am not very happy about North's reference to 'the
prophetic consciousness', for this is an expression which seems
to me to stand in need of definition, the point of his criticism is
clear enough, and, I am bound to say, seems to me to be perfectly sound. Further, one outstanding contribution which North
makes in this article is the view which he advances, following the
lead of Professor G. R. Driver,[2] in connexion with the supposed
obvious reference to divine kingship in Psalm xlv. 7 (EVV. 6),
'Thy throne, O god, is for ever and ever.' As North points out,[3]
on the analogy of such an idiomatic expression as that of Cant. i.
15 and iv. 1, 'Thine eyes are doves', which must be rendered
more freely as 'Thine eyes are like doves' eyes', the Hebrew of
the passage in question need mean no more than 'Thy throne is
like God's throne for ever and ever' or 'Thy throne is everlasting
like that of God.'

In this same year, however, Professor S. H. Hooke and the
team which he had gathered about him delivered the now
famous series of lectures which were ultimately published under
the general title *Myth and Ritual*[4] and so gave currency to the
idea of a 'Myth and Ritual School'. I need not dwell on the fact
that in these lectures another attempt was made, along much the
same lines as those of Mowinckel, to arrive at a more balanced
appraisal of the Hebrew scriptures than that which was characteristic of the dominant school of literary criticism; in short,
that an attempt was made to study the ritual and mythology of
ancient Israel from the standpoint of what Hooke regarded as a
culture pattern characteristic of the ancient Near East, in which
the ritual and mythology associated with the figure of Marduk
(or Bel) at the Babylonian *akitu* festival and the partially analogous features of the corresponding Osiris–Horus complex in the
worship of ancient Egypt were all thought to share, a governing
factor being the importance attached to the king in what was at

[1] Loc. cit.
[2] Cf. *The Psalmists*, ed. D. C. Simpson, 1926, p. 124.
[3] Op. cit., pp. 29 f.
[4] *Myth and Ritual. Essays on the Myth and Ritual of the Hebrews in relat on to the Culture Pattern of the Ancient East*, ed. S. H. Hooke, 1933.

basis an elaborate effort to promote the well-being of the community. Nevertheless, at the risk of repeating what has probably been said more than once before in the course of this book,
I must remind you of Hooke's fundamental theory; i.e. that, if
allowance be made for the possible adaptation, disintegration, or
degradation of a basic pattern, one may think in terms of an
annual festival which, whether it was held in the spring or the
autumn, bore the character of a New Year festival and originally
took the following form:[1]

(*a*) The dramatic representation of the death and resurrection of the
god.
(*b*) The recitation or symbolic representation of the myth of creation.
(*c*) The ritual combat, in which the triumph of the god over his
enemies was depicted.
(*d*) The sacred marriage.
(*e*) The triumphal procession, in which the king played the part of
the god, followed by a train of lesser gods or visiting deities.

As it happens, the traces of this hypothetical myth and ritual
pattern were found to be very slight and indeed quite fragmentary
so far as ancient Israel was concerned. Indeed the only evidence
adduced which went beyond that already offered by Sigmund
Mowinckel and Hans Schmidt for the celebration of Yahweh's
Kingship over the gods and His power in creation, the enactment
of a ritual combat in which He gained the victory over His
enemies, and the holding of a procession in which He returned
in triumph to His sanctuary on Mount Zion, was of a somewhat
tenuous kind. In fact the only additional matter which could be
regarded as having anything like a direct bearing on this supposed
myth and ritual pattern was that which had to do with the theory
of the sacred marriage. That is to say, there is the evidence
afforded by contemporary Aramaic papyri for the association of
the goddess Anath with Yahweh in the worship of the Jewish
colony at Elephantine in the fifth century B.C.;[2] and in the
second place there are the regulations for the construction of the
booths which are the distinguishing feature of the so-called
'Feast of Tabernacles' as described in the Code of Holiness; for,

[1] Op. cit., p. 8.   [2] Op. cit., pp. 140 and 185.

it is claimed, the association of these booths with the period of the Wandering is simply an adaptation of what was originally the bridal chamber connected with the sacred marriage and its reinterpretation in terms of the historical traditions of the Hebrews.[1] For the rest, the evidence advanced in support of the claim that Yahweh was thought of as a dying and rising god was of a much more circumstantial kind, and was practically confined to the mourning customs presupposed by such passages as Judges xxi. 19–21 and Hos. vi. 3, which were held to offer traces of what was once the annual wailing for the death of Yahweh.[2] On this basis Professor T. H. Robinson, in the final lecture of the series, offered the following statement as a conjectural reconstruction of the supposed myth and ritual pattern in the form in which it may have existed in ancient Israel during the pre-exilic period.[3]

It necessarily began with the removal of Jahweh and Anath from their home in the Temple, and with the occupation of a sacred hut in the neighbourhood of the sanctuary, probably a vineyard. Then began the story of Creation, opening with the great contest of Jahweh against the powers of Chaos. This probably took different forms in different sanctuaries, but the issue was everywhere the victory of Jahweh. The divine marriage followed, consummated in the sacred hut, and this was succeeded by the death of Jahweh. After a period of lamentation He was restored to life, and, with His consort, was led to His home in the Temple, there to reign until the changes of the year brought back again the festal season.

As I have already said, the actual evidence offered in support of this theory was throughout very slight and indeed quite fragmentary; and, if I may say so, it has always seemed to me quite remarkable that in the examination of Hooke's theory, as in Mowinckel's own treatment of the autumnal festival, so little consideration was given to the royal psalms with their rich mythological colouring and the indications which they give of the part played by the king in the ritual of the cultus.[4]

I suppose that I have always found this remarkable for the

---

[1] Op. cit., pp. 12 and 139 f.   [2] Op. cit., pp. 186–8.   [3] Op. cit., pp. 188 f.
[4] Cf. the passing reference to Hans Schmidt's theory, op. cit., p. 126.

simple reason that just at that time I was studying the Psalter in connexion with a piece of research into Greek and Israelite ideas of a life after death, and in so doing found myself forced into a partial acceptance of Mowinckel's views concerning the dramatic aspect of the autumnal festival, but with a greater emphasis upon the role of the king, through reading the discussion of √*hyh* in what was for me the revolutionary work of Wolf Wilhelm Graf Baudissin on the Adonis–Esmun–Tammuz relationship and its possible bearing on the conception of Yahweh as a (or the) 'living God'.[1] Linking Ps. ii, xviii, lxxxix, cx, cxviii, and cxxxii, as royal psalms, with several of the psalms which celebrate the Kingship of Yahweh, I advanced the thesis that the autumnal festival, in the modified form of Mowinckel's theory which I was prepared to accept, had its roots in the pre-Davidic worship of '*ēl* '*elyôn* (R.V. 'God Most High'), and that in the ritual drama the kings or nations of the earth, as representing the forces of darkness and death in opposition to those of light and life, united in an attempt to destroy Yahweh's chosen people by attacking them and destroying the Davidic king upon whom their 'life' (*ḥayyîm*), i.e. their well-being and indeed their survival, was held to be dependent. At first the king, who could be referred to as the Son, the Servant, and the Messiah of Yahweh, suffered humiliation and defeat, and as a result was nearly swallowed up by the chaos of waters through which man sinks at death into the Underworld; but ultimately, in acknowledgement of his proven loyalty to the Davidic covenant and his complete obedience to the will of the heavenly King, he was delivered through the personal intervention of Yahweh Himself, as the 'Most High', and brought back in triumph to the land of light and life to be enthroned afresh on Mount Zion. Such a restoration to life on the part of the king, however, was nothing less than a ritual rebirth; it was an indication that this suffering

---

[1] *Adonis und Esmun. Eine Untersuchung zur Geschichte des Glaubens an Auferstehungsgötter und an Heilgötter*, 1911. As I have indicated elsehwere (*E.T.* lxii (1950–1), p. 39 n. 5), while there is much in this work with which I am unable to agree, my reading of it led to a complete reorientation of my views concerning the Old Testament and, indeed, what seems to me to be a deeper understanding of the Bible as a whole.

Servant and humble Messiah had been adopted once more as the Son of the 'Most High' or, to express this vitally important point in another way, that he had been restored to office as priest 'after the order of Melchizedek'. In this way the 'life' or well-being of the nation, for which the king was directly responsible, found provisional assurance for yet another cycle of the year.

At this point, however, it seems desirable that I should add a personal word of explanation with regard to my own association with the so-called 'Myth and Ritual School'; for my conclusions were ultimately delivered as one of a second series of lectures, organized by Professor Hooke, which subsequently appeared as a volume of essays forming a sequel to *Myth and Ritual*.[1] The point which I wish to make here is that I arrived at my conclusions quite independently of any associations with the 'Myth and Ritual School'. It was only after Professor W. O. E. Oesterley had read through my work, as he had been in the habit of doing for the previous two or three years, that he suggested that I should give Professor Hooke the opportunity of accepting it for his second series of lectures. Accordingly, if I am to be regarded as a member of this 'Myth and Ritual School', it is only right that it should be known that I entered it, so to speak, through the back door! I hasten to add that I do not mention this because I have any wish to be dissociated from my old friend Professor Hooke, although it will be clear that I do not see eye to eye with him and his colleagues on every point; in fact it must be obvious that I am highly sceptical about the conjectural reconstruction of the supposed myth and ritual pattern in Israel which I have already quoted. I am merely anxious to prevent students of the history of interpretation from jumping to hasty conclusions which are not warranted by the facts, and inferring, for example, that my own conclusions were reached in an effort to lend support to Professor Hooke's theory of a culture pattern common to the ancient Near East and displaying the characteristics to which I have already referred.

[1] i.e. 'The Rôle of the King in the Jerusalem Cultus', in *The Labyrinth. Further Studies in the Relation between Myth and Ritual in the Ancient World*, ed. S. H. Hooke, 1935, pp. 71–111.

The only other feature of the pre-war years to which I ought, perhaps, to draw attention is the theory advanced by Harris Birkeland, a pupil of Mowinckel, in 1933 (and indeed recently reiterated)[1] to the effect that the enemies referred to so frequently in the Psalter are almost invariably foreigners, and that the 'I' who speaks is, therefore, the king or, in some cases perhaps, the leader of the armed forces other than the king or, again, so far as the post-exilic period is concerned, a native governor or high-priest. In my opinion Professor Birkeland overstates his case, but his argument is one which may not be ignored; and it is important in the present connexion, because it opened up the possibility that the royal psalms were more numerous than had hitherto been supposed.

The end of the war, however, revealed the fact that the two lines of approach to our problem, represented by the work of Mowinckel and of the Myth and Ritual School, had been taken up enthusiastically by Professor Geo Widengren and his associates, notably Docent (now Professor) Ivan Engnell, in what has come to be known as the Uppsala School. The background to the ideas of kingship in the Old Testament which is supplied by the faith and practice of the ancient Near East has been examined by them more widely and in greater detail; but, for the most part, what they have to say about the subject in the Old Testament itself remains much too summary or fragmentary in character to enable one to arrive at anything like a complete picture of the views held by this new school of thought.

Thus Engnell has published a general survey of the myth and ritual pattern as he seeks to reconstruct it, paying added attention to the important comparative data available from Hittite and Ugaritic sources; and in conclusion he gives a short account of the way in which he proposes to follow up his findings with respect to the Old Testament.[2] He advances the view that in the area under survey the fertility aspect of a primitive high

---

[1] *Die Feinde des Individuums in der israelitischen Psalmenliteratur*, 1933; 'The Evil-doers in the Book of Psalms', *A.N.V.A.O.* ii, 1955, No. 2, 1955. The latter work also contains some helpful comments on the views of the Myth and Ritual School and the whole question of 'patternism'.

[2] *Studies in Divine Kingship in the Ancient Near East*, 1943, pp. 174–7.

god was split off into a fertility god of the dying and rising type, and that this was done in such a way that normally the original identity was not altogether lost; accordingly the king, who was regarded as the embodiment of this dying and rising 'young god', might also be regarded as an incarnation of the high god. As already indicated, however, the way in which Engnell applies his findings to the conceptions of kingship in the Old Testament is difficult to determine, as his views in this connexion can only be discovered from summary statements of the type already indicated[1] and a few occasional articles.[2] It seems clear, however, that he finds evidence for more royal psalms, whether strictly such or only so in what is known as a 'democratized' sense, than is generally thought to be the case, and, therefore, still more evidence for the motif of the king's descent to the Underworld.[3] Hence, if the king is to be regarded as an incarnation of the high god and, therefore, is to be identified with Yahweh, this means, presumably, that we have still more evidence for the view that Yahweh was thought of as a dying and rising god.

This picture may be filled out a little by reference to Widengren's own special studies in the ritual and mythology of the

[1] e.g. *Gamla Testamentet. En traditionshistorisk Inledning*, i (1945), pp. 109–18, 135–47; and articles such as those on 'Konung, kungadöme' and 'Psaltaren' in *Svenskt Bibliskt Uppslagsverk*, ed. I. Engnell and A. Fridrichsen, i (1945), cols. 1221–6, and ii (1952), cols. 787–832.

[2] e.g. as cited in the following notes.

[3] e.g., in addition to Ps. xviii, lxxxix, and cxviii, as employed by me in the work referred to above, pp. 227 ff., Ps. xxii, xlix, lxxxviii, and cxvi. Cf. op.cit. i, cols. 1223–4; also 'Till fragan om Ebed Jahve-sångerna och den lidande Messias hos "Deutero-jesaja" ', *S.E.Å.* x (1945), pp. 31–65 and the revised English translation of this work, *B.J.R.L.* xxxi (1948), pp. 54–93; 'Kain och Abel. En rituell interpretation', in *S.J.F.T.* xlvi (1947), pp. 92–102. Cf., too, Widengren's discussion of the ideas which he finds expressed in the language of Psalm lxxxviii, 'Konungens vistelse i dodsriket. En studie till Psalm 88', *S.E.Å.* x (1945), pp. 66–81. In *E.T.* lxii (1950–1), p. 41 n. 1, I cited Engnell's article 'Kain och Abel' as an example of the way in which, as it seems to me, one may exaggerate the influence of such supposed royal ideology on the literature of the Old Testament; and in connexion with his essay ' "Know-ledge" and "Life" in the creation story', in *Wisdom in Israel and in the Ancient Near East* (Rowley *Festschrift*), pp. 103–19, specifically p. 118 n. 1, Engnell objects that 'apparently through difficulty with the language' I have 'missed the most essential point, the reactionary re-interpretation of the motive'. I take this opportunity of saying that I was perfectly well aware of this feature in his argument, but that it has no bearing whatsoever on the point at issue.

ancient East[1] together with his recent monograph on the theme
of sacral kingship in the Old Testament and in Judaism.[2] Here
it seems to me that the most important elements, even though
the Old Testament evidence is not very convincing, are those
which touch upon the king's connexion with the 'Tree of Life'[3]
and the 'Water of Life'[4] and the bearing which these ideas may
have upon the Paradise story and the conception of the 'Primal
Man'.[5] As for the autumnal festival, it is clear that Mowinckel's

[1] See especially 'Det sakrala kungadömet bland öst- och västsemiter', *R.o.B.* ii
(1943), pp. 49–75; *Mesopotamian Elements in Manichaeism = King and Saviour II*,
U.U.Å. 1946: 3, 1946; *The Ascension of the Apostle and the Heavenly Book = King
and Saviour III*, U.U.Å. 1950: 7, 1950; *The King and the Tree of Life in Ancient
Near Eastern Religion = King and Saviour IV*, U.U.Å. 1951: 4, 1951.

[2] *Sakrales Königtum im Alten Testament und im Judentum*, 1955. See also *Psalm
110 och det sakrala kungadömet i Israel*, U.U.Å. 1941: 7. 1, 1941.

[3] See *R.o.B.* ii, pp. 60 ff.; *King and Saviour IV*, pp. 36 ff., 49 ff.; *Sakrales Königtum*, pp. 48 and 56. Cf., too, the preliminary discussion of this feature by Engnell in
Studies in Divine Kingship, esp. pp. 24 ff. For myself I find it difficult to follow Widengren when, turning to the Old Testament, he cites such passages as Isa. iv. 2, xi. 1,
xiv. 19; Jer. xxiii. 5, xxxiii. 15; Zech. iii. 8, vi. 12, and concludes that 'there existed
long ago and for a long period in Israel a very concrete symbolical notion of the ruler
as the mighty tree, growing in Paradise, the Garden of God, "in the midst of the
earth", and providing shadow and protection to all living beings. That this assumption
is justified is shown by an impressive passage in Lamentations where we read of the
Davidic king:

> The breath of our noses, the Anointed of Yahweh,
>   caught in their pits!
> We had said: "In his shadow
>   we shall live among the peoples!"
>   Lamentations 4: 20.

In this text we meet again with the idea of the peoples' living in the shade of the
king, i.e. the ruler is seen symbolically as the mighty tree in whose shadow his subjects
take their refuge.' (*King and Saviour IV*, p. 58.) As I see it, in all these cases we have
no more than simple metaphorical language of the type to be found, say, in Jotham's
fable, as cited above, p. 206 n. 5 (i.e. with special reference to Judges ix. 15). Cf.,
too, I. Engnell, ' "Planted by the Streams of Water" ', *Studia Orientalia Ioanni
Pedersen septuagenario a.d. VII Id. Nov. anno MCMLIII a collegis discipulis amicis
dicata*, 1953, pp. 85–96, where it is suggested that the simple simile of Ps. i. 3 should
be seen against the background furnished by the thought of the 'Tree of Life'.

[4] Cf. *King and Saviour IV*, pp. 36 f.; *Sakrales Königtum*, pp. 48 f.

[5] This point was taken up and developed by Aage Bentzen in 'Messias–Moses redivivus–Menschensohn', *A.T.A.N.T.* xvii (1948), pp. 37 ff., and in the revised English
translation *King and Messiah*, 1955, pp. 39 ff. Cf., too, his earlier work *Det sakrale
kongedømme. Bemærkninger i en løbende diskussion om de gammeltestamentlige salmer*,
1945, pp. 76 f.; and especially the debate between Mowinckel, 'Urmensch und
"Königsideologie" ', *S.T.* ii (1948, published 1949–50), pp. 71–89, and Bentzen,

general theory with regard to its New Year aspect and my own views as already outlined have been accepted in part but with the following major differences. In the first place, room is found, along much the same lines as those advanced by members of the Myth and Ritual School, for the king's part in a sacral marriage;[1] and, in the second place, an attempt is made to reinforce the view that Yahweh Himself was thought of as a dying and rising god by citing, for example, a number of passing references to the thought of His being asleep and needing to be roused[2] and by stressing the obviously cultic cry 'Yahweh lives'.[3] For my own part I must say that I find nothing in the evidence cited which warrants such a view; and in my opinion one of the basic mistakes made in this connexion is that of taking the Hebrew text too literally and with insufficient regard for the use of idiom or purely figurative language.[4]

During recent years Mowinckel has restated his own views along much the same lines as before within the framework of several wider studies covering the Psalter as a whole,[5] the origin and development of the Messianic Hope,[6] and the significance of the cultus for the religious life;[7] and it is to be observed that

'King Ideology–"Urmensch"–"Troonsbestijgingsfeest" ', ibid. iii (1949, published 1950–1), pp. 143–57, specifically pp. 148–53, which reveals the fact that we have nothing here which has any bearing on the actual ideas of kingship in ancient Israel.

[1] Cf. G. Widengren, 'Hieros gamos och underjordsvistelse. Studier till de sakrala kungadömet i Israel', *R.o.B.* vii (1948), pp. 17 ff.; *Sakrales Königtum*, pp. 76 ff.; and see above, pp. 226 f.

[2] e.g. Ps. vii. 7–8 (EVV. 6–7), xxxv. 23, xliv. 24 25 (EVV. 23–24), lix. 5–6 (EVV. 4–5), lxxviii. 65–66.

[3] Ps. xviii. 47 (EVV. 46).

[4] Cf. my concluding remarks, *E.T.* lxii (1950–1), pp. 41 f.

[5] *Offersang og sangoffer. Salmediktningen i Bibelen*, 1951; 'Salmeboken', in Michelet–Mowinckel–Messel, *Det Gamle Testamente*, iv. 1 (1955), pp. 9–292. The objection which Mowinckel raises to my use of the royal psalms in connexion with the autumnal festival (*Offersang og sangoffer*, pp. 570 ff.) reveals again that strange contradiction in Mowinckel's thinking to which I have referred above, p. 223 n. 2.

[6] *Han som kommer. Messiasforventningen i det Gamle Testament og på Jesu tid*, 1951.

[7] *Religion og Kultus*, 1950, and, in a revised German edition, *Religion und Kultus*, 1953. Cf., too, the subsidiary studies, *Zum israelitischen Neujahr und zur Deutung der Thronbesteigungspsalmen*, A.N.V.A.O. ii. 1952, No. 2, 1952; *Der achtundsechzigste Psalm*, A.N.V.A.O. ii. 1953, No. 1, 1953. Attention should also be drawn to the way in which the autumnal festival, regarded as the great festival for the renewal

he now avoids any suggestion that the king should be regarded as an 'incarnation' of Yahweh and makes it quite clear that in his opinion one should think rather of the king's being equipped with supernatural power through the gift of the 'Spirit'.[1]

I should add, to complete this short survey, that I have just reissued my own conclusions in an expanded and, what is more, a revised form, the most important difference being that I now reject the view that the autumnal festival was concerned with the cyclic revival of the social unit, and argue instead that its orientation was not merely towards the following cycle of twelve months but towards a completely new era.[2] That is to say, if ever it had its roots in a complex of myth and ritual which was primarily concerned with the cycle of the year and an annual attempt along magico-religious lines to secure a renewal of life for a specific social unit, this had been refashioned along morally persuasive lines in terms of Yahweh's eternal Kingship and Israel's experience of His activity on the plane of history, and the thought in question was really the creation of a new world order and the introduction of an age of universal righteousness and peace. In short, while I continue to reject the historical interpretation of the psalms which celebrate the Kingship of Yahweh, I now hold that from the first they were not only cultic in origin but also, like the associated royal psalms, eschatological in their orientation. If I am right, this means that the theory of royal psalms does not preclude their sometimes being 'Messianic' in what is now the established eschatological sense of this term;[3]

of Israel's covenant with Yahweh, dominates the very attractive commentary by A. Weiser, *Die Psalmen*, A.T.D. 14–15, 1950, 4th ed. rev., 1955. It is interesting to note, however, that, despite Weiser's sympathetic reception of Mowinckel's theory in this connexion, he shows (op. cit., p. 35) the common misunderstanding of Mowinckel's position to which I have referred above, p. 221 n. 2. For the work of H. J. Kraus, 'Die Königsherrschaft Gottes im Alten Testament', *B.H.T.* xiii, 1951, and 'Gottesdienst in Israel. Studien zur Geschichte des Laubhüttenfestes', *B.E.T.* xix, 1954, see my comments in the Society for Old Testament Study's *Book List 1952*, pp. 54 f., and ibid. *1954*, p. 65.

[1] See above, p. 208 n. 8.
[2] *Sacral Kingship in Ancient Israel*, as cited above, p. 206 n. 6.
[3] Cf., as an example of current discussion in this field, A. Bentzen, 'Kan ordet "Messiansk" anvendes om Salmernes kongeforestillinger?', *S.E.Å.* xii (1947), pp. 20 ff.

and in that case the Messianic Hope, in its association with the House of David, is much earlier than is now commonly thought.

Finally, if I am asked what bearing this has on Professor Hooke's theory of a culture pattern common to the ancient Near East, I can only say (without in any way committing myself with regard to the validity of his claim) that the following features, at least, seem to me to be present in the autumnal festival of the Jerusalem cultus during the period of the monarchy: (*a*) The celebration of Yahweh's original triumph, as leader of the forces of light, over the forces of darkness as represented by the monstrous chaos of waters or primeval ocean; His subjection of this cosmic sea and His enthronement as King in the assembly of the gods; and the further demonstration of His might and power, not only in the creation of the habitable world, but also on the plane of history. (*b*) A dramatic representation of the dawn of the great eschatological 'Day', when Yahweh will finally triumph over the rebellious gods and nations of the earth, and so affirm His Kingship over the moral realm as well as the realm of nature. (*c*) The corresponding dramatic representation of the descent of the true Messiah to the Underworld and his ultimate deliverance by Yahweh from the forces of darkness and death. (*d*) A triumphal procession in which the Ark, as the symbol of Yahweh's presence, and the king, who in this dramatic ritual has proved to be the true Messiah and the accepted 'Son' of Yahweh, proceed to the Temple for the final act of enthronement which is to mark the beginning of this new era. Only, let me repeat, this is no cultic act of a magico-religious kind; it is worship which, if it exposes the participants to all the dangers of an exaggerated nationalism, also reveals a quite lofty spiritual aim.

RITUAL AND THE HEBREW
PROPHETS

by H. H. ROWLEY

IT is curious how labels get attached to men and to schools. In 1933 Professor Hooke edited a volume of essays published under the title *Myth and Ritual*, and since then he has been either praised or blamed as the leader of the 'Myth and Ritual School'. In reality those essays were largely a *mise au point* of studies which had been going on for some time, but mainly outside this country. There had been a growing recognition of common elements in the culture and outlook of the peoples of the ancient Near East from the Nile to the Euphrates, and Professor Hooke and his colleagues underlined those common elements.[1] Little was then known of the Ras Shamra texts, which were only beginning to see the light, but from which a good deal of additional material can now be drawn for some aspects of the subject.

Some scholars, such as the late Henri Frankfort,[2] have since reacted strongly against the whole idea of a common pattern of culture, and have emphasized the diverse elements of Egyptian and Babylonian civilization, and have dismissed 'patternism' as something irrelevant to our studies. On the other hand, what has come to be known as the 'Scandinavian School' has sometimes gone beyond Professor Hooke and his colleagues in emphasizing the common elements and in pressing 'patternism' in ways which cannot be attributed to them. In truth, it is as misleading to speak

---

[1] O. Eissfeldt, in *The Old Testament and Modern Study*, ed. by H. H. Rowley, 1951, p. 122, says that in this book and its sequel, *The Labyrinth*, ed. by S. H. Hooke, 1935, 'The external analogies have been given precedence over the illustrative material to be found within the Old Testament itself.' The measure of over-emphasis on what had hitherto been under-emphasized was less than in some more recent studies, and some, at any rate, of the writers had no desire to minimize the evidence of the Old Testament or to impose an alien pattern on the whole.

[2] Cf. the summary of his paper read to the 7th Congress for the History of Religions, held in Amsterdam in 1950, published in the *Proceedings* of the Congress, ed. by C. J. Bleeker, G. W. J. Drewes, and K. A. H. Hidding, 1951, pp. 99 f., and *The Problem of Similarity in Ancient Near Eastern Religions*, 1951.

of the 'Scandinavian School' as to speak of the 'Myth and Ritual School', since there are very real divergencies amongst the members of that supposed school. Professor Hooke and his colleagues were in some respects anticipated by Sigmund Mowinckel, in his very important *Psalmenstudien*,[1] and to him must be given a significant place in the history of 'patternism'. But since the headquarters of 'patternism' moved to Sweden, Mowinckel has sharply repudiated some of its developments, and has been in turn severely criticized by Swedish colleagues. That there were common elements and diverse elements in the culture and practice of the peoples of the region with which we are concerned is hard to deny, and it is possible to repudiate the extremer views on either side without assuming a merely negative attitude to either.

Ivan Engnell, of Uppsala, has been a storm centre in recent Old Testament studies, partly by reason of his championship of Oral Tradition instead of Literary Criticism, and partly because of his development of one aspect of the 'Myth and Ritual' views in his *Studies in Divine Kingship in the Ancient Near East*.[2] With the question of Divine Kingship I am not concerned in this paper. It may not be out of place to observe, however, that one of my predecessors in my chair in the University of Manchester, Professor M. A. Canney, in the very year in which *Myth and Ritual* was published, and quite independently of Professor Hooke's 'school'—with which his name is never associated—issued an article ten years before Engnell's book saw the light, in which the self-same ideas were put forward in brief outline.[3] Canney argued that throughout our area and beyond kings were thought of as divine, and that in Israel the king was 'virtually an incarnation of the deity'.[4] In 1933 Manchester was as deeply involved in the ideas of the so-called 'school' as any of its members, either then or later, whether in this country or in

---

[1] These *Psalmenstudien* were published in six parts in the *Skrifter* of the Norwegian Academy, 1921–4. For an estimate of their contribution to the study of the Psalter, cf. A. R. Johnson, in *The Old Testament and Modern Study*, pp. 189 ff.
[2] Published in 1943.
[3] Cf. *Oriental Studies in Honour of Cursetji Erachji Pavry*, 1933, pp. 63 ff.
[4] Ibid., p. 74.

Scandinavia. Certainly not all of the members of Professor Hooke's team would have gone so far as Professor Canney, and I should stop a long way short of this.

The special aspect of the general subject which has been assigned to me for the present essay is one in which I think we owe the so-called 'school' a debt of gratitude for the important contribution it has made to the study of the Old Testament—though again there are extremer expressions of that contribution which I do not endorse. The view that the Hebrew prophets were an entirely unique phenomenon in the religious history of the world—unique not only in the spiritual level they attained, but in the whole character of their work—is one that cannot be maintained. The recognition that there were prophets outside Israel very much like some of the early groups of prophets who come before us in the Old Testament has long been widespread, and more than forty years ago Hölscher's *Die Profeten*[1] empha- sized what has come to be called the 'ecstatic' character of Hebrew prophecy.[2] In the hands of some this character has been ascribed to all Old Testament prophecy, and it has been main- tained that every oracle arose out of some 'ecstatic' experience.[3] This tendency to overpress evidence, and indeed to outrun it, is a constant danger to scholarship, and we shall find further in- stances of it as we proceed.

That the Egyptian story of Wen Amon[4] presents us with prophecy closely similar to that of the early Israelite prophets cannot be gainsaid. In that story we are told that a youth became possessed and continued in this state all the night, declaring that

[1] Published in 1914.
[2] For the present writer's views on this subject cf. *The Servant of the Lord*, 1952, pp. 91 ff.
[3] Cf. W. Jacobi, *Die Ekstase der alttestamentlichen Propheten*, 1920, p. 4: 'Ecstasy is of the essence of prophecy'; H. Gunkel, *The Expositor*, 9th series, i (1924), p. 358: 'The fundamental experience of all types of prophecy is ecstasy'; also T. H. Robinson, *Prophecy and the Prophets in Ancient Israel*, 1923, p. 50. In *E.T.*, xlvi (1934–5), p. 43, T. H. Robinson maintains that an objective criterion, in the form of some kind of ecstatic experience, was demanded by both prophet and hearers for each oracle.
[4] A translation of this story may be found in *Ancient Near Eastern Texts*, ed. by J. B. Pritchard, 1950, pp. 25 ff.

he was the mouthpiece of the god. More recently evidence of prophets at Mari at a much earlier date has come to light.[1] It is therefore quite impossible to treat Hebrew prophecy as an isolated phenomenon. It grew out of a background of ancient Near Eastern prophecy, going back very far and spreading widely.[2] In the Old Testament we read of prophets of Baal,[3] and evidence of similar prophets in neighbouring countries at a later time has long been familiar.[4]

Nevertheless, if Hebrew prophecy grew out of this background, we should not forget that it did grow. All should not be seen in terms of a particular manifestation, and that especially characteristic of an early period. That there was an abnormal element in even the greater prophets of the Old Testament may be allowed; but this does not mean that all prophecy was 'ecstatic', or that every oracle was born in a special abnormal experience. Wheeler Robinson thought it unlikely that 'a prophet of the classical period would have dared to prophesy without an inaugural vision such as Isaiah's in the temple, or an audition such as Jeremiah's, or such a characteristically peculiar experience as that of Ezekiel', and added: 'Moreover, we may expect such experiences to recur from time to time, and our expectation is fulfilled.'[5] Whether these experiences of vocation are rightly described as 'ecstatic' need not detain us.[6] Quite apart from these experiences we find the prophets sometimes

---

[1] Cf. A. Lods, in *Studies in Old Testament Prophecy*, ed. by H. H. Rowley, 1950, pp. 103 ff.; M. Noth, *B.J.R.L.* xxxii (1949–50), pp. 194 ff., and *Geschichte und Gotteswort im Alten Testament*, 1950; F. M. Th. de Liagre Böhl, *Nederlands Theologisch Tijdschrift*, iv (1949–50), pp. 82 ff.; W. von Soden, *Die Welt des Orients*, 1950, pp. 397 ff.; and H. Schmökel, *Theologische Literaturzeitung*, lxxvi (1940), cols. 54 ff.

[2] Cf. A. Neher, *L'Essence du prophétisme*, 1955, pp. 17 ff.

[3] 1 Kings xviii. 19 ff. Their conduct as described in verse 28 was 'ecstatic'.

[4] Cf. Hölscher, *Die Profeten*, pp. 132 ff.; T. H. Robinson, *The Classical Quarterly*, xi (1917), pp. 201 ff., and *Prophecy and the Prophets*, pp. 33 f.

[5] Cf. *Redemption and Revelation*, 1942, pp. 143 f. Cf. also J. P. Hyatt, *Prophetic Religion*, 1947, p. 17.

[6] J. Skinner admitted the use of the term. Cf. *Prophecy and Religion*, 1922, p. 4 n.: 'The fact that the great prophets far surpassed their predecessors in their apprehension of religious truth is no reason for denying the reality of the ecstatic element in their experience, or for explaining it away as a mere rhetorical accommodation to traditional modes of expression.'

behaving in ways which would soon get them into trouble in the modern world. Isaiah on and off over a period of three years was liable to be seen walking through the streets of Jerusalem naked and barefoot;[1] and Jeremiah appeared in the Temple wearing a wooden yoke.[2] These were acted prophecies, usually described by the term 'prophetic symbolism'. They are not evidence of prophetic 'ecstasy', to be put on the same level as Saul's stripping off his clothes and rolling about on the ground naked all night,[3] but they are evidence of abnormal behaviour. Nevertheless, no study of Hebrew prophecy can end with the outer behaviour of the prophet. The prophet claims to be the mouthpiece of God,[4] and it is by the message he delivers that his claim is to be judged. It is here that the development of Hebrew prophecy shows itself. Linked with prophecy elsewhere in its beginnings and in some of its forms of expression, it rises in the greater prophets whose oracles are preserved for us in the Bible to great spiritual heights.

We must not close our eyes to the fact that all the prophets of Israel did not rise to these sublime heights. If one thing is clear to the student of the Old Testament, it is that there were many varieties of prophet in Israel, and the uniqueness that may be claimed for Hebrew prophecy is something that belonged to but a few of the prophetic figures that come before us, and something that lies in the content of their message rather than in the form of its delivery.[5]

A generation ago it was common amongst scholars to set the prophets and the priests over against one another in the sharpest way. The prophets were presented as men who had no use whatever for any of the practices of the cultus, and who thought it

---

[1] Isa. xx. 2 ff.

[2] Jer. xxvii. 2, xxviii. 10.

[3] 1 Sam. xix. 24.

[4] Cf. Exod. vii. 1 f., iv. 16; Jer. i. 9; also the common prophetic formula, 'Thus saith the Lord'.

[5] Cf. H. Birkeland, *The Evildoers in the Book of Psalms*, 1955, p. 18: 'A text translated from Hebrew as opposed to Akkadian literature reveals such immense differences that everybody who can read discovers them at once. Common patterns existed, it is true. But in most cases they have to be detected by the scholarly work of specialists.'

was wholly alien to the will of God.[1] Professor Volz wrote:

The Old Testament prophetic religion stands in the sharpest contrast to priestly religion, or Cult Religion. Priestly religion is the religion of sacrifice; the priest brings the gifts of men from below up to the Deity. Prophetic religion is the religion of the word; it brings the voice of God from above down to men.[2]

On such a view the prophets were limited for all practical purposes to the canonical prophets, and the familiar passages in which they denounce the ritual observances of their day were given an extreme interpretation and held to mean that they condemned the cultus root and branch. The passages on which this view was based were mainly Isa. i. 10 ff., Amos v. 21 ff., Hosea vi. 6, Micah vi. 6 ff., Jer. vi. 20, vii. 21 ff., and together they were held to show that in the eyes of the prophets all sacrifice was an abomination to God, and the Temple itself was an offence in His eyes. Not all scholars took this extreme view, and I have more than once argued from the study of the prophetic books themselves that it cannot be maintained.[3] I agree with A. C. Welch that 'the judgment that the prophets were unanimous in their attitude toward the cult, and that they agreed in condemning it *per se*, does not do justice to the facts',[4] and that the claim 'that their common view was one which condemned the cult *in toto* can only be proved from isolated passages pressed beyond the terms of a just exegesis'.[5] If the prophets had really meant that sacrifice under all circumstances was evil, they would not have needed to bring condemnation of the lives of men into association with their denunciation of the sacrifices. Isaiah condemns sacrifice, sacred festival and prayer, and says 'Your hands are full of blood.'[6] If it was for this reason that their ritual

---

[1] Cf. J. A. Bewer, *The Literature of the Old Testament in its Historical Development*, 1922, p. 267: 'Religion was a matter of the cult. The earlier prophets had violently protested against such a conception of religion and rejected the entire cultic apparatus as contrary to the will of God.'

[2] Cf. *Prophetengestalten des Alten Testaments*, 1938, p. 56.

[3] Cf. *Melilah*, ed. by E. Robertson and M. Wallenstein, i (1944), 185 ff.; *B.J.R.L.*, xxix (1945–6), pp. 326 ff.; xxxiii (1950–1), pp. 74 ff.; and *The Unity of the Bible*, 1953, pp. 30 ff.   [4] *Prophet and Priest in Old Israel*, 1936, p. 17.

[5] Ibid., pp. 17 f. Cf. also K. Roubos, *Profetie en Cultus in Israël*, 1956, pp. 68 ff., 113.   [6] Isa. i. 15.

observances were condemned, this would be understandable;
but we should not then conclude that the condemnation of the
observances was absolute. If the prophet meant that even if their
hands were not full of blood, their sacrifices and their prayers
would equally be an offence to God, he would have been wiser
not to mention the irrelevance. Jeremiah spoke of the coming
destruction of the Temple, but made it clear that if men would
amend their ways, the Temple might be spared.[1] He could
scarcely have thought that the Temple was in itself an offence to
God. We ought therefore not to go beyond our text, but to be
content to say that these prophets declared that the religious
observances of their day were meaningless in the eyes of God
because they were the observances of men whose lives were an
offence to Him. They were not the expression of the devotion
of their hearts, but rather the proud expression of the defiance
of their spirit. That the prophets who spoke in this way say little
in praise of the cultus is to be understood. For they were dealing
with the situation of their own day, when for many the ritual
was an end in itself.

By the 'Myth and Ritual School' this question has been
approached from another side, and the simple antithesis between
priests and prophets has now few defenders. So long ago as 1914
Hölscher had already suggested that there were prophets who
stood beside the priests in the shrines, where they belonged to
the cultic staff.[2] These prophets he differentiated from the
canonical prophets, however. Since then, as we shall see, much
water has flowed under the bridge. In the third part of his
Studies in the Psalms, published in 1923,[3] Mowinckel took up
the question of cultic prophets, and argued that there were such
officials functioning in the shrines beside the priests, and that not
a few of the psalms were, at least in part, composed by them.
Amongst the psalms he notes are some which he associates with
the 'great festivals',[4] some which he classes as prophetic oracles,[5]

[1] Jer. vii. 5 ff.   [2] Cf. *Die Profeten*, p. 143.
[3] *Psalmenstudien III: Kultprophetie und prophetische Psalmen.*
[4] Ps. cxxxii, lxxxix. 20–38 (E.V. 19–37), lxxxi and xcv, l, lxxxii, lxxv, lxxxvii,
lxxxv, xiv, and xii.
[5] Ps. lx, cviii, xx, and xxi.

some which he calls royal oracles,[1] and some which were for private cultic use.[2] His fundamental view of the psalms was that they were ritual texts, used to accompany the sacred acts of the worship. It will be seen at once how closely this ties up with the ideas of the 'Myth and Ritual School'. For in the opening essay of *Myth and Ritual* Professor Hooke defined what was meant by 'myth' in the words:

In general the spoken part of a ritual consists of a description of what is being done, it is the story which the ritual enacts. This is the sense in which the term 'myth' is used in our discussion. The original myth, inseparable in the first instance from its ritual, embodies in more or less symbolic fashion, the original situation which is seasonally re-enacted in the ritual.[3]

That has relevance to much more than the Psalter, of course, but Mowinckel's understanding of the use of the psalms was not dissimilar. In this he was followed by Welch,[4] who also rejected the view that prophets and priests were diametrically opposed to one another[5]—though Welch was not a member of the 'Myth and Ritual School'.

By older writers the Psalter had often been referred to as 'The Hymn Book of the Second Temple', and the composition of most of the psalms had been assigned to the post-exilic period. Now, on the contrary, the antiquity of many of the psalms was maintained, and they were related to the pre-exilic ritual of the Temple in a more intimate way than the term 'Hymn Book' suggests to us. The psalm was believed to express the meaning of the ritual it accompanied, and particular psalms were thought to belong to particular rites. Where all this concerns our subject

---

[1] Ps. ii, cx, lxxii, and xlv.   [2] Ps. xci and lxii.

[3] p. 3.

[4] Cf. *The Psalter in Life, Worship, and History*, 1926, pp. 62 ff. On p. 59 Welch observed that 'the psalter is remarkably acultic', but this did not mean unrelated to the cult; for on p. 63 he says: 'It needs, then, to be emphasized at the beginning that the psalter was far more closely related to the cult-practice and its recurrent ritual than has been generally recognized in the ordinary English commentaries.' While Welch makes no reference to Mowinckel in his chapter on 'The Psalter and Worship', his footnote on p. 94 shows that he was familiar with the Norwegian scholar's work.

[5] Cf. *Prophet and Priest in Old Israel*, 1936.

in the present essay is in that Mowinckel held that many of the psalms arose in the prophetic responses in the worship. The cultic prophets were believed to have been the representatives of the congregation, who were caught up into ecstasy in all the excitement of the religious festival, and who fulfilled the function which all the congregation should ideally have fulfilled, and made the response to which they were prompted by the divine power.[1] In later times, Mowinckel argued, their place was taken by the Temple singers.[2]

Some of these ideas of Mowinckel's were taken up and presented to English readers in a brief paper by A. R. Johnson twenty years ago.[3] Following Mowinckel he developed the view that there were cultic prophets beside the priests, with a defined place in the ritual of worship, and that in post-exilic times they developed into the singers of the Second Temple. Following Mowinckel again he held that some of the psalms were composed by cultic prophets for use in the ritual of the Temple.[4] More recently he has published a monograph dealing with the first part of this thesis,[5] leaving the second part to be developed in a forthcoming monograph, of which only the title is yet available.[6]

That there is not a little evidence in the Old Testament to support this view is beyond question. It is impossible to cite all the evidence here, and unnecessary since it can be found in the works of Mowinckel and Johnson. Briefly it may be noted that it rests on the frequent association of priests and prophets with one another and with the Temple, and of prophets with cultic occasions. A few examples, all from the Book of Jeremiah, may suffice. In Jer. xxvi we read that prophets and priests together heard Jeremiah's utterance in the Temple and together accused

---

[1] Op. cit., pp. 16 ff. Cf. the view of H. Junker (*Prophet und Seher in Israel*, 1927, pp. 22 f.), where the prophets are associated with the sacred dance at the shrines, and with the sacred poetry which was sung as its accompaniment.

[2] Op. cit., pp. 24 ff.

[3] Cf. *E.T.*, xlvii (1935–6), pp. 312 ff.

[4] Cf. *The Labyrinth*, pp. 80, 109, where Ps. cxxxii. 11–18 and cx are so interpreted. Cf. also H. Junker, op. cit., pp. 38 ff.

[5] *The Cultic Prophet in Ancient Israel*, 1944.

[6] *The Cultic Prophet and the Psalter* (cf. *The Cultic Prophet in Ancient Israel*, p. 5 n.). There is as yet no indication when this monograph may be expected.

him to the authorities.[1] Elsewhere Jeremiah links prophet and priest together, and declares that their wickedness has been found in the Temple.[2] In yet another passage he speaks of prophets uttering false prophecies and the priests ruling at their direction.[3] Moreover, in the Book of Jeremiah we find a reference to a room in the Temple belonging to the sons of a prophet.[4] All of this and much more would seem to establish an association between prophets and priests, and in particular between prophets and the Temple.

Moreover, when the Shunammite woman wished to go to Elisha to tell him of the death of her child, her husband expressed surprise that she should go on a day which was neither new moon nor sabbath.[5] From this it is clear that it was customary to visit prophets on cultic occasions. An association between prophets and religious festivals, as well as between prophets and the Temple, seems therefore to be established.

This once more leaves open the question of the relation between the canonical prophets and such cultic prophets. Mowinckel distinguished between them, though, as will be seen, he blurred the distinction to some extent. One of the Swedish scholars has failed to find any distinction, and has claimed that all the Israelite prophets belonged to guilds of cultic prophets. Writing of him Eissfeldt says: 'The question whether the writing prophets belonged to the cultic associations is answered with an emphatic affirmative, and it is plainly laid down that no more difference is to be made between the writing prophets and their predecessors in this respect than in any other.'[6] The Swedish

[1] Jer. xxvi. 7, 11.

[2] Jer. xxiii. 11.

[3] Jer. v. 31 (R.S.V.; R.V. has 'by their means').

[4] Jer. xxxv. 4. The term 'man of God' which stands in this verse is elsewhere frequently used for a prophet. Cf. 1 Sam. ix. 6 ff., 1 Kings xiii. 11, 18, 2 Kings v. 1. The phrase 'nš 'lm is found in Ugaritic (C. H. Gordon, *Ugaritic Handbook*, 1947, p. 129, Text 1, line 22); and E. Dhorme (*R.B.*, xl (1931), p. 36) and H. L. Ginsberg (*The Ugarit Texts*, 1936, p. 112) connected this with the Hebrew *'îsh* *'elōhîm* = 'man of God'. Whether this stands for 'prophet' in Ugaritic is uncertain, however. Dhorme (loc. cit.) thought it meant 'the servant of the gods', and Gordon (*Ugaritic Literature*, 1949, p. 112) renders 'the servitors of the gods'.

[5] 2 Kings iv. 23.

[6] Cf. *The Old Testament and Modern Study*, pp. 123 ff.

scholar in question is A. Haldar, who has carried 'patternism' to the length of equating all the Israelite prophets with guilds of diviners found in Babylonia.[1] There we find evidence of guilds of diviners who bear the names of *bārū* and *maḥḥū*. The *bārū* is defined as one whose divination depended on technical methods,[2] and the *maḥḥū* as one who received his oracle in a state of ecstasy,[3] but their functions are said to have overlapped, so that there was a 'cumul des fonctions'.[4] Haldar says it is 'obvious' that the Hebrew 'seer' and 'prophet' are essentially different from one another—though it will be seen later that this is by no means obvious—and he equates the 'seer' with the *bārū* and the 'prophet' with the *maḥḥū*, and then proceeds to use the Babylonian material to interpret the function of the Hebrew seers and prophets.[5] Mowinckel had brought the cultic prophets into association with non-Israelite groups,[6] but had not involved the theory of cultic prophets in such embarrassment as this extreme view threatened to do. Engnell had earlier held that Amos was a cultic official,[7] and in this he was followed by Haldar.[8] More recently it has been claimed that Amos was a hepatoscoper,[9] a mere technician in the art of reading liver omens on which to base his oracles. That there were diviners amongst the Israelite prophets is, indeed, quite certain from references found in the Old Testament. Micah says: 'The priests give direction for payment, and the prophets divine for money.'[10] It is almost certainly true that there were classes of diviners found in Israel, despite the condemnation of divination which we find

---

[1] Cf. *Associations of Cult Prophets among the Ancient Semites*, 1945.
[2] Ibid., pp. 6 ff.   [3] Ibid., pp. 21 ff.
[4] Ibid., p. 28.
[5] Ibid., p. 124.
[6] Cf. *Psalmenstudien*, iii. 5.
[7] In *Studies in Divine Kingship*, p. 87, Engnell argued that the term *nōḳēdh*, which is used of Amos in Amos i. 1 and of Mesha of Moab in 2 Kings iii. 4, denoted a cultic official, and in *Svenskt Bibliskt Uppslagsverk*, i (1948), cols. 59 f., he directly states that Amos was a cultic official.
[8] Op. cit., pp. 79 n., 112. Against the view of Engnell and Haldar, cf. K. Roubos, op. cit., pp. 4 ff.
[9] Cf. M. Bič, *Vetus Testamentum*, i (1951), pp. 293 ff. Against this cf. A. Murtonen, ibid. ii (1952), pp. 170 ff.
[10] Mic. iii. 11; cf. Ezek. xiii. 6, 9, xxii. 28.

in several passages.[1] Indeed, it is unlikely that we should have found such frequent condemnation if the practice had no footing amongst the people. But it is an abuse of 'patternism' to read the Babylonian situation into the Hebrew, and to reduce all the Old Testament prophets to divining classes.[2] The 'Myth and Ritual School' did not begin in such doctrinaire rigidities.

It might seem, then, that we should draw as sharp a line between two sorts of prophet as was formerly drawn between prophet and priest, and that cultic prophets should be linked with the priests and set over against the canonical prophets as persons of a wholly different order, who should never have been designated by the same name.[3] We know beyond a peradventure that there were inner divisions between the prophets, and that each side accused the other of being false prophets. Jeremiah issued a sustained attack on the false prophets of his day,[4] and charged

---

[1] Cf. Lev. xix. 26, Deut. xviii. 10, 1 Sam. xv. 23, xxviii. 2, 2 Kings xvii. 17, xxi. 6; also Isa. iii. 2, Mic. iii. 11, Jer. xxvii. 9, xxix. 8, Ezek. xiii. 6, 9, xxii. 28, Zech. x. 2.

[2] H. J. Kraus (*Gottesdienst in Israel*, 1954, p. 110) says it is an undue simplification of the problems to dispose of the relations of the prophets to the cultus by the slogan 'cult-prophecy'. It is curious that he shows no acquaintance with the work of Haldar, but justifies this comment by a reference to the works of Mowinckel and Johnson. Probably both authors would say that this comment is an over-simplification of their view, and would doubt whether Kraus had read their works with sufficient care to understand them. As the present essay may sufficiently show, their work arose out of a protest against the older simplification, and they are careful not to fall into a new simplification, but to recognize that in dealing with Old Testament religion no simple dichotomies are justified.

[3] A. Jepsen, *Nabi*, 1934, endeavours to establish this kind of sharp line between the greater prophetic figures of the Old Testament and the prophets of the *nābhî'* type, whose name has unfortunately become attached to them. His distinction is not between cultic prophets and non-cultic, but between professional prophets and non-ecstatic prophets. Its mistake lies, as so often, in the desire for something clear cut. N. W. Porteous (in *Record and Revelation*, ed. by H. W. Robinson, 1938, p. 233) says: 'It is difficult to believe that Jepsen is right in making the cleavage between *nebi'im* and canonical prophets as absolute as he does. His theory has the weakness of every theory which depends on a thoroughgoing revision of the text that is not at all points convincing. . . . It seems likely that they (i.e. the great prophets) had something in common with the *nebi'im* which made it natural for men to group them together with the latter.' A. Neher (*L'Essence du Prophétisme*, 1955, pp. 207 ff.) identifies 'nabism' with cultic prophecy, and holds that after the destruction of Shiloh the prophets substituted themselves for the priests and assumed priestly functions.

[4] Jer. xxiii. 9 ff.

them with being poor technicians who stole one another's oracles to disguise their incompetence and lack of divine direction.[1] The Book of Deuteronomy bears witness to the prevalence and the danger of false prophets, when it twice offers guidance for their detection.[2] Unfortunately that guidance is not very clear. In one case it says that the prophet whose word does not come true is a false prophet; but in this case the guidance is too late to save people from being misled by his specious promises. In the other passage it says that even if the prediction comes true the prophet who draws people away from God is a false prophet; but since the prophets on both sides spoke in the name of God and claimed to be His mouthpiece, the bewildered hearers were not helped to distinguish between them. The fact that the compilers of Deuteronomy, who clearly wished to help men in this respect, could find no satisfactory way of doing so is sufficient to show that we cannot simply identify the false prophets with the cultic prophets and divorce the true prophets from the cultus. Had there been so unmistakable a principle of discrimination, Deuteronomy might have been expected to indicate it.

The inner division between true and false prophets first comes before us in the story of Micaiah, in the time of Ahab and Jehoshaphat.[3] But Micaiah and the prophets who were opposed to him were as much, or as little, cultic prophets. They were clearly prophets of the same order, making like claims to utter oracles which Yahweh gave them, and Micaiah can only offer the explanation that Yahweh had suffered a lying spirit to mislead Zedekiah the son of Chenaanah.[4] Similarly, when Jeremiah was ridiculed in the Temple by a prophet who spoke with a different

---

[1] Jer. xxiii. 30. [2] Deut. xiii. 1 ff, xviii. 22.
[3] 1 Kings xxii. 5 ff.

[4] 1 Kings xxii. 21 ff. Kraus (op. cit., pp. 114 f.) makes the astonishing assumption that this vision must have taken place at 'the amphictyonic centre', and that it provides evidence for his theory that the call of the prophets was associated with the Ark. This is pure eisegesis. There is no reference whatsoever to the 'call' of Micaiah, who was known to be a prophet long before this incident (cf. 1 Kings xxii. 8), and there is no suggestion whatever that when he was sent for he was in any shrine, or had to visit a shrine for this vision before he could come into the King's presence. Moreover, since Micaiah was a northern prophet, it is not clear how the Ark, which was at Jerusalem, comes into the picture at all.

voice from his,[1] it is apparent that both claimed a like status and a like inspiration, and once more the difference between true and false prophet is one which could not easily be discerned by the common people.

Clearly we cannot draw sharp lines to divide off the different classes of prophet from one another. That there were many varieties of them may be known with certainty. Apart from the term 'man of God', which stands for a prophet, we find the terms *rō'eh* and *ḥōzeh*, both meaning 'seer', and *nābhî'*, whose precise etymological meaning is not agreed,[2] but which certainly stands for various kinds of prophet. In 1 Sam. ix. 9 we find the terms *rō'eh* and *nābhî'* equated, and though it is probable that originally they stood for identifiably different varieties of sacred person, it is impossible to carry any distinction through the passages where the various terms are used. The passage in 1 Sam. ix. 9 says 'he that is now called a prophet (*nābhî'*) was formerly called a seer (*rō'eh*)'. Both terms are applied to Samuel, and we find that Gad is called both a prophet and a seer in the same verse (the term for 'seer' being there *ḥōzeh*).[3]

Of the varieties of the functioning of the persons described by these various terms a few examples must suffice. Samuel is found available for consultation at Ramah,[4] where he apparently presides at a sacred feast,[5] and he tells Saul to await him at the shrine of Gilgal.[6] Ahijah is available for consultation at Shiloh,[7] though it is improbable that there was a shrine there in his day.[8] Gad is the king's seer,[9] and there is no suggestion that he functioned in any shrine. Elisha is consulted in his own home by Naaman,[10] and is summoned to the presence of the kings of Israel and

---

[1] Jer. xxviii. 1 ff.
[2] Cf. *The Servant of the Lord*, 1952, pp. 96 ff., where I discuss this question with reference to the views of other scholars.
[3] 2 Sam. xxiv. 11.
[4] 1 Sam. ix. 6 ff.
[5] 1 Sam. ix. 22 ff.
[6] 1 Sam. x. 8.
[7] 1 Kings xiv. 1 ff.
[8] The Danish excavations at Shiloh have shown that the place was destroyed in the eleventh century B.C. and that its occupation thereafter was very slight for some centuries. Cf. H. Kjaer, *Quarterly Statement of the Palestine Exploration Fund*, 1927, pp. 202 ff., 1931, pp. 71 ff., and A. Mallon, *Biblica*, x (1929), pp. 369 ff.
[9] 2 Sam. xxiv. 11.
[10] 2 Kings v. 9.

Judah on a campaign against Edom.[1] Nathan waylaid David on the roadside when he went to rebuke him for his conduct in relation to Bathsheba and Uriah,[2] and an unnamed prophet similarly waylaid Ahab after a battle,[3] and Elijah on another occasion waylaid the same king.[4] In all these cases the prophet appears to have functioned as an individual figure in various places, and certainly not always in relation to any religious observance in a shrine, though sometimes he is found there. The prophet Samuel even exercised the priestly function of sacrifice.[5] On the other hand we sometimes find prophets in companies. There were such companies living at Bethel,[6] at Jericho,[7] and at Gilgal,[8] or prophesying by the wayside under the hill of Gibeah,[9] or with Samuel at Ramah.[10] Large numbers of Baal prophets were maintained by Jezebel,[11] and at the end of Ahab's reign we find a similar group of Yahweh prophets at his court.[12] Evidence that some of the prophets found their oracles by divination has already been mentioned. Others were stirred to prophecy by music,[13] or found their messages through dreams.[14] It is quite impossible to reduce all these to a single category of prophet, or to define which were true and which were false in terms of the place where they functioned or whether they functioned alone or in groups. All we can say with confidence is that the prophet was a sacred person, who could exercise his prophetic ministry in a shrine or elsewhere, and that hard and fast lines could not be drawn between the various kinds of prophet, or the relation of a prophet to God be deduced from the circumstances in which he prophesied.

[1] 2 Kings iii. 11.   [2] 2 Sam. xii. 1.   [3] 1 Kings xx. 38.
[4] 1 Kings xxi. 17 ff.   [5] 1 Sam. x. 8.   [6] 2 Kings ii. 3.
[7] 2 Kings ii. 5.   [8] 2 Kings iv. 38.   [9] 1 Sam. x. 5, 10.
[10] 1 Sam. xix. 18 ff.   [11] 1 Kings xviii. 19.   [12] 1 Kings xxii. 6.
[13] 2 Kings iii. 15; cf. 1 Sam. x. 5. T. J. Meek (*Hebrew Origins*, 1936, p. 168; 2nd ed., 1950, p. 173) notes that in the latter of these passages there is no indication that the music was more than the accompaniment of the prophetic state, whereas in the former it was used to bring on that state. He therefore holds that this was a development of professionalism. 'One mark of this growing professionalism', he says, 'was the use of mechanical means to induce the prophetic ecstasy.' H. Junker (op. cit., p. 32) thinks the prophets in 1 Sam. x. 5 were returning from the shrine, and brings this passage into association with the procession psalms.
[14] Num. xii. 6, Jer. xxiii. 28.

If there were cultic prophets who had a defined place in the ritual of the shrines, and who shared with the priests in the services which took place there as officials of the cultus,[1] it is impossible to suppose that the major canonical prophets exercised their ministry in this way. Here I am in the fullest agreement with T. J. Meek, who says: 'It is questionable whether many of the canonical prophets were cult officials, despite the opinion of modern scholars to the contrary.'[2] It is true that Amos prophesied in the shrine at Bethel,[3] but it is scarcely likely that it was as an official sharing in the sacred rite of the sanctuary that he functioned. Isaiah received his call in the Temple,[4] either when he was actually in the Temple or present in vision only, but there is no reason to suppose that he was on its staff.[5] Jeremiah prophesied in the Temple when he announced its destruction,[6] but it could hardly have been as a participant in any official service. Haldar asserts that Jeremiah 'obviously' belonged to the Temple staff,[7] but to other scholars this is anything but obvious. On another occasion we find him prophesying in the

---

[1] N. W. Porteous (*Expository Times*, lxii (1950–1), p. 8) suggests that the cultic prophets were priests with an added gift. He says: 'May the supposed cult prophets not merely be priests who, like Jeremiah and Ezekiel, were specially endowed to undertake the sacramental side of worship, but unlike them, did not feel forced into an attitude of criticism toward the cult? Haldar's principle of cumulation of functions might very well apply here.'

[2] Cf. *Hebrew Origins*, 2nd ed., pp. 178 ff.

[3] Amos vii. 10 ff.

[4] Engnell, in *The Call of Isaiah*, 1949, offers an interpretation of Isa. vi in terms of the New Year festival and the royal rites that belonged to it as the background of the prophet's experience.

[5] Cf. T. J. Meek, *Hebrew Origins*, 2nd ed., p. 179: 'It has sometimes been said that Isaiah was in the temple as a cult official when he had the vision of his call, but because he had a vision of Yahweh in the temple it does not follow that he was a functionary there, or that he was in the temple; he could have had such a vision anywhere and in any capacity.' Cf. also Roubos, op. cit., pp. 17 ff.

[6] Jer. vii. 2 ff., xxvi. 2 ff.

[7] Op. cit., p. 121. Haldar refers to Jer. i. 1 *et passim*. Jer. i. 1 states that he was 'of the priests that were in Anathoth'. This would not make him a member of the staff of the Jerusalem Temple, and if it did it would be *qua* priest and not *qua* cultic prophet. It is commonly supposed that Jeremiah may have been a descendant of the Abiathar who was priest in Jerusalem in the days of David, but who was dismissed to Anathoth in the reign of Solomon (1 Kings ii. 26 f., 35). Cf. Roubos, op. cit., pp. 22 ff.

Temple,[1] but following that incident we find that the exiles in Babylon ask why the Temple authorities cannot keep him in order.[2] Within the Temple he is subject to the discipline of the Temple authorities, but there is no indication that the activities complained of were part of the organized worship of the Temple. Within the Temple precincts much went on besides the organized worship. In the New Testament we find Jesus teaching in the Temple,[3] though He cannot be supposed to have been a member of the Temple personnel. Just as He could gather a group around Him and speak to them, so, it may be presumed, Old Testament prophets could gather groups around them within the precincts of Temple or shrine, without necessarily being officially associated with the sanctuary.

Not all of Jeremiah's prophesying was done in the Temple. He could be sent for by Zedekiah to give him privately the word of the Lord;[4] he could go to the house of the potter,[5] there to find a message for men, or the sight of two baskets of figs could prompt an oracle.[6] Similarly Isaiah could go outside the city to meet the king and there deliver to him the word of the Lord.[7] Though Ezekiel was a priest,[8] his oracles are said to have been delivered in Babylonia, and there is no suggestion that any of them were given as part of a service of worship, or that he belonged to the personnel that conducted such a service. The theory of cultic prophets—and I would emphasize that it is a theory, though much seems to point to its soundness—does not mean that all the prophets of the Old Testament are turned into such prophets. On the other hand, it does not mean that all the cultic prophets are turned into false prophets. If the prophetic psalms were recited by cultic prophets in the ritual of the Temple, we must recognize that there were probably good and bad, true and false, amongst these prophets as there were amongst the others. At the same time, if this view is correct, it would reinforce the conclusion that the antithesis between priests and

---

[1] Jer. xxviii. 1 ff.
[2] Jer. xxix. 24 ff.
[3] Mark xi. 15 ff., 27 ff., xii. 1 ff., John vii. 14 ff.
[4] Jer. xxxvii. 17 ff.
[5] Jer. xviii. 2 ff.
[6] Jer. xxiv. 1 ff.
[7] Isa. vii. 3 ff.
[8] Ezek. i. 3.

prophets is not to be overstressed, and lend support to the belief that while the prophets of reform certainly denounced the hollowness of much of the religious observance of their day, they were not opposed to all religious observance and did not advocate a religion without any corporate expression in worship. It is improbable that men whose function is denoted by a common term were at such irreconcilable cross purposes as they would in that case have been with the cultic prophets. There were good and bad prophets, and there were probably good and bad priests, and the divergence between the reform prophets on the one hand and the good cultic prophets and good priests on the other was probably that the former saw no value in the ritual of the shrines of their day—since men did not validate the rites by the spirit they brought to them—and saw no hope of any real amendment of men's evil ways, while the latter sought to invest the forms of religion with their true meaning.[1] Beside them were doubtless the mere formalists on the cultic side, who were unconcerned for the spirit so long as the ritual was duly carried out, and the popular prophets on the non-cultic side, who would provide the oracle that won them approval and profit, but who were insensitive to the Spirit of God.

Are we then to conclude that the only remains of the compositions of the cultic prophets are to be found in the Psalter, and that while the oracles of non-cultic prophets have been preserved in the prophetic canon, those of their cultic brethren have been anonymously preserved only in so far as they have secured a place in the Psalter? This would certainly be surprising. Most of the oracles in the prophetic books arose out of a given historical situation and were directed to people who lived in that situation. It is, of course, impossible to attach a precise date to the individual oracles, but the work of each prophet bears the marks of the period in which he lived. The psalms, on the other hand, do

---

[1] Cf. H. F. Hahn, *Old Testament in Modern Research*, 1954, p. 141: 'With this altered perspective on the prophetic function, it was possible to see the priest and prophet, each in his own sphere, working for the furtherance of religion without being continually at cross-purposes. The priest had the help of the cult-prophet in teaching the significance of ritual actions; the canonical prophet added yet more by infusing religious worship with an ethical content.'

not appear to be addressed in general to a precise historical situation, and all attempts to date them with reference to such a situation have failed—with rare exceptions, such as Ps. cxxxvii. The failure here is quite different from the failure to give a precise date to the individual oracles in the prophets. It is impossible to date the psalms within centuries, and the widest differences have prevailed amongst the scholars who have sought to define their age. The psalms appear to be related to ritual situations, which were recurrent, and therefore to have been used repeatedly in the appropriate circumstances. On Mowinckel's view many of them were related to the royal festivals, and especially to the New Year festival, in which he believed the cultic prophets played an important part.[1]

It will be remembered that in Mowinckel's formulation of the theory of cultic prophets he suggests that they did not merely recite stereotyped formulae, but that they experienced a rush of the Spirit and formulated on the spot the response which they made in the name of the congregation. Such impromptu responses would not all be equally impressive, and it is antecedently likely that the more successful would be recorded and found to be a present help in trouble by the less original technicians in this service.[2] But if there were creative cultic prophets, it might be expected that on special occasions, and especially in moments of crisis for the nation, the responses of such prophets would have some relation to the situation, and would therefore be less suitable for inclusion in the Psalter, since they would not be the sort of

---

[1] Engnell says roundly that the only possible interpretation of the relevant psalms is that *'in their original situation* the psalms at issue are to be judged as rituals directly referring to the functioning in the cult of the sacral King' (*B.J.R.L.*, xxxi (1948), p. 56). On the function of the King in the cult cf. A. R. Johnson, *Sacral Kingship in Ancient Israel*, 1955, and his essay in the present volume.

[2] Cf. *Psalmenstudien*, iii. 8. N. W. Porteous criticizes Mowinckel's theory that there were two sorts of cultic prophets. He says: 'He (i.e. Mowinckel) suggests that, while the *nebhi'im* were undoubtedly associated with the sanctuary, it was only certain among them who were actually admitted to be cult functionaries, the great majority being representative of the congregation and performing the orgiastic exercises on its behalf. The prophets, therefore, are to be thought of as representatives of the lay element in the worship. Is it then really necessary to suppose that we have two classes of prophets associated with the sanctuaries, namely a majority of lay prophets and a minority of cult prophets?' (*E.T.*, lxii (1950–1), p. 8).

responses that could be recurrently used. Moreover, apart from such responses, if many of the psalms were used to accompany ritual acts and were therefore liturgical texts, they may well be the composition of cultic prophets—not simply impromptu creations, but carefully and artistically prepared. For the special occasions special liturgical texts might have been prepared, and again these would be less suitable for inclusion in the Psalter.

It is not, therefore, surprising that some scholars have found traces of cultic liturgies preserved in the prophetic books, and one of the features of recent study of the prophets—not merely amongst members of the 'Myth and Ritual School' or the 'Scandinavian School'—has been the detection of such liturgies within the prophetic canon. Mowinckel believed that Joel and Habakkuk were liturgies to be attributed to cultic prophets,[1] on the ground that they contain a mixture of passages in the style of psalm and prophecy. Humbert propounded the view that the book of Nahum was a prophetic liturgy, composed for the celebration of the fall of Nineveh in 612 B.C.[2] Balla took the view that Habakkuk was a liturgy,[3] and this was adopted by Humbert in an extended study of this prophet.[4] Engnell followed the view that Joel was a cultic liturgy,[5] but Kapelrud has maintained that it was composed in the style of such a liturgy, rather than that it was ever used in the actual service of the Temple.[6]

---

[1] Ibid., pp. 27 ff.

[2] Cf. *Z.A.W.* xliv (N.F. iii, 1926), pp. 266 ff., *AfO.* v (1928–9), pp. 14 ff., *R.H.Ph.R.* xii (1932), pp. 1 ff.; cf. also A. Weiser, *Einleitung in das Alte Testament,* 2nd ed., 1949, p. 192. A. Haldar (*Studies in the Book of Nahum,* 1947, pp. 3 ff.) rejects the view that the book is a liturgy (so also O. Eissfeldt, *Einleitung in das Alte Testament,* 1934, pp. 462 f.), but thinks it arose in a cult-prophetic circle and had a propagandist aim. Cf. Haldar's view as expressed in *Svenskt Bibliskt Uppslagsverk,* ii (1952), cols. 417 ff.

[3] Cf. *Die Religion in Geschichte und Gegenwart,* 2nd ed., ii (1928), cols. 1556 f. Balla was followed by E. Sellin, *Einleitung in das Alte Testament,* 6th ed., 1933, p. 120. Cf. Weiser, op. cit., pp. 195 f.

[4] Cf. *Problèmes du livre d'Habacuc,* 1944, pp. 296 ff.; also Engnell, in *Svenskt Bibliskt Uppslagsverk,* i (1948), cols. 769 ff.

[5] Cf. *Svenskt Bibliskt Uppslagsverk,* i (1948), cols. 1075 ff.

[6] Cf. *Joel Studies,* 1948; cf. also Weiser, op. cit., p. 179. T. H. Robinson (in Robinson–Horst, *Die zwölf Kleinen Propheten,* 1938, p. 63) had regarded Joel ii. 12–14 as a fragment of a penitential liturgy, and held ii. 19 to be taken from a liturgical text.

Once the suggestion of surviving cult liturgies in the prophetic books had been made, there was a tendency to find ever more such passages.[1] Engnell has gone so far as to divide the material found in the prophetic books into two main categories, the one being what he calls the 'diwan type', which consists of direct oracle, and the other the liturgical type, which is modelled on the cultic usage.[2] He maintained that Isa. xxiv–xxvii, the so-called 'Isaiah Apocalypse', is of a liturgical character,[3] and further argues that the whole of Deutero-Isaiah is of this type. It is to be clearly emphasized, however, that he does not mean that the author was a cultic prophet attached to any sanctuary. Just as Kapelrud says that Joel was composed in the style of a cultic liturgy, so Engnell holds that Deutero-Isaiah was a prophetic imitation of a cultic liturgy. He therefore uses the word 'liturgy' in 'a strict form-literary sense, so that the question of its possible directly cultic connexion is left open'.[4]

I am doubtful if cultic liturgies form any large part of the prophetic canon, though it may well be that some such passages have been preserved. Whatever can be read as oracle is more naturally to be read as oracle, and so far as the major figures are concerned—such as Amos, Isaiah, and Jeremiah—it is very hard to suppose that they were cultic prophets. Even if, as I believe, they did not hold the cult to be essentially and ineradicably evil, they regarded the worship of their day as hollow and vain, and it is more than doubtful if they took part as leaders and minis-trants in ceremonies which they declared to be meaningless in their day. It is impossible, for instance, to think that Isaiah,

---

[1] H. Gunkel found Isa. xxxiii to be such a liturgy (cf. *Z.A.W.* xlii (N.F. i. 1924), pp. 177 ff.), and also the end of Micah (cf. *What Remains of the Old Testament*, E. tr. by A. K. Dallas, 1928, pp. 115 ff.; cf. also A. S. Kapelrud, in *Svenskt Bibliskt Uppslagsverk*, ii (1952), cols. 278 f.); G. Gerleman found the book of Zephaniah to be such a liturgy (cf. *Zephanja textkritisch und literarisch untersucht*, 1942).

[2] Cf. *S.E.Å.*, xii (1947), pp. 128 f., *The Call of Isaiah*, 1949, pp. 59 f., and *Svenskt Bibliskt Uppslagsverk*, ii (1952), cols. 763 f.

[3] Cf. *Svenskt Bibliskt Uppslagsverk*, i (1948), col. 1031.

[4] Cf. *B.J.R.L.* xxxi (1948), p. 64. W. Caspari (*Lieder und Gottessprüche der Rückwanderer*, 1934, pp. 129 ff.) offers an elaborate examination of Deutero-Isaiah from the point of view of the cult, with which he associates it closely. The argument is often forced, however. K. Elliger (*Die Einheit des Tritojesaia*, 1928, pp. 15 ff., 24 ff., 29 ff.) finds liturgical passages in Isa. lix. 1–4, 9–18, lxi, lxii, and lxiii. 7–lxiv. 11.

who declared that it was idle for men to trample the courts of the Temple, and to keep sacred festival and offer sacrifice, since God could only see the blood that was upon their hands—it is impossible, I say, to think that he should have participated in the service as a spokesman of the people whose sacrifice God repudiated by his mouth. It is even more difficult to think of Jeremiah fitting into the service as an official ministrant. Many scholars have believed that he declared that God had never ordained sacrifice at all, and not merely that contemporary sacrifice was an offence to Him. Though I do not share this view, I find it impossible to think that he had any use for the kind of services he witnessed in his day. In a city in which evil of all kinds was rampant, where men neighed after one another's wives and cheated and oppressed, where he felt that corruption had reached such a pitch that even if a single righteous person within it might guarantee its safety it yet could not be saved,[1] the thronging of the Temple courts was an idle mockery and an affront to God, which he could only view with impatience.

So far as Ezekiel and Deutero-Isaiah are concerned, their work fell in Babylonia, in the period of the exile, and throughout most of the ministry of both the Temple was no longer standing. We know too little of the organization of the synagogue in that age—if indeed it existed—and there is too little evidence of cultic prophets ever functioning in the worship of the synagogue for it to be reasonable to treat Ezekiel and Deutero-Isaiah as cultic prophets. Only within very modest limits does it seem to me to be reasonable to find cultic liturgies preserved in the prophetic canon. It is not easy to think of the major prophets in that role, or to suppose that cultic liturgies which were composed by others have been attributed to them. The book of Nahum, which is so unlike the other prophetic books in character that some thought of Nahum as one of the false prophets against whom such men as Jeremiah stood, may have been such a liturgy. Its author was a brilliant poet, who described the fall of Nineveh, whether before or after that fall, with superb skill, and whether it was prophecy or liturgy, it is probable that it

[1] Jer. v. 1 ff.

was recited with great satisfaction more than once after Nineveh had fallen.

Though I am not inclined to find any large collection of cultic liturgies in the prophetic canon, I think it possible that some of the oracles were based on such liturgies. It is probable that the haunting and effective Song of the Vine in Isa. v was modelled on some well-known vintage song. It was only as it developed that the prophet's hearers began to realize that it was more than a vintage song. It is possible that occasionally the prophets may have modelled other passages on familiar liturgical compositions, in the way that Kapelrud supposes was done in the case of Joel, and Engnell in the case of other passages.

If, then, I may sum up the fruits of the discussions of recent years, as they appear to me, they are far less substantial than some scholars have supposed. My own attitude to all these studies is one of great caution, and the more extreme of the positions I have indicated I have no hesitation in rejecting. It is wrong in method to impose the pattern of one culture upon another, and especially in this case. For we know that while Israel dwelt in a cultural milieu from which she undoubtedly derived much that found a permanent place in her religion, her prophets fought hard against some elements of that cultural milieu. Clearly, therefore, Israel is not to be understood simply in terms of that milieu, and that which she did not share with others is never to be forgotten. On the other hand, it is dangerous to forget the heritage she drew from the distant past and the influences she was subject to from those around her. The tendency of the more extreme exponents of 'patternism' to reduce all to a single character takes too little account of the evidence, and is much too simple to be probable. So far as the prophets are concerned, the imposition of a uniform type on them and the making of them all into cultic prophets seems to me to be another example of the same lack of penetration.

Happily not all of these studies have been of this Procrustean variety, and it is on this account that I find something of real value to have come out of them. The view that there were cultic prophets rests not on *a priori* ideas, and the forcing of foreign practices on the Old Testament, but on evidence that lies within the Old Testament. But that evidence tells of many varieties of prophet in Israel—varieties not alone of spiritual level, but of means of functioning. The prophet was always a sacred person because he was believed to be possessed by the spirit of God, but he was not necessarily, in virtue of being a prophet, appointed to a defined place in the worship of some shrine.[1] Hence I accept the view that there were cultic prophets without turning the major canonical prophets into members of such guilds.[2] On the other hand I do not divide the prophets into two sharply separated groups, but think they were divided as the colours of the rainbow are divided. The evidence that they were on the staff of any particular shrine is wanting, though there is no evidence against this; it seems to me to be more likely that any prophet was free to function in a shrine though not limited to such functioning, and the extent to which prophets exercised this freedom and the intimacy of their relationship to the ritual of the shrines varied greatly. The softening of the lines between the various groups of prophets, without their reduction to a common type, seems to me to be a great gain.

Similarly the softening of the lines between priests and prophets is in my view a gain. But once more the abandonment of the older, hard antithesis between these classes does not mean that no difference of attitude towards the cultus is to be found amongst prophets and priests. To think of prophets only in terms of the best and priests only in terms of the worst is unwise. There were good prophets and good priests, and while there was undoubtedly a difference of emphasis between them, they were all exponents of the same religion. The Bible contains the Law and the Prophets, and it would be curious if these were governed

---

[1] Cf. what the present writer has said in *The Servant of the Lord*, 1952, p. 105: 'Since prophets were religious persons, devotees of their God, it is natural to find them in the shrines in which religion centred. But that does not make them members of the staff of the shrines.'

[2] Cf. N. W. Porteous, *E.T.* lxii (1950–1), p. 7: 'It may be admitted that an impressive case has been made out for the existence in Israel of cult prophets forming a regular part of the personnel of the sanctuaries.' Porteous earlier on the same page says: 'Like the priests the prophets seem to have an official standing. Whether that inevitably points to their being actually cult officials is not so clear.'

by irreconcilably opposed ideas as to the nature of religion and the will of God. The growing emphasis on the unity of the Old Testament reflected in the many books devoted to the theology of the Old Testament is not unrelated to the studies we have been reviewing.

So far as the preservation of prophetic liturgies in the prophetic books is concerned I am sceptical of the claims that are made to detect them. A few may have survived, and some passages may be based on such liturgies. But it is not here that I look for the solid fruits of these studies. Rather is it in the new light they have shed on the Psalter by bringing it into relation with both prophecy and the cultus. Here once more there has been a significant perception that beneath all its variety of form and of idea, the Old Testament has a deep unity, and that not alone the Law and the Prophets, but the Psalms have a real place in that unity, and that all belong essentially together.

THE MYTH AND RITUAL POSITION
CRITICALLY CONSIDERED

by S. G. F. BRANDON

SINCE the year 1795, when Charles-François Dupuis set forth the view[1] that behind the figures of Christ and Osiris, of Bacchus and Mithra, there lay a common tendency to personify the sun in its annual course, the comparative study of religions has been generally characterized by attempts to find some common interpretative principle which will account either for the origin of religion or for its essential structure. The motive behind such attempts is intelligible, and it may well be compared to the tendency manifest in many other disciplines to seek one simple formula which will explain an immense corpus of otherwise amorphous data. But these attempts, which have generally occurred successively and often in consequence of each other, have resulted in the history of the comparative study of religions assuming the appearance of a chronological record of the rise and fall of various so-called 'schools', which are severally distinguished by the peculiar theories concerning the origin or nature of religion which their members advanced or defended. Thus, to name but a few representative examples: the so-called 'Philological School' of Max Müller and his followers sought to account for religious origins in terms of a solar mythology by means of comparative philology;[2] the reactions which this line of interpretation provoked found a common expression in the efforts of those scholars who turned for a solution to anthropological research and of whom one of the earliest and most distinguished representatives, Sir Edward B. Tylor, set forth animism, i.e. 'belief in Spiritual Beings' as what he termed 'the minimum definition of Religion'.[3] An even greater name in this

---

[1] *L'Origine de tous les cultes ou la religion universelle* (nouv. éd., Paris, 1822). On Dupuis see *La Grande Encyclopédie*, t. 15, p. 97. Cf. G. Berguer in *Histoire générale des religions*, ed. M. Gorce et R. Mortier, t. i (Paris, 1948), p. 8.

[2] e.g. Max Müller, 'Comparative Mythology' (1856), in *Chips from a German Workshop* ii (London, 1867). Cf. L. Spence, *Introduction to Mythology* (London, 1921), pp. 47–51.

[3] *Primitive Culture* i (London, 1929, 1st ed. 1871), 424.

'Anthropological School' is that of Sir James G. Frazer—indeed by reason of his prodigious labours in assembling material and in advancing certain hypotheses in the interpretation of it his name still remains, despite criticism and changing modes of thought, the most significant in this field of study. The work of Frazer, based as that of the 'Anthropological School' generally on the assumption of the soundness of the evolutionary principle in the interpretation of culture,[1] was largely devoted to showing how profoundly the needs of the agriculturalist's life had affected religious concept and practice. The spectacle of the annual cycle of Nature's year, with its recurrent drama of the death and revival of vegetation, inspired, so he maintained, the pregnant idea of the dying-god, of which Adonis, Attis, and Osiris are the classic examples, and from which derived the institution of divine kingship, whereby communities at a certain level of cultural development believed that their well-being was essentially bound up with the well-being of their king, who impersonated or was the incarnation of the spirit of vegetation.[2]

Frazer in his interpretation of religious origins had also advanced the thesis that an 'Age of Magic' had preceded the 'Age of Religion',[3] and in support of this view he had cited a great abundance of evidence concerning the magical rites practised by primitive peoples whereby mainly by the action of miming they sought to cause the recurrence of phenomena advantageous to themselves. This evaluation of the importance of ritual was in due course so developed by the late Professor Gilbert Murray[4] and the late Dr. Jane Harrison[5] in interpreting ancient Greek religion that the claims of ritual magic to be one of the

---

[1] But Frazer fully realized the complexity of the issue and the vital part played by cultural diffusion, cf. *Balder the Beautiful* (*Golden Bough*, *VIII*), i, Preface, pp. vi-vii; *Folklore in the Old Testament*, i. 106–7; 'Sur l'étude des origines humaines' in *The Gorgon's Head and other Literary Pieces* (London, 1927), pp. 348–55.

[2] The theme in its various aspects finds expression throughout the constitutive parts of *The Golden Bough*.   [3] *The Dying God* (*Golden Bough*, iii. 1936), p. 2.

[4] 'Excursus on Ritual Forms preserved in Greek Tragedy', in J. E. Harrison, *Themis* (Cambridge, 1912); *Five Stages of Greek Religion*, chap. i (the substance of the book was originally delivered as lectures in 1912).

[5] *Prolegomena to the Study of Greek Religion* (Cambridge, 1907); *Ancient Art and Ritual* (London, 1913).

primary factors in the origin of religious concept became generally recognized. Closely associated with this new appreciation of ritual came a re-evaluation of myth. In early times myth had been generally regarded either as the poetic imaginings of primitive peoples or it was interpreted aetiologically, i.e. as being the naïve explanations of natural phenomena concocted by the primitive mind. But now attention was given to the close connexion holding between ritual and myth, and since the former was generally believed to be prior in order of appearance, myth in its original form was held to be an explanation of the ritual, a kind of libretto designed to make intelligible sacro-magical acts when the original emotions which prompted them were no longer remembered or understood.[1]

It was in this setting, constituted by the trend of thought in the field of *Religionsgeschichte*, that the so-called 'Myth and Ritual School' emerged in the third decade of the present century. As seen in that context, it appears as an intelligible derivation from the work of Frazer[2] and the new estimate of the function of ritual and myth, and it may also be fairly regarded as another instance of that same tendency to seek a formula which will neatly explain the origin or nature of a complex of religious faith and practice.

Intelligible though it be when seen in such a context, the 'Myth and Ritual' thesis is not thereby adequately explained in the matter of original inspiration, and it would seem that there is yet another factor of considerable significance concerning which a reckoning must be made. A clue to the nature of this factor is surely to be found in the fact that the majority of those scholars who co-operated with Professor S. H. Hooke in the original publication of the thesis in 1933 were men who were

---

[1] Cf. W. R. Smith, *Religion of the Semites* (3rd ed., London, 1927), pp. 17–20, see also S. A. Cook's notes, op. cit., pp. 500–3; A. N. Whitehead, *Religion in the Making* (Cambridge, 1927), pp. 8–17; E. O. James, *Comparative Religion* (London, 1938), pp. 97–100; G. van der Leeuw, *La Religion dans son essence et ses manifestations* (Paris, 1948), pp. 404–5; M. Éliade, *Traité d'histoire des religions* (Paris, 1949), pp. 350–73; Chantepie de la Saussaye, *Lehrbuch der Religionsgeschichte* (ed. A. Bertholet u. E. Lehman, Tübingen, 1925), i. 93–94; E. Cassirer, *An Essay on Man* (New Haven, 1944), pp. 79–83; T. H. Gaster, 'Myth and Story', *Numen*, i (1954), pp. 184–212.

[2] The work of A. M. Hocart should also be noted in this connexion: his *Kingship* was published in 1927 and he contributed to the symposium *The Labyrinth*.

profoundly concerned with the interests of the Christian religion; most of them, moreover, were Old Testament scholars.[1] It is, therefore, not altogether surprising that five out of the original eight lectures, which formed the symposium *Myth and Ritual*, were concerned with the various aspects of the so-called 'Myth and Ritual pattern' as manifest in the cultures of Palestine, and as constituting issues which ultimately had significance for Christian theology.[2] And to what may be described as this general professional interest there may have been an even deeper-lying motive, which can be reasonably defined, although its existence cannot be demonstrated. It is that the 'Myth and Ritual' thesis represents a reaction on the part of certain scholars to the great emphasis which had hitherto been laid upon the essential significance of the prophetic movement and tradition in the religion of Israel. The prophet had been exalted to the detriment of the priest, the inspirational element in religion at the expense of the cultic. Whether such considerations were consciously felt or subconsciously operative,[3] the 'Myth and Ritual' thesis did in fact help to redress the balance by showing that in the cultus of Israel there was a factor which proved as influential as that of prophecy in shaping the thought and aspirations, not only of Israel, but also of Christianity, and it is surely significant that this tacit *apologia* for the cultus coincided with a renewed interest in this country and on the Continent in the liturgical heritage of the Christian Church.[4]

To complete the account of those factors which appear to have been influential in the genesis of the 'Myth and Ritual' thesis consideration must also be given to the theory concerning

[1] The Preface to *Myth and Ritual* (Oxford, 1933) by Canon D. C. Simpson is significant in this connexion.

[2] In the succeeding symposium edited by S. H. Hooke entitled *The Labyrinth* (London, 1935) the same interest manifests itself in the majority of the essays.

[3] In his Preface to *Myth and Ritual*, pp. xiii–xiv, Dr. Simpson was evidently conscious of the issue.

[4] The controversy aroused by the measures to revise the *Book of Common Prayer* in 1927 and 1928 and the publication by the S.P.C.K. of the symposium *Liturgy and Worship* in 1932 may be mentioned in this connexion.

[*Editor's note*: The statements on this page must be corrected by what is said in the first essay.]

the diffusion of culture propounded by Sir Grafton Elliot Smith and W. J. Perry, according to which certain fundamental inventions and institutions of human society, having been first achieved in Egypt, had gradually been diffused among the other peoples of the ancient world: among such institutions was notably that of divine kingship.[1] As will be noticed at greater length presently, the exponents of the 'Myth and Ritual' thesis have variously based themselves upon the diffusionist and the evolutionary theories of culture; nevertheless it is evident in the earliest statements of the thesis that the view that the pharaonic kingship of Egypt had powerfully influenced the ideas and institutions of neighbouring peoples was accepted as virtually axiomatic.[2]

As seen now across more than twenty subsequent years of discussion, discovery, and research, the original exposition of the 'Myth and Ritual' thesis may also be reckoned as the first notable effort to reap the harvest which the archaeology of the Near East had been steadily producing. From the discovery of the celebrated Amarna tablets in 1887 to the uncovering of the ancient city of Ugarit, at the modern Ras Shamra, in 1929, evidence had been accumulating to show that among the peoples occupying what the late Professor J. H. Breasted had aptly called the 'Fertile Crescent' there had been a lively commerce, with its consequent intermingling of cultural elements and influences, so that justification was given for thinking of the ancient Near East as an integral culture-area.[3] Viewed in this light, similarities which were found to exist between the ideas

[1] The chief works in which the diffusionist theory was expounded prior to 1933 were G. Elliot Smith, *The Ancient Egyptian and the Origins of Civilization* (London, 1911, 2nd ed. 1923), *Human History* (London, 1930); W. J. Perry, *The Children of the Sun: a Study in the Early History of Civilization* (London, 1923); *The Growth of Civilization* (1924). Cf. A. J. Toynbee, *A Study of History* i (London, 1935), 424–40.

[2] *Myth and Ritual*, pp. 6, 8–9, 11–12, 71–73, 86 (S. H. Hooke), 87–88 (F. J. Hollis), 117, 118, 121, 123–4, 129 (W. O. E. Oesterley), 149 (E. O. James). It is significant that the Egyptologist, Prof. A. M. Blackman, who contributed to the volume, ends his essay by noting 'an indication that the original "pattern" was not a product of Egypt but was imported thither, possibly from Syria' (op. cit., p. 39).

[3] Cf. Ed. Meyer, *Geschichte des Altertums* (Stuttgart u. Berlin, 1913), i. 680–3; A. Moret, *Des clans aux empires* (Paris, 1923), pp. 185–6, 246, 341–8, 401–3; W. F. Albright, *From the Stone Age to Christianity* (Baltimore, 1946), pp. 1–33, 35–36.

and institutions of the various peoples dwelling in that area were naturally suggestive of a common attitude and response to certain situations. Moreover, this predisposition in particular was conducive to an appreciation of that which in the culture of Israel, traditionally regarded as the 'peculiar people', attested the basic integration of Israelite culture with that which seemed common to the area. But, as will be shown in greater detail presently, by making of the undoubted similarities occurring in the cultures of the ancient Near East the basic assumption of the existence throughout the area of a common cultural tradition in the matter of the institution of kingship, the exponents of the 'Myth and Ritual' thesis tended to disregard the equally or even more significant differences which existed in the *Weltanschauungen* of the cultures concerned.

With this basic assumption there was closely linked in the 'Myth and Ritual' thesis another, namely, the validity of the concept of 'culture-pattern' and the possibility of its effective diffusion outside the sphere in which it was created. In the two volumes in which the 'Myth and Ritual' thesis was first published no formal definition of a 'culture-pattern' was given,[1] but from the use of the term in many passages it is evident that the authors believed that in certain cultures there can be perceived a number of interrelated ideas and practices which may be considered as constituting a unified whole which has its own logic and is expressive of a specific communal endeavour to deal with some situation which threatens the common good and/or which might be made to serve the common welfare. This complex of idea and practice, or in the 'Myth and Ritual' terminology the 'culture-pattern',[2] it is further maintained, can be, in fact has

---

[1] In *Myth and Ritual*, p. 8, S. H. Hooke does give this partial definition: 'The ritual pattern represents the things which were done to and by the king in order to secure the prosperity of the community in every sense for the coming year.' In *The Labyrinth*, p. 260, E. O. James makes what may be deemed a definition of certain aspects of the 'pattern': 'Around the divine kingship a series of religious activities was set in motion in the great agricultural civilizations of the ancient East which had for their purpose the maintenance of the food supply and the prosperity of society in general, as well as the satisfaction of individual needs.' Cf. E. O. James, *Comparative Religion*, pp. 94–95.

[2] It is to be noted that often the term 'ritual pattern' is used when its connotation

been, diffused from the culture in which it originated and established effectively within alien cultures or at least among alien peoples. Now the mode of such a diffusion is never explicitly described, and the most that may be inferred from various allusions and references is that such 'culture-patterns' were diffused in consequence of war or trade or colonization. But the issue involved here is too important to permit the assumption to be passed without a closer scrutiny of its practical aspects. Accordingly it may be noted that in a pertinent passage Professor Hooke maintains that, just as the symbol of the winged sun-disk was diffused from Egypt to Assyria, Cappadocia and Persia, so 'it is also possible to conceive of the carrying of the larger ritual pattern with its associated myth from one country to another by one of the various ways of "culture spread", such as commerce, conquest, or colonization'.[1] However, the very example which is here chosen in support of the theory does itself raise doubt about the soundness of that theory, because it is evident that, while Hittite, Assyrian, and Iranian artists did copy this famous Egyptian symbol, its original significance was not understood by them—quite obviously it was the general form of the symbol which impressed the foreigner and he reproduced it without insight into its intrinsic meaning, changing its pregnant details according to his own fancy or needs.[2] If this then happened in the transmission of the concrete symbol of the winged sun-disk of Egypt, the question may well be asked how far is the assumption justified that a complex of religious ideas and practice, such as that presupposed in the 'Myth and Ritual' thesis, which had been created by a particular people in response to its experience of life in a given geographical environment, could be effectively

is clearly meant to include other elements than the 'ritual'. Cf. R. F. Benedict, *Patterns of Culture* (New York, 1934), pp. 23–24, 46, 254. See also J. de Fraine, *L'Aspect religieux de la royauté israélite* (Roma, 1954), pp. 27–32; A. Bentzen, *Messias-Moses redivivus Menschensohn* (Zürich, 1948), p. 16; *King and Messiah* (London, 1955), p. 83 n. 8, p. 84 n. 11.   [1] *Myth and Ritual*, p. 4.

[2] An example of this can be noted in op. cit., fig. i, in the reproduction of the *uraeus* serpents by the foreign artists: quite clearly they did not appreciate this part of the symbol and treated it as a pair of decorative streamers. On the significance of the Egyptian winged sun-disk see H. Bonnet, *Reallexikon der ägyptischen Religionsgeschichte* (Berlin, 1952), *sub nominibus* 'Behdeti' and 'Uräus'.

transmitted to alien peoples? It will be well here to consider again the instance of the winged sun-disk, since it has further significance in this connexion. Because such a symbol was a visible object and could be seen by a traveller on many Egyptian buildings or on objects circulated outside Egypt through trade or diplomatic policy, it was easy for a foreign artist to reproduce it, or something like it, in his own land; but, if the foreigner had not been content merely with an approximate reproduction of such a symbol and had sought to understand its spiritual meaning, he would have been obliged to make special inquiry of the competent Egyptian authorities, an undertaking which would have required considerable knowledge of a foreign language and insight into alien modes of thought.[1] It may accordingly be asked who in the countries of the ancient Near East would have been sufficiently interested in, or capable of, surmounting such immense difficulties in order to transmit to their own people the esoteric 'culture-pattern' of some alien folk? Merchants, soldiers, or colonists are certainly not cast for this role, and it is instructive to note what happened when educated men in the ancient world did specially seek to understand and interpret a culture alien to their own—the strange accounts which Herodotus gave of Egyptian customs and Plutarch's version of the Osirian myth have provided several generations of Egyptologists with a fascinating task of trying to identify their queer statements with what is known of ancient Egyptian faith and practice from the native records; and the general verdict is that these Greek savants utterly failed to apprehend the true nature of Egyptian religion.[2]

[1] The Egyptians' fear of dying and being buried in a foreign land, which is graphically described in the Middle Kingdom story of Sinuhe (Erman–Blackman, *Literature of the Ancient Egyptians*, pp. 14–29), is evidence of their conviction that foreigners could not really understand the essentials of Egyptian religion. The Phoenician attempts at embalming the bodies of certain magnates and their burial in anthropoid sarcophagi were obviously inspired by knowledge of Egyptian funerary practice, but it is equally obvious that such imitation did not imply an intelligent adoption of the Egyptian mortuary faith; cf. G. Contenau, *La Civilisation phénicienne* (Paris, 1949), pp. 155–6, 197–202, plates xi, xii; E. A. W. Budge, *The Mummy* (Cambridge, 1925), p. 431. See also H. Frankfort *The Art and Architecture of the Ancient Orient* (London, 1954), pp. 66, 117, 157–61, 197–201.

[2] Cf. Sourdille, *Hérodote et la religion de l'Égypte* (Paris, 1910), pp. 363, 365–6, 401; W. Spiegelberg, *Die Glaubwürdigkeit der Herodots Berichte über Ägypten im*

The assumption that 'culture-patterns' existed and could be effectively disseminated from their original centre among the peoples of the ancient Near East prepares the way for the next assumption, namely, that there existed a definitive 'culture-pattern' centred on the institution of divine kingship which was thus disseminated and which came to constitute a common tradition of faith and practice throughout that area. It is a crucial part of the 'Myth and Ritual' thesis that this 'culture-pattern' found dramatic expression at an annual festival in which the king played an essential part. The constitutive elements of the ritual enacted at this festival are defined as 'the dramatic representation of the death and resurrection of the god'; 'the recitation or symbolic representation of the myth of creation'; 'the ritual combat, in which the triumph of the god over his enemies was depicted'; 'the sacred marriage'; 'the triumphal procession, in which the king played the part of the god followed by a train of lesser gods or visiting deities'.[1] The clarity with which these liturgical moments are defined and their articulation in the assumed ἱερὸς λόγος demonstrated is certainly impressive, but when a search is made in the relevant expositions of the 'Myth and Ritual' thesis for an account of the actual origin of this 'ritual-pattern' and for evidence of its occurrence as such in the records of the various cultures concerned, the result is curiously vague and unsatisfactory. If the influence of the pharaonic kingship had been such as is assumed, it is reasonable to expect that in the Egyptian records there should be ample evidence of the existence of this 'ritual pattern' as a regular feature of the state-religion of Egypt and, further, of its great antiquity. However, the essay which was contributed to the original symposium by the Egyptologist, Professor A. M. Blackman, despite its considerable value to Egyptological studies, is notable for its generally negative character in this respect. Although, by ranging throughout the

---

Lichte der ägyptischen Denkmäler (Heidelberg, 1926), pp. 16–18, 34–40; A. Erman, *Die Religion der Ägypter* (Berlin u. Leipzig, 1934), pp. 86–87, 333, 425–6; E. A. W. Budge, *Osiris and the Egyptian Resurrection* i (London, 1911), 18. Megasthenes's identification of two Indian gods with Dionysos and Herakles is also significant in this connexion; cf. C. Eliot, *Hinduism and Buddhism* ii (London, 1954), 137–8, 139 n. 1.

[1] *Myth and Ritual*, p. 8 (S. H. Hooke).

whole course of Egyptian history, a number of instances were found which had a certain degree of correspondence to certain moments of the hypothetical 'ritual-pattern', nowhere was it shown that there was a regular annual festival in Egypt which reproduced this 'pattern' in its essential entirety and thus presumably provided the prototype of such a festival, which was diffused from the valley of the Nile throughout the lands of the Fertile Crescent.[1]

The most convincing evidence of the occurrence of such a 'ritual-pattern' at an annual festival is actually provided by the records of the New Year festival at Babylon.[2] But the significance of this evidence may well be questioned; the actual documents concerned are relatively late in date and Babylon cannot, without qualification, be regarded as representative of Mesopotamia generally back to the era of Sumerian hegemony,[3] and still less may it be taken as typical in the matter of the religious faith and practice of various states, not all of them of Semitic origin, lying far to the west and north, unless it can be shown that the culture of Babylon or of some older Mesopotamian state was effectively diffused throughout the area of the Near East.

[1] See the statement of Blackman quoted on p. 265 n. 2, above. Cf. H. Frankfort, *Kingship and the Gods* (Chicago, 1948), pp. 34–35, 183–5, 204, 207–9. See also the account of Egyptian kingship given by Bonnet, op. cit., *sub nomin.* 'Dreißigjahrfest', 'Feste', 'König', 'Krönung', 'Kult', 'Theokratie'; see also under 'Ernte'. Reference might also be made to the account of H. W. Fairman ('Worship and Festivals in an Egyptian Temple', in *B.J.R.L.*, xxxvii. 1954) of the annual festivals, in which the king participated, at the Ptolemaic temple of Edfu: the sacred marriage there had nothing of the character of that assumed in the 'Myth and Ritual' thesis (cf. op. cit., pp. 196–7, 200).

[2] Cf. C. J. Gadd, *Myth and Ritual*, pp. 47 ff.; S. H. Hooke, *The Origins of Early Semitic Ritual* (Schweich Lectures, 1935), pp. 8–19, *Babylonian and Assyrian Religion* (London, 1953), pp. 58–60, 103–11; I. Engnell, *Studies in Divine Kingship in the Ancient Near East* (Uppsala, 1943), pp. 18 ff.

[3] The Babylonian evidence for the sacred marriage is actually wanting and the 'pattern' has to be completed in this respect from other sources, see Gadd, op. cit., p. 56. 'La spéculation théologique doit adapter les anciens mythes au nouvel état politique et puisque rien n'existe en ce monde, si ce n'est par l'ordre des dieux et le destin qu'ils ont fixé, à l'élévation de Babylone au-dessus des autres cités doit répondre nécessairement l'exaltation de son dieu au-dessus de tous les autres dieux', L. Delaporte, *La Mésopotamie* (Paris, 1923), p. 154. Some allowance must also be made for the religious 'reformation' effected about the time of Ḥammurabi, cf. Delaporte, *Le Proche-Orient Asiatique* (Paris, 1948), p. 139–40.

This consideration leads back to an issue which has already been briefly noticed. It is that in the exposition of the 'Myth and Ritual' thesis there appears to be some uncertainty as to whether an original 'myth and ritual pattern' was diffused throughout the Near East from some single centre or whether in various places throughout that area similar 'patterns' were independently evolved in response to the challenge of similar environments. Each of these alternatives has its own particular set of problems. Generally it would seem that the diffusionist view has prevailed, but with uncertainty as to the original source of the movement. The continuous reference which is made to the pharaonic monarchy as the supreme example of divine kingship suggests that often Egypt is regarded as the original source of the 'myth and ritual pattern'.[1] But no attempt is made to demonstrate this, which perhaps is not surprising in view of the fact just previously noticed that the Egyptian records provide no evidence of the hypothetical 'cult-pattern' having existed as such in the state-religion of the land. That Mesopotamia is assumed to be the original point of diffusion seems to be indicated in certain other statements of the thesis,[2] but here again no definitive attempt has been made to prove that this was so; moreover, as has already been noted, there is a vagueness about the presumed place of origin of the 'pattern' in Mesopotamia itself, which in view of the nature of the relevant data is understandable. It is, accordingly, found on examination that not only have the exponents of the 'Myth and Ritual' thesis neglected to deal with the practical problems which the idea of a diffusion of an esoteric complex of religious concept and practice inevitably entails, but they themselves do not appear to be clear in their minds on the fundamental point of the location of the original centre from which the 'pattern' was diffused.[3]

---

[1] See above, p. 265 n. 2; to which may be added the later references of E. O. James, *The Labyrinth*, pp. 244, 249–50, 253–4, *Christian Myth and Ritual* (London, 1937), pp. 1–6, 40–41, 58–62.

[2] Cf. *Myth and Ritual*, pp. 66 (Gadd), 70, 81, 86 (Hooke—in this essay a compromise sometimes seems to appear in the use of the term 'Egyptian-Babylonian pattern'), 112–13, 120, 124, 129, 135 (Oesterley): Hooke, *Origins of Early Semitic Ritual*, p. 1.

[3] That the 'pattern' might have been diffused from two separate centres, namely,

In the final paragraph of his contribution to the symposium *Myth and Ritual* Professor W. O. E. Oesterley suggested that, while the diffusionist theory accounted for the recurrence of the 'pattern' among various peoples in what might be termed its classic form, the true cause of its being lay deeper. The passage deserves quotation:[1]

Behind the central 'pattern' with all its varying modifications in different centres among diverse peoples, there were certain underlying conceptions common to the entire world of the Near East, and beyond. Whether expressed in the developed and elaborate ritual of the city-god of Babylon, or in the somewhat similar rites in Erech and Asshur, or in those of the Egyptians on the morning of their New Year, or in those of the Zoroastrian *Naurūz* (New Year Festival), or in the celebrations in Jerusalem in honour of Jahweh, the underlying *motif*, expressed in various ways by different peoples, was the attempt to explain the mysteries of the dying vegetation at the approach of winter, and of the revival of Nature in the spring. While it is clear that in the case both of ideas and ritual the influence of more powerful and cultured peoples exerted itself on the less advanced, yet behind and beneath all was the insistent urge to answer the questions: Why does the vegetation die; how can it be revivified?

In this passage Dr. Oesterley touches upon an issue which must be much in the mind of one who seeks to study religion with comparative reference when he finds himself confronted with the 'Myth and Ritual' thesis. If the alleged recurrence of the

Egypt and Mesopotamia, as some statements seem to imply, must encounter the objection either that it is very improbable that such a 'pattern' would have been spontaneously and contemporaneously generated in two different places, or, that, if one of these centres had originally borrowed from the other, there is still the same 'diffusionist' problem to be solved.

[1] *Myth and Ritual*, p. 146. In this connexion the curiously obscure statement of Engnell (op. cit., p. 72) should be noted: 'However, as a possible contrary conception one may consider the west-Semitic type as an autochthonous development of an otherwise homogeneous schedule that has actually never been brought together and worked out or, in a word, urbanized, but has remained standing half-way. . . . It offers greater possibilities of doing justice to the original features found in the western area. Yet I am fully aware of the fact that we have at the same time to reckon with an extraordinarily strong influence from abroad, from the Egyptian and the 'Hittite', but far more still from the eastern Sumero-Accadian culture. We come, I think, nearest to the truth if we merely say that this western pattern is only an offshoot of the general Near East pattern.'

so-called 'pattern' is not to be explained by some theory of cultural diffusion but is regarded as constituting specific expressions of a common endeavour to answer some problem basic to the life of man (in this case that of the death and revival of vegetation), ought not similar manifestations of the 'pattern' to be found among other peoples than those of the Near East, when they were at a similar state of cultural development and living under similar environmental conditions? A test case at once suggests itself, namely, ancient China, where civilized life was based on agriculture and where climatic conditions produced those tensions arising from the need of certain kinds of weather at different times of the year, which were such potent factors in the religious conception of the Near Eastern peoples. Here indeed the ruler had an essential part in securing the prosperity of the land and this role involved him in the performance of an elaborate ritual, which was regulated by the calendar; he was, moreover, the 'Son of Heaven', who alone could perform those sacrifices which, it was believed, were vital to the well-being of the state.[1] However, despite all this apparent similarity between Chinese kingship and that which existed in the Near East, in Chinese faith and practice there is no trace of those elements which are fundamental to the Near Eastern 'ritual-pattern', namely, the concept of the 'dying-rising god', the ritual combat, or the sacred marriage.[2] And it may further be noted that in ancient India at a comparable stage of cultural development the

---

[1] Cf. M. Granet, *Chinese Civilization* (London, 1930), pp. 379–89, 400–2; L. Wieger, *History of Religious Beliefs and Philosophical Opinions in China* (Hsien-hsien Press, 1927), pp. 57–60, 63–64; W. E. Soothill, *The Hall of Light* (London, 1950), *passim*. See also 'The Mythico-Ritual Pattern in Chinese Civilization', by J. J. L. Duyvendak, and 'Zur konfuzianischen Staatsmoral' by E. Haenisch in *Proceedings of the 7th Congress for the History of Religions* (Amsterdam, 1951). The issue here is discussed at length by D. H. Smith in an article entitled 'Divine Kingship in Ancient China', which is due to appear in a future number of *Numen*.

[2] The thesis recently advanced by H. G. Quaritch Wales (*The Mountain of God*, London, 1953, pp. 38 ff) that 'a new religion, as part of a cultural pattern originating in Mesopotamia, was introduced to the Yellow River basin in the middle of the second millenium B.C.', must be considered improbable on two basic points (i) its interpretation of the role of Enlil in Mesopotamian religion is not demonstrated, (ii) the diffusion of the 'cultural pattern' from Mesopotamia to China is rather assumed than proved: indeed on the evidence available for that period it could not be otherwise.

power of the Brahman caste effectively prevented the political rulers from acquiring and exercising sacerdotal status and function, and, so far as a claim was made to divinity, it was made pre-eminently by the Brahmans themselves.[1] Accordingly, it seems necessary to conclude that the so-called 'ritual-pattern' cannot be regarded as the natural expression in cultic imagery and practice of human societies when living at a specific cultural level and faced with the common challenges of the agriculturist's life. The 'pattern', as it has been defined, is clearly an artificial composition and as such it must have had its origin in some specific community of peculiar genius, which inference naturally points to the necessity of adopting some theory of diffusion to account for the alleged recurrence of the 'pattern' in a number of different localities; but of the soundness of such a theory it has been found that serious doubt exists.

From this critical estimate of what might be called the assumptive basis of the 'Myth and Ritual' thesis attention must now be turned to the interpretation of the data relevant to the establishment of that thesis. Here invaluable work has been done by Professor H. Frankfort in his great study entitled *Kingship and the Gods*[2] and in his Frazer Memorial Lecture;[3] and his demonstration of the fundamental difference between the insti-

[1] 'Verily, there are two kinds of gods; for, indeed, the gods are the gods, and the Brahmans who have studied and teach sacred lore are the human gods', *Satapatha Brahmana*, 11. ii. 2–6, trans. J. N. Farquhar, *A Primer of Hinduism* (Madras, 1911), p. 19. 'An examination of all passages in which the masculine *brahmán* is found shows that it denotes in general a distinct class, if not a caste, with their dependents, and is frequently used in direct contrast with the king', A. Hillebrandt in *Encyclopaedia of Religion and Ethics* (ed. J. Hastings), ii. 798a. Divinity was ascribed to kings in honorific titles, but the fact is without significance in the present context, cf. J. Filliozat in *Anthropologie religieuse* (ed. C. J. Bleeker, Leiden, 1955), pp. 115–17. Cf. L. H. Gray in *Encyclopaedia of Religion and Ethics*, vii. 720–1; A. L. Basham, *The Wonder that was India* (London, 1954), pp. 34, 81–93, who shows that ancient Indian kingship was essentially a political institution; see also pp. 120, 138, 141. It is also significant that the only instance of a 'dying-god' in Hindu mythology, namely, the death of Krishna, appears in that part of his legend which contains other non-Indian *motifs*.

[2] Chicago, 1948.

[3] *The Problem of Similarity in Ancient Near Eastern Religions* (Oxford, 1951). Cf. S. G. F. Brandon, 'Divine Kings and Dying Gods', in *The Hibbert Journal*, liii (1955). For a criticism along somewhat different lines see de Fraine, op. cit., pp. 27–54.

tution of kingship in Egypt and in Mesopotamia is so satisfactory that the case may be deemed established,[1] so that consideration may now be given to some other issues.[2]

The exponents of the 'Myth and Ritual' thesis have rightly emphasized the essentiality of the connexion of the god Osiris with the pharaonic kingship. Osiris was indeed the vegetation god *par excellence* of Egypt, and his cultus, as it found expression in the royal ritual and in certain annual festivals, made manifest the Egyptian belief that the prosperity of the land was vitally integrated with the king's being and function. But to concentrate interest on this aspect of Osiris is to run the risk of misunderstanding or misrepresenting what appears to have been the greater significance of this deity for the inhabitants of the valley of the Nile. Osiris, the 'dying-rising god' of Egypt, was preeminently the centre of one of the most remarkable mortuary cults ever practised by mankind.[3] Whatever may have been the origins of this deity and whatever part he had in the state cult as a vegetation god,[4] from the earliest documents of Egyptian thought Osiris is the god to whom the individual turned in fervent hope when confronted by the dread prospect of death. It is of the pharaoh's faith in this respect that we are first informed, but a process of democratization can be traced until by the New Kingdom period the ordinary man and woman sought salvation through Osiris.[5] The means by which it was believed

---

[1] But cf. above, p. 69, n. 1. Ed.

[2] The evidence assembled by T. Fish in his article 'Some Aspects of Kingship in the Sumerian City and Kingdom of Ur' (*B.J.R.L.*, xxxii. 1951) should also be noted in this connexion. The account of kingship which C. J. Gadd gives in his Schweich Lectures entitled *Ideas of Divine Rule in the Ancient East* (London, 1948), pp. 33 ff., is significant in view of the fact of his being one of the original contributors to *Myth and Ritual*.

[3] H. Kees, *Totenglauben und Jenseitsvorstellungen der alten Ägypter* (Leipzig, 1926), p. 190; Erman, *Die Religion der Ägypter*, pp. 40, 68–69, 217–21; G. Roeder, *Volksglaube im Pharaonenreich* (Stuttgart, 1952), pp. 156–60; Bonnet, op. cit., sub *nomin*. 'Osiris', 'Jenseitsglaube' (pp. 344b ff.); J. Vandier, *La Religion égyptienne* (Paris, 1949), pp. 81–107; J. Černý, *Ancient Egyptian Religion* (London, 1952), pp. 84–90.

[4] Cf. A. Moret, *Le Nil et la civilisation égyptienne* (Paris, 1926), pp. 92–112; Vandier, op. cit., pp. 67–69; Frankfort, *Kingship and the Gods*, pp. 200–3, 207–9.

[5] This was first done in a masterly way by the late J. H. Breasted in his *Development of Religion and Thought in Ancient Egypt* (London, 1912), lecture viii. Cf.

that this salvation might be achieved was that of the magical assimilation of the deceased with the god, so that, as the devotee was identified with the god in death, he would be one with him in his resurrection.[1] And this death and resurrection was no piece of mystical symbolism, but was conceived of in the most realistic terms. Thus, the myth of Osiris is set forth essentially as a human drama, and the horrors of death are depicted with a brutal realism—for example in the *Pyramid Texts*, in a passage in which the ritual of embalmment is represented in terms of the Osirian drama, a spell against physical decomposition is provided for the deceased pharaoh Pepi:

> Isis comes and Nephthys: the one from the right and the other from the left. . . . They find Osiris, as his brother Set laid him low in *Nḏi̓.t.* Then speaks Osiris Pepi: 'Hasten thou to me!' and thus he exists in his name Sokaris. They prevent thee from perishing in thy name *i̓npw* (Anubis); they prevent thy putrefaction from flowing on the earth according to thy name *sȝb šmⸯ*; they prevent the odour of thy corpse from being evil for thee in thy name of *Ḥrw ḫȝti̓*. . . .[2]

Then:

Isis brings a libation to thee, Nephthys cleanses thee; thy two great sisters restore thy flesh, they reunite thy members, they cause thy two eyes to appear in thy face.[3]

It is seen then that primarily for the Egyptians Osiris was not a vegetation deity, with whose being the king was intimately associated and whose life-cycle constituted critical points in the course of the year; rather Osiris was the saviour to whom men

Frankfort, *Ancient Egyptian Religion* (New York, 1948), pp. 103–5. There is evidence in the Pyramid Texts that Osiris was an ancient mortuary deity whose prestige the Heliopolitan priesthood sought to controvert in favour of their god Atum. Cf. H. Kees, 'Das Eindringen des Osiris in die Pyramidtexte', Excursus XXVII in S. A. B. Mercer, *The Pyramid Texts* (London, 1952), iv. 123–39.

[1] The pattern is set in the Pyramid Texts: see P.T., 167 (K. Sethe, *Die altägyptischen Pyramidtexten*, i. 93–94). Cf. G. Thausing, *Der Auferstehungsgedanke in ägyptischen religiösen Texten* (Leipzig, 1943), pp. 21–22.

[2] P.T., 1255–7 (text in Sethe, op. cit. ii. 210–11; trans. L. Speleers, *Les Textes des pyramides égyptiennes* (Bruxelles, 1923), i. 83; S. A. B. Mercer, *The Pyramid Texts*, i. 207). Cf. Thausing, op. cit., pp. 115–16. See also P.T. 722, 725.

[3] P.T. 1981 (text in Sethe, op. cit. i. 478; trans. Speleers, op. cit. i. 115; Mercer, op. cit. i. 295). Cf. Thausing, op. cit., p. 133; Mercer, op. cit. iii. 892.

and women turned for the assurance of immortality and before whom they believed that they would be judged in the next world.[1] Hence, although he may have been solicited for a good harvest, the real significance of Osiris lay in his mortuary role, a fact which is graphically attested by his iconography, for he is ever represented as one who is embalmed for burial and yet holds the emblems of sovereignty and power.[2] And it is only by appreciating this aspect of Osiris that the peculiarity of the Egyptian *Weltanschauung* may be understood. Although the Egyptian was intensely concerned with the prosperity of his land and enthusiastically participated in those festivals which were designed to promote it, he was obsessed by the thought of his own personal fate when death should strike him down.[3] Consequently it is not strange that the vast bulk of the evidence which has survived of Egyptian life and thought is of a mortuary character, while little remains to illustrate concern with those issues which, according to the 'Myth and Ritual' thesis, should have been primary.

This conclusion in respect of Egypt inevitably raises the question whether the impression created by the 'Myth and Ritual' thesis in its interpretation of the Mesopotamian data may not similarly place too great an emphasis on certain aspects of religious faith and practice in that land and so obstruct the forming of a balanced estimate. If the New Year festival at Babylon, thus interpreted, were representative of a long-established tradition of faith and practice throughout that cultural area, it must next be asked to what degree was that tradition influential in the formation of the Mesopotamian *Weltanschauung*. At first sight it would appear that, in comparison with the Egyptian faith, religion in Mesopotamia was singularly

---

[1] Eloquent witness of the reality of this judgement before Osiris is afforded by the vignettes to Chapters 30 and 125 of the *Book of the Dead*. Cf. *The Book of the Dead: Facsimile of the Papyrus of Ani* (British Museum, 1894), sheet 3.

[2] Cf. Budge, *Osiris and the Egyptian Resurrection*, i. 30–54.

[3] Cf. S. G. F. Brandon, *Time and Mankind* (London, 1951), pp. 32–39; to the references there given add C. E. Sander-Hansen, *Der Begriff des Todes bei den Ägyptern* (Copenhagen, 1942); C. J. Bleeker, 'Die Idee des Schicksals in der altägyptischen Religion', in *Numen*, ii (1955), pp. 28–46.

deficient in encouraging those who professed it to look beyond the scope of this life—indeed, far to the contrary, its grim eschatology was calculated to invest death with the utmost terror.[1] However, despite the consequent concentration of interest on life in this world, it does not appear that state rituals, such as those in which the 'Myth and Ritual pattern' presumably found expression, satisfied the spiritual needs of the people, however necessary they were felt to be to the well-being of the community as a whole. Instead the great mass of divinatory and exorcismal texts, which have been recovered by archaeological research, attests the preoccupation of the people with warding off all manner of ills which were believed to be due to the action of evil spirits.[2] And of particular significance is it that in those texts in which Dumu-zi or Tammuz, the dying-rising god of vegetation, is invoked, the deliverance which is sought through his instrumentality is never from the common fate after death but from some evil which spoilt the enjoyment of this life. Indeed, if the *Epic of Gilgamesh* may be taken, as it surely must be in view of its great popularity, as a faithful reflection of the Mesopotamian view of life, then the advice which Siduri gives to the hero in his quest constitutes the best comment on the matter at issue here:

> Gilgamesh, whither runnest thou?
> The life thou seekest thou wilt not find;
> (For) when the gods created mankind,
> They allotted death to mankind,
> But life they retained in their keeping.
> Thou, O Gilgamesh, let thy belly be full;

---

[1] See the *Epic of Gilgamesh*, Tab. VII, vol. iv. 31–41, Tab. XII, 84–153; *Ishtar's Descent to the Underworld* (trans. A. Heidel in *The Epic of Gilgamesh and Old Testament Parallels*, Chicago, 1949, pp. 60, 99–101, 119–28; A. Ungnad, *Die Religion der Babylonier und Assyrer*, Jena, 1921, pp. 86–87, 117–18, 142–50). Cf. A. Jeremias, *Die babylonisch-assyrischen Vorstellungen vom Leben nach dem Tode* (Leipzig, 1887); F. Jeremias in Chantepie de la Saussaye, *Lehrbuch der Religionsgeschichte* (Tübingen, ed. 1925), i. 585–8; M. David, *Les Dieux et le destin en Babylonie* (Paris, 1949), pp. 39–40; T. Jacobsen, in *The Intellectual Adventure of Ancient Man* (Chicago, 1946), pp. 202–18, in *Before Philosophy* (Penguin Books), pp. 217–34.

[2] Cf. E. Ebeling, *Tod und Leben nach Vorstellungen der Babylonier* (Leipzig, 1931), pp. 122–62; Hooke, *Babylonian and Assyrian Religion*, pp. 77 ff.; Ed. Dhorme, *Les Religions de Babylonie et d'Assyrie* (Paris, 1945), pp. 260 ff.

Day and night be thou merry;
Make every day (a day of) rejoicing.
Let thy raiment be clean,
Thy head be washed, (and) thyself bathed in water.
Cherish the little one holding thy hand,
(And) let thy wife rejoice in thy bosom.
This is the lot of [mankind. . . .]¹

It has already been noted that many of the original exponents of the 'Myth and Ritual' thesis were evidently profoundly concerned with the interests of Christian theology; indeed on consideration it may fairly be asked how far the idea of the 'pattern' was itself suggested by the Christian *mythos*, because the form which that *mythos* had attained by the end of the first century reproduced in a remarkable way all the constitutive elements of the 'pattern'. The Christ was a god incarnate and of royal status by virtue of His Davidic descent; He had struggled with the power of evil and descended into Death but had revived again to a new and more glorious life; in triumph He had ascended into the heavens, where He reigned in majesty and dispensed new life to those who served Him. The *motif* of the sacred marriage was there too: the Bride of Christ was the Church and from that union was born the company of the faithful.² Indeed so complete did the parallels appear that Professor E. O. James was led to write:

Thus at the beginning of the Christian era the stage was set for a new act in the ancient drama of the divine kingship and its ritual pattern. . . . With the break-up of the Roman Empire the scattered fragments were again brought together, like the dismembered body of Osiris, this time round the figure of a spiritual Divine king 'incarnated once and for all in order ever after to rule the souls of men'; invested in a scarlet robe, a crown of thorns, and a reed for a sceptre, and dying to live on a cross which has become symbolized as the tree of life.³

¹ Tab. X, col. iii. 1–14; translated by A. Heidel, *The Epic of Gilgamesh and Old Testament Parallels* (University of Chicago Press, 1949), p. 70. For another recent translation see that of E. A. Speiser in *Ancient Near Eastern Texts* (ed. J. B. Pritchard, Princeton, 1955), p. 90a.
² Rev. xxi. 2, xxii. 17; cf. Eph. v. 23–32; 2 Cor. xi. 2. Cf. the vision of the Church as a woman in the *Shepherd of Hermes*.
³ *Christian Myth and Ritual*, pp. 40–41. See also his essay in *The Labyrinth*

The apparent fulfilment in the Christian *mythos* of the ancient 'pattern' is truly impressive, and Professor James ably interpreted it as a notable instance of the *Praeparatio Evangelii*, but it must be recognized that it could with equal aptness be interpreted adversely to the orthodox Christian claim, in that it might be contended that the ancient 'Myth and Ritual' pattern provided a set of inherited categories in terms of which Christian soteriology was inevitably formed. However, it appears on closer examination of the issues involved here that the definitive form which the Christian *mythos* achieved by the end of the first century is not to be explained primarily as due either to divine predestination or to the influence of inherited modes of thought, but as the outcome of a peculiar combination of events which can only be properly understood by a detailed investigation of the relevant data. Although such an investigation cannot be attempted here, a summary of a study published elsewhere[1] may be conveniently utilized to demonstrate the need of substantiating each alleged instance of the occurrence of the 'Myth and Ritual' pattern by an adequate examination of its historical context.

In the history of Christian doctrine there is perhaps no more significant fact, although it has been consistently disregarded by Christian scholars, than St. Paul's attestation that within some twenty years of the Crucifixion there were current two different and rival interpretations of the faith. This attestation is contained in two distinct passages in his Epistles, namely, Gal. i. 6–8 and 2 Cor. xi. 3–4. In view of the fundamental importance of the witness of these passages they must be quoted *in extenso*. In the Galatian passage Paul writes to his converts:

I marvel that ye are so quickly removing from him that called you in the grace of Christ unto a different gospel (εἰς ἕτερον εὐαγγέλιον); which is not another gospel (ὃ οὐκ ἔστιν ἄλλο);[2] only there be some

entitled 'The Sources of Christian Ritual'. It should be noted that A. Ehrhardt has attempted to show that Christian myth and ritual originated in reaction to Roman emperor-worship (see 'Myth and Ritual from Alexander to Constantine', in *Studi in onore di Pietro de Francisci* (Milano, 1955), iv, pp. 423–44.

[1] S. G. F. Brandon, *The Fall of Jerusalem and the Christian Church* (London, 1951, 2nd. ed. 1957).

[2] 'This is not an admission in favour of the false teachers, as though they taught the

that trouble you, and would pervert the gospel of Christ. But though we, or an angel from heaven, should preach (unto you) any gospel other (or contrary to: παρ' ὅ) than that we preached unto you, let him be anathema.

In the other passage the Apostle writes in admonition to his Corinthian converts:

But I fear, lest by any means, as the serpent beguiled Eve in his craftiness, your minds should be corrupted from the simplicity and the purity that is toward Christ. For if he that cometh preacheth another Jesus (ἄλλον ᾿Ιησοῦν), whom we did not preach, or if ye receive a different spirit (πνεῦμα ἕτερον), which ye did not receive, or a different gospel (εὐαγγέλιον ἕτερον), which ye did not accept, ye welcome it (καλῶς ἀνέχεσθε).[1]

Quite clearly in these two places Paul acknowledges that the interpretation of the person and mission of Jesus, of which he was the protagonist, was being challenged in its authority for his converts by another interpretation, which seriously differed from it. Now the significance of the situation obviously depends upon the identity of the exponents of this rival version of the faith. Unfortunately Paul nowhere explicitly states who they were, but it is patent from the profound concern which he shows about their activities that they were no mere group of irresponsible heretics but men who were capable of challenging his authority among his own converts. On further investigation there can be little doubt that these exponents of the rival gospel were none other than the emissaries of the Church of Jerusalem, which means that their teaching represented the interpretation of the status and role of Jesus held by those original apostles and 'eye-witnesses' who constituted the *Urgemeinde* of Christianity.[2]

one Gospel, however perverted (comp. Phil. i. 15, 18)', J. B. Lightfoot, *Saint Paul's Epistle to the Galatians* (London, 1881), p. 76. After a survey of the comparative meanings of ἄλλος and ἕτερος, Lightfoot concluded (ibid.); 'Thus while ἄλλος is generally confined to a negative of identity, ἕτερος sometimes implies the negation of resemblance.' Cf. K. Lake, *The Earlier Epistles of St. Paul* (London, 1930), p. 267 n. 1. ἄλλος ein anderer v. Art'., W. Bauer, *Wörterbuch zum Neuen Testament* (Giessen 1928), p. 61a, cf. p. 491a *sub* ἕτερος.

[1] Cf. A. Menzies, *The Second Epistle to the Corinthians* (London, 1912), p. 78.

[2] Cf. *Fall of Jerusalem*, chap. 4 and pp. 136–153; to the references given therein add M. Simon, *Les Premiers Chrétiens* (Paris, 1952), pp. 70–82.

That the teaching of the Mother Church of the faith differed so seriously from that of Paul is clearly a matter of supreme moment, but one also that is most unfortunately complicated by the fact that no documents of that church survived its obliteration when Jerusalem was destroyed by the Romans in A.D. 70. However, the situation is not completely hopeless, and it is possible by patient research to reconstruct the main tenets of its gospel from scattered allusions and references found in the writings of Paul, in the Acts of the Apostles, the Gospels, in the surviving fragments of Hegesippus, and in the Pseudo-Clementine literature. Accordingly it is found that Jesus was primarily proclaimed as the Messiah of Israel, who would shortly return with supernatural power and glory to 'restore again the kingdom to Israel'. This proclamation had apparently encountered the serious objection that Jesus had died the accursed death of the Law, and, to meet it, it had been necessary to elaborate an apologetic whereby it could be shown that this death had been foretold by the prophets, pre-eminently by Isaiah in the figure of the Suffering Servant of Yahweh. But such an apologetic, it must be noted, contained no elements of soteriology; the invocation of the Isaianic Servant as a prototype of the crucified Jesus was strictly a defensive move, for it could not have been otherwise in a Judaic milieu, where such an idea as that of the Messiah of Israel dying to save the Gentiles would have been an inconceivable, let alone an outrageous, thing. Consequently, in the definition of their gospel the Jerusalem Christians represented the Crucifixion as an unfortunate accident done in ignorance, but which had been anticipated by divine revelation; no emphasis was placed upon its significance and attention was directed instead to the imminent return of Jesus to redeem Israel. There seems to be evidence also for thinking that the prominence given to the Davidic descent of Jesus meant that his Messiahship was interpreted in a political sense.[1]

To this presentation of Jesus and His mission we know that Paul was vehemently opposed, but unfortunately no formal

[1] Cf. *Fall of Jerusalem*, chap. 5; H. J. Schoeps, *Theologie und Geschichte des Judenchristentums* (Tübingen, 1949), pp. 71–73, 78–98, 157.

statement of his own gospel appears in his writings which have survived; however, it is possible to piece together from various parts of the Epistles a coherent outline of the contents of that gospel.

Of key importance is the fact that for Paul the Crucifixion was of supreme significance and its proclamation stood in the forefront of his message. To him it was a supernatural event preordained by God before the aeons. Its explanation was comprised in an esoteric doctrine of mankind's state and destiny which is briefly sketched in 1 Cor. ii. 6–8 and Gal. iv. 1–7. Herein man is represented as held in bondage by the daemonic powers which ruled in the present world-order and which were closely associated with the celestial phenomena; to rescue men from this dire condition God had sent a supernatural pre-existent being, a veritable *deuteros theos*, to earth in an incarnated human form, and the daemonic powers, not recognizing his true nature, had crucified him and so, presumably by exceeding their rights, they had forfeited their hold over man. Paul, of course, identified this divine saviour with the historical Jesus, whom he accordingly calls 'the Son of God', *Kyrios* and *Soter*. Thus Paul's gospel was a soteriology of universal significance. The *mythos* also had its ritual expression, for in his references to baptism in Rom. vi. 2–5 it is evident that the Apostle taught that salvation was effected by the ritual assimilation, through the baptismal rite, of the neophyte to the saviour in both his death and resurrection.[1]

What would have been the outcome, if these two rival inter-pretations of the faith had been left to struggle together for the allegiance of the Church, is unknown. Judging by the resources of the rival exponents of them it would seem that victory must ultimately have gone to the Jerusalem leaders, because their authority and prestige as the first disciples far outweighed the claims of Paul. However, it was fated that the issue should be decided by extraneous forces. In the year 66 the Jewish nationalists revolted against the Roman suzerainty and four years later, after a disastrous struggle, the cause of Israel was

[1] Cf. op. cit., chap. 4.

lost with the utter destruction of Jerusalem and its Temple. In this catastrophe the Christian community of Jerusalem was in some way involved, because after A.D. 70 it disappears completely from the life of the Church. It was in the reconstruction of Christian life and thought which followed these shattering events that there was born that synthesis of the rival gospels of Paul and the Jerusalem *Urgemeinde* which constitutes the classic *mythos* of Christian soteriology and which first found expression in the Markan Gospel. Herein were fused into a single figure the picture of the historical Jesus, of royal descent, the Messiah of Israel, and the concept of the incarnated divine saviour of Paul, who by his vicarious death had redeemed mankind and whose mystic bride was the Church.[1] And thus in the Christ of Catholic theology was sublimely manifest the apparent fulfilment of those ancient adumbrations of a divine king who dies to give his people new life. But the fulfilment was apparent only, because it was not the achievement of forces of which the operation may be consistently traced; it was the fortuitous result of a combination of disparate and generically unconnected factors— yet to the eye of faith, it must be admitted, the fortuitous element here may be deemed providential and the events of A.D. 66–70 be seen as evidence of that divine intervention in history which is the basic concept of the Christian interpretation of the past.

The 'Myth and Ritual' thesis by implication raises an important question in another field, but one which is also of vital concern for the comparative study of religion.

By postulating the 'Myth and Ritual' complex as the basic religious pattern common to the cultures of the ancient Near East and by attempting to show that this pattern found expression in a series of annual festivals which were related to the course of Nature's year, a situation is implied from which it may reasonably be inferred on *a priori* grounds that a cyclic view of existence must have been held by those who practised such rituals.[2] That

---

[1] Cf. op. cit., chaps. 7, 9, 10.

[2] Cf. M. Éliade, *Traité d'histoire des religions* (Paris, 1949), pp. 332–49; *Le Mythe de l'éternel retour* (Paris, 1949), pp. 83–99.

such a view was actually held there is a certain amount of confirmatory evidence in Egyptian[1] and Mesopotamian[2] documents, although the fact leaves unanswered the question whether such a view had been inspired by some 'myth and ritual' pattern or whether that pattern, if it existed, would have been a specific expression of a *Weltanschauung* which had been formed by the operation of other causes. However that may be, the vital issue here lies in the fact that among the cultures of the ancient Near East there were two of which the *Weltanschauungen* were notably teleological and not cyclic in outlook. The cultures concerned were the Iranian, as conditioned by Zarathustra's reform, and the Hebrew. Since in the present context the significance of the Iranian estimate is more peripheral, attention may be devoted to that of the Hebrews.

If the 'Myth and Ritual' thesis be sound in its suggestion that the 'pattern' had once an effective currency in Israel through the institution of kingship, it would appear that, not only did a cyclic view of the temporal process never establish itself there, but, on the contrary, the teleological interpretation emerged at a very early period.

The origin of what might justly be called the 'Hebrew philosophy of History' is admittedly obscure, but there is reason for thinking that its roots are to be found in the propaganda of the Yahwist party which sought to maintain allegiance to Yahweh among the Israelite tribes after the settlement in Canaan.[3] If Professor Martin Noth's interpretation of the original confederacy of the Twelve Tribes on the analogy of the Greek and

---

[1] 'Re showeth himself in the morning, and Atum goeth down in Manu. Men beget, women conceive, and every nose breatheth air—day dawneth, and their children go one and all to their place.' (Quoted from the so-called 'Song of the Harper' of the New Kingdom period; Eng. trans. by A. M. Blackman in A. Erman's *Literature of the Ancient Egyptians* (Methuen, London, 1927), p. 252.)

[2] Cf. A. Jeremias, *Handbuch der altorientalischen Geisteskultur* (Leipzig, 1913), pp. 193–204, in Hastings, *Encycl. Rel. and Ethics*, i. 185: A. Rey, *La Science orientale avant les Grecs* (Paris, 1930), pp. 155 ff. The decreeing of destinies for the ensuing year was an important factor in the Babylonian New Year festival as C. J. Gadd shows in *Myth and Ritual*, pp. 55–56. Cf. Éliade, *Le Mythe de l'éternel retour*, pp. 89–94; F. Jeremias in Chantepie de la Saussaye, *Lehrbuch der Religionsgeschichte* (Tübingen, 1925), i. 505–12.

[3] Cf. S. G. F. Brandon, *Time and Mankind* (London, 1951), pp. 63–72.

Italian amphictyonies be accepted,[1] and there is much reason for so doing, then a situation can reasonably be envisaged after the invasion of Canaan, in which the constituent tribes tended to revert to their former independence, which meant devotion to their own tribal deities and a corresponding forgetfulness of Yahweh, under whose patronage they had achieved their first successful lodgement in the Promised Land. This centrifugal movement had the effect of weakening the invaders militarily, the consequences of which were soon felt in terms of conquest by the reviving power of the Canaanites and perhaps by the newly-arrived Philistines. The situation provided the devotees of Yahweh with a unique opportunity to press the claims of their deity with considerable assurance of success. Their message to their compatriots naturally took the form of an appeal to the memory of the past—that, when they had been faithful, Yahweh had done mighty deeds for their fathers: if now they would return to their allegiance to him, he would forgive them and redeem them. The appeal rested on a sound military logic, for return to Yahweh meant the unification of their forces, and, hence, increased military strength and a better chance of victory against their oppressors.

Thus Yahwism acquired its characteristic preoccupation with history, or at least an accepted tradition about the past. In its earliest form this attitude probably found expression in cultic formulae[2] and the exhortations of prophets. Whether it would have survived long in such form is a matter for speculation, but its survival was guaranteed from about the ninth or tenth century by a creation which is quite unparalleled in any other ancient religion. A writer (or a school of writers), usually designated the Yahwist, composed out of various fragments of tradition, legend, and folk-lore, a unique conspectus of the past from the very act of Creation. The composition was a work of

---

[1] M. Noth, *Das System der Zwölf Stämme Israels* (*Beiträge z. Wiss. v. Alt. u. N. Test.*, Vierte Folge, Heft 1, Stuttgart, 1930). Cf. W. F. Albright, *From the Stone Age to Christianity* (Baltimore, 1946), p. 215; H. H. Rowley, *From Joseph to Joshua* (Schweich Lectures, 1948, London, 1950), pp. 102 ff., 126; Brandon, op. cit., pp. 71–72.

[2] Cf. Brandon, op. cit., pp. 69, 72.

genius, because out of such disparate material a coherent narrative was fashioned in which Yahweh was shown as guiding the course of history in order to fulfil his promise to the nation's ancestor, Abraham, that of his descendants he would make a great people and settle them in the land of Canaan. Yahweh's character as the 'Lord of History' was thus exhibited in a dramatic narrative and the Israelite tribes acquired thereby the sense of a common ancestry and a divinely guided past.[1]

The influence of this Yahwist achievement was profound, and it set the pattern for all subsequent Hebrew thought. Even the great vicissitudes of fortune which the nation subsequently suffered failed to shake its conviction in the providence of its god, and the darker Israel's political situation became the more fervent grew Israel's hopes that Yahweh would eventually intervene to save them and destroy their enemies. Accordingly, the distinctive Hebrew *Weltanschauung* was formed, whereby the passage of time was regarded teleologically as the gradual unfolding of the divine purpose and its irresistible achievement. Hence, whatever encouragement the periodic festivals of kingship may have given to a cyclic view of existence, that encouragement was too weak a thing to challenge the teleologically conceived *Weltanschauung* of Yahwism.

And the Yahwist teleological interpretation of the past was destined to exercise an even greater influence, outside the bounds of Judaism, through Christianity. The scheme of Jewish apocalyptic clearly shows itself in the earliest Christian documents, and from their testimony it is evident that primitive Christian thought was essentially teleological in outlook. Even the problem caused by the continued delay of the expected *Parousia* of Christ did not disturb this mode of thought, nor did the subsequent process of Hellenization, which might have introduced the cyclic view of time which was native to Greek thought. Indeed, far to the contrary, by utilizing Paul's apologetic theory of 'Godly Remnant', which was the true Israel, the Church was able to lay claim to the traditional Jewish philosophy of History and so

[1] Cf. Brandon, op. cit., pp. 63–84, and the references there given. See also G. Hölscher, *Geschichtsschreibung in Israel* (Lund, 1952), pp. 119, 134–5.

to formulate the theory of the two divine covenants, the Old and the New, which eventually found abiding expression in the chronology which divides the stream of time by the Incarnation into two parts, designated respectively the era 'Before Christ' and that of the *anni domini*.[1]

Accordingly, it must be deemed remarkable, if the 'myth and ritual pattern' had succeeded in establishing itself in both Hebrew religion and Christianity, that the influence of the concomitant cyclic view of existence never seriously challenged the dominance of that peculiar teleology of Yahwism which by its very genius was inimical to the premisses of the 'myth and ritual' complex.

In the phenomenology of religion the ritual pattern envisaged in the 'myth and ritual' thesis belongs to the class of seasonal rites which expresses a consciousness that human life is faced with recurrent crisis through the cyclic process of nature's year.[2] In this sense it is to be distinguished from another class of ritual practice which is concerned with the perpetuation or re-creation of the efficacy of a unique event of the past.[3] The principle involved here may be described as the magical or ritual perpetuation of the past, and it represents a mode of primitive thought and action which has had a very long and remarkable history. It appears in Palaeolithic times in the famous painting of the so-called 'Dancing Sorcerer' in the cavern of the Trois Frères in the *département* of Ariège. The motive behind the production of this picture would seem to be that of perpetuating the potency of a magical dance after the action of that dance had finished in time.[4] The idea which was thus adumbrated at this remote period finds some notable forms of expression in subsequent ages. One of the most remarkable is that enshrined in the

---

[1] Cf. Brandon, op. cit., chap. viii and the references given therein.

[2] See p. 284 n. 2 above.

[3] Cf. Brandon, op. cit., p. 23. 'Le temps qui a vu l'événement commémoré ou répété par le rituel en question est *rendu* présent, 're-présenté' si l'on peut dire, si reculé qu'on l'imagine dans le temps', Éliade, *Traité d'histoire des religions*, p. 336.

[4] Cf. Brandon, op. cit., pp. 17–18. For a photograph and drawing of this figure, which is partly painted and partly engraved, see the Abbé Breuil, *Quatre cents siècles d'art pariétal* (Montignac, 1952), p. 166, see also pp. 176–7.

Osirian mortuary ritual, which we have already noticed. Herein it was sought by the use of imitative magic to make available to the devotee, on whose behalf the rites were being celebrated, the efficacy of a past event, namely, the resurrection of Osiris.[1] The same principle found expression in the ritual of the Christian Eucharist; indeed it may truly be said that therein it achieved its classic form. The quintessence of the rite lies in a ritual re-presentation of the historical death of Christ on Calvary for the purpose of pleading that Sacrifice again before God and for making its efficacy available to the faithful, then assembled, or on behalf of certain specified objects. Although in the course of the liturgical calendar this rite assumes the guise of a cyclically recurring festival, its reference to a unique historical event remains essential.[2]

In view of these considerations, doubt must again surely be felt about the presumed ubiquity of the so-called 'Myth and Ritual' pattern in the ancient Near East and also about its supposed influence. Indeed it would be ironical, if the 'Myth and Ritual' hypothesis be sound, that it was just in that cultural area in which the 'pattern' was supposed to have originated and flourished that the tradition of a teleological *Weltanschauung* developed, while in India, where it had no such currency, a cyclic view of existence was generated to become the basic premiss of both Hinduism and Buddhism.

According to its terms of reference this essay has been consistently critical of the 'Myth and Ritual' thesis. Moreover, since it is designed to be a contribution to a symposium on this subject, care has been taken not to enter too deeply into those fields which were being specifically covered by other contributors. Observance of these limitations has inevitably meant that little or no account has been given here of those aspects of the thesis which have met with general approval in the academic circles concerned and which have been very adequately and ably described by Professor Hooke and Professor Widengren in their papers. But the present

---

[1] Cf. Brandon, op. cit., pp. 29–30, 31.
[2] Ibid., pp. 169, 177–8, 180–1.

contributor would not like the impression to be given by his own critical consideration of the thesis that he is not appreciative of the significance of those aspects and that he does not recognize the achievement of those scholars who originally expounded the thesis. He sees the 'Myth and Ritual' thesis as one of the major developments in the comparative study of religion, and he believes that, despite all the opposition which it has encountered, when the final adjustments are made it will be found that its contribution has been of the highest importance and that its value is abiding.[1] To particularize, it would seem that the exponents of the thesis have established beyond all doubt the fundamental importance of kingship as a religious institution throughout the various cultures of the ancient Near East. Secondly, that they have succeeded in showing that kingship in Israel must be evaluated in this light, and that, if this is done, many hitherto obscure passages in Hebrew literature gain a new and convincing meaning, and truer appreciation of the peculiar genius of Israelite religion is thereby made possible. Another aspect of this contribution, which is of the highest import for the study of religion, is constituted by the demonstration which has thereby been given of the fundamental importance of the evidence of ritual and myth for understanding both the ethos and the *Weltanschauung* of ancient cultures.

But what is perhaps the most significant indication of the achievement of the 'Myth and Ritual' thesis is to be found by way of a comparison. Between the years 1903 and 1921 the twelve volumes comprising Hastings's *Encyclopaedia of Religion and Ethics* were published. In this great corpus of information under 'Ritual' only a cross-reference was given to 'Prayer' and 'Worship', while the article on 'Mythology' treated the question

---

[1] A measure of the influence of the 'Myth and Ritual' thesis is to be seen in the fact that the theme of the 7th International Congress for the History of Religions, held at Amsterdam in 1950, was 'the mythical-ritual pattern in civilization', and that of the 8th Congress, held in Rome in 1955, was 'the king-god and the sacral character of kingship'. Cf. *Proceedings of the 7th Congress for the History of Religions* (Amsterdam, 1951); *Atti dell'VIII Congresso internazionale di Storia delle Religioni* (Florence, 1956). The full text of the relevant papers is to be published under the title of *La royauté sacrée*.

of the ritual origin of myth solely from the aetiological point of view.[1] When one contemplates the great output of works which has been inspired by the 'Myth and Ritual' thesis and the interest and reorientation of view which those works represent, it would seem that a veritable renaissance (or reformation) was inaugurated in this field of study in 1933, when Professor Hooke and his colleagues published their symposium.

[1] In vol. x, p. 666a of this work, some notice is given of the 'myth versus ritual' controversy, reference being made to such books as W. R. Smith, *Religion of the Semites*. Reference to other standard works in the field of *Religionsgeschichte* is of significance in this connexion. The *Histoire générale des religions* (ed. M. Gorce et R. Mortier), 5 tomes, Paris, 1948–52, pays no attention to the 'Myth and Ritual' thesis. In the 1950 edition of the *Encyclopaedia Britannica* an article is given under 'Myth and Ritual', but it contains no reference to the thesis of Professor Hooke or the work of the so-called Uppsala school in this respect. The last (French) edition of G. van der Leeuw's great work on the phenomenology of religion (*La Religion dans son essence et ses manifestations*, Paris, 1948) takes no cognizance of the thesis. M. Éliade, in his *Traité d'histoire des religions* (Paris, 1949), accepts A. R. Johnson's interpretation of Yahweh's victory over Rahab (p. 343), but has nothing to say of the thesis as a whole beyond making a bibliographical reference to it (p. 371). The *Eranos-Jahrbuch*, Bd. XVII, 1949 (Zürich, 1950), contains a paper by E. O. James entitled 'Myth and Ritual'; A. Bertholet in his *Wörterbuch der Religionen* (Stuttgart, 1952), pp. 327–8, says briefly that 'die Begründung des Kultus durch den Mythus das Sekundäre ist'. He does not apparently discuss 'Myth and Ritual' as such. G. Mensching, in his *Vergleichende Religionswissenschaft* (Heidelberg, 1949), merely mentions *Myth and Ritual* in a bibliographical note (p. 100). It may also be noted that the 'Myth and Ritual' thesis appears to have played no part in the 'Entmythologisierung' controversy associated with Rudolf Bultmann. H.-C. Puech in the *Bibliographie générale* to the *Mana* collection on the History of Religion (printed in J. Vandier, *La Religion égyptienne*, Paris, 1948), after noticing the two fundamental studies, contents himself with a reference to C. Kluckhohn's estimate 'Myth and Ritual' in the *Harvard Theological Review*, xxx (1942) (p. xxx). N. Turchi in his *Storia delle religioni*, 2 vols. (Florence, 1954), merely gives a bibliographical reference under 'Myth and Ritual' (vol. i, p. 73) to Kluckhohn's article in the *Harvard Theological Review* and to the *Eranos-Jahrbuch*, xvii (1949). No notice is taken of the 'Myth and Ritual' thesis in the following general works: *De Godsdiensten der Wereld* (ed. G. van der Leeuw, Amsterdam, 1948, 2 vols.); *Christus und die Religionen der Erde* (ed. F. König, 3 Bände, Vienna, 1951); *Christus* (*Manuel d'histoire des religions* (ed. J. Huby, 8th ed., Paris, 1947); *Histoire des religions* (ed. M. Brillant et R. Aigrain, t. i, Paris, 1953); *Storia delle religioni* (ed. P. T. Venturi, 2 vols., Turin, 4th ed., 1954).

GENERAL INDEX

INDEX OF AUTHORS CITED
OR REFERRED TO

INDEX OF SCRIPTURAL CITATIONS
AND REFERENCES